Domingo Felipe Cavallo and his daughter Sonia Cavallo Runde, have produced a masterful book. Superb! Full of fascinating insights. Highly instructive, thoughtful and very well researched. The authors provide a compelling analysis of Argentina, connecting its historical episodes with current events. Domingo Cavallo presents a first-hand insider's view from the battlefields of economic policies. He is a courageous and patriotic warrior who fought hard to save Argentina from itself. This book is a must read!
> Dr Jacob A. Frenkel, *Chairman, JPMorgan Chase International, Chairman, Board of Trustees of the Group of Thirty (G30) and former Governor of the Bank of Israel*

Argentina's history of policy mistakes and corrections has important lessons for all countries. Bad policies created high rates of inflation that weakened growth and destroyed financial institutions. Argentina has recovered in the past and is trying to do so again. This book is the best source for understanding this complex history. Domingo Cavallo brings unique insights and technical understanding to these complex issues.
> Martin Feldstein, *Professor of Economics at Harvard University*

Cavallo's book superbly travels the economic history legacy of Argentina to give a unique pespective on the contemporaneous policymaking process in a resilient conflictive society.
> Gerardo della Paolera, *Professor of Economics at Universidad de San Andrés and Central European University (CEU)*

The history, the economics and the politics of Argentina, which promised so much at the onset, have been a long tragedy. This book provides a fascinating account that will benefit all those who want to understand better, students, scholars and practioners. Domingo Cavallo has been fully engaged, with all his energy, in the workings of that history and he takes the reader with him in his passion.
> Christophe Chamley, *Professor of Economics at Boston University and Directeur d'Etudes, Ecole des Hautes Etudes en Sciences Sociales (EHESS) at Paris School of Economics*

Argentina's Economic Reforms of the 1990s in Contemporary and Historical Perspective

Why has Argentina suffered so much political and economic instability? How could Argentina, once one of the wealthiest countries in the world, have failed to meet its potential for decades? What lessons can be taken from Argentina's successes and failures?

Argentina is irresistibly intriguing: its economic history, with its crises and its triumphs, cannot be explained in purely economic terms. As Argentina's economic history is also intertwined with ideological struggles, it can only be examined in the context of conflicts of interest, politics, war and peace, boom and bust.

This volume comprises two distinct components: an economic history of Argentina from the Spanish colonial period to 1990, followed by a narrative on the last 25 years of reform and counter-reform.

Domingo Felipe Cavallo has been at the centre of Argentina's economic and political debates for 40 years. He was one of the longest serving cabinet members following the return of democratic government in 1983. He is uniquely qualified to help the reader make the connection between historical and current events. Domingo Felipe Cavallo and his daughter, Sonia Cavallo Runde, offer academics and students of economics and finance a long form case study. The volume also seeks to offer researchers and policymakers around the world relevant lessons and insights into similar problems from the perspective of Argentina.

Domingo Felipe Cavallo was Minister of the Economy twice and Minister of Foreign Affairs in Argentina. He is currently a Partner at Global Source Partners LLC and the Chairman and CEO of DFC Associates LLC. Dr Cavallo is the author of numerous books written in Spanish, including *Pasión por Crear* (2001), *Estanflación* (2008) and *Camino a la Estabilidad* (2014).

Sonia Cavallo Runde is a lecturer in the politics of development at The Catholic University of America. She was a co-founder of CIPPEC, a think tank in Argentina.

Europa Perspectives: Emerging Economies

The *Europa Emerging Economies* series from Routledge, edited by Robert E. Looney, examines a wide range of contemporary economic, political, developmental and social issues as they affect emerging economies throughout the world. Complementing the *Europa Regional Surveys of the World* series and the *Handbook of Emerging Economies*, which was also edited by Professor Looney, the volumes in the *Europa Emerging Economies* series will be a valuable resource for academics, students, researchers, policy-makers, professionals, and anyone with an interest in issues regarding emerging economies in the wider context of current world affairs.

There will be individual volumes in the series which provide in-depth country studies, and others which examine issues and concepts; all are written or edited by specialists in their field. Volumes in the series are not constrained by any particular template, but may explore economic, political, governance, international relations, defence, or other issues in order to increase the understanding of emerging economies and their importance to the world economy.

Robert E. Looney is a Distinguished Professor at the Naval Postgraduate School, Monterey, California, who specializes in issues relating to economic development in the Middle East, East Asia, South Asia and Latin America. He has published over 20 books and 250 journal articles, and has worked widely as a consultant to national governments and international agencies.

The Islamic Republic of Iran
Reflections on an emerging economy
Jahangir Amuzegar

Argentina's Economic Reforms of the 1990s in Contemporary and Historical Perspective
Domingo Felipe Cavallo and Sonia Cavallo Runde

Argentina's Economic Reforms of the 1990s in Contemporary and Historical Perspective

Domingo Felipe Cavallo and
Sonia Cavallo Runde

LONDON AND NEW YORK

First published 2017 by Routledge

2 Park Square, Milton Park, Abingdon, Oxfordshire OX14 4RN
711 Third Avenue, New York, NY 10017

Routledge is an imprint of the Taylor & Francis Group, an informa business

First issued in paperback 2018

Copyright © 2017 Domingo Felipe Cavallo and Sonia Cavallo Runde

The right of Domingo Felipe Cavallo and Sonia Cavallo Runde to be identified as the authors of the editorial material has been asserted in accordance with sections 77 and 78 of the Copyright, Designs and Patents Act 1988.

All rights reserved. No part of this book may be reprinted or reproduced or utilised in any form or by any electronic, mechanical, or other means, now known or hereafter invented, including photocopying and recording, or in any information storage or retrieval system, without permission in writing from the publishers.

Notice:
Product or corporate names may be trademarks or registered trademarks and are used only for identification and explanation without intent to infringe.

Europa Commissioning Editor: Cathy Hartley
Editorial Assistant: Eleanor Simmons

British Library Cataloguing in Publication Data
A catalogue record for this book is available from the British Library

Library of Congress Cataloging in Publication Data
A catalog record for this book has been requested

ISBN: 978-1-85743-804-8 (hbk)
ISBN: 978-1-857-43975-5 (pbk)

Typeset in Times New Roman
by Taylor & Francis Books

To Sonia Abrazian, wife and mother, for her patience, encouragement, loyalty and love

Contents

List of illustrations   xi
Preface   xiv
Acknowledgments   xviii
List of contributors   xix
Abbreviations   xx

Introduction   1

PART I
The southernmost territory of imperial Spain turns into the Argentine Nation   9

1. The Spanish heritage   11
2. From the May Revolution to the National Organization   22

PART II
1853–1913: six decades of increasing integration into the global economy   41

3. From the National Organization to the First World War   43
4. Split, reunification and the 'historical presidencies'   51
5. The years when Roca dominated politics   60

PART III
From the beginning of the First World War to the end of the Second World War   75

6. The traumatic 30 years from 1914 to 1944   77

x *Contents*

  7 The 'Radical Republic'   80

  8 From the fall of Yrigoyen to the rise of Perón   90

PART IV
Four-and-a-half decades of political and economic instability   105

  9 Inflation, stagflation and hyperinflation   107

10 Perón and Evita   112

11 The 18 years when Peronism was outlawed   130

12 The return of Perón and the military   147

13 Transition to democracy and Alfonsín's presidency   161

PART V
Reform and counter-reform   175

14 The Latin American consensus of the 1990s   177

15 Menem and De la Rúa   188

16 The origin of Duhalde's decisions and Kirchner's metamorphosis   224

17 Duhalde and the Kirchners   239

PART VI
Conclusions   267

18 Conclusions   269

    Index   284

List of illustrations

Figures

2.1	Terms of trade and exports per capita 1810–1852	34
2.2	Average height of Argentine soldiers 1785–1839	35
2.3	Price level and exchange rate Argentina, USA and Great Britain 1820–1860	38
3.1	Investment and foreign savings 1885–1913	48
4.1	First convertibility experiment	58
7.1	Imports 1900–1929	86
7.2	Public expenditure and fiscal deficit 1910–1929	86
7.3	Real wage index	87
8.1	GDP per capita Argentina, USA and Canada 1929–1940	98
8.2	GDP per capita, Argentina, Great Britain and Australia 1929–1940	98
8.3	Price level Argentina, USA, Great Britain 1929–1940	99
8.4	Domestic and foreign terms of trade 1913–1943	102
8.5	Nominal and real wages indices 1929–1943	103
9.1	Annual rate of inflation 1943–1990	109
9.2	Cultivated land	110
9.3	Average yield of wheat, corn and soybean	110
10.1	Real wage index and urban employment 1943–1955	117
10.2	Domestic and foreign terms of trade 1929–1955	122
10.3	Public expenditure and fiscal deficit 1929–1955	123
10.4	Prices relative to cost of living 1945–1955	128
10.5	Exchange rates relative to cost of living 1945–1955	129
11.1	Domestic and foreign terms of trade 1955–1973	136
11.2	Public expenditure and fiscal deficit 1955–1972	139
11.3	Relative price indices 1958–1963	143
12.1	Annualized rate of quarterly inflation I-73 to IV-76	151
12.2	Real exchange rate and domestic and foreign terms of trade 1975–1983	155
13.1	The initial success of Plan Austral: monthly inflation	167
13.2	The melting down of Plan Austral: monthly inflation	170

xii *List of illustrations*

13.3	Monthly inflation rate during the hyperinflation	171
15.1	Monthly inflation rate from March 1990 to December 2001	196
15.2	Course of the inflation rate after launching of the stabilization	196
15.3	Domestic and foreign terms of trade 1973–2001	200
15.4	Comparative export performance, 1980/1990 and 1990/2000	200
15.5	Comparative exports performance, Argentina, Brazil and Chile	201
15.6	Per capita GDP 1973–1998	202
15.7	Average yield of wheat, corn and soybean 1942–2001	203
15.8	Per capita GDP 1990–2001	210
16.1	Participation and employment rates 1974–2001	226
16.2	Unemployment rate 1974–2001	227
17.1	Evolution of relative prices after peso-ification	244
17.2	Domestic and foreign terms of trade 1990–2014	246
17.3	Bilateral and multilateral real exchange rate	247
17.4	Comparative export performance, 1989/2001 and 2001/2015	247
17.5	Comparative export performance, 1989/2001 and 2001/2015	248
17.6	Average yield of wheat, corn and soybean, 1980–2014	249
17.7	Evolution of salaries in real terms, 2001–2004	249
17.8	Prices relative to CPI index, 2001–2015	250
17.9	Participation and employment rate 2001–2016	262
17.10	Unemployment rate 2001–2015	263
17.11	Poverty rate 1988–2015	264

Tables

2.1	Comparative per capita GDP growth in Argentina and other countries 1820–1850	38
3.1	Comparative per capita GDP growth between 1850–1929	45
3.2	Comparative export growth between 1870–1913	46
3.3	GDP growth, total, agriculture and manufacturing 1875–1914	47
3.4	Origin of population growth by five year periods between 1870 and 1914	49
3.5	Participation of immigrants in the population by censuses	49
5.1	Territorial expansion of provinces in the pampas	69
5.2	Land tenure system 1895 and 1914	71
6.1	Comparative per capita GDP growth between 1913 and 1945	79
7.1	Bank deposits in 1912–1914 crisis	88
8.1	Main economic indicators 1928–1943	96
8.2	GDP growth, total, agriculture and manufacturing 1875–1943	103
8.3	Participation of exports of manufactures from 1934–1936 to 1943	103
8.4	Contribution of some industries to the increase in the share of non-traditional exports between 1939 and 1943	104

List of illustrations xiii

9.1	Comparative per capita GDP growth between 1870–1913 and 1945–1990	109
10.1	Participation of exports of manufactures in total exports and real wages from 1943 to 1947	118
10.2	Rate of inflation 1943–1955	126
10.3	Evolution of agriculture sector GDP and exports from 1941–1943 to 1950–1952	127
11.1	Rate of inflation and rate of per capita growth 1956–1972	142
11.2	Investment the driver of growth from 1958 until 1962	143
11.3	Macroeconomic indicators from 1967 to 1972	145
12.1	Macroeconomic indicators from 1972 to 1976	150
12.2	Slow pace of fiscal adjustment 1975–1989	154
12.3	Real interest rates after financial liberalization 1977–1981	157
12.4	Per capita GDP growth by main sectors 1976–1981	157
12.5	Financial indicators 1976–1982	159
13.1	Financial indicators 1982–1989	165
13.2	Government expenditure and fiscal deficit 1982–1989	167
15.1	Course of annual inflation rate in the years after launching the stabilization plans	197
15.2	Rate of growth of per capita investment in constant local prices	201
15.3	Factor productivity growth in Argentina and Brazil in the 1980s and 1990s	203
15.4	Evolution of the number of retirees and of pensions 1989–2001	205
15.5	Fiscal accounts for the consolidated public sector, 1989–1996	207
15.6	Evolution of the public debt between 1989 and 1996	208
15.7	Bonds and treasuries in circulation, 1989 and 1996	208
15.8	Fiscal accounts for the consolidated public sector, 1996–2001	212
15.9	Fiscal accounts for the consolidated public sector, 1996–2001	212
15.10	Evolution of the public debt between 1996 and 2001	213
15.11	Bank deposit's monthly variation	218
17.1	Evolution of poverty rate 2001–2003	244
17.2	Fiscal account for the consolidated public sector, 2001–2003	245
17.3	Fiscal accounts for the consolidated public sector, 2003–2015	251
17.4	Evolution of the number of retirees and of pensions 2001–2015	254
17.5	Monetary policy indicators 2001–2015	258
17.6	Growth and inflation 2001–2015	259

Preface

Over the years I have held various offices and many times I was challenged to explain, convince, justify, or defend my positions. And I did plenty of that in writing and in the media. The purpose of this book is different, the latter part in particular. In the autobiographical portion of this book I recount my front-seat view of events and put them in historical perspective.

I have always believed in the value of studying and learning from history, and from a young age, I did. I studied economics in Argentina at the time of the slow recovery that followed the recession of 1962–1963 that had created doubts about the merits of President Frondizi's attempt at modernization through the 1958 Stabilization and Development Plan. I started to work professionally during the years of Krieger Vasena's 1967 Stabilization and Growth Plan and the lead up to Perón's return to power in 1973 in the middle of the tragic confrontation between the guerrilla movements and the military government.

The country went through several attempts to reverse the isolationist and interventionist policies it inherited from the first two Peronist governments that were in power between 1945 and 1955. At that time the leading economic theories were Keynesianism in North America and Structuralism and Dependency (or Centre-Periphery) Theory in Latin America. To describe the prevailing thinking of the time, I like to remember that when I was a student in Córdoba and read Mario Vargas Llosa's novels, the then-young Peruvian writer was a strong supporter of the Cuban Revolution.

Disillusioned with the course of events during the early 1970s, particularly at the time of the aggravation of the climate of violence from 1972 to 1974, and feeling that my knowledge of history and economics was insufficient to understand what was happening in Argentina, I decided to distance myself from current events in my own country and use this opportunity to deepen my knowledge of economic theory and the economic experience of other Latin American countries.

Harvard gave me the opportunity to achieve both goals at the same time. While I wrote my PhD dissertation on monetary policy in a stagflationary context, I benefited from the interest of several professors at Harvard and MIT in the inflationary experience of Argentina: Rudiger Dornbusch, Stanley Fisher, Martin Feldstein, Benjamin Friedman, Richard Musgrave and Yair Mundlak.

Preface xv

I also benefited from my interaction with classmates and economists who were completing post-doctoral studies at Harvard and MIT or visiting for conferences and seminars. Pedro Aspe, Sebastian Piñera, Eduardo Aninat, Jorge Dosermeaux, Roberto Dagnino, Larry Kotlikoff, Larry Summers, Jeffrey Sachs, Michael Bruno, Edmar Bacha, Eliana Cardozo, Alejandro Foxley, Alvaro Pachón and Christophe Chamley are persons whom I met at Harvard and then continued to interact with as a scholar and a policymaker.

Of particular note was as a participant in the Musgrave Mission for Tax Reform in Bolivia, on which I had the opportunity to interact with Professor Arnold Harberger. Some years later and thanks to the relationships with the academics and the professionals that I established in my Harvard years, I had the privilege to interact frequently with Jacob Frenkel, Vito Tanzi and Robert Mundell. I learned much from all of them.

Upon my return to Argentina I continued to study the Argentine economy with updated theoretical tools and much greater knowledge of what was happening in the rest of Latin America and the world. I founded the Instituto de Estudios Económicos sobre la Realidad de América Latina (IEERAL) a think tank financed by the Fundación Mediterránea, a private foundation located in Córdoba. IEERAL hosted a team of like-minded researchers, each seeking better understanding of a sectorial or regional problem in Argentina, but together trying to build a comprehensive understanding of the workings of the Argentine economy.

Our research, debates and conferences influenced public policies when Argentina returned to democracy. In 1987 I got my first opportunity in politics. Until then I had stayed out of politics and was not registered with either political party. I was invited as an independent to run on the Peronist ticket for Congress from my home province of Córdoba.

From 1987 to 1989 I served in Congress. My participation was highly visible and I explained why Sourrouille's Austral Plan was falling apart and criticized the generalized fiscal indiscipline in the federal government and the provinces.

When Menem succeeded Alfonsín as President, I was invited to join his government. I was appointed Minister of Foreign Relations and I did my part in integrating Argentina with the rest of the world. Having in mind the consequences of isolation which throughout history had kept Argentina backwards, I felt it was paramount to integrate with the world. What held us back was a poor relationship with the USA, no diplomatic relations with the United Kingdom after the South Atlantic War of 1982, and our border problems with Chile and our nuclear race with Brazil. It took several months of negotiations, but we made significant progress on all fronts. Argentina started to get involved in world affairs with a constructive attitude and regained the respect that it had only achieved in the Golden Age years from 1870 to 1914 and in the short period of Frondizi's government between 1958 and 1962.

The consequences of reconnecting to the world were immediately felt and similar to the two periods just mentioned, the improved foreign relations facilitated economic reforms that would expand foreign trade, attract investment, and introduce technological advances in the production of goods and services.

When in early 1991 I moved from the Foreign Ministry to the Economic Ministry, I had the chance to implement the policies that over a decade I had preached from the outside.

For the Convertibility Law, I was inspired by the experience of Carlos Pellegrini in the 1890s and in the observation of the behaviour of the people during the years of hyperinflation. In those circumstances, Argentines decided to use the dollar instead of the local currency, the austral, to protect their savings, even when holding dollars was illegal. The complementarity between the currency board which created the convertible peso and the legalization of the use of the dollar as an alternative currency was crucial to restoring confidence, creating stability and reinitiating growth.

The debt situation was no different than what President Avellaneda in the 1870s and President Pellegrini in the 1890s had to face. We, like them, had to restructure external debt to normalize financial relations with the main capital markets and, at the same time, had to recreate trust in the local markets.

When I ran for President in 1999 my view was that Argentina needed to deepen the reforms of the 1990s, particularly in the provinces that had run large fiscal deficits financed with borrowing from the local banks at high floating interest rates. My opponents had the benefit of the apparatus of two big and traditional political parties. In the end I did not win but my ideas helped shape the campaign and the policies of De la Rúa's government.

In 2001 I was called into government again. The boat was sinking and I sank with it, but I tried.

When confronted with the financial crisis that followed the recession and deflation that had started at the end of 1998, it reminded me of the problems debt deflation created during the 1890s that convinced Roca convertibility had to be restored at a parity different from that prevailing until the crisis of 1890. But the change in parity or the flotation of the convertible peso could have only been implemented after a successful restructuring of the public debt, something we started, but that the institutional coup of December 2001 interrupted.

In the few months I was in De la Rúa's government, we tried hard to avoid a disorderly default and an explosive devaluation similar to what Presidents Saenz Peña and Victorino de la Plaza had successfully done between 1914 and 1916, when convertibility had to be suspended to face the crisis generated by the First World War. Similarly, Presidents Uriburu and Justo, when faced with the impact on the local economy of the Great Depression, succeeded in abandoning the gold standard without disorganizing the economy through the valuable advice of Prebisch and Pinedo. Unfortunately, in 2001, politics crushed policies and, in the end, corporatism and special interests prevailed as I explain in Chapter 16.

The simultaneous default on the foreign debt and the forced 'peso-ification' of domestic debt, which was in fact default on domestic debt, provoked a large devaluation of the peso so that the economy jumped from deflation into a period of high and variable inflation that has endured until these days. In turn, inflation is again the main problem of the Argentine economy that Macri's government has to cope with today.

We title Part V of this book 'Reform and counter-reform' because my successors undid most of what was done during the period that I was directly involved in economic policy. I was on the opposing political side, powerless and politically persecuted. Duhalde and the Kirchners not only made me a scapegoat, but tried to silence me. I kept writing, sometimes defending myself from attacks, other times criticizing the policy mistakes that in my mind and experience they were making. I wrote two books in Spanish describing the consequences of the policies that had reintroduced inflation and once more isolated the Argentine economy from the world.

After commenting on my book *Camino a la Estabilidad*, published in Spanish in 2014, one of the most respected economic historians of Argentina, Gerardo della Paolera, suggested that I write a book for the English-speaking public explaining my evaluation of the economic reforms of the 1990s and the subsequent counter reform of the last 14 years. He found that the comparison between historical episodes and the events of the last quarter of a century I present in that book is useful to understand why stabilization and economic liberalization plans have frequently failed permanently to reverse the isolationist and interventionist policies that since the mid-1940s generated persistent inflation, stagflation and hyperinflation.

When my daughter agreed to co-author this book, I decided to follow della Paolera's advice. Once we jointly decided what historical episodes to focus on, she did most of the research and writing of the historical part, Chapters 1 to 13, allowing me to concentrate on Chapters 14 to 17. In this part of the book, I try to merge an objective description of events with my subjective interpretation of the ideas, circumstances, conflicts, and prejudices that once again undid economic reforms that brought stability and economic development to Argentina.

As we wrap up this book, Argentina seems to have changed course again. A responsible government is trying hard to open up the economy to trade once more, reinsert it in the world and fight inflation. I wish them the best. My main advice to them is: do not ignore our past because the problems our current leaders face are similar to those faced in the past after periods of similar statism and international isolation. There is much to learn from our nation's experience. I sincerely hope this book helps not only our people, but also those citizens of the world that look at the future of Argentina with interest and hope.

Domingo Felipe Cavallo

Acknowledgments

Over many years of research and policy development, many scholars and professionals helped me to assemble the information and ideas summarized in this book. The list of colleagues would be so long that I would need several pages to list all of them. But I want to mention four people who helped us during the preparation of the manuscript. Agustin Cavallo, who organized all the figures and tables, and Daniel Runde, Paxton Helms and Conor Savoy for their excellent editorial efforts. Of course, none of them are responsible for any errors that may remain.

Contributors

Domingo Felipe Cavallo was Minister of the Economy twice and Minister of Foreign Affairs in Argentina. He was twice elected as a member of the National Congress. He also served as President of the Central Bank of Argentina. He is honorary President of Fundación Mediterránea, the research institute in applied economics which he created in 1977. He has taught at the National University of Córdoba, the Stern Business School at New York University, Harvard University and Yale University. Dr Cavallo is the author of numerous books written in Spanish, most recently, *Pasión por Crear* (2001), *Estanflación* (2008) and *Camino a la Estabilidad* (2014).

Dr Cavallo is a Correspondent Member of the Royal Academy of Moral and Political Sciences of Spain. He is also a member of the Group of Thirty. He has received honorary doctorates from the University of Bologna, the Université Paris 1 Panthéon-Sorbonne, the University of Turin, Ben Gurion University and Genoa University.

He is currently a Partner at Global Source Partners LLC and the Chairman and CEO of DFC Associates LLC. Dr Cavallo resides in Buenos Aires. He is married to Sonia Abrazian and has three children and seven grandchildren.

Sonia Cavallo Runde is a lecturer in the politics of development at The Catholic University of America. She was a co-founder of CIPPEC, a think tank in Argentina. She studied economics at the Universidad de San Andrés in Argentina. She holds a Master's Degree in Public Policy from the Harvard Kennedy School of Government. Sonia Cavallo Runde is married and has three children. She splits her time between Buenos Aires and Mclean, VA, USA.

Abbreviations

ANSES	Administración Nacional de la Seguridad Social
ARSAT	Argentina Satelital
BOCONs	Bonos de Consolidación de Deudas
CEPAL/ECLAC	Comisión Económica para América Latina/Economic Comission for Latin America and the Caribbean
CGT	Confederación General del Trabajo
CIPPEC	Centro de Implementación de Políticas Públicas para la Equidad y el Crecimiento
CNAP	Caja Nacional de Ahorro Postal
CPI	Consumer Price Index
ERP	Ejército Revolucionario del Pueblo
EU	European Union
EXIM Bank	Export-Import Bank of the United States
FIEL	Funcación de Estudios Latinoaméricanos
FORA	Federación Obrera Regional
FORJA	Fuerza de Orientación Radical de la Jóven Argentia
FREPASO	Frente País Solidario
GATT	General Agreement on Tariffs and Trade
GDP	Gross domestic product
GOU	Grupo de Oficiales Unidos
IADB	Inter-American Development Bank
IAPI	Instituto Argentino para la Promoción del Intercambio
IEERAL	Instituto de Estudios Económicos sobre la Realidad Argentina y Latinoamericana
IMF	International Monetary Fund
INDEC	Instituto Nacional de Estadística y Censos
INTA	Instituto Nacional de Tecnología Agropecuaria
ISI	Import Substitution Industrialization
ITDT	Instituto Torcuato Di Tella
LEBACs	Letras del Banco Central
MERCOSUR	Southern Common Market (Mercado Común del Sur/Mercado Comum do Sul)
M0	Monetary Base

NAFTA	North American Free Trade Agreement
PPI	Producer Price Index
SOMISA	Sociedad Murta Siderúrgica Argentina
UCA	Universidad Católica Argentina
UCeDe	Unión de Centro Democrático
UCRI	Unión Cívica Radical Intransiquente
UCRP	Unión Cívica Radical del Pueblo
UDELPA	Unión del Pueblo Argentino
UGT	Unión General de Trabajadores
UIA	Unión Industrial Argentina
US(A)	United States (of America)
USTR	United States Trade Representative
YPF	Yacimientos Petrolíferos Fiscales

Introduction

Argentina's economy is intriguing: many economic episodes throughout its 200 years as an independent nation are difficult to explain on purely economic terms. It is necessary to relate the economic events, plagued by conflicts of interest, to political circumstances, external conditions and ideological discussions. The purpose of this book is to help the reader make the connection between historical and current events through all these angles.

It also seeks to offer researchers and policymakers who confront similar problems in other economies relevant lessons from the Argentine experience.

The book has two distinct components: an economic history of Argentina from the Spanish colonial period to 1990, which is coauthored by Domingo Felipe Cavallo with Sonia Cavallo Runde and a narrative by Domingo Felipe Cavallo on the last quarter of a century of reform and counter-reform.

There are many excellent accounts of Argentinean history for the long period ending in 1990. We drew heavily on the works of Luis Alberto Romero, Tulio Alperín Donghi, José Ignacio García Hamilton, David Rock, Jonathan Brown, Mario Bunge, Carlos Díaz Alejandro, Roberto Cortés Conde, Gerardo della Paolera, Alan Taylor, Juan José Llach, Juan Carlos De Pablo and the many others referenced.

The only originality we claim for Parts I to IV of the book results from the selection of episodes we focus on. The events selected, we believe, deserve detailed attention because they are important to understanding Argentina's current problems and offer lessons for other countries. In addition, there is some originality in our political approach. Deliberately, we seek to link economic and political events with ideological discussions and shed light on the many conflicts of interest among increasingly organized pressure groups. The purpose of this sociological analysis is to explain why administrations frequently and drastically changed the rules of the game, or could not carry out the policies that needed to be done.

Part V is a first-hand account. The author played a crucial role as a decision maker during a large part of that period and has strong views on both the merits and the shortcomings of the decisions adopted in the period 1990–2015. The author's view is very different from the narrative that the governments of Nestor and Cristina Kirchner offered over their 12 years in power. Their narrative was strong and persistent during the entire time they held political power. The Kirchners were not reluctant to spend taxpayer money to publicize or even propagandize their narrative. Argentina experienced favourable external conditions during the commodity boom from 2003 to 2012 that helped them hide the problems they created. This part of the book is the sole responsibility of Domingo Felipe Cavallo and that is why despite the advice of professional editors we use the first person singular.

***

In the 200 years since the birth of independent Argentina, the most relevant episodes that help understand its economic history are two long waves of globalization. The first lasted from 1860 to 1930, and the second began in 1945 and continues to this day.

Great Britain led the first wave of globalization until 1914. It started to weaken with the First World War and ended when the Great Depression erupted in the USA, the country that had started to displace Great Britain as the world's production leader.

The second wave of globalization began in 1945 as the USA emerged from the Second World War as the leading global economic power. After seven decades and many vicissitudes, this process continues. There are new strong actors disputing the economic and military power of the USA, particularly China and Russia, that until 1990 still functioned as autarchic economic systems but have entered the global economy during the last quarter of a century.

During the first wave of globalization, Argentina was one of the most successful emerging economies of the time. The political system functioned under the National Constitution enacted in 1853 and subscribed by the Province of Buenos Aires in 1860. Between 1870 and 1913, the Argentine economy grew faster than that of the USA, Canada, Australia and Brazil, four countries that, like Argentina, are rich in natural resources and attracted large inflows of capital and immigrants from Europe. Economic historians refer to this period as the 'Golden Age' of the Argentine economy.

As with most countries actively engaged in international trade and finance, Argentina suffered from the numerous shocks that emerged after the First World War such as the European hyperinflations of the 1920s, the Great Depression and the Second World War.

Economic troubles fuelled defensive attitudes of increasingly organized interest groups. Democratic institutions weakened allowing these interest groups, including the armed forces, to capture greater political power.

Argentina suffered its first military coup in 1930, and until 1946 the governments were either military or civilians elected in rigged elections.

In contrast with the first wave of globalization, Argentina delayed its participation in the second wave of globalization for 45 years. From 1945 to 1990, economic policies turned both populist and internationally isolationist.

The Argentine economy suffered rampant inflation and suffered a long period of slow and unstable growth.

After being a prominent member of the military government that seized power in 1943, Juan Perón won the election to become president in 1946. From the beginning of his ascent to power, Perón viewed the promotion of labour intensive manufacturing, construction and domestic services as a way to shift the distribution of income away from capital and land intensive agriculture in favour of urban workers. To implement this strategy, Perón relied upon multiple exchange rates, high import duties and quantitative restrictions on imports, and implicit or explicit taxes on exports of agricultural goods.

The desired effect on urban real wages was short lasting because the policies triggered stagnation of agricultural production, a drastic reduction in exports, and difficulties in financing for imports of intermediate and capital goods required for the efficient production of manufactured goods and domestic services.

In addition to its import substitution growth and redistribution strategy, the government of Perón increased government expenditures that resulted in fiscal deficits. Initially, levies on wealth and past savings financed these fiscal deficits, but eventually the government relied on monetary expansion. Inflation became a persistent phenomenon: with the exception of a peak in 1959 (a year of a drastic release of repressed inflation), inflation varied at around 30 per cent per year. The worst inflationary experience, however, was yet to come.

Supply constraints and low productivity during the early 1950s restricted the expansion of industry. Even when industrial expansion resumed, particularly after the opening up to foreign direct investment during Arturo Frondizi's presidency (1958–1962) overall growth was lower than during the Golden Age, lower than in the USA, Australia and Canada in the same period, and significantly lower than in neighbouring Brazil.

In 1973, Perón became President for a third time. This was a time of favourable external terms of trade, not dissimilar to those that existed at the beginning of his first presidency. In two years, Perón implemented similar policies to those applied earlier: heavy taxes on agriculture, active encouragement of manufacturing, construction and domestic services, a sharp increase in public spending, and large fiscal deficits financed by massive monetary expansion.

This time, terms of trade reversed much more rapidly than in the late 1940s. The death of Perón and the intensification of the war between the military and the guerrillas curtailed the political power of Isabel Perón. In this context, her attempt to reverse the policies, as Perón himself had done after 1949, generated protests, strikes and riots, and ended in an inflationary explosion in June 1975.

The 15 years that followed the inflationary explosion of 1975 were dramatic. Inflation always ran above 100 per cent per year and attempts to introduce partial economic reforms failed to reverse the climate of stagnation and high inflation.

4 *Introduction*

The growth performance during this period was poor. Per capita income declined at a rate of 1.5 per cent per year while the world expanded at a rate of 1.6 per cent per year. By the end of this period, the Argentine economy experienced hyperinflation. Between March 1989 and March 1990, the annual rate of inflation reached 11,000 per cent.

The traumatic experience of 1975–1990 created the political conditions for a complete reorganization of the economy: an ambitious economic reform that pursued a full integration of Argentina into the global economy framed by a monetary system similar to that of the initial decades of the 20th century.

During the first quarter of 1991, the Argentine government passed the Convertibility Law that created a new monetary system based on the peso convertible at 1 to 1 to the dollar and fully backed by foreign reserves. The same law legalized the use of the dollar in competition with the peso.

At the same time, the government eliminated taxes on agricultural exports, reduced import duties, and removed quantitative restrictions on imports. It also privatized state owned companies after reinstating competition in the markets or regulating services that operated under conditions of natural monopoly. The government reduced public expenditures, simplified the tax system and eliminated the fiscal deficit.

Inflation fell to 3 per cent per annum in 1994. The country enjoyed four consecutive years of rapid growth. In 1995, a sudden stop of capital inflows because of the crisis in Mexico generated a recession, but the International Monetary Fund (IMF) and other financial institutions, including international private banks, provided lending of last resort and the country recovered in one year without any alteration of the rules of the game. Argentina again experienced rapid growth from 1996 until 1998.

Because of several external shocks, particularly the devaluation of the Brazilian real in February 1999, the depreciation of the euro from 1999 until the middle of 2002, Argentina entered into recession in the late 1990s. With a sharp deterioration of terms of trade and an inability to devalue the peso, deflation accompanied the recession and created a climate of virtual depression. Unemployment and poverty increased continuously.

Beginning in 1999, government expenditure as a percentage of gross domestic product (GDP) increased because of both the recession's impact on GDP and the augmented interest costs on the public debt, particularly that of the provinces with the local banking system. For the same reason, revenues started to decline and the fiscal deficit increased. This fiscal deterioration caused another sudden stop in capital inflows.

In the last quarter of 2000, foreign capital started to leave the country and in 2001, the country suffered another abrupt reduction in net capital flows that produced illiquidity in the banking system. At this point the Provinces had trouble servicing their debts, which caused several banks to become insolvent, and neither the Central Bank nor the government had resources to help them.

The IMF, that earlier provided some funding, decided in November 2001 to withdraw its support when the government announced an orderly restructuring of the public debt. A run on the banks forced the government to restrict withdrawing in cash of bank deposits. This move triggered riots and forced the fall of the De la Rúa government.

In the middle of this political chaos, a new provisional government led by interim President Eduardo Duhalde decided to abandon convertibility, transforming all financial obligations, including bank deposits, from dollars into inconvertible pesos. This caused the peso to suffer a large devaluation: the price of the dollar jumped from 1 to 3.8 pesos between January and September 2002. In 2002 the consumer price index increased 42 per cent and the devaluation and the reintroduction of inflation dramatically increased unemployment and poverty in the first half of 2002.

The government froze wages, pensions and public utility rates, and introduced taxes on agricultural exports and price controls on beef and other basic consumption items. In 2003, as foreign terms of trade improved and the US dollar weakened, the Argentine economy that between 1998 and 2002 had suffered a 25 per cent decline in GDP started to recover rapidly and the peso appreciated. The price of the dollar went down from 3.8 pesos to slightly below 3 pesos and inflation declined to 3 per cent in 2003.

The new government led by Nestor Kirchner allowed wages to increase gradually in 2003 and more rapidly beginning in 2005. Government expenditure also started to increase rapidly. In 2006, despite the fact that the compulsory debt restructuring of 2005 allowed for a sharp reduction in the interest cost of the public debt, government spending returned to the same proportion of GDP as in 2001.

Monetary policy targeted growth rather than inflation so the Central Bank intervened to stop the appreciation of the peso. Beginning in 2005, as wages started to recover, government expenditures increased at a rapid pace. Since monetary expansion was committed to preventing the appreciation of the peso, inflation started to increase again.

Inflation accelerated to 6 per cent in 2004 and increased up to 24 per cent in 2008. The government, instead of using monetary policy as an anti-inflationary tool, decided to cheat on the official measurement of inflation which beginning in 2007 was 'fixed' (by data manipulation) at around 9 per cent per year. Domestic debt was indexed to officially measured inflation and holders of debt suffered a new devaluation of their assets. This policy prevented voluntary domestic debt financing for deficits and deeply discredited Argentina in the world.

The economy continued growing quickly, except in 2009 when the global recession and a conflict with farmers produced a recession. Favourable external terms of trade and large fiscal and monetary stimulus for domestic demand continued to drive economic growth.

The government intervention in markets, the restrictions on foreign trade, the freezing of public utility rates, the renationalization of public utility companies, and the large increase in government expenditure and tax pressures was tantamount to a counter-reform of the reform carried out in the 1990s.

By 2012 the Achilles heel of the Argentine economy was not only inflation, by then a persistent phenomenon, but also the many relative price distortions that discouraged efficient investment and instead encouraged capital flight, land speculation, and inefficient real estate investment. After 2012, stagflation became the new reality.

***

At the beginning of 2016, as we are writing this introduction, Argentina's economy is once again in the middle of economic turmoil. The current type of crisis has historically followed episodes of populist and isolationist policies.

The policies of the last decade have left Argentina with a 40 per cent annual inflation rate, increasing unemployment, a three-year long recession, declining foreign trade, and almost no foreign direct investment. Not surprisingly, around US $80 billion have fled the country during the last seven years.

On 10 December 2015 a new government took power. In order to find sustainable solutions, President Mauricio Macri is attempting reforms and policies that have already been tested in the past. Similar attempts have historically proved to be politically difficult and the prelude and consequences are both worth reviewing.

At least twice in its recent past, the country has gone through similar crises. In both those instances, the crises came after several years of high government spending, big and persistent fiscal deficits financed mainly by printing money, government-imposed restrictions on exports and imports, exchange controls, and widespread market interventions. These expansionary policies unfolded during years of favourable external terms of trade and became unsustainable at the point when those terms reversed.

The first crisis dates to 1949, the fourth year of the first government of Juan Perón. The other happened in 1975, in year three of the third Peronist government, when Perón had already passed away and his third wife and vice-president, Maria Estela Martinez de Perón (popularly known as Isabelita), succeeded him in power.

These crises were similar to the current one, but were certainly not the only economic crises that Argentina has endured during its history. Crises also developed after periods of relatively orthodox policies aimed at integrating the country into the world economy. There was a crisis in 1914 and another in 1930, in both cases after decades of active and successful engagement by Argentina in the first wave of globalization. There was also another crisis of that kind at the turn of the 21st century, after a decade of economic policies seeking to again integrate Argentina into the revitalized process of globalization that followed the fall of the Berlin Wall and the Iron Curtain.

These two types of crises are different in nature, but external circumstances were crucial in explaining the moment when the crises started. The crisis that followed periods of active participation by Argentina in the global economy happened at times of significant decline in external demand for Argentine exports which generated domestic deflationary pressures. The crisis that followed periods of populism and international isolation came when the improvement in foreign terms of trade that had made possible the application of those policies, reversed.

The macroeconomic conditions of the economy in these two types of crises differed significantly. The macroeconomic problem at the time of the 1914, 1930 and 2001 crises was *deflation*. The problem at the time of the crisis of 1949 and 1975 was *inflation*, the same challenge that Argentina faces now.

Finally, throughout Argentine history there are many other currency and debt crises that originated in domestic fiscal and monetary disturbances rather than in external shocks. This was the case of the 1876 and the 1890 crises and the crisis of 1958, 1962, 1981 and 1985. The policies applied to overcome the crises of 1876 and 1890 were able to restore price stability after a few years. But, for the crises that followed populist and isolationist episodes, price stability was elusive. To make matters worse, a few years after each attempt to overcome the crisis, inflation accelerated. The only successful stabilization process was that of 1991 after the country had suffered hyperinflation.

Now that Argentina once again confronts the consequences of unsustainable populist and isolationist policies, it is fitting to ponder the future course of events. Should we expect that the Macri government will encounter the same difficulties that governments had in 1949 and 1975 undoing populist policies similar to those of the Kirchner government?

Will the Macri government and Argentina's citizens have to endure hyperinflation again before being able to restore price stability and growth? Could the experience of the traumatic 20 years that followed 1949, and the even more traumatic 15 years that followed 1975, be used to design a strategy that can achieve success and revive the stable and globalized environment that began in Argentina, as in most Latin American countries, around 1990?

This book tries to answer those questions by digging into the economic history of the country and by reviewing the play-by-play of its numerous and recurrent crises. It goes back to the centuries when Argentina was still part of the Spanish Empire and to the first 50 years of the United Provinces of Río de la Plata that preceded the formation of the unified Argentine Nation. Several of the institutional pitfalls and the confrontational behaviour of the political and economic elites are a legacy of Argentina's history: more than three centuries of highly centralized and interventionist governments failed to build a peaceful and modern society. Very different outcomes were achieved in the USA, Canada and Australia, to name only a few earlier emerging nations that had human and geographical characteristics similar to Argentina, but with institutional arrangements that allowed for a much higher degree of human liberty and showed a much higher respect for the rule of law and property rights.

***

8 *Introduction*

Hopefully, the discussion of the vicious consequences of persistent inflation, stagflation and hyperinflation as clearly demonstrated by the Argentine historical experience, will serve as a warning to avoid the use and abuse of monetary policy as an instrument to inflate debts away. This is a relevant warning at times when influential economists encourage countries with widespread debt overhangs to apply an 'Argentine style' solution. Using monetary policy, or even worse, redesigning monetary regimes in order to facilitate collection of the inflation tax instead of engaging in an orderly process of fiscal consolidation and debt restructuring is misleading. It merely replicates all the policy mistakes that transformed Argentina from the poster child of price stability and growth in the 1990s to the basket case of the past 15 years.

The evidence of the consequences of populism and isolationism on investment and productivity that emerge from the historical experience of Argentina may be useful for countries that are trying to integrate their economies into world trade and finance. Is it possible to take advantage of opportunities offered by globalization? Is it possible to protect from the negative external shocks that result from globalization? For an answer, we can look back once again. In matters of growth and globalization, Argentina likewise turned from a poster child in the period 1870–1913 to a basket case in the period 1945–1990.

***

Crucial to the explanation of the course of events that characterized the intriguing economic history of Argentina is the clash between leading ideologies and the interaction of increasingly organized interest groups and corporations, particularly in the interwar period when, instead of creating synergies, they nurtured conflicts, violence and permanent institutional instability.

The return of democracy in 1983 created positive expectations that the political system would reverse the institutional shortfalls left behind by more than 50 years of successive coups, military rule, weak constitutional governments elected in restricted elections, and Peronism as the hegemonic political party. However, the experience of the last 15 years has demonstrated that the weaknesses in Argentina's democracy persist, particularly within its republican institutions.

We hope that the present and future governments of Argentina succeed not only in re-establishing economic order but also, and above all, fully restoring the federal, democratic and republican institutions of the National Constitution.

Part I
The southernmost territory of imperial Spain turns into the Argentine Nation

1 The Spanish heritage

Latin America's Spanish heritage has been valuable in many respects; but, it is clear that it did not leave a great legacy in economic matters. Argentina, like all Latin American countries colonized by Spain, inherited a highly bureaucratic administration and a backward economic structure.[1]

This administrative arrangement imposed by the Spanish Empire responded to the Crown's desire to add new land to its sovereign domain, convert natives[2] to Christianity and vassals of the Crown, and increase the wealth of Spain through the exploitation of the new territories' abundant mineral resources.

The Empire had many administrative units, viceroyalties, governments, general captaincies, and courts that required the appointment of a large number of public officials, administrators, tax collectors and judges. Furthermore, defending these territories, which had poorly defined borders, and maintaining domestic law and order required large and complex military forces.

In Argentina, the particular economic structure that the country inherited upon independence stemmed from three key socio-economic phenomena that had been in place for centuries: the exploitation of the silver mines in Potosí, the Jesuit missions' contribution to human development, and the export-led economy of Buenos Aires based on cattle raising ranches known as *estancias*.

The exploitation of the silver mines of Potosí and its supply chain along the Royal Road to Alto Perú was the engine of growth for more than two centuries and provided the bulk of the money that financed civil servants, soldiers and the Church. Its productivity declined, however, during the 18th century and its financial contribution to the United Provinces of Río de la Plata ceased with the loss of Alto Perú in 1813.

The Jesuits and other Catholic regular orders organized communal settlements of natives, called 'reductions' or 'missions'. The missions became increasingly active and productive in interregional trade. There were missions not only in the cities on the Royal Road but also in those on the Río de la Plata waterways and on both sides of the Andes. Unfortunately, the missions had lost their economic role by the time of the creation of the Viceroyalty of Río de la Plata. After the expulsion of the Jesuits by King Carlos III, the inhabitants of the old missions migrated to nearby cities or to Buenos Aires to work as artisans and peasants or were recruited by private merchants that were well connected with the government. These same private merchants also purchased most of the land and capital equipment of the old missions, thereby creating a class of large landowners not much different from the class of cattle ranch proprietors then emerging around Buenos Aires.

During the 18th century, the development of cattle ranches and the exports of hides, tallow and grease caused the port of Buenos Aires to become the new engine of growth of the economy that would allow Argentina to join the more open and dynamic world economy of the 19th century.

After Buenos Aires became the capital of the Viceroyalty of the Río de la Plata, and legal trade shifted from Lima to the port of Buenos Aires, its political and economic role enlarged significantly. Other European colonial powers became increasingly interested in the Río de la Plata area. The British invasions of Buenos Aires and Montevideo in 1806 and 1807 had two effects. First, creoles realized that it was they, not the Spanish Viceroyalty, who were the true defenders of the city. Second, it helped the creoles ponder the value of freer trade similar to that long pursued by the British. These local events together with Napoleon's invasion of Spain helped trigger the May Revolution.

The Royal Road to Alto Perú and the Río de la Plata waterways

The Spanish conquerors founded cities and established a European presence in what is today Argentina beginning in the 1530s. In 1532, *Adelantado*[3] Francisco Pizarro subjugated the Inca Empire and started to expand Spanish control along the west coast of South America. Settlements on the east coast started soon after. In 1536, *Adelantado* Pedro de Mendoza founded Buenos Aires on the western edge of the Río de la Plata. Members of Mendoza's expedition navigated the Paraná River and founded the city of Asunción next to a river that the native inhabitants of those territories, the *Guaraníes*, called Paraguay. The Buenos Aires settlement did not survive the attacks of the native people (though Asunción did), but Juan de Garay re-founded Buenos Aires in 1580.

From the beginning of the conquest, the *Adelantados* searched for the mines from which the natives obtained the gold and the silver that they wore as ornaments and used as ceremonial implements. In fact, the name *Río de la Plata* comes from the first explorers who believed that the river would take them to rich mines in the Andes. Even the name Argentina, first used in a poem by Martin Del Barco Centenera published in Lisbon in 1602, comes from *argentum,* the Latin name for silver. Argentine was used as a poetic synonym for an inhabitant of Río de la Plata. Despite this optimistic nomenclature, the conquerors did not find silver in the territory of Argentina, which limited the area's Spanish population for more than two centuries.

During the colonial era, the population clustered around the richest mines or in places endowed with human and natural resources. In these areas the indigenous populations were enslaved and forced to provide goods and labour for the mines. Around 1540 the conquerors discovered *Cerro Chico*, one of the richest mines in Spanish America, and founded Potosí nearby in 1545. By the mid-17th century, Potosí was one of the biggest cities in the world with a population of 150,000.

To exploit the natural and human resources of the newly conquered territories, the Spanish Crown used an institution called *encomienda*. The *encomendero* was given charge of a certain number of natives who were obliged to pay tribute in money or in labour. When appropriate for his productive activities, the *encomendero* was also given licenses to extract minerals or develop land either for cultivation or to raise horses, mules, or cattle. The natives, having no money to pay the tributes, provided the much-needed labour. The Inca had used a similar institution, the *mita*, long before the arrival of the Spaniards. The *mita* provided them labour to extract gold and silver from the mines of Perú and Alto Perú.

From the 16th to the 18th centuries, the economy of today's Argentina slowly developed along two main north–south axes: the Royal Road to Alto Perú connecting Potosí with Buenos Aires and the Río de la Plata waterways connecting Buenos Aires with Asunción. To the west of the Royal Road to Alto Perú, the Spaniards founded cities that connected to the Captain Generalcy of Chile across the Andes. To the east of the Río de la Plata waterways, the Spaniards founded cities and native missions in an attempt to block Portuguese occupation of the same territories. During the 17th and 18th centuries, the Portuguese expanded their sovereign domains westward from their first locations on the eastern coast. Primitive nomadic tribes, native to the area, populated the territory between the two north–south settlement axes.

Connecting these two axes from west to east, the Europeans controlled two slices of territory: the areas surrounding the road from Santa Fe to Córdoba and the lands north of a line of *fortines* (small forts) that went from Buenos Aires to San Rafael in Mendoza across the south of today's provinces of Córdoba and San Luis.

Coins minted in Potosí supported trade along the Royal Road to Alto Perú and the Río de la Plata waterways. Córdoba, Salta and Jujuy provided mules, horses, oxen and carts; Tucumán provided sugar; Mendoza and San Juan produced wines; and Paraguay produced a herbal tea called *yerba mate*.

Unlike the Alto Perú, the territories that would later become Argentina did not have silver or gold and the Spanish empire was not interested in cultivating the fertile *pampas*. Furthermore, the native population (with the exception of the *guaraníes* of Paraguay) preferred to move from their lands or die rather than become virtual slaves on an *encomienda*.

All trade between the colonies and the outside world was under a Spanish-controlled mercantile monopoly. All shipments in and out of the Viceroyalty of Perú, incredibly including today's territory of Argentina, went through

Lima and other ports on the Pacific. This continued until the creation of the Viceroyalty of Río de la Plata in 1776. The long distances that people and merchandise had to move in Argentine territory was a large barrier to Argentina's human and economic development.

Between the second half of the 16th century and the second half of the 18th century the bulk of government revenue came, directly or indirectly, from the mines of Potosí. The government also collected custom duties and other internal taxes but these revenues represented less than one-third of total government revenue. Silver coins and, to a lesser extent gold coins, minted in Potosí were the only means used in non-barter transactions. Many of the exchanges did not involve the use of money.

Only the *encomenderos*, the public officers, and religious authorities received income that allowed them to accumulate wealth. The bulk of the population earned incomes that barely allowed them to subsist and many did not even participate in the monetary economy, bartering just as they had in pre-Spanish colonial era.

The Jesuit missions

A concession by the Pope expressed in several bulls granted the Spanish Crown rights that previously were the exclusive privilege of the Church. The Crown could organize the presence of the Catholic Church in the Americas, receive the *Diezmo*,[4] organize and distribute missionaries in the new territories, decide on the location of churches and cathedrals, and select candidates for clerical positions in the Americas. These rights and responsibilities were defined under the rules of royal patronage and the *Vicariato Regio* which granted the Spanish Crown the right to supervise and the obligation to protect the Catholic Church in the region.

The first religious orders that arrived in America were the Dominicans and the Franciscans. The Mercedarians and the Augustinians followed with the Jesuits the last to arrive, towards the end of the 16th century. The *encomienda* and the *mita* functioned in places where there was a strong concentration of natives. The Crown wanted to secure the evangelization of the natives that lived dispersed or in small communities that were not useful for the *encomenderos*. To assist with evangelization, the crown decided that the natives were to be 'congregated and reduced in comfortable and convenient locations' called reductions or missions. The missions were religious and socio-cultural institutions created and administered by religious orders, the Jesuits and Franciscans being the most prominent. The *Guaraní* missions in Paraguay played an important role in the 17th and 18th centuries.

The natives' reductions were a social and economic development experiment that stood out from the rest of the social and economic structures that emerged from the interaction of the public officers, the *encomenderos*, and the private landowners. Once the missionaries set up the first reductions at the beginning of the 17th century, the majority of the natives that up until then had resisted the *encomiendas* voluntarily chose to abandon their communities and join the missions. At the missions, they received land to produce their food and accepted the rules imposed by the missionaries. The natives in the missions were well treated; they participated in the life of the community, received religious instruction, and learned more advanced European agricultural techniques to cultivate the land.

The most successful Jesuit reductions were located around the Paraná, Paraguay and Uruguay rivers in territories that today belong to Argentina, Paraguay and Brazil, but they also played an important role in almost all the cities on the Royal Road to Alto Perú. The Jesuits first settled in Córdoba in 1599 which became their headquarters in the region. There were six missions scattered throughout Córdoba. They were called *estancias* because they were agricultural and trade centres. In Córdoba, the Jesuits created the first University. In fact, in the 17th century, the city of Córdoba, the heart of the former Jesuit Province of Paraguay, was bigger and more important than Buenos Aires.

In the *Guaraní* missions, the main product produced was *yerba mate*, a herbal tea that the *Guaraní* natives had been cultivating for centuries. They supplied *yerba mate* to all the cities on the Royal Road to Alto Perú and the Río de la Plata waterways, down to Buenos Aires, and to places as distant as Alto Perú and Chile. Contrary to the practice of the *encomenderos*, the missions reinvested the surplus produced by the commercial activities. They invested in common facilities for the communities and churches and financed armies. These armies played an important role in the wars that the governments of Asunción and Buenos Aires fought against the expansionary ambitions of the Portuguese, not only on the territories occupied by the missions, but also along the east coast of the Río de la Plata in today's Uruguay.

Throughout the 17th century, the *Guaraníes* continued migrating to the reductions, attracted by the opportunity to receive an education and attracted by a higher standard of living. They also looked for protection from the Portuguese slavers that besieged them from the east and from the *encomenderos* and public officers in Asunción who were always anxious to capture the human and material resources of the missions.

The *Guaraní* militias of the missions contributed around 4,000 men to the successive campaigns organized by the Government of Buenos Aires to displace the Portuguese from Colonia de Sacramento. Colonia was a strategic location that the Portuguese controlled and used to dispute Spain's claim to the territory of today's Uruguay and to share control of navigation on the Río de la Plata.

Unfortunately, diplomatic negotiations between authorities in Madrid and Lisbon did not adequately take into account the interest of the *Guaraní* missions. In 1750, Spain and Portugal signed the Treaty of Madrid. Spain got Colonia de Sacramento and in return Portugal got all of the missions to the east of the Uruguay River. The natives of the missions rebelled against this decision which led to the so-called '*Guaraní* Wars' between 1752 and 1756.

The circles of power in Lisbon and Madrid, influenced by the practices of enlightened despotism, considered the Jesuits as a state within the state and not compatible with royal absolutism. Eventually, the combined forces of Portugal and Spain defeated the *Guaraníes*. The Jesuits, accused of being instigators of the war, were expelled from Portugal in 1758, from Spain in 1767, and forced to give up their missions.

For Córdoba and the main cities on the Royal Road to Alto Perú, the expulsion of the Jesuits was a harsh blow. The expulsion of the Jesuits deprived the viceroyal system of communal and private property that would have contributed to a less concentrated distribution of economic power when it became the United Provinces of Río de la Plata. The decline of the missions after the expulsion of the Jesuits was the largest setback of the colonial era to the social and economic development of what are today Argentina's Central and Northern provinces.

From *vaquerías* (cattle hunting) to *estancias* (cattle raising ranches)

Until the beginning of the 17th century, Córdoba was, after Potosí, the second most important religious and economic centre in what would became the Viceroyalty of Río de la Plata. Córdoba was located at the intersection of the roads that led from Asunción del Paraguay on the east, through the cities of Santa Fe, with San Luis, Mendoza and Chile in the west, along with San Juan, Catamarca and La Rioja towards the northwest and with Santiago del Estero, Tucumán, Salta and Jujuy, to reach Potosí in the Alto Perú. Until that moment, Buenos Aires was still a village of less than 2,000 inhabitants; it was a marginal port that traded in smuggled merchandise.

The city of Buenos Aires grew in importance throughout the 17th and 18th centuries. Its population increased from less than 2,000 in 1615 to more than 30,000 in 1776, when the Viceroyalty of Río de la Plata was created. From the second half of the 16th century to the second half of the 17th century, cattle ranching developed in the Jesuit Missions and on the properties of the *encomenderos* from Córdoba northwards. The lands assigned to the missions and the *encomenderos* raised mules that were much needed for transportation in Alto Perú, horses for riding, and oxen for pulling carts and wagons. In Córdoba, Mendoza and San Juan the missions and the *encomenderos* also raised cows and goats for milk and beef cattle for export, mainly to Chile.

By the end of the 16th century, wild descendants of the cattle brought from Spain by Juan de Garay had populated the *pampas*. Cows and bulls abounded in the entire territory which was rich with grass and had abundant fresh water. During the second and third decades of the 17th century some merchants and *encomenderos* began to organize groups of horse riders that, with a good pack of dogs, would hunt wild cattle that were valuable for their hides and tallow. Occasionally they would consume the meat but most of the time it remained in the fields and fed vultures and other meat-eating animals. As soon as the *Cabildos*[5] discovered the animals' commercial value, they started to control cattle hunting by issuing authorizations to a limited number of hunters, specifying the volume, area, and period of each authorization.

This hunting of wild cattle developed initially in Córdoba but grew more intensively in Buenos Aires during the 18th century. In the beginning, the hides and tallow trade supplied the domestic market but gradually Buenos Aires merchants started to export to Europe through their port. In this way, cattle hunters and hide traders rapidly increased their wealth and social standing. This social group then lobbied the government to forbid the killing or sale of unmarked animals; and the *Cabildo* of Buenos Aires created a register of marks and distributed mark rights to some 40 hide traders and landowners. Eventually, when the herds of wild cattle started to decline, the same social group started to purchase land to replace cattle hunting with cattle raising. This was the genesis of the cattle ranches that are so characteristic of the Argentine *pampas*.

Up until the expulsion of the Jesuits, only religious orders had owned large tracts of land. The decline and dismantling of the missions after the expulsion of the Jesuits and the rise of cattle ranching for the production and export of hides and tallow to Europe through the port of Buenos Aires started a process of land concentration. A small number of powerful landowners had the money and the political connections to acquire large properties and were the principal beneficiaries of those developments.

The *pampas* remained uncultivated throughout the 16th, 17th and 18th centuries. The production of wheat and maize took place on land close to urban areas and supplied local markets. The powerful bakers' guilds strictly controlled the production and price of wheat flour. The Spanish tradition considered cattle raising which required horse riding a high-order activity but considered farming an inferior activity fit for natives and slaves. Consequently, farming did not develop while cattle ranching for export became the new engine of growth of the economy of Río de la Plata, especially in the hinterlands around the port of Buenos Aires.

From landowners and ranchers to *caudillos*

There were a relatively small number of large landholders and ranch owners linked to the hides and tallow trades. They lived in the cities and often held public office, served in the public militias, or became merchants. The income from those roles allowed them to obtain and expand their properties. The ranchers and landowners were wealthy, and commissioned horsemen to act as private militias against the natives and whomever threatened their property.

The *gauchos*, free-spirited men, were nomadic and did not possess land or cattle. The *gauchos* would either work on the ranches for short periods or participate in wars against the natives. The presence of the natives was a latent and diffuse threat that created a natural synergy between the *gauchos* and their *patrón* (boss).

This economic and social structure was firmly in place in the Viceroyalty of Río de la Plata at the time of the May Revolution; but, two new powerful and ideologically opposed groups would emerge from this structure after the Revolution. On one extreme were the urban elites consisting of lawyers, military leaders and clergymen that aspired to become the enlightened elite of the United Provinces of Río de la Plata. Ideologically, they were liberals and favoured a strong, central government. On the other extreme, landowners and ranchers had become federalist strongmen, ideologically more conservative and committed to the defence of their properties and their economic power. For the five decades after the May Revolution, the clashes between these two social groups would drive the civil wars that challenged the peace and order needed for economic and social progress.

The creation of the Viceroyalty of Río de la Plata

The administration of the new American territories conquered by the Spanish relied on a large and complex bureaucracy. To finance this system, the Crown needed to collect taxes. Taxes included the *Quinto* (one-fifth) imposed on the production of minerals. Other tributes included the *alcabalas,* a transaction tax charged on merchandise entering each city; and the *almojarifazgo* that was a sort of customs duty applied to imports. In addition, the crown charged for the appointment of public officers and clerical posts, as well as for the granting of monopolies for the production and sale of tobacco, playing cards, explosives and other products the production of which required the government's authorization.

At the beginning of the 17th century, Spain suffered a decrease in the income from its American colonies. The production of gold and silver in Potosí had started to decline. Accounts from the time reported that only 700 natives remained alive out of the thousands that had worked in the mines through the *Mita* system. It had become necessary to employ slaves or hire workers. The cost of production had also increased significantly and the Crown had to reduce the *Quinto* (one fifth) to a *Diezmo* (one tenth). Smuggling through the port of Buenos Aires also meant duty tax was not being collected on that trade.

In the face of declines in tax income from America and increased interest of rival European powers in the ports on the Río de la Plata, King Carlos III introduced important changes to the administration of the colonies.

A few years after the expulsion of the Jesuits and as part of his changes, King Carlos III created the Viceroyalty of Río de la Plata with Buenos Aires as the capital. The new Viceroyalty comprised what are today Argentina, Bolivia, Paraguay and Uruguay that until then had been part of the Viceroyalty of Perú and had been obliged to trade and communicate with Spain through Lima. By legalizing the maritime connection with Spain through the port of Buenos Aires, the Crown was able to reduce transportation costs between Potosí and the Spanish ports. This had a positive impact on the development of Buenos Aires. It also increased the size of the military forces located in the city and permitted the arrival of non-Spanish vessels, especially Portuguese and British, as long as they accepted the authority of Spanish customs.

Simultaneous with the creation of the Viceroyalty of Río de la Plata, the Crown decided to increase taxes on domestic sales and imported goods, but exempt exports of hides and tallow. The increase in taxes generated violent uprisings in Alto Perú, but the tax exemption on exports of hides and tallow generated a sharp increase in the official exports of those products. In 1780 the first industrial transformation of meat (into beef jerky) began. The first export of jerky was to Havana in 1785; and in 1796, there were already some 30 *saladeros* producing beef jerky on the west coast of the Río de la Plata.

One of the matters that required the viceroy's attention was the defence of the cattle ranches from attacks by natives. During the course of the 18th century, the *Mapuches* and *Araucanos* from the Chilean central and southern territories started to ride into the pampas looking for wild cattle to bring back. When the wild cattle became scarce, the *Mapuches* and *Araucanos*, sometimes in alliance with the local *Tehuelches*, started raiding the ranches that raised cattle north of the Salado River with the goal of capturing their domesticated cattle. Until the mid-18th century, no military forces had defended the frontier land from these attacks. In 1752, the government of Buenos Aires organized the first militias to undertake this role: the *Blandengues*. In 1778, after the creation of the Viceroyalty of Río de la Plata, Viceroy Vértiz reinforced the defences and created a line of *fortines* tasked with defending the frontier (by then the actual frontier was the Salado River). The *fortines* were small villages that supported the development of cattle ranches. Thanks to this protection, the landowners were able to enlarge their properties and expand cattle production.

The British invasions

Important political developments in the Viceroyalty of Río de la Plata were associated with the impact of Napoleon's France on the connection of the British, the Portuguese and the Spanish empires with their colonies in America. One of those events was the invasion of Buenos Aires in 1806 and 1807 by British forces and the forced abdication of Fernando VII of the Spanish Crown in favour of Napoleon's brother in 1808.[6]

The reaction of the people of Buenos Aires to the British invasions of 1806 and 1807 set a precedent that influenced the events of 1810.

In 1806, an army led by Santiago Liniers, an officer of French origin who had been loyal to Spain for more than three decades, defeated a British army that occupied Buenos Aires for 45 days. Viceroy Rafael de Sobremonte had abandoned Buenos Aires and moved to Córdoba with the royal treasury in his possession following procedures that the law had established many years before. The people of Buenos Aires considered him a coward and did not welcome him back. Meanwhile, the Royal Court of Buenos Aires designated Liniers as the military authority of Buenos Aires. From this position Liniers organized the people to defend the city from new attacks and created several new militias made exclusively of *Creole* soldiers and officers who had voluntarily decided to take up arms. The *Patricios* army corps with Cornelio Saavedra as General and Manuel Belgrano as the commander of one of its three battalions would play an important role in the May Revolution and its aftermath.

A second British invasion occupied Montevideo, in spite of the fact that Viceroy Sobremonte had marched from Córdoba with 3,500 men. When in February 1807 the news of the fall of Montevideo reached Buenos Aires, a *Cabildo Abierto* (town hall assembly) decided to remove Sobremonte and asked the Royal Court of Buenos Aires to designate Santiago de Liniers as the new Viceroy without the approval of the King of Spain. A few months later, when the British attempted to occupy Buenos Aires again, they faced a vigorous and effective defence by the militias and had to surrender just a few hours after entering the city. In this episode, the new Creole militias, organized by Liniers, supplemented the traditional Spanish militias led by Martín de Álzaga, a Spanish merchant and the mayor of the city.

On 1 January 1809, Martín de Álzaga and a group of Spanish residents tried to force the resignation of Viceroy Liniers with the support of the Spanish militias. The Creole militias, led by Cornelio Saavedra, blocked the coup and coup's leaders were exiled to Carmen de Patagones, a town on the southernmost edge of the Viceroyalty. The role played by the Creole militias in defending Liniers encouraged the Creole leaders who were increasingly dissatisfied with the Spanish political and economic order on the River Plate. The Supreme Central Council of Spain, the institution that had accepted the abdication of Fernando VII and designated Joseph Bonaparte as the new king, decided to remove Liniers and designate Baltazar Hidalgo de Cisneros as the new viceroy since they realized that the political environment was starting to threaten the integrity of the Empire.

Even though the leaders of the emerging independent movement discussed the possibility of disobeying the order with Cornelio Saavedra and other members of the Creole militias, they decided that the time had not come to oppose the decision of the Supreme Central Council (which was loyal to Spain) again. Cisneros became the new and last Viceroy of Río de la Plata.

The clashes between the Creoles and the Spanish authorities took place not only in Buenos Aires but also in some cities of the Alto Perú. In May 1809, a coup in Chuquisaca deposed the governor and the Royal Court of Charcas. In July of the same year, a similar movement in La Paz forced the resignation of the governor and the bishop. The Viceroy of Perú sent troops to La Paz and the Viceroy of the Río de la Plata sent troops to Chuquisaca and the movements were crushed.

In November 1809, Cisneros created the 'Political Vigilance Tribunal' to prosecute and punish the *afrancesados* and those that promoted the creation of political regimes that favoured independence from Spain. This decision displeased the Creoles.

In 1809, the Junta de Sevilla instructed Viceroy Hidalgo Cisneros to allow trade with Great Britain as a way to honour the alliance between Spain and the British against Napoleon. At the same time, Viceroy Cisneros saw it as an opportunity to dampen the negative effect that the Napoleonic wars had on trade between Río de la Plata and Spain. The consulate of Cadiz and the merchants that had benefited from the trade monopoly between Spain and America objected to the decision.

Cisneros, under pressure, reversed the policy, but a group of important Buenos Aires landowners asked Mariano Moreno to speak up and demand the re-establishment of free trade. His writing, known as the '*Representación de los Hacendados*' echoed the liberal ideas of English economists and the social philosophers of the Enlightenment period. Manuel Belgrano, in charge of the Consulate of Buenos Aires had already expressed similar opinions, although not as emphatically as Moreno's manifesto. Cisneros finally restored free trade with Great Britain but it lasted only until 19 May 1810.

Notes

1 See García Hamilton (2003).
2 We will use the word 'native' as a synonym for: indigenous tribes/peoples, First Nations or Indians. These were inhabitants of the region before the European colonists arrived in the 16th century. We use the term 'natives' for brevity and to allude to the term Native Americans used in North America.
3 *Adelantado* is the Spanish title given to the explorer commissioned by the King of Spain.
4 Ten per cent tax.
5 A *cabildo* or *ayuntamiento* was a Spanish colonial and early post-colonial, administrative council that governed a municipality.
6 A very good account of these events can be found in Jonathan C. Brown (2010).

References

Brown, Jonathan (2010) *A Brief History of Argentina*, 2nd edn, New York: Checkmark Books.
García Hamilton, José Ignacio (2003) *El Autoritarismo y la improductividad*, Buenos Aires: Sudamericana.
Rock, David (1987) *Argentina 1516–1987: From Spanish Colonization to Alfonsín*, Berkeley: University of California Press.
Szuchman, Mark D. and Brown, Jonathan C. (1994) *Revolution and Restoration: The Rearrangement of Power in Argentina, 1776–1860*, Lincoln and London: University of Nebraska Press.

2 From the May Revolution to the National Organization

In May 1810, as soon as news of the dissolution of the Supreme Central Council of Spain reached Buenos Aires, the leaders of the revolutionary movement decided to remove the Viceroy and organize a local government, arguing that Joseph Bonaparte was illegitimate. The leaders claimed loyalty to the deposed Fernando VII.

The new government in Buenos Aires immediately launched a campaign to convince other cities in the interior of the country to adopt and support the ideals of the May Revolution. This campaign, however, evolved into long and violent wars that would ultimately last five decades.

The idea of independence from Spain eventually prevailed in all of the provinces of the former Viceroyalty of Río de la Plata; but, the United Provinces of Río de la Plata lost the territories of Bolivia, Paraguay and Uruguay which eventually became new nations, independent not only from Spain but also from Argentina.

Most political historians describe the conflicts and wars that involved the United Provinces of Río de la Plata during the five decades that followed the May Revolution as conflicts between the 'unitarist' elites of Buenos Aires and the 'federalist' strongmen (*caudillos*) of the interior. This is a fair description of the conflicts up to 1830. And the confrontation does explain why Bolivia, Paraguay, and Uruguay separated from the United Provinces of Río de la Plata.

However, it is our thesis that the conflicts that prevailed after 1830, when Juan Manuel de Rosas imposed himself as the strongman of Buenos Aires and led an authoritarian government, can be better described as a clash between the liberal intellectual and military elites with the more conservative and nationalist strongmen who were nostalgic for the conservative values of Spain.

Even though Rosas built a narrative in which he was the champion of federalism and characterized his opponents as savage unitarists, his government was extremely centralized and authoritarian, so, in essence, unitarist. In conducting the foreign affairs of the United Provinces of Río de la Plata, Rosas defended Buenos Aires' monopoly on maritime trade to increase customs revenue. This attitude infuriated the governments of Paraguay, Uruguay and

Corrientes who wanted to share in the use of the waterways. This explains the continuous state of war between these provinces and the province of Buenos Aires.

In the provinces of the northwest, linked to Córdoba, all of which demanded a Constitutional Assembly, Rosas imposed his authority by force. Rosas was reluctant to call for a Constitutional Assembly and opposed the idea of a Constitutional Republic.

When Urquiza defeated Rosas at Caseros in early 1852 it was a confrontation between liberal and conservative ideals, much more than the clashes between the unitarists and federalists, that shaped the change in the economic and political paradigm. Urquiza was a true federalist strongman who had supported Rosas in the past but by the early 1850s was convinced that Rosas' authoritarianism and monopolistic ambitions for the Port of Buenos Aires were preventing the constitutional organization of the new nation.

The long-standing aspiration of Buenos Aires to prevail with respect to the rest of the provinces – the unitarism that Juan Manuel de Rosas had kept alive but disguised – led the Province of Buenos Aires to reject the Agreement of San Nicolás and the new constitution, and to choose not to join the newly created Argentine Confederation.

Primera Junta (First Council) and *Junta Grande* (Great Council)

The new government that emerged from the 1810 May Revolution was a council of nine members, two of them military figures: President Cornelio Saavedra, and council member Miguel de Azcuénaga, Four other members were creole lawyers: Manuel Belgrano, Juan José Castelli, Mariano Moreno and Juan José Paso. There were also two Spanish merchants, Domingo Matheu and Juan Larrea, and a clergyman, Manuel Alberti. The official name of the Council was the 'Provisional Governmental Council of the Provinces of the Río de la Plata in the name of Fernando VII' but it is better known as the *Primera Junta* (the First Council).

Confrontation and conflict began immediately after the designation of the First Council. The members of the Royal Audience refused to accept the oath of its members. Instead, the Royal Audience declared loyalty to the Regency Council of Spain that had replaced the Supreme Central Council dissolved at the beginning of 1810. The Regency Council was intended to be the custodian of the power of the Crown of Spain after Napoleon had forced the abdication of Fernando VII. Furthermore, the Royal Audience sent messages to the cities and provinces of the interior of the Viceroyalty instructing them to disregard the orders of the First Council. In response, the revolutionary government arrested the members of the Royal Audience and, arguing that the Audience members' lives were in danger, sent them back to Spain on a British vessel. After successfully vacating the Royal Audience, the First Council appointed pro revolution Creoles to the empty seats.

There was no immediate response in the cities and provinces to the request of the First Council to elect delegates that would represent the interests of their respective jurisdictions in an expanded council. In some places, there was not only indecision but also clear opposition to the revolutionary movement. This was the case in Córdoba, where the governor, the bishop and the most influential members of the community asked Santiago de Liniers, the hero of the reconquest and defence of Buenos Aires, to lead a counter-revolutionary movement.

He accepted but the First Council dispatched a militia that defeated Liniers after three months of chaotic fighting. Juan José Castelli, who like Mariano Moreno was a passionate revolutionary, ordered the execution of Liniers, the governor, and other leaders of the counter-revolution.

Fortified by the quick success in Córdoba, the First Council decided to assemble two larger armies. The first would fight the authorities of Alto Perú which had declared loyalty to Spain and had asked to become part of the Viceroyalty of Perú. The second would pressure the governments of the provinces of Santa Fe, Corrientes, Montevideo and Asunción, where royalists still prevailed. To organize those emerging armies, the First Council ordered all families to contribute their young men to military service. The rich families were able to send their slaves instead; families without slaves had no alternative but to send their young males.

The army led by Castelli was able to occupy Potosí and Charcas in mid-November 1810. It adopted drastic measures against the previous royalist authorities including confiscation of properties belonging to families that had openly opposed the First Council. Emboldened by this success, the majority of the members of the First Council, with the exception of Moreno, decided that it was important to incorporate the delegates from Corrientes, Santa Fe, Tucumán, Córdoba, Tarija, Salta, Jujuy, Catamarca, Mendoza, San Luis, San Juan, La Rioja and Santiago del Estero. Potosí, Cochabamba, Santa Cruz de la Sierra and La Paz had designated delegates, but the First Council did not incorporate them because Castelli did not trust their commitment to the revolutionary cause.

In December 1810, the First Council morphed into the so-called *Junta Grande* (Great Council) with the incorporation of thirteen new delegates. At the suggestion of Dean Gregorio Funes, the delegate from Córdoba, the Great Council created provincial councils with one member, the president, designated by the Great Council and the rest elected by the local *cabildos* (town halls).

Moreno argued that the Great Council should be a legislative assembly with its executive power concentrated in a smaller council of just three members. A very influential group of Creoles backed his idea. They believed that Buenos Aires ought to continue to lead the revolution through a centralized government that it controlled.

Saavedra, who wanted to prevent more clashes with the provinces, decided to send Moreno on a diplomatic mission to Europe as a means of distancing him from the centre of power.

General Manuel Belgrano's army then marching towards Asunción was not as effective as the previous campaign in Alto Perú. The royalist Governor of Paraguay received support from Brazil and defeated Belgrano at Tacuarí in March 1811. A few months later, there was a rebellion in Asunción against that region's governor, and the new creole government proclaimed independence from not only Spain but also Buenos Aires.

Supporters of Moreno attempted a revolt in April 1811. Saavedra and Dean Funes, together with the majority of the members of the Great Council, quickly quashed those attempts.

The Triumvirates

Montevideo continued under the control of the royalists but in early 1811 Gervasio de Artigas, the strongman of the Banda Oriental (the west bank of Río de la Plata), subverted the rural population in support of the revolutionary movement and started fighting the royalists. General Belgrano tried to support Artigas' fight but was ineffective.

Two pieces of bad news reached Buenos Aires by June 1811. First, Castelli had been defeated in Huaqui by an army of the Viceroy of Perú and the revolutionary troops had retreated to Jujuy. Second, the Spanish fleet continued to blockade the port of Buenos Aires as a way to help the royalist government in Montevideo resist the siege of the city by Artigas' militias. These events strengthened the position of the supporters of Moreno in the *Cabildo* of Buenos Aires and forced a negotiation with the Great Council.

Moreno had died at sea on his way to Britain, but his ideas continued to influence events in Buenos Aires. Cornelio Saavedra left Buenos Aires to lead the Army of the North and the *Cabildo* forced the creation of a three party executive authority comprised of a president and two secretaries. The so-called First Triumvirate was created in September 1811. Bernardino Rivadavia, one of the secretaries of this first Triumvirate, was the most influential member of the new executive authority.

The government of the United Provinces faced a difficult situation with the royalist forces of Montevideo controlling navigation in the rivers with the support of the Spanish fleet. At the beginning of 1811, the Regency Council of Spain had decided to move the capital of the Viceroyalty of the Río de la Plata to Montevideo and designated Francisco Javier de Elío as the new viceroy. De Elío requested and obtained the support of Portugal.

Artigas entered into a conflict with the First Triumvirate in October 1811 when Portugal sent troops to Montevideo and Buenos Aires to negotiate a truce with Elío, thereby recognizing him as the ruler of Montevideo and lifting the siege. Even though Gervasio de Artigas organized an exodus of the population of the countryside of Uruguay and moved his troops to Salto Chico (today Concordia) in the province of Entre Ríos, he believed that the First Triumvirate was betraying the revolutionary cause and prioritizing the interest of Buenos Aires.

The Great Council continued as a legislative assembly until its dissolution in December 1811, when the soldiers and officers of the 1st infantry regiment *Patricios* rebelled against the decision of the Triumvirate to transform the militia into a regular army with Manuel Belgrano in command.

The delegates of the provinces that had been represented in the Great Council were ousted from Buenos Aires and accused of insurgency. Cornelio Saavedra, forbidden to return to Buenos Aires, went into exile in Chile. Ten of the officers and soldiers who had led the rebellion were executed by firing squad. This was the second episode, after the execution of Liniers and the leaders of the counter-revolution in Córdoba that ensured that the infighting within the revolution would be violent and bloody.

Manuel Belgrano was designated commander of an army whose mission was to prevent the occupation of the cities from Jujuy to Córdoba by the royalist forces and to retake the Alto Perú region for the revolutionary cause.

Between April and September 1812, General Belgrano devoted his efforts to reorganizing the army. Then, he disobeyed the order of the First Triumvirate to retreat with his troops to Córdoba. Instead, he organized the exodus of the civil population of Jujuy and ordered the army to burn what was left of the city to prevent the royalist army from finding human and material support on their way south. Finally, he confronted the royalists in Tucumán and Salta, where he achieved two significant victories. He then continued north to reoccupy Potosí in June 1813.

While Belgrano undertook the difficult mission of reconquering the Alto Perú region, the fighting between local factions in Buenos Aires intensified. In fact, by mid-1812 the First Triumvirate thought that the former supporters of Moreno, led by Martín Álzaga, were organizing a revolt. Bernardino Rivadavia accused Moreno's supporters formally and they were condemned to death. Martín de Álzaga and his colleagues were shot and then their bodies were hung in Plaza de la Victoria for several days.

By March 1812, a group of military men that had fought against the French in the Spanish Army, with José de San Martín and Carlos María de Alvear as the most prominent members, arrived in Buenos Aires to support the revolution. They offered their services to the First Triumvirate and created the Lautaro Lodge (*Logia Lautaro*) in an attempt to breathe new life into the revolution.

The First Triumvirate faced a difficult decision. They could proceed to declare the independence of the United Provinces of Río de la Plata or they could choose to return to Spain since the Cádiz Parliament (*Cortes de Cádiz*) had by then approved a constitution that provided the same rights as the provinces in the European territories to the viceroyalties of America.

The decision of the First Triumvirate to order the retreat of the army commanded by Belgrano to Córdoba displeased the members of the Lautaro Lodge and they pushed for a change in the Triumvirate's membership. They prevailed and the Second Triumvirate replaced the First in October 1812. Two civilian members of the Lautaro Lodge joined Juan José Paso, the only member of the First Triumvirate to remain in office. The Members of the Second Triumvirate were compelled to call for a General Constitutional Assembly with representation of all the provinces that was committed to declaring independence and establishing a Constitution.

The Constitutional Assembly of 'Year XIII' and the Directorates

The Assembly started in Buenos Aires in January 1813. The Assembly of Year XIII (*Asamblea del Año XIII* in Spanish) included representatives of Buenos Aires, Salta, Córdoba, Corrientes, San Juan, Mendoza, Santiago del Estero, Catamarca, La Rioja, Tucumán, San Luis, Jujuy, Entre Ríos, Santa Fe and the cities of the Alto Perú that designated delegates while Belgrano still occupied that territory.

The tension between Artigas and the government of Buenos Aires continued until the beginning of 1813, because Miguel de Sarratea had tried to assume leadership over Artigas' troops. Due to the mediation of Great Britain the Portuguese left Montevideo. Sarratea organized a new siege of that city. Only when Sarratea left the command of the army that was besieging Montevideo did Artigas resume his participation in the fight against the royalists and sent delegates to the Assembly.

The Assembly did not accept the delegates of the Banda Oriental sent by Artigas, because they sought to declare independence and transform the United Provinces of the Río de la Plata into a Federal Confederation. In fact, one of the first decisions of the Assembly was that the delegates represented the People of the United Provinces and not the Provinces themselves, a clear indication that their intention was to organize a unitarist government.

The decision of the Assembly not to accept the delegates sent by Artigas increased the climate of confrontation between the strong men of the provinces that advocated federalism and the elites of Buenos Aires that favoured the creation of a unitarist government.

Regardless of the tensions, the Assembly played an important legislative role in 1813. It endorsed political representation and the sovereignty of the people in place of the sovereignty of the Spanish crown. It ordered the removal of all symbols of Spain and replaced them with the Argentine coat of arms. It ordered the minting of the first national silver and gold money in Potosí. It ended various forms of slavery by eliminating the obligation of the natives to provide personal services and pay tributes, ended the *encomienda* system, the legacy *mita* system, and the *yanaconazgo*. It declared that the newborn children of slaves would be free and banned the slave trade. It also proclaimed freedom of the press and of religion.

In the same year the Assembly endorsed all the ideals of the May Revolution. In addition, it decided to concentrate the executive power in only one person and replaced the Second Triumvirate with the Directorate.

Following the appointment of Gervasio Posadas as the first Supreme Director, the government of the United Provinces of Río de la Plata became indisputably unitarist and was indisputably led by Buenos Aires. It was, at this time, that the struggle between the central government and the federalist strongmen of the provinces grew into a civil war.

Posadas made two decisions that proved to be crucial for defeating the royalists in Montevideo and to laying the grounds for San Martín's campaigns to liberate Chile and Perú. He ordered the organization of the first national navy under the leadership of William Brown and designated San Martín as Governor of Cuyo.

Continuing the pattern of internal fighting and alleged treachery, Posadas accused Artigas of sedition. This action led to the creation of the League of the Free People of the United Provinces, a coalition formed by the Banda Oriental, Entre Ríos, Corrientes and Santa Fe, that strongly advocated federalism.

A revolt in the Army of the North and Fernando VII's return to the throne weakened Posadas' leadership and in January 1815 Carlos María de Alvear replaced his uncle as Supreme Director. Alvear governed only for a few months. A military revolt in April removed him from power after he clashed with San Martín on the approach to the campaign to liberate Chile and Perú.

The declaration of independence

After the dissolution of the Assembly of the Year XIII, the new Supreme Director, Ignacio Alvarez Thomas, agreed to call for a Constitutional Congress to declare the Independence of the United Provinces of the Río de la Plata.

The fall of Alvear did not affect the prevalence of the idea of a unitarist government. Ignacio Álvarez Thomas, Antonio González Balcarce and Juan Martin de Pueyrredón, the three immediate successors of Alvear in the Supreme Directorate, continued to fight the strongmen in the interior while providing support to the army of San Martín that was trying to defeat the royalist forces in Alto Perú by first liberating Chile and Perú.

The Congress of Tucumán declared independence with the participation of the representatives of Buenos Aires, Córdoba, Tucumán, Salta, Mendoza, San Juan, San Luis, Catamarca, La Rioja, Santiago del Estero, Salta, Jujuy and the three cities of Alto Perú that were still under the control of the Army of the North, Charcas, Chichas and Mizque. The rest of the cities of Alto Perú did not send their representatives because the royalists had regained control. The cities of Paraguay did not send representatives, because Paraguay had already disengaged from the United Provinces of the Río de la Plata. The provinces that made up the League of the Free People led by Artigas did not send representatives, because they were fighting a war against the Directorate.

The anarchy of 1820

Conflict with the provinces intensified during the Directorates presided over by Juan Martín de Pueyrredón and his successor Juan Rondeau. After the federalists defeated the unitarists in the Battle of Cepeda, the Directorate disbanded in a climate of anarchy that characterized the year 1820. The provinces regained their autonomy, but the Province of Buenos Aires continued to guide external affairs and to support the campaign against the royalists in Montevideo, Chile, Perú and the Alto Perú.

After several interim governors, Martín Rodriguez became Governor of the Province of Buenos Aires in September 1820 with the support of the large merchants and landowners of Buenos Aires, one of whom was Juan Manuel de Rosas.

Martín Rodriguez negotiated peace with the Governor of Santa Fe, Estanislao López, who after defeating Buenos Aires at Cepeda had betrayed his allies in the League of Free People. Juan Bautista Bustos, the federalist strongman and Governor of Córdoba, acted as a mediator and Juan Manuel de Rosas provided crucial help.

Rosas was a merchant and landowner who had built a fortune in the sale and export of hides and salted meat. He had organized an army of gauchos to defend his ranches from natives on the frontier. He became the guarantor of a secret clause of the peace agreement between Martín Rodriguez and Estanislao López. The clause consisted of the payment of 25,000 heads of livestock as compensation to Santa Fe for the cost of the war. This negotiation created a partnership between Rosas and López that would be crucial to Rosas' acquiring the power he would eventually exercise. López converted Rosas to the federalist cause even though Rosas' instincts and interests were more closely aligned with the unitarist merchants and landowners who benefited from trade with the British.

In the meantime, San Martín, having already crossed the Andes with his army at the beginning of 1817 and liberated Chile after defeating the royalists in the Battles of Chacabuco and Maipú, was now preparing a campaign to liberate Perú with support of the Chilean government. Due to the anarchy on the eastern side of the Andes, he would have to launch his campaign without the resources of the government of the United Provinces of Río de la Plata.

Despite this obstacle, he went ahead with his campaign and in July 1821 he declared the independence of Perú and was named its Protector. In that capacity, he governed Perú for one calendar year even though the royalists still controlled part of the territory of Perú and Alto Perú.

Simón Bolivar led the army of the Gran Colombia and was marching south trying to defeat the royalists in today's Ecuador, Perú and Alto Perú. Bolivar had occupied the coast of Ecuador and was preparing his campaign to Quito. In 1822, Bolivar summoned San Martín to a meeting. San Martín met him in Guayaquil in July 1822. Discouraged by the lack of support from Buenos Aires and aware of Bolivar's better prospects for success, San Martín offered his troops to Bolivar, resigned his position as Protector of Perú, and returned home.

The government of Buenos Aires had accused San Martín of disobeying its orders to return with his troops to fight the war against the local *caudillos.*

San Martín only stayed a few weeks in Buenos Aires, just enough time to visit the grave of his wife and arrange for his daughter and him to travel to Europe. They left for France in February 1824.

The Unitarist Constitution and the short lived Presidency of Rivadavia

Martín Rodriguez governed until 1825. Gregorio Las Heras, a former general in San Martín's army, succeeded him. The true power behind the governors during this period, however, was the unitarist Bernardino Rivadavia. Rivadavia was a strong advocate of liberalism. He wanted to encourage trade and financial relations with the British in order to build the infrastructure the country needed for development.

Bernardino Rivadavia was able to pass a unitarist constitution and was appointed president. Under his rule, Rosas was designated commander of the troops in charge of defending the frontier from attacks by the natives.

The new national government was short-lived. The provinces opposed the unitarist constitution. Brazil invaded the territories east of the Uruguay River and occupied Montevideo. Rivadavia had to resign and there was no new national government until the enactment of the National Constitution in 1853. Furthermore, the country defaulted in 1927 on a £1 million loan from Baring Brothers in London that prevented Argentina from accessing the international financial markets for the next three decades.

Juan Manuel de Rosas

After the resignation of Rivadavia, there were several provisional governors, one of whom was a prominent federalist military leader, Manuel Dorrego, a business partner of Rosas. The peace negotiations with Brazil had already forced the resignation of Rivadavia so Dorrego had to accept the independence of Uruguay, not only from Brazil but also from Argentina. This decision infuriated the unitarists led by former governor Juan Lavalle who decided to revolt against Dorrego.

Instead of retreating to Santa Fe to look for the support of Estanislao López, as Rosas recommended, Dorrego stayed in Buenos Aires and Lavalle captured him and ordered his execution. This execution was another act of cruelty feeding the ongoing antagonism between the unitarists and the federalists.

In 1829, after the resignation of Rivadavia, San Martín tried to return with the intention of helping to end the civil war between federalists and unitarists. As he neared the port of Buenos Aires, he heard about the climate of violence and hate triggered by the execution of Dorrego. He decided not to disembark in Buenos Aires, stayed a few months in Montevideo, and returned to France where he lived until his death in 1850.

Governor Lavalle ordered José María Paz to organize the fight against the federalist strongmen of the interior after the execution of Manuel Dorrego. General José María Paz had fought under Belgrano in the Army of the

North. Afterwards, he had participated in the war against Brazil and Juan Martín de Pueyrredón had sent him to fight Estanislao López in Santa Fe. He had also served under Rivadavia.

General Paz decided to initiate his campaign against the federalist strongmen in 1829 and marched to Córdoba forcing the resignation of Juan Bautista Bustos who had governed the province since 1820. Bustos sought the support of Facundo Quiroga of La Rioja; Paz defeated Quiroga in La Tablada in 1829 and again in Oncativo in 1830.

Estanislao López and Rosas joined forces to defeat Lavalle and forced him into exile in Uruguay. Rosas became the new Governor of Buenos Aires, and started to exercise power that he would not abandon until 1852. The civil war and external conflicts would not subside during his more than two decades of rule.

In August 1830, nine of the fourteen provinces had joined the Unitarist League led by Paz. For his part, Rosas had created the Federalist League with Santa Fe and Entre Ríos. But, soldiers of Estanislao López captured and imprisoned General Paz. After his liberation in 1839, Paz briefly went into exile in Montevideo but soon resumed the fight against Rosas, helping the governors of Corrientes and Uruguay between 1840 and 1850.

Rosas resigned as governor in 1832 after he defeated the Unitarist League. Over the next three years he devoted his efforts to securing the frontier from the natives. Since the time of the Viceroyalty, the Mapuches and Ranqueles had led raids that attacked rural villages and cattle ranches. Rosas took charge of the military efforts to defeat them, an unfinished task dating from the time of Martín Rodriguez and Bernardino Rivadavia. During the new campaign, Rosas killed around 3,200 natives, took 1,200 prisoners, and rescued 1,000 captives. His strategy was to give reasonable treatment to tribes that he considered friends allowing him to extend the frontier further south and west and add some 200,000 square kilometres in the provinces of Buenos Aires and Córdoba. Rosas allowed friendly tribes to settle in the conquered territories; and, he gave allied tribes permission to keep their territories.

In 1835, Rosas became Governor of Buenos Aires, this time with dictatorial powers and in charge of the foreign relations of the Argentine Confederation, the new name given to the United Provinces of Río de la Plata. The ongoing civil war intensified as neighbouring countries provided support to the unitarist governors.

In 1837, one year after the creation of the Peruvian–Bolivian Confederation, the Confederation's leader Andrés de Santa Cruz, was preparing to invade Tucumán and declare war against the Argentine Confederation. France supported the Peruvian–Bolivian Confederation by imposing a naval blockade on Buenos Aires that lasted two years. Rosas reacted to the threat.

The liberal intellectuals living in Montevideo urged Lavalle, who was then exiled in that city, to resume his fight against Rosas with the support of the French and the Peruvian–Bolivian Confederation. Lavalle expected to get ample support from the provinces but that support did not materialize.

Additionally, as the French started peace negotiations with Rosas, they withdrew their financial support from Lavalle. His troops were demoralized and many deserted. Lavalle avoided the federalist troops and retreated north with a small group of supporters. He was killed when attempting to escape after suffering a defeat in La Rioja in 1841. The death of Lavalle did nothing to ease the on-going civil war.

In neighbouring Uruguay, two political parties represented opposing ideologies and interests. The conservative Blancos (Whites) represented the agricultural interests of the countryside. Manuel Oribe, a close friend of Rosas, was their leader. The liberal Colorados (Reds) represented the business interests of Montevideo. Their leader was Fructuoso Rivera, who favoured the exiled Argentines.

In June 1838, an army led by Rivera overthrew President Oribe and declared war on Rosas. The conflict would last thirteen years. In 1843, the Argentinean army invaded Uruguay on Oribe's behalf and laid siege to Montevideo for nine years. During this period José María Paz resumed his fight against Rosas and relocated to Corrientes, Asunción and Montevideo, championing a coalition of the Uruguayan, Paraguayan and Corrientes Government in a new attempt to defeat Rosas. The Paraguayans feared that Rosas wanted to reclaim their territories for the Argentine Confederation.

This virtual coalition was interested in keeping foreign vessels freely navigating the Paraná and Uruguay rivers to facilitate external trade without the intermediation of Buenos Aires. With the support of France and Great Britain, they blockaded the port of Buenos Aires and organized naval expeditions to guarantee that Asunción, Corrientes and Montevideo could trade freely among themselves and with Europe. The blockade started in 1845, but by 1849, when the two European powers concluded that the blockade was ineffective, they moved on to peace negotiations with Rosas.

The outcome of those negotiations was a very favourable agreement for Rosas. Were it not for an uprising against Rosas led by Justo José de Urquiza from Entre Ríos, Montevideo would have fallen. But Brazilian intervention on behalf of the Colorados defeated Oribe and Rosas had to lift the siege of Montevideo.

Justo José de Urquiza had been an ally of Rosas during the civil war period, but like many other *caudillos* and all the liberals and unitarists, Urquiza disapproved of the delays and excuses that Rosas used to justify indefinitely postponing the constitutional organization of the country. As Governor of Buenos Aires in charge of the foreign relations of the rest of the provinces, Rosas exercised a very centralized dictatorial government, was cruel to his enemies, and continuously engaged in costly civil and external wars.

The intellectuals exiled in Chile, Uruguay, Paraguay and Brazil supported Urquiza who fought and defeated Rosas in the Battle of Caseros on 3 February 1852. These intellectuals accepted a move away from the unitarist ideals of the past that had generated so much opposition in the provinces. They brought forward proposals for organization of the country. Consensus was built around the idea of a representative and republican government that would also be federal.

The economic system of the United Provinces of Río de la Plata

The economic system of the United Provinces of Río de la Plata was as bureaucratic as it was during the time of the Viceroyalty. However, other aspects of the economy had changed quite significantly. Free trade benefited the people of Buenos Aires and the interior. The mercantile trade monopoly with Spain, already weakened during the last years of the Viceroyalty, ended with the May Revolution. The United Provinces of Río de la Plata adopted free trade with Europe and the rest of the world. Given that Buenos Aires controlled the Río de la Plata waterways, it played a natural intermediary role in all trade. At the same time the previously active land trade routes to neighbouring territories (today's Chile, Bolivia and Paraguay), were negatively impacted by the wars of independence and subsequent civil wars.

Separately, the fiscal situation hurt the provinces of the interior. As early as 1813, after the defeat of the Northern army by the royalists during the second campaign to Alto Perú, fiscal resources ceased to flow from the mines of Alto Perú and Potosí stopped demanding goods and services from the cities on the Road to Alto Perú.

Consequences of the liberalization of foreign trade

The people of Buenos Aires had sought to open trade even before the May Revolution. After the May Revolution, the United Provinces of Río de la Plata were finally able to trade freely with all European and American nations.

The opening of trade overlapped with the transition from the Viceroyalty to the United Provinces of Río de la Plata. This shift is crucial to explain the significant improvement in the well-being of the population of what would later become the Argentine nation, at least for the population living in the hinterland of Buenos Aires.

Buenos Aires and its hinterland, enlarged by the addition of frontier territories acquired during the campaigns against the natives led by Rodriguez, Rivadavia and later Rosas, became one of the most open economies in the world. Diversification in markets and products allowed the economy of Río de la Plata to escape the trap of being a single staple economy and allowed it to sustain its economic growth for over five decades.

Between 1810 and 1850, per capita exports from Buenos Aires were three times higher than the per capita exports of other advanced economies. Terms of trade almost quadrupled between 1810 and 1837 as a result of the combined effect of declining textile prices and rising prices for livestock products (see Figure 2.1). Hides, tallow, jerked beef, wool and other livestock-related products were the main export products. The ranch economy was also responsive to relative price changes. As wool and tallow appreciated in terms of hides, producers shifted their product mix towards the new products.

Economic historian Ricardo Salvatore discovered interesting information to document this phenomenon. The heights of soldiers born in the years before and after the May Revolution show that people in low-income groups had suffered serious deterioration in nutrition and health in the years preceding the revolution, but that the rise in height after 1810 was remarkable (see Figure 2.2). Salvatore writes:

> Free trade had a salutary effect on the nutritional status of the population. The cost of imported food (flour, olive oil, wine, sugar, manioc flour, and other dried goods) went down. Cheaper imported textiles helped improve hygiene. The shift from wheat to livestock produced a greater volume of calories than before. The increased exports of hides, tallow, and grease created a surplus of beef for internal consumption.
>
> (Salvatore and Newland 2003, p. 3)

Consequences of the interruption of the supply of fiscal resources by Potosí

The evolution of the economy of the United Provinces as a whole was not as positive as that of Buenos Aires. On the contrary, the interruption of regional trade with Bolivia, Paraguay, Uruguay and Brazil, caused by the wars and the precarious road infrastructure, severely thwarted economic activity in the interior of the country. To make matters worse, Buenos Aires continuously

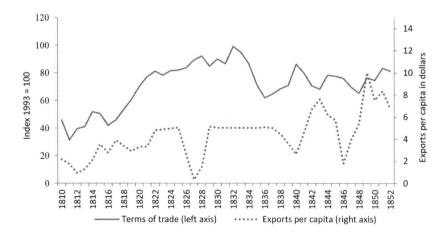

Figure 2.1 Terms of trade and exports per capita 1810–1852
Source: authors' own calculations, based on material originally published in Ferreres (2010).

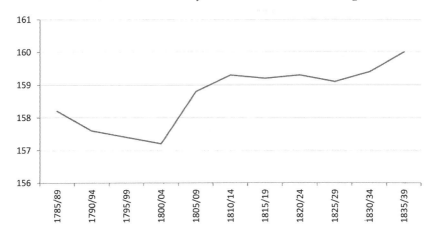

Figure 2.2 Average height of Argentine soldiers 1785–1839 (in cm)
Note: Average height refers to birth cohorts.
Source: Salvatore (1998).

imposed restrictions on navigation of the Río de la Plata waterways and the Buenos Aires Custom's authorities virtually monopolized maritime trade.

In terms of the wellbeing of the population, the benefits of cheaper imported goods that arrived from Buenos Aires did not compensate for the scarcity of fiscal resources that followed the interruption of the transfers from Potosí and the collapse of trade along the Royal Road to Alto Perú.

At the time of the Viceroyalty of Río de la Plata, there was a tax collector in each of the main cities, but the two most important coffers were those of Potosí and Buenos Aires. Potosí collected more than the cost of its bureaucracy, but that was not the case in Buenos Aires. The expenses devoted to administration and defence largely exceeded the revenue collected by the custom's authorities of Buenos Aires, so Alto Perú actually subsidized Buenos Aires through all the years of the Viceroyalty. Only the strong political force of centralized Spanish rule in the American territories kept these two regions, which had very different interests, functioning as an integrated economic and political unit. But, after the war of independence Alto Perú had no reason to keep sending fiscal resources to the other parts of the former Viceroyalty. The loss of these resources was a severe setback for the finances of the United Provinces of Río de la Plata. While the tax collection by custom's authorities of Buenos Aires in the period 1811–1815 was 6.4 million pesos, the transfers from Potosí, net of remittances to Spain, had been 16.7 million pesos in 1791–1795.

In addition, trade with Potosí declined significantly, so Bolivian pesos were hard to come by. This mainly affected the provinces of the interior because Buenos Aires received gold and bills of exchange in gold or pounds through the trade of hides with Great Britain. When provincial governments borrowed money they documented them in the form of bearer bonds. These bonds became legal tender for taxes and later circulated as money.

The liberalization of trade brought about an increase of imports and simultaneously an increase in the exports of hides and other livestock by-products. Not surprisingly, there was a sharp increase in the revenue generated by the Buenos Aires Custom. Meanwhile, public financial resources to the interior country took a hit.

In order to compensate, the provinces of the interior increased tax rates on merchandise entering their respective territories. These taxes replicated the old *alcabalas* under Spanish rule, but over time developed into an inefficient system of internal customs that, along with the wars, restricted internal trade. The economy of the interior of the United Provinces of Río de la Plata became a set of fragmented and isolated regional markets with weaker trade networks than had existed during the Viceroyalty.

The wars of independence and the civil and external wars of the following years meant increased expenses everywhere so the need for financing of fiscal deficits became a widespread and permanent problem in the United Provinces of Río de la Plata.

Between 1810 and 1820, Buenos Aires took over the role of treasurer for all of the provinces. To finance its deficits the government sought out unusual sources: delaying payments to suppliers; confiscating properties and goods; and, eventually, taking loans offered by local merchants that then used those credits to pay their custom duties.

Following the dissolution of the national government in 1820, the Province of Buenos Aires gained its autonomy like the rest of the provinces. Since the customs at the port of Buenos Aires were in its jurisdiction, Buenos Aires could manage its fiscal situation. However, some reforms such as the creation of the Bank of Buenos Aires in 1822 helped provide supplementary financing without generating inflation for five consecutive years. Access to capital markets was also important. The Province of Buenos Aires obtained its first foreign loan from Baring Brothers for £1 million. The government deposited the proceeds of that loan, meant to pay for infrastructure, in the bank that financed merchants and landowners. The bank had limited capital and its assets were illiquid because even though it was supposed to discount bills of exchange up to 90 days, in practice the debtors would request continuous refinancing.

This period of fiscal discipline and monetary order ended around 1825 due to the war with Brazil. The government had to finance the army that was fighting east of the Uruguay River while it suffered a drastic reduction in revenues collected from customs due to the blockade of the port of Buenos Aires by the Brazilians. Under these pressing circumstances, the government decided to use the loan obtained from London and requested an additional loan in gold to the Bank of Buenos Aires. The bank granted the loan but requested that the government declare the inconvertibility of the paper money it had issued. The bank changed into the Banco Nacional and its notes became inconvertible. The government made the bank's notes legal tender that could cancel any obligation at face value.

The bank returned to the province of Buenos Aires after the dissolution of the National Government in 1827. This succession of events prompted the Province of Buenos Aires to enter a long period of inflationary financing. From 1826 to 1831, the inconvertible peso suffered a sharp devaluation and inflation was 20–22 per cent per year for the first time in the history of the United Provinces and the Viceroyalty.

During his first term in government Rosas was able to restore fiscal and monetary discipline and stabilize the inconvertible peso. The peso remained stable during the initial two years of his second government. However, in 1837, customs revenues dwindled when the French blockaded the port of Buenos Aires in support of the Confederation of Perú and Bolivia. Rosas relied once again on printing inconvertible pesos to finance the fiscal deficit. He closed the Bank of Buenos Aires so the money was minted by the Casa de la Moneda, a new institution that was granted a monopoly on printing paper money. When the bank closed, the quantity of paper pesos amounted to 15 million pesos. By 1852 it had increased to 126 million pesos.

The inconvertible peso suffered continuous devaluations until 1842. Between 1838 and 1842, inflation ranged between 25 per cent and 45 per cent per year. The end of the war and the blockade contributed to the peso's appreciation. For three years, there was deflation. By the time of the new war with Montevideo and the French and British blockade from 1845 to 1849 the peso devalued again and inflation resumed at a rate of around 14 per cent per year. Monetary instability continued after the fall of Rosas and during the period when the Confederation of Argentina and the Province of Buenos Aires functioned as separated entities. It was only after the reunification and the consolidation of the Argentine nation that the government pursued monetary and financial reforms geared towards the creation of a convertible currency and a banking system.

Both the liberal intellectuals in exile and the politicians noticed that the monetary system and inflation behaved very differently in Argentina compared to Great Britain, the British Empire and the USA (see Figure 2.3). This evidence convinced them of the need to undertake a monetary and financial reform after the constitutional organization of the country.

The United Provinces' growth struggle

Inflationary financing had an important impact on the saving and investment decisions of merchants and landowners. At a time of high inflation, they would hoard gold, purchase land, and invest liquid capital in livestock. While the exporters and merchants could deal with inflation, workers and farmers saw their wages and farming proceeds decline with inflation. Consequently, immigration was discouraged and the expansion of the domestic economy was severely constrained.

38 *The Argentine Nation*

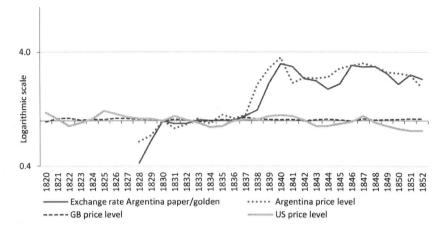

Figure 2.3 Price level and exchange rate Argentina, USA and Great Britain 1820–1860
Source: authors' own calculations, based on material originally published in Ferreres (2010) and methodology used by della Paolera and Taylor (2001).

Table 2.1 Comparative per capita GDP growth in Argentina and other countries 1820–1850

Country	1820	1850	Annual change 1820–1850
	(in thousand 1990 I. dollars[*])		
Argentina	1,096	1,274	0.5%
USA	1,257	1,806	1.2%
Australia	518	1,975	4.6%
Canada	904	1,330	1.3%
Brazil	646	686	0.2%
Mexico	759	758	0.0%
Great Britain	1,706	2,330	1.0%

Note: [*] I. dollars means 'International dollars' as defined by Maddison (2006).
Source: authors' own calculations, based on material originally published in Maddison (2006) and Ferreres (2010).

The uncertainties associated with wars and currency instability discouraged long-term investment and technological change in activities other than livestock production for export, particularly in farming, manufacturing and infrastructure. Making things worse, when the government of Buenos Aires stopped servicing the £1 million loan from Baring Brothers just a few years after disbursement the country lost access to the London financial market for the next four decades. The 'western offshoots countries'[1] were able to develop infrastructure, borrow capital and receive immigrants. Argentina, on the other hand, could not do those things until the organization of a united Argentine nation.

Maddison's research estimates that from 1820 to 1850 performance of the Argentine economy was superior to that of Brazil and Mexico, but inferior to that of the USA, Australia, Canada and Great Britain (see Table 2.1).

Note

1 Maddison (2006) calls 'western offshoot countries' the USA, Canada, Australia and New Zealand.

References

Della Paolera, Gerardo and Taylor, Alan M. (eds) (2003) *A New Economic History of Argentina*, New York: Cambridge University Press.

Ferreres, Orlando (2010) *Dos Siglos de Economía Argentina*, Buenos Aires: El Ateneo.

Halperin Donghi, Tulio (2005) *Guerra y Finanzas en los Orígenes del Estado Argentino*, Buenos Aires: Prometeo Libros.

Maddison, Angus (2006) *The World Economy*, Paris: OECD Publishing.

Rock, David (1987) *Argentina 1516–1987. From Spanish Colonization to Alfonsín*, Berkeley: University of California Press.

Salvatore, Ricardo D. (1998) 'Height and Welfare in Late-Colonial and Post-independence Argentina' in J. Komlos and J. Baten (eds) *Biological Standard of Living in Comparative Perspective*, Stuttgart: Franz Steiner Verlag.

Salvatore, Ricardo D. & Newland, Carlos (2003) 'Between Independence and the Golden Age: The Early Argentine Economy' in Gerardo Della Paolera and Alan M. Taylor (eds) *A New Economic History of Argentina*, New York: Cambridge University Press, Chapter 2, pp. 19–45

Szuchman, Mark D. and Brown, Jonathan C. (1994) *Revolution and Restoration: The Rearrangement of Power in Argentina, 1776–1860*, Lincoln and London: University of Nebraska Press.

Part II
1853–1913: six decades of increasing integration into the global economy

3 From the National Organization to the First World War

The adoption of the Argentine Constitution in 1853 coincided with the beginning of what economic historians call 'the first wave of globalization' led by Great Britain.

During these decades of globalization, from roughly the mid 19th century to 1914, Argentina was one of the world's most successful emerging economies. Between 1870 and 1914 the Argentine economy grew faster than the economies of the USA, Canada, Australia and Brazil, four countries with similarly abundant natural resources, attracted large inflows of capital, and large numbers of immigrants from Europe.

In addition to the favourable external conditions offered by international trade, capital movement and immigration, a key driver of Argentina's success was that Argentina's intellectual and political leaders learned from past mistakes.

During the first wave of globalization, Argentina's leaders were uniformly enthusiastic supporters of the country's engagement with the world. They realized that trade with the rest of the world would allow increasing expansion of production which in turn would lead to improvements in people's quality of life.

They had also learned that integrating into the world trade system was important, but insufficient: it was essential to be able to tap international sources of capital. Foreign capital was required for the country to be able to finance the expansion of infrastructure and the investment necessary to incorporate technological advances required for more efficient local production of goods and services.

Two intellectuals and politicians who observed what was going on in Europe and in the USA, Alberdi and Sarmiento, emphasized the importance of immigration and education. It was necessary to bring people who would work, produce and consume in Argentina in order to populate a vast and almost empty country, and it was essential to educate those people to make them knowledgeable and productive, and fully integrate them into the culture and values of the emerging nation.

Succession of constitutional governments

After the Battle of Caseros, the Argentine Confederation focused on its institutions. A Constitutional Assembly convened in Santa Fe approved the Argentine Constitution of 1853. This constitution organized the nation as a Federal Representative Republic.

The Argentine Confederation itself dated to 1835 and initially included the provinces of Buenos Aires, Santa Fe, Entre Ríos, Corrientes, Córdoba, Tucumán, Salta, Jujuy, Santiago del Estero, Catamarca, La Rioja, San Juan, San Luis and Mendoza. Patagonia, La Pampa, Chaco and Formosa were still frontier territories populated by natives. Rosas had never recognized the independence of Paraguay, but Paraguay was also never integrated into the Argentine Confederation. Misiones was an underpopulated frontier territory and coveted by Paraguay.

The province of Buenos Aires seceded from the Argentine Confederation and presented itself as a separate nation called the State of Buenos Aires. This split was a consequence of the opposition of the business elite of Buenos Aires who did not accept a national government led by a federal strongman from the interior and did not want to hand over control and revenues from the Custom of Buenos Aires.

Buenos Aires's leaders, the unitarist Valentín Alsina and Bartolomé Mitre, were not part of the Constitutional Assembly, refused to participate in elections, would not accept the authority of the elected president, and were prepared to confront the Confederation militarily.

Justo José de Urquiza was elected President of the Argentine Confederation in 1854. He governed the Argentine Confederation from Paraná in Entre Ríos but without the revenue of Buenos Aires.

The interior of the country was mired in a long economic depression since the interruption of trade and the inflow of resources from the Alto Perú. Despite its backwardness Urquiza and his successor Santiago Derqui confronted the army of Buenos Aires. In 1859, the Confederation defeated Buenos Aires in the Battle of Cepeda. The governments of the Confederation and of the State of Buenos Aires signed the pact of San José de Flores and the Province of Buenos Aires finally joined the Argentine Confederation. In 1860, the National Constitutional Assembly made a few reforms to the National Constitution proposed by the Legislature of Buenos Aires and the official name of the country changed from the Argentine Confederation to the Argentine Nation.

Military conflicts continued for two more years between the national government and the government of the Province of Buenos Aires on who would actually lead the nation. This power struggle was settled after the Battle of Pavón in 1862 when Urquiza conceded victory to Mitre. Derqui resigned and Bartolomé Mitre became President of the Argentine Nation. During his administration Argentina started to function as a truly reunified nation. The ideal of a Constitutional Federal Republic finally became a reality.

The prevalent political ideology during the six decades that followed 1862 was the liberal republicanism embedded in the National Constitution of 1853. Nevertheless, the electoral methods and the way successive governments exercised power evolved over time. The presidencies of Bartolomé Mitre, Domingo Faustino Sarmiento and Nicolás Avellaneda were more aristocratic than democratic. In the quarter-century in which Julio A. Roca dominated politics, the governments were oligarchic rather than aristocratic. After 1910 when Roque Saenz Peña became president the government made progress towards democracy. However, even though the changes in political orientation had some influence on economic policymaking, none of the governments deviated from the prevalent economic ideology of free trade combined with the fiscal and monetary orthodoxy imposed by the gold standard.

The new governments learned from historical experience

From 1853 to the beginning of the First World War, Argentina tried to keep its economy fully integrated in the world economy. The domestic structure of production reacted rapidly to the changes in demand, relative prices, and new technology. This strategy delivered impressive results that explain why economic historians call the period 1870–1913 'the golden age of the Argentine economy'.

From 1850 to 1913 Argentina's GDP per capita grew in line with the USA, Australia and Canada (see Table 3.1); but, from 1870 to 1913, both global and per capita GDP growth were much higher in Argentina than in most countries of the world, including the USA, Australia, Canada and Great Britain. The difference was particularly large in comparison with neighbouring Brazil.

Table 3.1 Comparative per capita GDP growth between 1850–1929

Country	1850	1870	1913	Annual change 1850–1913	Annual change 1870–1913
	(in thousand 1990 I. dollars)				
Argentina	1,274	1,311	3,797	1.7%	2.5%
USA	1,806	2,445	5,301	1.7%	1.8%
Australia	1,975	3,273	5,157	1.5%	1.1%
Canada	1,330	1,695	4,447	1.9%	2.3%
Brazil	686	713	811	0.3%	0.3%
Mexico	758	674	1,732	1.3%	2.2%
Chile	1,200	1,300	2,653	1.3%	1.7%
Great Britain	2,330	3,190	4,921	1.2%	1.0%

Source: authors' own calculations, based on material originally published in Maddison (2006).

Exports were indisputably the main driver of economic expansion. Export growth reflected the higher performance of Argentina compared to other major countries (see Table 3.2).

As in previous decades, production and export of agricultural products continued to grow quickly. Over time, these came from a larger geographical area as the frontier was conquered, settled, and railroads were expanded. Large numbers of immigrants, mainly adult males coming from Italy, Spain and other European nations, provided the labour that allowed the transformation of agriculture from land-intensive livestock production to labour-intensive production of wool and grain crops.

The shift from production and export of hides, tallow and jerked beef to the production of wool actually started in the 1850s and continued during the decades that followed. Production of beef also shifted from low quality to higher quality when the technology of refrigeration and transportation boosted the exports of frozen beef to European markets.

Even accounting for beef exports, the main driver of growth during the golden period was agriculture. Its share of GDP increased from 4.4 per cent in the years 1876–1880 to 15.4 per cent in 1911–1915. At the same time livestock production declined from 56.5 per cent of GDP in 1876–1880 to 16.2 per cent in 1911–1915. The rural production scheme consisted of rotating crops and pasturing animals. Crops, mainly wheat, corn and flax, expanded with railroad development and falling maritime transportation costs. Land-intensive cattle ranching tended to move towards marginal lands making more land available for rotating between crops and pasture and creating space for more labour-intensive techniques that facilitated further expansion. After 1880, the 'campaign to the desert'[1] incorporated 45 million hectares to the territory. Cultivated land (crops and pastures) increased by 30 million hectares. Between 1884 and 1913, there was a 9 per cent annual increase in cultivated land and a production increase of 10.5 per cent per annum, reflecting a solid 1.5 per cent annual productivity growth.

Table 3.2 Comparative export growth between 1870–1913

Country	1870	1913	Annual change 1870–1913
	(in thousand 1990 I. dollars)		
Argentina	29	515	6.9%
USA	403	2,380	4.2%
Australia	98	382	3.2%
Canada	58	421	4.7%
Brazil	76	317	3.4%
Mexico	28	150	4.0%
Chile	27	149	4.1%
Great Britain	971	2,555	2.3%

Source: authors' own calculations, based on material originally published in Maddison (2006).

The growth of manufacturing industries was as noteworthy as that of crops. Manufacturing growth was above the rate of GDP growth and higher than growth of non-crop agriculture and livestock combined. Roberto Cortés Conde has estimated that industry grew almost 5.9 per cent per year between 1875 and 1914, while GDP for the economy as a whole grew by 5.4 per cent and agriculture grew by around 4.2 per cent (see Table 3.3). New agriculture-related industries developed in this period. The industrial census of 1914 shows that in that year food, beverages and tobacco represented 53 per cent of total production; textiles and leather represented 21 per cent; and wood items were 5 per cent.

By 1870 leading countries, particularly Great Britain and the USA, had adopted the gold standard. This monetary system gave them stability and drove fruitful engagement with the international trade and finance systems. Argentina's intellectual and political leaders doggedly tried to make the Argentine currency convertible into gold at a fixed rate; but, they were unable to stick to the gold standard because of periodic fiscal and monetary crises that forced the country to abandon convertibility. After every crisis, however, they resumed the country's commitment to convertibility, convinced that it was essential to keep the country well integrated in international capital markets. At the same time, they worked to develop a domestic banking system and local capital markets; however, they were less successful in this enterprise.

In the 1850s the State of Buenos Aires, still alienated from the Argentine Confederation, reached an agreement with bankers in the city of London for the repayment of the debt they had defaulted on in 1827. This normalization of financial relations with London encouraged the inflow of capital into Argentina, particularly during the 1870s and the 1880s. Capital inflows fluctuated in the subsequent decades (see Figure 3.1). They were drastically reduced during the early 1890s because of the crisis of 1890, resumed between 1893 and 1898, fell again between 1899 and 1905, and became particularly strong from 1906 until 1913 when Argentina's commitment the Gold Standard gained credibility.

The important inflow of capital was one of the main economic differences between the first five decades of the United Provinces of Río de la Plata and the Argentine Confederation. This inflow of capital permitted enormous investments in railroads, telegraph systems, ports and farm infrastructure.

Table 3.3 GDP growth, total, agriculture and manufacturing 1875–1914

	Annual change 1875–1914
GDP (total)	5.4%
Agriculture	4.2%
Crops	10.9%
Livestock	10.9%
Manufacturing	5.9%

Source: Cortés Conde (1994).

48 *Integration into the global economy*

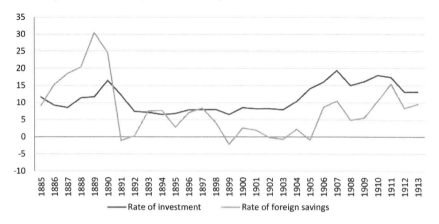

Figure 3.1 Investment and foreign savings 1885–1913
           (in percentage of GDP)
Source: authors' own calculations, based on material originally published in Taylor (1998).

The investment in infrastructure was remarkable. By 1913, the country had more than 33,000 kilometres of railroads connecting most of the country. Buenos Aires had a new port. Rosario was on its way to becoming an important trading centre and port for Argentina's agricultural production. Other new ports were developed in Santa Fe, Zarate and San Pedro. And the province of Buenos Aires built a city for its new capital, La Plata.

GDP growth resumed after four years of recession following the First World War and the economy continued to expand until 1929.

For the expansion of agriculture, the millions of European immigrants that came attracted by wages significantly higher than those paid in their home countries were just as important as the availability of arable land, the investment in crops, pastures, improved livestock, and the expansion of railroads and ports.

The government promoted European immigration even before the Argentine Confederation and the State of Buenos Aires were reunited. During the period of the Argentine Confederation, the government supported the creation of settlements where immigrant farmers became proprietors. Mitre, Sarmiento and Avellaneda all favoured this process. When Roca became president, policies changed. Settlement with land ownership was discouraged and immigrants became tenants or sharecroppers of the big landowners, particularly in the areas occupied after the extension of the frontier.

Between 1870 and 1914, net migration accounted for 49 per cent of population growth. That percentage was as high as 70 per cent in 1885–1889 and slightly negative only during the First World War (see Table 3.4).

The censuses of 1869, 1895 and 1914 show how important immigrants were as a percentage of total population, particularly immigrants that came from Italy and Spain (see Table 3.5).

Table 3.4 Origin of population growth by five year periods between 1870 and 1914

Period	Net migration	Population growth	Population growth explained by net migration
	(in thousand persons)		
1870–1874	100	268	37%
1875–1879	43	259	17%
1880–1884	150	393	38%
1885–1889	602	856	70%
1890–1894	157	454	35%
1895–1899	301	643	47%
1900–1904	244	704	35%
1905–1909	785	1,374	57%
1910–1914	737	1,465	50%
1870–1914	3,119	6,416	49%

Source: Recchini de Lattes and Lattes (1975).

Table 3.5 Participation of immigrants in the population by censuses

	1869	1895	1914
Population (million)	1,737	3,955	7,885
Percentage of immigrants in population	12.1	25.5	30.3
Immigrants by origin (percentage)			
Border countries	19.7	11.5	8.6
Rest of the world	80.3	88.5	91.4
Spain	20.2	22.3	38.5
Italy	42.3	55.3	43.1
Others	37.6	22.4	18.4

Source: Recchini de Lattes and Lattes (1975).

Education played a crucial role in integrating and educating immigrants. From Sarmiento's time, but mainly during the governments of Avellaneda and Roca, the creation of primary, secondary and training schools for teachers allowed most of the children of those immigrants and many illiterate adults to be educated resulting in an effective and productive integration of those newcomers into Argentine society.

Note

1 'Campaña del Desierto' is the name historians give to the military occupation of southern territories still controlled by native inhabitants in the late 1870s.

References

Cortés Conde, Roberto (1994) *La Economía Argentina en el Largo Plazo (Siglos XIX y XX)*, Buenos Aires: Editorial Sudamericana.

Della Paolera, Gerardo and Taylor, Alan M. (2003) *A New Economic History of Argentina*, New York: Cambridge University Press.

Galiani, Sebastian and Gerchunoff, Pablo (2003) 'The Labor Market' in Gerardo Della Paolera and Alan M. Taylor (eds) *A New Economic History of Argentina*, New York: Cambridge University Press, Chapter 5, pp. 122–169.

Maddison, Angus (2006) *The World Economy*, Paris: OECD Publishing.

Recchini de Lattes, Zulma and Lattes, Alfred E. (1975) *La Población de Argentina*, Buenos Aires: INDEC.

Rock, David (1987) *Argentina 1516–1987: From Spanish Colonization to Alfonsín*, Berkeley: University of California Press.

Taylor, Alan M. (1998) 'Capital Accumulation' in Gerardo Della Paolera and Alan M. Taylor (eds) *A New Economic History of Argentina*, New York: Cambridge University Press, Chapter 6, pp. 170–196.

4 Split, reunification and the 'historical presidencies'

When the Constitutional Assembly enacted a National Constitution in 1853 the Province of Buenos Aires seceded from the Argentine Confederation and functioned as the State of Buenos Aires. Justo José de Urquiza was the first president of the Confederation and governed from Paraná. Santiago Derqui succeeded him. Only after the Battle of Cepeda in 1859 and the signing of the Pact of San José de Flores did the province of Buenos Aires re-enter the Confederation.

In 1860 the Constitution was reformed to incorporate the changes demanded by Buenos Aires; but, conflicts continued until the Battle of Pavón that ended with the resignation of Derqui and the designation of Bartolomé Mitre as the new president of the Argentine Nation.

Mitre, Sarmiento and Avellaneda completed three successive six-year terms from 1862 to 1880. This period is known as the 'historical presidencies'. In spite of persistent violent conflicts with several of the provinces, a long war with Paraguay, and fighting against the natives on the frontier, these three presidencies made significant contributions to the institutional and economic development of the country. And, the three governments not only continued, but actually emphasized the promotion of immigration that began in the 1850s.

The governments also benefited from the normalization of financial relations with Britain that started before reunification with the restructuring of the Baring Brothers loan that Argentina defaulted on in 1827. Mitre's government, for example, was able to tap into the world's capital markets to finance the war with Paraguay and develop infrastructure.

Sarmiento's years were particularly prosperous and he focused on promoting widespread education. Public health became a salient issue after a yellow fever epidemic killed thousands in Buenos Aires.

Avellaneda faced the country's first financial and debt crisis after the normalization of external financial relations. His successful crisis management paired with territorial expansion after the Desert Campaign set the foundations for the impressive economic progress that began after 1880.

Argentine Confederation and the State of Buenos Aires

From 1853 to 1860 Argentina was split in two: the Argentine Confederation with its capital in Paraná, and the State of Buenos Aires that kept control over its custom revenue and its bank. The provinces elected Justo José de Urquiza as President of the Argentine Confederation in 1854. He completed his term in 1860 and Santiago Derqui succeeded him. The same year, Pastor Obligado became governor of the State of Buenos Aires. Valentin Alsina succeeded him in 1858.

Bartolomé Mitre was commander of the army of the State of Buenos Aires. Meanwhile, one of the most prominent liberals that had returned from exile after the fall of Rosas, Juan Bautista Alberdi, supported the Government of the Confederation and drafted the National Constitution of 1853. Most of the other liberals exiled during the government of Rosas, among them Domingo Faustino Sarmiento and Dalmacio Velez Sarsfield, supported the government of the State of Buenos Aires.

The different alignment of the intellectuals and politicians that had opposed Rosas from exile and had applauded the campaign of Urquiza did not rely only on the traditional aspiration of Buenos Aires to lead Argentina, but also on some liberals' perception that there were still remnants of the characteristic conservatism of the strongmen of the provinces in the Confederation. In his book *Facundo* Sarmiento called those strongmen 'barbarians' in contrast to the liberal intellectuals and politicians whom he characterized as 'civilized'.

Institutional change was imminent and came quickly. President Urquiza created the National Army. He called for the first election of senators and representatives and inaugurated the first National Congress. Congress approved the law that created the federal judiciary system and appointed the first Supreme Court. Urquiza nationalized the University of Córdoba and several secondary schools, and pursued an immigration policy that established settlements of immigrant farmers in the provinces of Santa Fe and Entre Ríos.

In terms of foreign policy, Urquiza achieved Spain's recognition of Argentina's independence, granted Great Britain the right to navigate Argentine rivers, and restored diplomatic relations with the Holy See. The discussions on the right to navigate the rivers dominated relations with Brazil and Paraguay. Urquiza was able to establish good relations with Paraguay by mediating between its government and the USA in a conflict that intensified in 1859 when an American fleet with 2,400 men appeared in the port of Rosario with the intention of attacking Paraguay. Solano López, the president of Paraguay, rewarded this help by mediating the reunification of the Argentine Confederation and the State of Buenos Aires.

The Confederation faced great difficulties implementing the changes set forth in the Constitution. And it was not able to finance its ambitious plans to modernize the infrastructure, eliminate domestic customs, create a national bank and a national currency, and promote immigration of European farmers to create agricultural settlements. The Confederation's not controlling the Custom of Buenos Aires and not receiving its revenue was ruinous. The attempt to create an alternative customs office in the port of Rosario did not succeed either. Ultimately the lack of fiscal resources made the Argentine Confederation unmanageable.

In contrast, the State of Buenos Aires, which kept its customs revenue and whose bank continued to print money, enjoyed a period of prosperity that strengthened its determination to either enter the Confederation while keeping its prerogatives or declare independence. Mitre was the leader of the political party (Partido Nacional) that advocated the first alternative. Valentín Alsina led the party that advocated the second (Partido Autonomista).

Thanks to the strength of its finances, the State of Buenos Aires could not only recreate its bank but also renegotiate with Baring Brothers. It committed to pay the debt plus the accumulated interest and signed a repayment agreement. Baring Brothers resumed its role as a financial agent with the right to place Argentine debt in the London market.

In 1859, Valentín Alsina, the then Governor of Buenos Aires, ordered Mitre to invade Entre Ríos. Governor Justo José de Urquiza defeated Mitre at Cepeda and Alsina was forced to resign. Mitre became Governor and finally agreed to negotiate the incorporation of Buenos Aires into the Confederation contingent upon a constitutional reform that would guarantee the privileges of his province.

These negotiations resulted in the Agreement of San José de Flores. It recognized the right of the Province of Buenos Aires to keep its bank and the right to print its own currency; but it maintained the constitutional provision dealing with the federalization of customs collected at the port of Buenos Aires. Mitre convinced Derqui that Buenos Aires should keep control of its customs for some time while offering the rest of the country monetary compensation. Buenos Aires would contribute 1,500,000 pesos fuertes per year to the treasury of the Confederation. In 1860, the Constitutional Assembly approved the reform. With this the Argentine Confederation and the Province of Buenos Aires became one Argentine nation.

The conflicts between the national government and the government of the province of Buenos Aires persisted on issues such as the intervention[1] of the national government in provincial matters. In particular, after a political revolt in San Juan to replace the federal governor with Antonino Aberanstain, a close friend of Domingo Faustino Sarmiento, President Derqui intervened. He sent the San Luis governor Juan Saá to fight against the leaders of the revolt and remove Aberanstain. The National Army captured Aberanstain and executed him. This decision infuriated Mitre who retaliated by suspending the committed monetary contribution to the national government.

Derqui moved to Córdoba and began organizing an army to declare war against Buenos Aires. Urquiza, from Entre Ríos, marched against Buenos Aires and met its army in battle in Pavón. Surprisingly, in spite of the successful initial attacks of his army, Urquiza decided to retreat. Urquiza probably realized that without the support of Buenos Aires the national government would never be able to govern the nation.

Mitre had won the battle and the war. Derqui left the country and Mitre was sworn in as interim President and later became President in 1862. The issue of establishing the city of Buenos Aires as the capital of the nation was still pending and led to a struggle between Mitre and Alsina. In 1880 the Legislature of Buenos Aires finally passed a law in which it was ordered that the national government would be hosted in Buenos Aires.

From 1854 until 1859 the state of Buenos Aires had tried to keep a balanced budget, introduced a tax reform extending the tax base to include exports, restored external credit, and avoided using inflationary financing. Nevertheless, between 1859 and 1862, because of the various military conflicts, it ran a significant deficit, issued a large amount of debt, and saw its bank put large amounts of money into circulation. The government of the Confederation on the other hand never had the possibility of printing money so it had accumulated significant debt to domestic creditors. In 1862 Mitre's government regained access to the Buenos Aires customs revenue but also inherited the debts of both the Province of Buenos Aires and the Confederation.

There were still many clouds on the horizon, but at least Argentina was an organized and unified nation with a widely accepted constitution, and civil wars and external conflicts behind it.

Politics from 1862 to 1880

Mitre was the first President of the unified Argentine Nation to complete his constitutional term. He governed between 1862 and 1868 with Marcos Paz as Vice-President. Throughout his term, strongmen (*caudillos*) in the interior of the country challenged him and in 1863 he sent troops to La Rioja to fight the Angel Vicente Peñaloza who had resumed his war against the National Government after revolts in San Luis and Catamarca. Peñaloza was defeated and killed later that same year.

In 1863, members of the Partido Colorado from Uruguay who were living in exile in Buenos Aires organized a revolt against the President of Uruguay, Bernardo Berro of the Partido Blanco. Led by former President Venancio Flores – and with the support of the Brazilian army– an invasion of Uruguay forced the resignation of Berro. Flores became president. President Solano Lopez of Paraguay came out in support of the ousted Partido Blanco and declared war on Brazil. It was in this context that Solano Lopez asked Mitre for permission to cross the Argentine provinces of Corrientes and Entre Ríos to fight the Brazilians in Uruguay. Mitre who had sided with the Colorados against former President Berro denied them permission and Mariscal López invaded Corrientes. Mitre declared war on Paraguay and signed an agreement with Brazil and Uruguay to create the so-called 'Triple Alliance' (La Triple Alianza).

And, further complicating matters, the last federal strongmen of the interior opposed Argentina's involvement in the war against Paraguay and rose up in Mendoza, San Juan, La Rioja and San Luis. They gathered an army of more than 10,000 men led by Juan Saá and Felipe Varela. Mitre had to withdraw from Corrientes where he was fighting the Paraguayans to deal with the federal insurgents. Ultimately, the war was costly for Paraguay, but also for Argentina. The rebellion was defeated but at a high cost of lives and presidential prestige.

In spite of these conflicts, Mitre focused on the organization of the national government. He did not get the approval of the Legislature of Buenos Aires for the federalization of the city of Buenos Aires. However, he did reach a compromise under which the province of Buenos Aires would host the federal government which would control the customs as long as the federal government provided enough resources to fund the provincial budget. In 1866, a constitutional reform nationalized customs.

Mitre organized the federal justice system and applied the Code of Commerce of the province of Buenos Aires to the whole country. He nationalized the 'Colegio San Carlos', a prestigious secondary school that had educated the elite of Buenos Aires and that from then on was known as the 'Colegio Nacional Buenos Aires'. He also created secondary schools in several provinces.

Mitre started the construction of a railroad, the Central Argentino from Rosario to Córdoba, as well as a railroad to the southern territories. A private company in the state of Buenos Aires had created the first railroad, the Ferrocarril Oeste, during Governor Pastor Obligado's term.

At the end of his mandate, Mitre's Partido Nacional and Adolfo Alsina's Partido Autonomista had different candidates for the presidency but neither seemed strong enough to defeat the other. Colonel Lucio Mansilla proposed the candidacy of Domingo Faustino Sarmiento who was serving as ambassador to the USA and had stayed out of the internal battles and divisions during Mitre's presidency. Adolfo Alsina in turn agreed to be the vice-presidential candidate and the slate was elected.

Sarmiento governed from 1868 to 1874. In 1869, he organized the first census of the population which counted 1.88 million in the country of which 187,000 lived in the city of Buenos Aires. That same year, the Congress approved the Civil Code drafted by Dalmacio Velez Sarsfield, a highly regarded lawyer from Córdoba, at the request of Mitre in 1863.

During his presidency, Sarmiento fought the last two years of the war with Paraguay and confronted the last rebellion of a strongman. General Ricardo López Jordan revolted against Justo José de Urquiza. The governor of Entre Ríos had developed a good relationship with Sarmiento in spite of their differences after the Battle of Caseros. Lopez Jordan's soldiers assassinated Urquiza at his house in San José and Sarmiento decided to declare war against the army of López Jordán. The war lasted until 1873 and required the mobilization of several thousand men from both sides. It was as costly in terms of lives and money as the war against Paraguay.

Domestically, during the presidency of Sarmiento there was a yellow fever epidemic that killed more than 14,000 in Buenos Aires.

In spite of the attention required for the wars and the epidemic, Sarmiento was a champion for education. With the help of his Minister of Education Nicolás Avellaneda, he created 800 new primary schools and increased the number of children attending classes from 30,000 to 110,000. To encourage the training of teachers he created the 'Escuelas Normales' and brought 61 teachers from Boston in the USA. He had been impressed with the primary school system of Massachusetts ever since his first visit to the USA. He continued expanding secondary education by creating new high schools in the provinces that did not have them.

Sarmiento also created several agricultural schools in the interior. In 1871 he organized the first exposition of arts and fruits of the land in the city of Córdoba. This exposition brought about the creation of the Academy of Sciences and the Astronomical Observatory of Córdoba. Upon Sarmiento's initiative, the University of Córdoba created the School of Engineering and Chairs in Mineralogy in the National College of San Juan and Catamarca that a few years later would become the San Juan School of Engineering.

Transportation and communications also saw impressive progress. During Sarmiento's presidency railroads expanded from 573 kilometres in 1868 to 1,331 kilometres in 1874 connecting cities such as Villa María with Río Cuarto, Córdoba with Tucumán, Concordia in Entre Ríos with Mercedes in Corrientes, and Buenos Aires with Campana. The government built new ports in Zárate and San Pedro. Sarmiento also extended the telegraph network along 5,000 kilometres connecting all the country's major cities. By the end of his term, Sarmiento had even inaugurated the first telegraphic connection with Europe. In 1873, he created a National Bank (Banco Nacional).

At the end of Sarmiento's presidency there was an unsuccessful coup attempt led by Mitre to block the swearing in of Nicolas Avellaneda. Mitre was imprisoned and Avellaneda was sworn in as President for the 1874–1880 term.

Avellaneda faced an economic and financial crisis at the beginning of his term. However, as soon as the crisis started to turn, he passed a law that promoted immigration. The number of immigrants significantly increased and most of them went into farming settlements in the provinces of Santa Fe, Entre Ríos and Córdoba.

In 1875, the Sociedad Rural Argentina, an association whose membership included the large cattle-raising landowners, organized the first Rural Exposition of Buenos Aires, initiating a tradition that continues to this day. In 1876, Argentina started to export frozen meat to Great Britain and sent the first cereal exports to Europe in 1877.

The railroad network continued to expand and by the end of Avellaneda's term, it had reached 2,500 kilometres. Avellaneda completed the railroad to Tucumán that was started during Sarmiento's presidency. He also extended the railroads to the west and to the south within the Province of Buenos Aires and from Río Cuarto to Villa Mercedes in San Luis.

When Adolfo Alsina, Avellaneda's first Minister of War died, the President appointed Julio Argentino Roca to that office. Avellaneda supported Roca's military strategy of expelling or subjugating the Mapuches, Ranqueles and Tehuelches that controlled the southern part of the Province of Buenos Aires and Patagonia. This campaign was not very different from the one that Rosas had led in the 1830s. Half a century later, the natives still controlled a broad territory that allowed them to transport the cattle they had stolen from Argentine ranches to southern Chile. The Campaign to the Desert (Campaña del Desierto) killed or imprisoned several thousand natives and expelled those that were not captured south of the Negro and Neuquén rivers.

Money and banking from 1862 to 1880

After the creation of the Argentine Nation, both the monetary system and financial intermediation system tried to emulate those of Great Britain and the USA. This was not a smooth process; in fact, it turned out to be a painful and slow process that would not succeed until the next century.

In 1862, a group of local and foreign merchants founded the Bank of London (Banco de Londres) a private bank. It would play an important role years later. Public and small private banks also sprouted up in the provinces.

Mitre had had no option, but to accept the nationalization of the debts of both the Argentine Confederation and the State of Buenos Aires. He had tried to create a national currency and a national bank, but could not get the approval of Congress due to the opposition of Buenos Aires. Therefore, he decided to negotiate the terms under which the Banco de la Provincia de Buenos Aires would conduct monetary policy, not only for the province of Buenos Aires but also for the Argentine Nation as a whole. He ultimately established 20-to-1 parity between the banks' paper peso and the peso fuerte.

Mirroring the prevailing monetary systems of successful systems in other countries, Mitre and his economic advisors tried to make the notes of the Banco de la Provincia de Buenos Aires convertible to gold. However, at first, instead of moving towards the value of the peso fuerte, the paper peso lost value. By 1864, the exchange, which had started at 20 to 1 in 1862, had fallen to 29 to 1. It took a significant monetary contraction and high interest rates to create deflation and finally achieve the monetary stability that prevailed during the presidency of Sarmiento.

Nevertheless, when Argentina was waging war on Paraguay, it was forced to borrow 3.5 million pesos fuertes from the Banco de la Provincia de Buenos Aires. This loan to the government crowded out credit for the private sector. In order to soften the monetary shortage the Argentine government asked Baring Brothers in 1865 to arrange a loan from the London capital markets. After long negotiations, the funds finally entered into the Treasury in 1868 and 1869.

The exchange rate stabilized at 25 paper pesos per peso fuerte and, in practice, the country met its goal of adopting the gold standard. Between 1868 and 1874 the provinces and the national government were able to get new loans from London. Between 1871 and 1872, the National Treasury received a loan for public works that was supposed to finance the construction of a new port in Buenos Aires, the port of Rosario, and the expanding railroad system. As the payments for such infrastructure projects would take some time, the National Treasury deposited the loan in the Banco de la Provincia of Buenos Aires. The bank then used them to grant loans to the private sector. From 1868 to 1873, a significant expansion of domestic credit contributed to the climate of prosperity that characterized the presidency of Sarmiento.

The crisis of 1876

In 1872, President Sarmiento got approval in Congress to create the Banco Nacional. One year later, the government transferred all the deposits from the Banco de la Provincia de Buenos Aires to the Banco Nacional. As the reserves in gold were dwindling in both banks, the government authorized the Banco de la Provincia de Buenos Aires to replace its reserves in gold with notes backed by gold. The purpose was to keep expanding the domestic money supply, but instead it had the effect of alerting the private sector to the fact that convertibility was at risk. Not surprisingly, the private sector started to demand gold instead of paper pesos and the reserves in gold of the banks declined further.

When Avellaneda took office in October 1874, the situation was critical. The difficulties Baring Brothers encountered in London to sell Argentine debt only aggravated the situation.

Figure 4.1 shows that the demand for paper pesos, represented by the monetary base measured in pesos fuertes, increased rapidly until 1871, when the private sector had confidence in convertibility, but it started to decline until 1875. This decline meant a withdrawal of gold from the banks. The yield

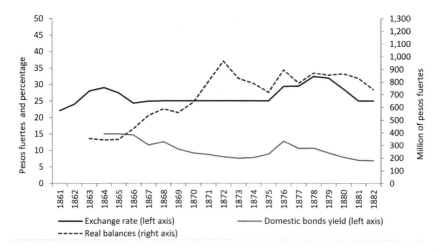

Figure 4.1 First convertibility experiment
Source: Della Paolera and Taylor (2001).

on domestic bonds (which had been declining until 1873) started to rise, reflecting a loss of confidence. By May 1876, Avellaneda had to suspend the convertibility of paper pesos and at the same time adopt very restrictive monetary and fiscal policies.

The fiscal adjustment came mainly from increased customs duties. Some economic historians have described discussions around this decision as a confrontation between free traders and protectionists. But none of the participants in the discussion were against free trade in the sense that they opposed Argentina's full integration into the world trade system.

All parties recognized that the increase in import duties was necessary to adjust the fiscal accounts. The dispute between the Treasury Minister, Norberto de la Riestra on one side and Vicente Fidel López and Carlos Pellegrini on the other, had to do with the structure of the customs duties. De la Riestra proposed a reduction of custom duties for finished consumer goods and an increase on intermediate inputs and capital goods that were used by agriculture and manufacturing. Vicente Fidel López and Carlos Pellegrini advocated the opposite in order to reduce the costs of production and preserve competitiveness. This so called 'protectionist' position ultimately prevailed.

The real economy immediately contracted. The trade deficit shifted back to a significant trade surplus in just a few years but the cost was a deep recession. The country was able to continue servicing its debt, but it was not until 1881 that Argentina regained access to external financing.

Note

1 The Argentine Constitution admits federal intervention in the provinces to remove the executive, the legislative and even the judiciary power in special circumstances. Federal intervention have been frequently used to remove authorities of public and private entities.

References

Cortés Conde, Roberto (1989) *Dinero, Deuda y Crisis*, Buenos Aires: Editorial Sudamericana.

Della Paolera, Gerardo and Taylor, Alan M. (2001) *Straining at the Anchor: The Argentine Currency Board and the Search for Macroeconomic Stability, 1880–1935*, Chicago, IL and London: The University of Chicago Press.

Rock, David (1987) *Argentina 1516–1987: From Spanish Colonization to Alfonsín*, Berkeley: University of California Press.

5 The years when Roca dominated politics

Julio Argentino Roca dominated the Argentine political scene from 1880 to 1906. He was President during two non-consecutive terms; and, even during the years between his presidencies, from 1886 to 1898, he played a decisive role in the candidacy, election, and later resignation of President Miguel Angel Juarez Celman and his replacement by Vice-President Carlos Pellegrini.

At the end of Pellegrini's presidency, Roca was able to block the candidacy of his main opponent in the Partido Autonomista, Roque Saenz Peña, by promoting Roque's father, Luis Saenz Peña for President and José Evaristo Uriburu for Vice-President. Unlike Roque Saenz Peña, both would accept Roca's patronage.

Roca was sworn in as president for the second time in 1898 and governed until 1904. He supported Manuel Quintana's presidential candidacy, but had to accept José Figueroa Alcorta, a close associate of Roque Saenz Peña, as Vice-President. When Manuel Quintana died in 1906 the ascension of Figueroa Alcorta to the presidency meant the beginning of an irreversible decline in Roca's influence.

Roque Saenz Peña himself was finally elected in 1910 and is credited with the electoral reforms that democratized the Argentine political system. Both Julio A. Roca and Roque Saenz Peña died in 1914, the year that marked the end of Argentina's first wave of globalization. Argentina was at the time of their death among the ten richest countries in the world.

There is no doubt that Roca and Pellegrini were the architects of the impressive infrastructure development and frontier expansion that productively employed millions of immigrants. A huge inflow of foreign capital provided the financing for this progress through the 1880s, but also fed the financial crisis that peaked in 1891. Pellegrini's political ability allowed Argentina to overcome the crisis, but not without pain and suffering throughout most of the 1890s.

Between 1899 and 1914, 15 years of currency convertibility and full integration into the world economy, the economy grew as it had never grown before and at a much faster pace than any other country in the world.

Politics from 1880 to 1906

When Nicolás Avellaneda proposed a law federalizing the city of Buenos Aires and then most of the provinces elected Julio Argentino Roca as the new President, Carlos Tejedor led a new rebellion trying to block both decisions. Carlos Pellegrini, the Minister of War who had succeeded Roca, defeated the rebellion. Pellegrini continued as Minister of War in Roca's government and became his close friend and associate.

Congress passed the federalization law and the new governor of the province of Buenos Aires, Dardo Rocha, founded the city of La Plata as the new capital of the province of Buenos Aires. Roca took over the leadership of the Partido Autonomista and engaged in negotiations with the provinces that tried to keep the opposition out of power everywhere. Like his predecessors, he relied on federal interventions in the provinces whenever local leaders disputed his power. Electoral fraud was widespread in most provinces.

There is no doubt that Roca was the most powerful political figure in Argentina not only during his presidency, but also in the quarter of a century following his ascension to power. Roca pursued and accomplished the conquest of the territories south of Río Negro and Neuquén. The Campaign to the Desert had already increased the availability of productive land but after the campaign extended to the south and to the north, practically all Argentine territory became potentially productive. In 1884, the National Territories Law created the national territories of Formosa, Misiones and Chaco in the north and La Pampa, Neuquén, Río Negro, Chubut, Santa Cruz and Tierra del Fuego in the south.

President Roca also created the first national currency, the peso moneda nacional. He gave the National Bank monopoly rights in issuing of the new currency. He sought foreign capital and invested heavily in infrastructure. During Roca's first term in office the railroad network expanded from 2,500 to 6,200 kilometres.

Roca's presidency also saw institutional changes, some of which challenged the Catholic Church's prevailing power and involvement in public matters. First, the creation of a Civil Registry took responsibility for registering births, marriages and deaths from the Church. Furthermore the Congress passed an important Education Law advocated by Sarmiento. This new law established compulsory primary education that was secular and free for all children. Both these policies triggered a suspension of diplomatic relations with the Holy See.

Despite controversy and opposition, the impact of the Education Law was significant. The number of primary schools increased from 1,200 to 18,000 and the number of students increased from 87,000 to 181,000 in just six years. The number of teachers rose from less than 2,000 to more than 5,000.

On the foreign policy front, President Roca favoured the relationship of Argentina with Great Britain though a secular orientation impeded relations with the Holy See. Chileans were in the midst of the Pacific War and Roca seized that opportunity to negotiate a territorial boundaries treaty with Chile in 1881 that helped consolidate the sovereignty of Argentina in its Patagonian territories.

Before leaving power, Roca nominated his brother-in-law Miguel Juarez Celman as a candidate for president with Carlos Pellegrini as his vice-president. They were sworn in in 1886. Roca maintained his support to Juarez Celman until 1890 when, due to a severe economic crisis, Leandro Alem's Unión Cívica party stirred an upheaval. Even though the government could overcome the revolt, having lost the support of Roca, Juarez Celman had to resign and cede power to his Vice-President, Carlos Pellegrini, who served out the remainder of Celman's term which ended in 1892.

The economic and financial crisis that dominated the administrations of both Juarez Celman and Carlos Pellegrini peaked in 1890. During the crisis, the Banco Nacional and the Bank of Buenos Aires declared bankruptcy. Carlos Pellegrini created the Banco de la Nación and a Currency Board (Caja de Conversión) that would commence operations once the country had rebuilt enough foreign reserves to maintain the convertibility of the peso at a fixed exchange rate with gold.

Near the end of his administration, focus shifted to who would be Pellegrini's successor. The newly created Unión Cívica party initially nominated Bartolomé Mitre and Bernardo de Irigoyen for president and vice-president for the election of 1892. Roca proposed, with Mitre's consent, a 'national unity' presidential formula presided over by Mitre but without Irigoyen as his running mate. Leandro Alem opposed this agreement and created the Unión Cívica Antiacuerdista soon renamed Unión Cívica Radical. Mitre's candidacy lost momentum and Bernardo de Irigoyen became the presidential candidate of the Union Cívica Radical.

A highly regarded lawyer and diplomat, Roque Saenz Peña, was the expected presidential candidate of Roca's Partido Autonomista. In order to block Roque Saenz Peña's strong candidacy, Mitre once more formed an alliance with Roca and proposed the candidacy of Luis Saenz Peña, Roque's father. Like his son, Luis Saenz Peña was a highly regarded lawyer, but unlike him, he loathed politics and power.

Pellegrini feared that the members of the Unión Cívica Radical were preparing an uprising and ordered the detention of most of its leaders. Therefore, in the end Bernardo de Irigoyen did not participate in the 1892 election. Luis Saenz Peña, who was uncontested, won the presidency from 1892 to 1898.

During his term, Luis Saenz Peña continued the expansion of the railroad network that connected all the main provincial capitals. Buenos Aires, Rosario and Santa Fe completed their ports. Buenos Aires was growing and changing its landscape. Lined with elegant buildings, a wide avenue, the Avenida de Mayo, connected Plaza de Mayo with Plaza del Congreso.

When Luis Saenz Peña suspected the insurgency led by the Unión Cívica Radical, he asked Aristóbulo Del Valle, who co-founded the party with Leandro Alem, to join his government. But the presence of Del Valle in the cabinet was not enough to avert the insurgency. In 1893 Hipólito Yrigoyen, a nephew of Leandro Alem, who distrusted the organizational capacity of his uncle, organized a revolt that came close to success, but was finally defeated by the army led by General Roca. The Unión Cívica Radical decided to abstain from elections arguing that there would be fraud. Luis Saenz Peña was powerless, most members of his cabinet paid more attention to the orders of Roca and Pellegrini than to his.

Luis Saenz Peña finally resigned in January 1895 and Vice-President José Evaristo Uriburu completed his term. Uriburu accepted the patronage of Julio Argentino Roca who was the president of the Senate. He pacified the political situation by granting an amnesty to the leaders of the rebellions of 1890 and 1893. Thanks to an improved economic situation he was able to complete his term without too many conflicts.

In 1896, Aristóbulo Del Valle died and Leandro Alem committed suicide. Hipólito Yrigoyen became the clear leader of Unión Cívica Radical and engaged in what he called revolutionary abstention.

Roca was sworn in as president again in 1899 and completed his second term in office in 1904. The Unión Cívica Radical led by Yrigoyen did not participate in the national election but Bernardo de Irigoyen ran for governor of the Province of Buenos Aires. Once elected governor, de Irigoyen reached an informal agreement with Roca to ensure governance at the cost of permanently distancing himself from Hipólito Yrigoyen.

On the economic front, in November 1899 President Roca enacted the Law that implemented the Currency Board and restored the Gold Standard. In 1901, Roca withdrew support for Pellegrini's debt unification project after the Senate had approved it. The law generated strong opposition when, in a congressional debate, Pellegrini noted that 8 per cent of the customs revenue would back repayment of external debt. Riots and protests ensued so Roca made Pellegrini accountable for the initiative. Pellegrini, distanced from Roca from then on, supported Roque Saenz Peña's initiatives in favour of a political reform that would eradicate fraud and democratize elections.

During Roca's second government, he modernized and professionalized the military. He created the War College (Escuela Superior de Guerra) for military training and research on national defence issues and military history. He also mandated a military draft and created new military bases outside the city of Buenos Aires. He also sought to reduce the risk of the military challenging civilian governments and promoted the military's use of the telegraph network. Like his predecessors, Roca supported the development of the telegraph network that in 1904 extended over 50,000 kilometres.

Roca's foreign policy was also very active. He restored diplomatic relations with the Holy See that had been suspended after secular laws were passed during his first presidency in 1901.

Early in his presidency, Roca reached an agreement with President Errázuris of Chile on a border dispute in Puna de Atacama. In 1902, his representative in Chile signed the 'Pactos de Mayo' that committed the two countries to stop their arms race and to submit present and future border disputes to the arbitration of Great Britain.

By December 1902, his foreign minister Luis María Drago led an international campaign against the use of military force by Great Britain and the German Empire against Venezuela to force repayment of its debt. The principle that public debts never justify military attack, known as 'the Drago Doctrine,' has since been widely accepted around the world.

During the initial years of President Roca's second term in office, social protests multiplied and trade unionism started. The Federación Obrera Regional (FORA) was created in 1901 and the Unión General de Trabajadores (UGT) was formed in 1903. The employers pushed back with police support and confrontations turned violent. Roca favoured repression rather than dialogue and negotiations, an attitude criticized not only by the Radicals and the Socialists, but also by Carlos Pellegrini and Roque Saenz Peña.

In 1903, Roca supported the candidacy of Manuel Quintana, but he had to compromise and accepted José Figueroa Alcorta, the former governor of Córdoba, and a close ally of Pellegrini as the vice-presidential candidate. Roca had sanctioned a political reform proposed by Lucio V. Mansilla that enacted the election of representatives by precincts in the Federal District. As a consequence of this electoral reform, Socialist party leader Alfredo Palacios won the election in La Boca, a neighbourhood popular with recently arrived immigrants. Palacios became the first socialist representative elected in the Americas.

Manuel Quintana took office in 1904 and accepted the patronage of Roca as José Evaristo Uriburu had done in 1897 and maintained the economic and foreign policies of Roca. Both the economy and the national railroad network continued to expand. Quintana nationalized the University of La Plata, regulated the professions, promulgated a law of Sunday rest proposed by Socialist Representative Palacios, and approved the 'Lainez Law' that promoted the creation of elementary schools in the provinces.

In 1905, the Radicals, led by Yrigoyen, were well-organized in most provinces and reappeared on the political scene. They rebelled against Quintana's government. The revolt was defeated, but the stress took a toll on Quintana's health. In August, 1905, there was an attempt on his life and in February 1906, he transferred power to José Figueroa Alcorta. Quintana died a few months later.

Money and banking from 1880 to 1906

The tough spending cutbacks during the presidency of Avellaneda opened the door for President Roca to create a new monetary system. The system established both gold and silver as the precious metal currencies and established a fixed parity between them. In practice, gold displaced silver and the system started to move towards the gold standard. The Casa de la Moneda would mint gold pesos and the Banco Nacional would put paper pesos (that were convertible into gold on a one-to-one basis) into circulation. President Roca, advised by Carlos Pellegrini, wanted to revoke the Banco Provincia de Buenos Aires' authorization to issue paper pesos thus ensuring the Banco Nacional's monopoly on issuing currency. However, in the face of opposition from Governor Dardo Rocha, they had to compromise and both banks would in practice conduct monetary policy.

To reinforce the ability of the Banco Nacional to create domestic credit for both the public and private sectors, President Roca got congressional approval for a law that increased the bank's capital by 8 million gold pesos. To integrate this capital, the government borrowed the necessary amount of gold from abroad. The Banco Nacional was subsequently able to issue more currency rapidly. It put small denomination notes into circulation and opened branches in the interior of the country making the Banco Nacional the strongest bank in the financial system.

Full convertibility of paper pesos into gold pesos was established in 1883. But it lasted for only 17 months. Banco de la Provincia de Buenos Aires was more judicious about issuing paper pesos, but together the two banks expanded the money supply without strictly maintaining the corresponding supply of precious metals. The drawback of the new monetary system was that bank reserves in precious metals had two roles. They backed the issuance of paper pesos as mandated by convertibility, but they also backed the deposits of the public in both gold and paper pesos. Banks, seeking to increase their profitability, kept only a small proportion of their deposits in the form of reserves. Consequently, at times when people decided to convert paper pesos or deposits into gold pesos, the reserves that the banks held in gold shrank rapidly. This was the case in 1884. By end of 1884, the banks were resisting convertibility. The government suspended it in March 1885 and decreed inconvertibility in December 1886.

After the suspension of convertibility, expansionary fiscal and monetary policies prevailed. The fiscal deficit increased from 7 million gold pesos in 1881 to 20 million in 1885 and to 52 million in 1891. That expansion and the corresponding currency issue caused (unlike the aftermath of 1876) an increase in the price level that reflected the depreciation of the paper peso. In 1891 the exchange rate reached 4 paper pesos per gold peso. Inflation peaked in 1891.

The Law of Guaranteed Banks and the crisis of 1890

At the onset of President Miguel Juarez Celman's term, the macroeconomic situation, in spite of aggressively expansionary fiscal and monetary policies, still seemed manageable because the inflow of foreign capital continued and the deflationary trend that prevailed abroad softened domestic inflationary pressures. In 1887, the President submitted a law to Congress for banking reform that would allow any bank meeting minimum capital requirements to issue paper pesos in the amount of the national government-issued gold bonds that they had purchased on the market or directly from the National Treasury. The law tried to emulate the US National Currency Act but deviated from it in two crucial respects. While in the USA the dollar was convertible into gold, in Argentina the peso was non-convertible so there was no obligation to keep gold reserves that backed the peso. In addition, while in the USA banks had to purchase the bonds in secondary markets, in Argentina the Treasury issued new gold bonds to sell directly to the banks willing to acquire the right to issue paper money.

To secure the gold needed to pay for the gold bonds that they wanted to purchase from the Treasury, the banks, particularly those owned by the provinces, issued and placed debt in pounds or in gold on the London market. The Treasury deposited in the Banco Nacional the precious metals obtained from selling the gold bonds to the banks. In theory, the Banco Nacional should have kept the gold in reserves to back the paper money issued by the guaranteed banks. But in practice, Banco National lent these reserves.

As a whole, during the period 1880 to 1889 the inflow of foreign capital was impressive and helped to finance investment in infrastructure, the purchase of land, and the purchase of gold bonds issued by the guaranteed banks. The gold bonds gave the banks the right to issue paper money that they could use to expand credit in paper pesos to the private sector, often with a longer term of maturity than the terms of foreign loans they had received before. Currency and maturity mismatches became widespread and made the whole system vulnerable to a sudden stop in capital inflows.

By early 1889, London banks and investors became reluctant to continue purchasing Argentine debt and some of the bondholders started to sell their Argentine bonds in the secondary market. The exchange rate of paper pesos started to depreciate rapidly and inflation accelerated. The public in Argentina tried to protect their savings from depreciation by exchanging their paper pesos for gold and in order to reduce the pace of currency depreciation the Banco Nacional started to sell its gold reserves. By 1891 gold had moved from the safes of Banco Nacional to private hands.

In London, the Bank of England was worried about Baring Brothers' high-risk exposure to Argentine debt. They engineered a rescue that generated what is known as the Baring Brothers crisis. The negative impact on the British economy was neither large nor long lasting. On the other hand, in Argentina the effects of the crisis were devastating. Most of the banks, starting with the Banco Nacional and the Banco de la Provincia de Buenos Aires became not only illiquid but also insolvent. They lost more than 50 per cent of their deposits and the value of their assets fell by more than 70 per cent.

The price of land in the Province of Buenos Aires that had increased from an index of 100 in 1886 up to 385 in 1888 fell to 95 in 1891. Inflation, that between 1886 and 1888 had been almost non-existent, jumped to 20 per cent in 1889, 41 per cent in 1890, and 56 per cent in 1891. The impact on GDP growth was also high. During 1890 and 1891 the cumulative fall in GDP averaged 15 per cent per year.

During the crisis, before it had reached its peak, Leandro Alem's rebellion, though defeated, forced the resignation of Miguel Juarez Celman. Pellegrini then inherited the responsibility to manage a country in the midst of an economic crisis. Pellegrini appointed to his cabinet two members of the moderate wing of opposition party Unión Cívica Radical. He also appointed Vicente Fidel Lopez as Minister of the Treasury and Victorino de la Plaza as debt negotiator.

In 1889, Juarez Celman had approved an increase of 15 per cent in import duties to generate additional revenue. Because importers paid duties in paper pesos, the revenue in gold pesos had actually fallen. In 1890, the first fiscal policy decision by Pellegrini was to determine that importers were to pay 50 per cent of the import duties in gold pesos. Nonetheless, revenue continued to fall. In January 1891, Pellegrini and Vicente Fidel López worked out a tax reform that required full payment in gold pesos of all import duties. It further established a temporary 4 per cent ad valorem tax on exports of hides, wool and beef and created consumption taxes collected for the first time at the federal level.

In spite of all these measures, revenue in gold pesos fell 31 per cent during 1891 due to the depreciating peso. The exchange rate that had been 2.65 paper pesos per gold peso in August 1890 had reached 4.21 paper pesos per gold peso by the third quarter of 1891. Pellegrini was convinced that the only way out of the crisis was stopping the inflationary process. He therefore shifted the focus to a contractionary monetary policy.

Following their bankruptcies, the Banco Nacional dissolved and the Banco de la Provincia de Buenos Aires remained inactive for several years. To create expectations of a return to gold standard at the parity prior to the suspension of convertibility in 1884, Pellegrini proposed a Convertibility Law that created a Currency Board (Caja de Conversion). The Currency Board would start to operate once the country had established adequate gold reserves.

To unlock the foreign exchange market Pellegrini started to negotiate a refinancing of the debt. In February 1891, the debt negotiator signed an agreement with a group of banks coordinated by the Bank of England. The agreement granted to Argentina a loan of £15 million at 6 per cent interest that allowed the government to service the debt normally during the next three years. The condition of the foreign loan was in line with the monetary policy implicit in the creation of the Currency Board.

With a stricter monetary policy on the horizon, the government decided to suspend the convertibility of paper pesos of deposits in the official banks. On the ruins of the old Banco Nacional the government created the Banco de la Nación which would operate with stricter rules than those of its predecessor. The charter of the new Banco de la Nación prohibited the bank from financing any public entity except the National Government, which would in turn get a maximum credit of 2 million pesos.

In February 1892, when Luis Saenz Peña, then President of the Supreme Court seemed likely to become the next president, the paper peso started to appreciate and the process accelerated when Luis Saenz Peña appointed Juan José Romero as Treasury Minister. Romero was a high profile advocate for the gold standard.

Minister Romero was displeased with the de la Plaza–Bank of England agreement because it was onerous and added to the fiscal burden. Therefore, he resumed negotiations and the parties reached a new agreement whereby from 1893 to 1898 Argentina would only pay half its beforehand agreed debt service. After 1898, it would pay full service and in 1901 would start repaying the principal. This new agreement reduced the fiscal burden of debt servicing. Consequently, the fiscal deficit fell from 52 million paper pesos in 1891 to 17 million paper pesos in 1892 and turned into a fiscal surplus of 2 million pesos in 1893.

In 1892, the paper peso appreciated sharply and between 1893 and 1894 it fluctuated between 3.2 and 3.6 paper pesos per gold peso. In 1892 the general price level fell 21 per cent and in 1893 it fell an additional 6 per cent. At the same time, the real economy recovered rapidly and during the remainder of the decade, GDP growth averaged 5 per cent per year, only slightly below the pre-crisis growth rate. The Argentine economy was recovering at the time of global recession with the lowest international prices of the period between 1870 and 1894.

Gold discoveries in the world were also generating international liquidity and inflation in the world economy. This new trend in international prices helped Argentina limit deflation to 13 per cent between 1895 and 1898 while the peso appreciated 37 per cent during the same period.

There is no doubt that the recovery of the economy was the result of more optimistic expectations by local and foreign investors; but, in 1897 exporters and merchants started to argue that the appreciation and the deflation was dangerously threatening profitability. Argentine businessman and self-trained economist Silvio Gesell, who anticipated the ideas of Irving Fisher on the effect of deflation on real interest rates, formalized the argument against deflation. In 1898 the nominal interest rates paid on a domestic bond were 7.9 per cent and inflation was −4 per cent, so the real interest rate was 11.9 per cent and in 1899, the same nominal interest rate with inflation of −14 per cent increased to 21.9 per cent per year.

Very likely, it was this argument and the influence of the exporters that convinced the authorities to implement the strict Currency Board with a parity of 2.27 paper pesos per gold peso rather than continue deflating the paper peso to restore the 1 to 1 parity of 1884. In his first speech in Congress, President Roca announced the return to convertibility; and, in October 1889, Congress approved the law that ordered the implementation of the Currency Board.

From 1899 to 1913, Argentina went through a period of growth and stability that inspired admiration from the rest of the world and generated significant benefits for most of the population. But the distribution of the benefits was not even. The landowners, exporters and foreign and domestic corporations that invested in railroads and other public services were often part of the political elite and got the highest share of the distribution of income. Workers, tenants and sharecroppers, most of them immigrants that had arrived in the country without capital, benefited much less. They worked on farms, in construction, in the service sector, or in the emerging industries and were paid just enough to keep them from returning to their countries of origin. During this period, workers, tenants and sharecroppers attempted to organize to defend their interests and push for higher wages, but they did not have significant political influence, though this situation would change in the subsequent decades.

The landowners

The process of land acquisition and appropriation and the distribution of economic power had changed relatively little since the end of the Viceroyalty. In fact, there was no major difference, particularly after the Campaign to the Desert, between the patterns of land distribution in the period 1880 to 1914 and the pattern during the last decades of the Viceroyalty and the five decades of the United Provinces of Río de la Plata.

Roberto Cortés Conde has estimated the territorial expansion in the Pampas between 1867 and 1914. Table 5.1 shows that the expansion of the frontier during the period increased privately owned land without high risk of attacks by the natives by 432,000 square kilometres.

The large increase in the availability of land led Cortés Conde and other scholars to argue that the scarce resource at the time was labour rather than land, and therefore immigrants that started to provide labour could have acquired land that was abundant and relatively cheap. James Scobie (1964) and Carl Solberg (1987) make a different argument in their books. They argue that while Canada adopted a policy of family farms (homesteads), the Argentinean government discouraged immigrant land ownership. Immigrants typically became rural tenants or sharecroppers. These authors show that after even the Campaign to the Desert, large landowners acquired new land the same way they did during the Viceroyalty period after the expulsion of the Jesuits and during the Argentine Confederation at the time of Rosas.

Table 5.1 Territorial expansion of provinces in the pampas (surface, thousands of km^2)

Province	1867	1876	1890	1914
Buenos Aires	117	237	311	307
Santa Fe	57	83	132	134
Entre Ríos	77	77	75	78
Córdoba	150	150	175	168
La Pampa	–	–	145	144
Total	401	547	838	831

Source: Cortés Conde (1979).

Even though this may not have been the intention of the government, in practice when the soldiers and officers of the Campaign to the Desert received land as payment, they did not become farmers, but rather sold their new properties to domestic and foreign investors. Most of the investors were landowners that either had liquid capital or could borrow from the banks. The big difference between the amount of foreign capital that came to Argentina during the 1880s and the amount invested in fixed capital may have been used to finance land acquisition by people and corporations that expected to make a profit once the railroads expanded. This may explain why between 1886 and 1888 the price of land in the province of Buenos Aires increased by a factor of almost four. The immigrants that came without capital did not have a chance to compete with the large landowners and investors who were purchasing the bulk of the land for sale.

A comparison of the census data of 1895 and 1914 on land tenure by Cortés Conde shows the process of land concentration and cultivation by tenants and sharecroppers rather than by proprietors continued after the crisis of 1890 when the price of land was, for several years, much cheaper than in the 1880s. Table 5.2 shows several interesting facts: the number of rural properties was significantly smaller in 1914 than in 1895 in the four provinces of the Pampas and the proportion of properties cultivated by tenants and sharecroppers was significantly higher in 1914 than in 1895. In the Province of Buenos Aires, there were 37,000 properties in 1895 and owners cultivated 18,000 of them. Nineteen years later, the number of properties had fallen to 29,000 and owners cultivated only 9,000 of them.

The tensions between landowners and their tenants and sharecroppers intensified at a time of bad harvests or low prices for their products. This explains why in 1912 the tenants and sharecroppers decided to organize in defence of their rights. It also explains why the Unión Cívica Radical, a new political party that represented the rural middle classes, the workers, and the immigrants, referred to the big landowners and the Conservative Party as an oligarchy and accused them of trying to preserve political and economic power at the expense of the rest of the population.

Electoral reform

Jose Figueroa Alcorta allied with Roque Saenz Peña in resisting Roca's influence. Pellegrini had died in 1906 and Roque Saenz Peña was his political heir. Roca's power, unchallenged since 1880, in 1906 started to decline rapidly and continued to do so until his death in 1914.

In trying to soften the opposition of the Union Cívica Radical and to get support for his fight against Roca's allies in Congress, President Figueroa Alcorta granted an amnesty to the revolutionaries of 1905 and initiated secret negotiations with Yrigoyen with the help of Roque Saenz Peña.

In 1907, while looking for water, a group of workers found oil in Comodoro Rivadavia, an isolated port in the National Territory of Chubut. Thanks

Table 5.2 Land tenure system 1895 and 1914

Province	Proprietors	Tenants	Sharecroppers	Total
1895				
Buenos Aires	18.0	15.0	3.8	37.8
	49%	41%	10%	100%
Santa Fe	9.8	7.5	2.6	19.8
	49%	38%	13%	100%
Entre Ríos	9.7	3.0	1.5	14.2
	69%	21%	11%	100%
Córdoba	13.9	2.4	2.2	18.6
	75%	13%	12%	100%
1914				
Buenos Aires	9.3	16.8	3.1	29.1
	32%	57%	10%	100%
Santa Fe	5.5	7.4	1.4	14.3
	39%	52%	10%	100%
Entre Ríos	3.2	6.9	1.3	11.4
	28%	61%	12%	100%
Córdoba	3.0	3.8	1.2	8.0
	38%	47%	15%	100%

Note: the number of proprietors, tenants and sharecroppers are in thousands.
Source: Cortés Conde (1979).

to the fact that a public entity had made the discovery on land that belonged to the state, President Figueroa Alcorta requested that Congress declare a large territory surrounding the oilfields a public preserve. He got only 10 per cent of the land he had requested but succeeded in creating the public preserve.

In 1907, President Figueroa Alcorta promulgated a law that put all of the railroads under the same legal regime, extended tax exemptions, obliged the railroad companies to create a fund to finance the construction of roads that would lead to railroad stations, and prohibited the building of roads that would compete with the railroads. In 1910 Figueroa Alcorta inaugurated the railroad connection between Mendoza and Santiago de Chile and the telegraphic cable that would connect Argentina with Europe. By 1910 the railroads covered 27,000 kilometres.

Trade union activity had started during the government of Roca with the creation of two rival worker's organizations: FORA in 1901 and the UGT. In 1903, FORA and UGT organized riots and strikes that intensified in 1909 under the influence of anarchists that competed with the socialists to represent the working class.

Police Chief Ramón Falcón ordered the police to break up protests on 1 May 1909 that resulted in ten deaths and more than a hundred injured. The next day the police confronted the workers that were accompanying the coffins of the victims with more death on both sides. History recorded these episodes as the 'red week'. A year after an unsuccessful attempt against the life of President Figueroa Alcorta, in November 1909 an anarchist assassinated Chief Falcón fuelling public outrage.

As the riots and strikes surged again in 1910, just a few months before the first Centennial Celebration of the May Revolution, Figueroa Alcorta declared a state of emergency and approved a law that authorized the imprisonment and expulsion of any suspected anarchist.

With the support of Figueroa Alcorta, in 1910 Roque Saenz Peña won the election and became president. Before taking the oath, he met with Yrigoyen. The leader of Unión Cívica Radical committed to abandoning his revolutionary stance and Saenz Peña promised to push for an electoral reform law that would prevent fraud in future elections.

Saenz Peña's main legacy was the changes he brought to Argentina's political system, and the law that he proposed was sanctioned by Congress in 1912. The Saenz Peña law made voting secret, universal and compulsory for all the men listed on the military roll.

But his contributions went beyond political reform. During his Presidency, he inaugurated the first subway of Buenos Aires and the monumental Retiro train station. In 1912, he endorsed a law to promote development in the National Territories. Railroads in Chaco, Formosa, Rio Negro, Chubut and Santa Cruz were built, completing the already impressive Argentine railroad system. He also inaugurated the first electrical railroad between Buenos Aires and Tigre.

In June 1912, tenant farmers experiencing worsening contractual conditions launched a protest known as the 'Grito de Alcorta'[1] (Cry of Alcorta). Through the creation of the Federación Agraria Argentina (Argentine Agrarian Federation), the rural middle classes erupted onto the national political scene.

Saenz Peña's deteriorating health forced him to take a leave of absence and hand power to his Vice-President Victorino de la Plaza in October 1913. Saenz Peña died in August 1914 and de la Plaza served out his term of office which ended in 1916.

Note

1 'Alcorta' is the name of the town where the tenant farmers met to deliberate and make explicit their demands. It is not related to the last name of President Figueroa Alcorta.

References

Cortés Conde, Roberto (1979) *El progreso argentino, 1880–1914*, Buenos Aires: Editorial Sudamericana.

Cortés Conde, Roberto (1989) *Dinero, Deuda y Crisis*, Buenos Aires: Editorial Sudamericana.

Cortés Conde, Roberto (1994) *La economía argentina en el largo plazo (siglos XIX y XX)*, Buenos Aires: Editorial Sudamericana.

Della Paolera, Gerardo and Taylor, Alan M. (2001) *Straining at the Anchor: The Argentine Currency Board and the Search for Macroeconomic Stability, 1880–1935*, Chicago, IL and London: The University of Chicago Press.

Rock, David (1987) *Argentina 1516–1987: From Spanish Colonization to Alfonsín*, Berkeley: University of California Press.

Scobie, James R. (1964) *Revolution on the Pampas: A Social History of Argentine Wheat 1860–1910*, Austin: University of Texas Press.

Solberg, Carl E. (1987) *The Prairies and the Pampas: Agrarian Policy in Canada and Argentina 1880–1930*, Stanford, CA: Stanford University Press.

Part III
From the beginning of the First World War to the end of the Second World War

6 The traumatic 30 years from 1914 to 1944

As with most countries engaged in international trade and finance, Argentina suffered a series of traumatic shocks beginning in 1913: the First World War, the Great Depression, and then the Second World War.

Despite the challenges, exports did increase in some years, but even when they did, difficulties in importing intermediate inputs and capital goods had a supply side negative effect on growth. The Great Depression reduced demand for exports and worsened the terms of trade.

Economic adversities fuelled the corporatist defensive attitudes of increasingly organized interest groups. Republican institutions that had become more democratic after the passage of the Saenz Peña Law in 1912 were weakened after 1930 when corporations and the armed forces captured ever more political power.

In 1930, Argentina suffered its first military coup that removed a democratically elected government. During the remainder of the interwar period, the governments were either military or civilian, but elected in rigged elections. In 1943, a second military coup brought a nationalistic military elite into power. From the beginning of the Second World War, the political and military elites were divided between pro-Allied and pro-Axis camps, but the country remained officially neutral until it declared war on the Axis powers in March 1945. Argentina did not participate in the Bretton Woods Conference in 1944, but did participate in the Conference of San Francisco that led to the United Nations but only after last-minute negotiations with the USA.

Argentina, which had been a successful participant in the global economy during the first wave of globalization, self-marginalized itself from the second wave of globalization led by the USA that began immediately after the Second World War.

Ideological conflicts during the interwar period

Crises originated in external shocks, the tensions between rural tenants and landowners, and the social conflicts created by the expansion of urban services and manufacturing controlled by foreign companies, all of which accentuated the ideological arguments between the defenders of the open market economy and the Nationalists. The Nationalists were deeply sceptical of the benefits of close connection with foreign capitalists and therefore globalization.

Furthermore, even among those that favoured an open market economy, there was a clear pro-British preference. The political and business establishment of Buenos Aires saw the USA, which started to challenge the economic leadership of the United Kingdom after the First World War, as more of a competitor than a potential partner in trade and finance. Other members of the Buenos Aires' elite saw Germany and Italy as potentially better partners.

The privileges extended by the United Kingdom to the members of its Commonwealth and Empire during the Great Depression added to the arguments of the Nationalists. The new circumstances shifted the emphasis in external relations towards the USA which began taking on an impressive amount of power at the beginning of the Second World War. Paradoxically, Nationalists added many of the pro-British and pro-German politicians and business leaders that disliked the USA to their ideological camp.

The influence of the Nationalists explains the neutrality of Argentina during the First World War. In the case of the Second World War, it was not only the influence of Nationalists, but also Argentina's traditionally distant relations with the USA and establishment members' sympathy with Germany and Italy that explains why Argentina stayed neutral until March 1945.

Economic performance during the First World War, the interwar period and the Second World War

Signs of recession were already present in the years preceding the First World War. They intensified in 1914 when the war began and were compounded by a severe drought that affected the domestic supply of and external demand for agricultural products. During the following four years, the impact of this foreign shock in the form of both deteriorating terms of trade and the sudden stop of capital inflows was extreme and the level of economic activity was sharply curtailed.

By 1918, the economy had started to come back to life and recover although not with the dynamism of the previous decades. Then, in 1929, it was dealt a new external shock, the Great Depression.

From the beginning of the Great Depression in 1930 to the end of the Second World War in 1945, the economic, political and military conflicts among the world's most powerful nations drove the collapse of international trade and finance and the disintegration of the global economy. Newly isolated national economies faced obstacles to overcoming crises and avoiding stagnation.

In those years, Argentina, like most nations, struggled with negative shocks from abroad while its intellectuals and politicians debated how best to reorganize the economy to cope with the unstable and confusing external environment.

Table 6.1 Comparative per capita GDP growth between 1913 and 1945

Country	1913	1929	1945	Annual change 1913–1929	Annual change 1913–1945
	(in 1990 I. dollars)				
Argentina	3,797	4,367	4,356	0.9%	0.4%
USA	5,301	6,899	11,709	1.7%	2.5%
Australia	5,157	5,263	7,133	0.1%	1.0%
Canada	4,447	5,065	6,928	0.8%	1.4%
Brazil	811	1,137	1,390	2.1%	1.7%
Mexico	1,732	1,757	2,134	0.1%	0.7%
Chile	2,653	3,396	3,630	1.6%	1.0%
Great Britain	4,921	5,503	7,056	0.7%	1.1%

Source: authors' own calculations, based on material originally published in Maddison (2006).

The economic performance of Argentina was poor in the interwar period and it was worse after 1929 than before. Until 1929 the slowdown in growth mirrored that of the United Kingdom, was very similar to the slowdown of Canada, and less pronounced than that of Australia.

Unlike Argentina, neighbouring Brazil and Chile were able to take advantage of the more rapid growth of the USA that began in 1939. The inability of Argentina to use the strength of the US economy to its advantage accentuated the slowdown it experienced during the early 1940s in spite of having softened the impact of the Great Depression during the 1930s. While the USA grew 2.5 per cent per year in per capita terms between 1913 and 1945, Argentina grew only 0.4 per cent. This growth was worst of all the countries shown in Table 6.1.

References

Cortés Conde, Roberto (1994) *La economía argentina en el largo plazo (siglos XIX y XX)*, Buenos Aires: Editorial Sudamericana.
della Paolera, Gerardo and Taylor, Alan M. (2001) *Straining at the Anchor. The Argentine Currency Board and the Search for Macroeconomic Stability, 1880–1935*, Chicago, IL and London: The University of Chicago Press.
Diaz Alejandro, Carlos D. (1970) *Essay on the Economic History of the Argentina Republic*, New Haven, CT: Yale University Press.
Ferreres, Orlando (2010) *Dos Siglos de Economía Argentina*, Buenos Aires: El Ateneo.
IEERAL (Instituto de Estudios Económicos de la República Argentina) (1986) *Revista Estudios Año IX-N39-Julio/Septiembre*, pp. 103–184.
Maddison, Angus (2006) *The World Economy*, Paris: OECD Publishing.

7 The 'Radical Republic'

The Saenz Peña law spurred the democratization of the republican, representative, and federal system created by the National Constitution of 1853 and paved the way for the Radical Party of Leandro Alem, Bernardo de Irigoyen and Hipólito Yrigoyen.

However, even before the election of Yrigoyen in 1916, the government of Victorino de la Plaza outlined the new foreign and domestic policies that would characterize the period that historians call 'The Radical Republic'. There would be an increased focus on working-class issues. And under the umbrella of neutrality, foreign policy during Yrigoyen's presidencies would be, in practice, anti-North American and less compliant with British interests than it had been during the years that Roca dominated Argentine politics.

In strictly political terms, during the Radical presidencies the governments shifted from a popular democracy under Yrigoyen to a liberal democracy under Marcelo Torcuato de Alvear. In economic terms, in spite of the severe recession triggered by the First World War, the policies continued to seek fruitful integration into the world economy, particularly during Alvear's presidency, when Argentina courted not only the British market but also that of the USA. The government not only strove to avoid devaluation of the peso, but returned to the gold standard in 1927.

The Great Depression that originated in the USA brought the popular democracy of Yrigoyen's second term and the Radical Republic itself to a tragic end.

Politics immediately before and during the Radical Republic

President Victorino de la Plaza addressed several working-class issues. He created the Caja Nacional de Ahorro Postal, a financial institution, to encourage the habit of saving small amounts through the purchase of postal stamps. He also sanctioned a labour law that protected workers in the case of industrial accidents and occupational diseases. Similarly, he championed an affordable housing law.

Just before the start of the First World War in 1914, President de la Plaza signed a pact with his Chilean and Brazilian counterparts in response to the

American occupation of Veracruz, Mexico. This was called the ABC Pact (for Argentina, Brazil and Chile). De la Plaza declared Argentina's neutrality during the First World War and made known his intention to continue to trade with both sides.

In 1915, de la Plaza granted Argentine citizenship to around three million immigrants and thereby granted them the right to vote. In 1916, Hipólito Yrigoyen, the legendary leader of the Unión Cívica Radical, won the presidential election.

Yrigoyen took office on 12 October 1916. The economy was mired in a deep recession that started in 1914 and would last four years. As in most other countries, the war opened the door to increased government intervention in the economy. The goal was to reduce the recessionary effects of the conflict and to respond to the sectorial pressures of increasingly mobilized economic and social actors.

The decline of real wages and unemployment caused by the recession fuelled the spread of anarchist and socialist ideals and generated increasingly violent social conflicts around the time the Bolsheviks came to power in Russia. Yrigoyen tried to pass legislation that offered workers more protection and ordered the Department of Labour to mediate in conflicts between workers and employers; but, his initiatives did not always find support in Congress. Mediation efforts were unsuccessful as the parties refused to negotiate and compromise.

Three episodes over the span of three years illustrate the great difficulties that Yrigoyen faced as he tried to pass progressive social legislation and restore order following violent social conflicts. First was the workers' insurrection that led to the tragic week of 1919. Second was the rural workers' 'Rebellion of Patagonia' in 1920 and 1921. Finally, there was labour unrest surrounding layoffs by the British-owned company La Forestal in the north of Santa Fe in 1921. Each episode was more violent and cost more lives than the one before.

The 'tragic week' of January 1919 started as a conflict between workers and the Vasena Metallurgic Workshops (Talleres Metalúrgicos Vasena). A confrontation between strikers and strike-breakers hired by the company turned violent initially resulting in four deaths and 30 injured workers. The next day, at the workers' funerals, there were new attacks by the strike-breakers, the police were overwhelmed, and the violence intensified. President Yrigoyen sent in General Luis Dellepiane to restore order but it took his forces a week to control the rebellion. The repression increased and the ultimate death toll was 65 workers and four policemen.

The rebellion in Patagonia started in November 1920 as a strike demanding wage increases and housing benefits for rural workers. Most protesters were Chilean immigrants led by an anarchist of the Workers Society of Rio Gallegos in the province of Santa Cruz. Strikers occupied numerous properties and took property owners hostage. Yrigoyen sent a military unit commanded by Colonel Hector Benigno Varela to restore order; Varela threatened to shoot those strikers who did not release the hostages and return to work and promised improvements for the workers and their families and the situation was controlled with only a few arrests (including several Chilean police officers that where helping the strikers). Colonel Varela blamed the rebellion on the Chileans and initially exculpated the workers. However, one year later, when riots started again and Colonel Varela returned with two military units, he declared that the strikers had betrayed his good faith and repressed the rebellion mercilessly. His men shot hundreds of workers and arrested even more. The conflict came to an end, but only at a high cost in lives and lost prestige for the national government. It would also cost the life of Colonel Varela. An anarchist assassinated him two years later in the streets of Buenos Aires.

The Forestal Land, Timber and Railways Company, created in 1872 by British, French and German investors, and known in Argentina as La Forestal, became the world's biggest producer of tannin and quebracho wood. In 1919 and 1921, the workers of La Forestal went on several strikes demanding better working conditions. They received support from anarchist and socialist activists and the Federación Obrera Regional Argentina. The Province of Santa Fe, then governed by the radical politician Enrique Mosca, formed a police task force called the Gendarmería Volante and financed by the company. This police force enforced company rules. With the support of national troops sent from Rosario, the repression of the strikes resulted in hundreds of deaths, a loss of life greater than in Patagonia.

Yrigoyen encouraged the expansion of trade unions hoping that they would organize workers, allowing them to negotiate working conditions in a peaceful way. In response to the demands of both the organized workers and the organized rural tenants and sharecroppers, President Yrigoyen proposed and Congress approved several social initiatives. The initiatives created a social security system for the workers and employees of public utilities such as the gas, electrical energy, telegraph, telephone and railroad companies. He also passed laws that regulated household employment, the work of minors as well as the relation between tenants and landowners. Congress did not approve all of Yrigoyen's social initiatives because powerful corporations and even President Alvear pressured legislators.

Yrigoyen promoted the creation of state-owned companies like state railroads (Ferrocarriles del Estado) and the State Oil Company, Yacimientos Petrolíferos Fiscales (YPF). In the case of the private railroad companies, most of them British-owned, he set limits on the fees companies could charge and enforced accurate accounting for the determination of profits and the issuing of dividends. In cases where monopolist producers were hoarding goods, he proposed the expropriation of the goods and their sale at market prices. In one case he expropriated and sold 200,000 tons of sugar.

Yrigoyen maintained the educational policies started by Sarmiento and continued by all the previous presidents; but in the universities, he supported the University Reform promoted by the Federación Universitaria Argentina, a student organization that originated in Córdoba and spread very rapidly to the other universities. The University Reform granted tuition-free education and unrestricted student admission. Students were also empowered to participate in the University's governance.

In foreign policy, Yrigoyen emphasized the estrangement from the USA that had started during the administration of Juarez Celman. In 1889 and 1890, Saenz Peña, then the Argentine representative to the First Pan-American Conference, led the opposition to the creation of a Continental Customs Union proposed by the USA. On the other hand, unlike his predecessors, Yrigoyen was also tough with British interests. Yrigoyen was the pioneer of the nationalist domestic and foreign policies that would become standard for most of the governments starting with the one created after the 1943 military coup and lasting until the government of Carlos Menem in 1989. In 1916, Yrigoyen criticized the US invasion of Santo Domingo. He would later withdraw the Argentine delegation from the Paris Peace Conference, because the British and other imperial powers did not accept the principle of equal treatment for all nations, with no distinction between victors and vanquished.

By the end of his term, Yrigoyen supported the nomination of his friend Marcelo Torcuato de Alvear as the Unión Cívica Radical's candidate. Alvear was the heir of a wealthy and patrician family. His ideas on economic and international matters were closer to those of conservative politicians than those of his predecessor, mentor and friend. In fact, as Ambassador to France, he had been a member of the delegation to the Paris Peace Conference, but had disagreed with the decision of Yrigoyen to withdraw the delegates when the British opposed Argentina's initiatives.

Alvear began his government in 1922 at a time when the economy was growing fast and international conditions had become more favourable. His inaugural speech took a conciliatory tone with the opposition that was different from the confrontational style of his predecessor. He filled his cabinet with people not connected with Yrigoyen and in some cases, like those of Admiral Manuel Domecq Garcia and General Agustín Pedro Justo, distant from the ideology of the Unión Cívica Radical.

Economic policies during Alvear's presidency were more liberal and less interventionist than those during his predecessor's presidency. Though, in the case of the livestock and meat markets, he applied stricter regulations that established minimum and maximum prices. He also created a state-owned meat processing company that many years later became the legendary Frigorífico Lisandro de la Torre. Alvear supported the State Oil Company, YPF, but did not go ahead with the idea of nationalizing the oilfields as Yrigoyen's followers proposed.

In terms of social legislation, Alvear continued the efforts of Yrigoyen to extend social security coverage to bank employees and teachers. In 1923 Congress approved a law that created a social security system to provide mandatory universal coverage for all workers. This was later repealed when both the Unión Industrial Argentina and the trade unions opposed the initiative because it imposed contributions to employers and workers that both considered too onerous. A deep crisis in the sugar cane industry ended in a strike by the independent sugar cane producers organized by the Federación Agraria Argentina. President Alvear set the price so that sugar mills had to pay the sugar cane producers and created a provincial agency to mediate future conflicts. He also passed a law to promote the creation of cooperatives through tax exemptions and credit from Banco de la Nación.

In educational matters, he continued the policies of his predecessors that supported public education but departed from Yrigoyen's policies regarding universities. He weakened support for the student movement and helped reverse some of the more controversial initiatives of the University Reform of 1918.

In foreign policy, Alvear signed several border agreements with Chile, Bolivia and Uruguay and unsuccessfully tried to have Congress forgive Paraguay's debt after the War of the Triple Alliance. Relations with the USA improved and brought about an impressive increase in investments, particularly in the automobile industry. For example, the Ford Motor Company established a car assembly plant in Argentina, the first in Latin America and the second outside the USA (the other was in London). The investment by other American companies was also important for the food processing industries and energy distribution businesses. This expansion of US investment in Argentina, and American companies' competition with British companies negatively impacted Argentina's diplomatic relations with Great Britain.

Early in Alvear's presidency, the Unión Cívica Radical split between the supporters of Alvear, who came to be known as the 'Anti-Personalists', and the supporters of Yrigoyen, known as 'Personalists'. The confrontation between the two groups was significant, even in Congress, and when it came time to nominate candidates for the 1928 election the Personalists supported an Yrigoyen–Francisco Beiró ticket and the Anti-Personalists supported a Leopoldo Melo–Vicente Gallo ticket. Even though the Anti-Personalist faction formed a coalition with the Conservatives, Yrigoyen won a landslide election and, on 12 October 1928, took the oath for his second term. But, popular support diminished rapidly during his second term due to political violence within the country and the impact of the economic crisis abroad.

In October 1929, the crash of the market on Wall Street in the USA set off the Great Depression that would dominate the picture for the next decade. Yrigoyen's government, like most governments in the world, was taken by surprise and did not know how to react.

On the domestic political front, early in his term, Yrigoyen decided to intervene in the provinces of Mendoza and San Juan which were governed by two opposition parties: the Lencinismo in Mendoza and the Bloquismo in San Juan. In November 1929 an unknown assassin killed Carlos Washington Lencinas, who had been recently removed from the Senate by Yrigoyen's majority. In December, an Italian anarchist attempted to assassinate Yrigoyen and the president's bodyguards killed him. In January 1930, an unidentified assassin killed the lawyer Manuel Ignacio Castellano, an important member of Bloquismo. In March, the Unión Cívica Radical lost the parliamentary elections in Buenos Aires, ending in third place after two socialist parties, the Partido Socialismo Independiente and the Partido Socialista Argentino. Nationwide, the Unión Cívica Radical got fewer votes than the opposition.

In 1929, Yrigoyen proposed that Congress pass a law nationalizing the oilfields. Rights given to the provinces under the Code of Mining had in turn been given as concession to private foreign companies. In August 1930, YPF decided to intervene in the oil market to try to break up the monopoly of the private oil companies.

In mid-1930, Yrigoyen granted a pardon to the anarchist that had assassinated Colonel Hector Benigno Varela in 1922. This decision infuriated conservatives.

On 6 September 1930, a military coup removed Yrigoyen from power. The press, the conservatives, the socialists, and even the Anti-Personalist Radicals applauded the coup. The middle classes that had been Yrigoyen's main support, who were also dissatisfied because of the economic crisis, also supported the move. This was the end of the Radical Republic and the beginning of a long period of political and economic instability very different from the six decades that had elapsed since the birth of Argentina as a unified constitutional nation.

The economy from the First World War recession to the beginning of the Great Depression

During the 15 years between the beginning of the First World War and the Great Depression in 1929, Argentina remained committed to fiscal and monetary orthodoxy and integrated itself into the world trade and finance system. As with most countries that were open economies and not directly involved in the war, Argentina suffered a deep recession that lasted four years. This time, though, the recession was not the consequence of misguided domestic policies, but of the collapse of international trade and finance attributable to the war.

The recession actually began towards the end of 1913, because of falling liquidity in the London market; the recession only became severe after the declaration of war in August 1914. Argentina suffered not only a sudden stop in the inflow of foreign capital (which went from a net inflow of 9.6 per cent of GDP in 1913 to a net outflow of 2.4 per cent of GDP in 1914), but also many restrictions on imports. The recession was aggravated in 1914 and 1916 by a drastic fall in agricultural production due to bad weather conditions that affected harvests. The evolution of exports, as reflected in Figure 7.1, shows the depth of the recession.

Since import duties represented a high proportion of revenues, to keep the fiscal deficit under control the government was forced to cut government expenditures. Fiscal policy became very restrictive as shown in Figure 7.2.

86 *The two World Wars*

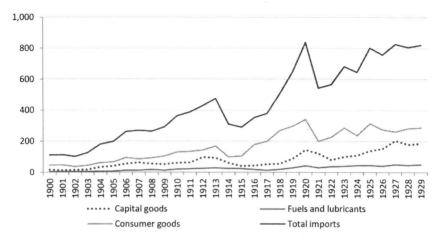

Figure 7.1 Imports 1900–1929
(in million dollars)
Source: authors' own calculations, based on material originally published in Ferreres (2010) and methodology used by Diaz Alejandro (1970).

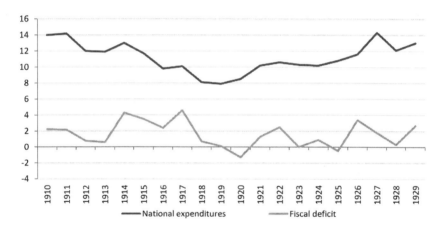

Figure 7.2 Public expenditure and fiscal deficit 1910–1929
(in percentage of GDP)
Source: authors' own calculations, based on material originally published in IEERAL (1986) and Cortés Conde (1994).

GDP fell 10.3 per cent in 1914 and 21 per cent in the four-year period from 1914 to 1917. The cost of living increased because of higher import prices and the devaluation of the peso. Nominal salaries fell only a few percentage points but, because of price increases, real wages fell almost 20 per cent between 1914 and 1918 as shown in Figure 7.3.

According to Mario Bunge (1940), unemployment rose to 19.7 per cent in 1917. Falling real wages and increased unemployment help to explain the

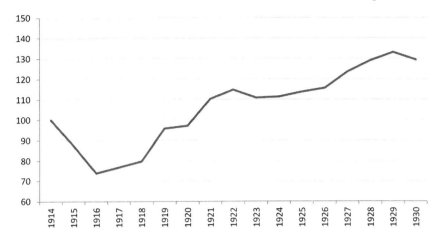

Figure 7.3 Real wage index
(1914=100)
Source: authors' own calculations, based on material originally published in IEERAL (1986).

increase in worker's unrest during the Yrigoyen's presidency, especially after migrants that had left the country during the years of the war started to come back and encountered working conditions that were much poorer than those they had known before.

The economy began to recover in 1918 and expanded rapidly until 1929. By 1922, real wages surpassed the level of 1913 which explains why social unrest vanished and people started to perceive a climate of prosperity again during the Alvear presidency. However, that prosperity was not uniform across sectors.

The restrictions on imports during the war cut two ways. On one hand they restricted production and generated a recession that lasted four years. On the other, restricting imports created incentives for the local production of import substitutes. Immediately after the war, several foreign industrial companies built factories in Argentina. The most important of these was the Ford Motor Company. There are no accurate figures on the rate of growth of industrial GDP for this period with estimates ranging from 4 per cent to 5 per cent. Cortés Conde, using census data, estimated that between 1920 and 1930 industrial GDP grew at 4.1 per cent per year. In their study on the economic development of Argentina, the Comisión Económica para América Latina (CEPAL) estimated annual industrial GDP growth of 5.1 per cent. Whichever source and method is applied, it is clear that the expansion of industrial production was significant.

The increase in foreign demand for beef immediately after the end of the war drove an increase in the price of livestock as cattle farmers increased the retention of cows for reproduction. However, when the livestock cycle produced a significant increase in the supply of finished steers, prices started to fall. The cattle farmers and breeders lobbied the government for protection. President

Alvear responded by intervening in the market and creating a state-owned meat processing company in spite of the fact that until then his economic policies had been, in general, less interventionist than those of Yrigoyen.

The price of wheat and other cereals started to fall in 1925. The same happened with the prices of imported manufacturing goods that competed with local industrial production. The farmers and the industrialists also lobbied for protection, particularly as wages started to increase more rapidly than productivity. Of course, lobbying by cattle ranchers, breeders, and farmers intensified during the 1930s when export prices for their products fell even more steeply than they had in the 1920s.

Money and banking from the First World War to the Great Depression

When the nations that were preparing for war decided to repatriate capital, the foreign reserves in the Caja de Conversion started to fall and de la Plaza decided to suspend convertibility. The paper peso started to depreciate but gold remained in the country. The private banks that had enjoyed several years of expansion leading up to 1912 encountered major difficulties. They were losing liquidity rapidly even before the beginning of the war and a high proportion of their assets became bad loans. The strict gold standard rule the country had followed until August 1914 did not have room for a lender of last resort. De la Plaza decided to authorize the Caja de Conversion to print money to lend to the Banco de la Nación in order to rediscount credits to private banks that needed liquidity.

The Caja de Conversion continued to put money in circulation at the same rate as gold reserves increased when the country was still on the gold standard. This means that it did not create money to lend to the Banco de la Nación. However, the Banco de la Nación acted as a lender of last resort with the huge increase in deposits it received as the public, scared by the war and the fragility of private banks, moved its liquidity to the state-owned bank. This is shown in Table 7.1.

Table 7.1 Bank deposits in 1912–1914 crisis

	1912	1914	Percentage of change
	(million of paper pesos, end of year)		
Total	1,480	1,189	−19.7%
Private domestic banks	674	365	−45.8%
Banco de la Nación	478	553	15.7%
Foreign banks	328	271	−17.4%

Source: authors' own calculations, based on material originally published in Della Paolera and Taylor (2001).

The private banks suffered losses not only in deposits but also capital because their assets were deteriorating rapidly. The banking crisis was also clearly reflected in the value of the stocks of the banks that fell far further than other equities.

The Banco de la Nación provided not only liquidity to the private banks in crisis but also rediscounted many of their bad loans at interest rates lower than the rate it paid to depositors. This helped private banks gain liquidity, but also to recover solvency. These measures avoided a collapse of the banking system similar to what had happened in 1890, but on the other hand the Banco de la Nación ended up absorbing most of the bad loans in the system and became a weaker institution than what Carlos Pellegrini had envisioned when it was created in 1891.

The accumulation of bad loans in the Banco de la Nación, as Gerardo Della Paolera and Alan Taylor (2001) have demonstrated, explains why the experience of the return to the gold standard between 1927 and 1929 was short-lived. To avoid the collapse of the Banco de la Nación Argentina had to exit the gold standard several months before Great Britain and two years before the USA. This decision helped Argentina dampen the effects of the Great Depression, but left a legacy of bank bailouts and insolvent debtors that created an addiction to the use of inflation as a way to transfer wealth from savers to imprudent debtors and their creditors. This poisonous legacy would infect economic policies for the next six decades.

References

Bunge, Alejandro (1940) *Una Nueva Argentina*, Madrid: Kraft.
Comisión Económica para América Latina (1958) *El Desarrollo Económico Argentino*, CEPAL: Santiago de Chile.
Cortés Conde, Roberto (1994) *La economía argentina en el largo plazo (siglos XIX y XX)*, Buenos Aires: Editorial Sudamericana.
Della Paolera, Gerardo and Taylor, Alan M. (2001) *Straining at the Anchor: The Argentine Currency Board and the Search for Macroeconomic Stability, 1880–1935*, Chicago, IL and London: The University of Chicago Press.
Diaz Alejandro, Carlos D. (1970) *Essay on the Economic History of the Argentina Republic*, New Haven, CT: Yale University Press.
Ferreres, Orlando (2010) *Dos Siglos de Economía Argentina*, Buenos Aires: El Ateneo.
IEERAL (Instituto de Estudios Económicos sobre la Realidad Argentina y Latinoamericana) (1986) *Revista Estudios Año IX-N39-Julio/Septiembre*, pp. 103–184.

8 From the fall of Yrigoyen to the rise of Perón

General José Felix Uriburu, a nationalist military officer who sympathized with the corporatist ideas that were spreading in Europe, led a military coup that removed Yrigoyen from power. Uriburu himself only governed a year and a half. The so-called Personalists, followers of Yrigoyen, still dominated the Radical Party. They were predominantly nationalist but were, of course, opposed to Uriburu's corporatism.

In November 1931, General Agustin P. Justo won the election with the Radical Party outlawed but with some support from the anti-Personalist Radicals. He completed his constitutional six-year term, but was in conflict with not only the Personalists but also the followers of Alvear.

Justo and Alvear, the leader of the anti-Personalist Radicals, shared liberal and republican ideals. However, while Justo accepted and was even ready to use fraud to take and maintain power, Alvear remained loyal to the democratic ideals of the Radical Party.

The creation of the Force of Radical Orientation for the Young Argentina (Fuerza de Orientación Radical para la Jóven Argentina, known by its Spanish acronym as FORJA) supported the nationalistic ideological stance of the followers of Yrigoyen. Uriburu, in turn, represented the anti-liberal and corporatist ideas supported by the military.

The ideological confrontations intensified during Justo's government and his successor, Roberto Ortiz, an anti-Personalist Radical, had to accept Ramon Castillo, a representative of the pro-Axis nationalists as vice-president.

During this period, a group of young economists led by Federico Pinedo and Raul Prebisch were able to manage the economy so as to soften the deflationary effects of the Great Depression. They also proposed ways to reorient the economy from the British market towards that of the USA and other Latin American countries. However, the political conflicts and the nationalistic sentiment that was intensifying not only in the pro-Axis circles, but also among the anti-Personalist Radicals impeded that reorientation.

After the military coup of 1943 and the rise of Juan Perón as the dominant political figure, the idea of keeping Argentina an open-market economy more in the circle of influence of the USA than in the traditional British sphere clearly lost ground.

Politics between 1930 and 1945

After leading the military coup of 6 September 1930, General Uriburu, a nephew of former President José Evaristo Uriburu, took power and governed until February 1932, when the newly elected president, General Justo, took office.

Uriburu was a nationalist military commander that disliked liberalism and favoured corporatism, the political system of Mussolini's Italy that had spread across Europe since the end of the First World War. He dissolved Congress, intervened in all the provinces governed by the Radicals, and repealed the University Reform of 1918.

Uriburu tried to organize a National Party that sought to unite all the political parties except the Personalists to ensure that the followers of Yrigoyen would never return to power. However, as soon as he called for the first election in the Province of Buenos Aires, the Radical Party candidate, Honorio Pueyrredón, a former minister in Yrigoyen's government, won the election with the support of Alvear.

Uriburu decided to intervene in the province triggering a rebellion in the armed forces. He defeated the revolt and sent its leaders, Pueyrredón and Alvear, into exile; however, the event eroded his power. In the national election he called in November 1931, he had to admit General Justo, a liberal former military commander that had been the Minister of War in Alvear's cabinet, as candidate for the presidency.

Justo was able to assemble a broad coalition of most of the political parties that had supported the military coup against Yrigoyen, but did not agree with Uriburu's anti-liberalism and corporatism. Uriburu prevented Marcelo T. de Alvear from running with the argument that a complete constitutional term of six years had not passed since his last election. This led most of the anti-Personalists to support General Justo.

Not all the parties of the coalition agreed on the candidate for vice-president leading Justo to run on two separate tickets. The anti-Personalists supported Justo and Nicolás Matienzo and the Conservative Party (Partido Demócrata Nacional) supported Justo and Julio Argentino Roca Jr. The Justo–Roca ticket won the election against the candidates Lisandro de la Torre and Nicolás Repetto of the Progressive Democrats and the Socialist Party which had not joined the coalition assembled by Justo.

Even though Justo was the new president and Alvear was the leader of the Radicals, and together they were able to dominate politics for the next ten years, the nationalist and corporatist ideas of Uriburu were still latent in certain military circles and reappeared in the military coup of 1943.

Justo and Alvear shared liberal and republican ideas, but they had very different approaches to gaining and exercising power. Justo accepted and was ready to use fraud while Alvear was loyal to the democratic ideas of the Radical Party. These differences, in spite of their shared distancing of themselves from Yrigoyen's nationalism and Uriburu's corporatism, explain the frequent conflict between them. In fact, Justo imprisoned Alvear and many other Radical militants and authorized the use of violence and fraud to keep the Radicals out of power at both the national and provincial levels in 1932 when a group of Radicals and military officers were planning a new revolt.

Even as Justo tried hard to keep Argentina economically engaged with Great Britain at a time when it extended privileged status to members of the British Commonwealth, he ended up making concessions to the foreign companies that dominated the transportation and export businesses linked with big local cattle breeders. These concessions, known as the Roca–Runciman Pact, harmed smaller cattle ranchers and generated strong opposition from the Progressive Democrats led by Lisandro de la Torre. The confrontation in Congress was so passionate and violent that one fanatic militant of the Conservative Party assassinated Enzo Bordabehere, an elected senator and close associate of de la Torre in the Senate.

In spite of all the political conflicts and British discrimination, under the Justo government the Argentine economy was able to recover faster than those of the USA and Canada thanks to the ability of a group of young economists led by Federico Pinedo. The expert in monetary affairs was Raúl Prebisch who had been the research director of the Banco de la Nación and undersecretary of finance during the government of Uriburu. Starting at the very beginning of Justo's government, they implemented policies similar to those that John Maynard Keynes would later recommend in his General Theory. Investment in infrastructure, particularly in roadways, bridges, hospitals, schools and public buildings was even higher than in the best years of the 1880s and the first decade of the 20th century.

Unfortunately, the institutions created to pull the economy out of recession would provide, after the military coup of 1943, the tools for the isolationist and populist policies that would generate inflation and stagnation in the economy for the next several decades.

Corporatism as a political regime never entirely replaced the republican political system of the constitution. However, workers and regional producers did start to organize corporations that would fight for the interests of their constituencies and try to counterbalance the strong influence that the landowners, bankers and foreign companies had exercised in previous decades and, particularly, during the years of the Great Depression. Therefore, economic corporatism was increasingly intertwined with the republican political institutions in generating regulations and state interventions in the market.

On the political front, in addition to the confrontations between the government of Justo and the Radical Party led by Alvear, there was a development that would have an important ideological impact in the following years. Two years after the death of Yrigoyen, a group of young intellectuals and politicians created the Force of Radical Orientation for the Young Argentina. One of its members was the writer Arturo Jauretche. Another, writer Raúl Scalabrini Ortiz, was an informal member in the beginning, because he was not a member of the Radical Party. In 1940, Scalabrini Ortiz formally joined

FORJA and supported Jauretche as the leader of the group. Their ideology was strongly nationalistic and they denounced the governments that had succeeded Yrigoyen as neo-colonialists. They argued that the Roca–Runciman Pact and the creation of the Central Bank and the Corporation for the Transport of Buenos Aires were decisions designed to protect foreign interests in Argentina and not to improve the standard of living of Argentine workers and producers. Their practical influence on politics during the short period of its formal existence – 1935 to 1945 – was small but their ideological influence on the events after the military coup of 1943 would be very important.

By 1936 workers already organized in sector-specific trade unions created the General Workers Confederation (Confederación General del Trabajo, known by its Spanish acronym CGT). In 1937, the CGT declared the first general strike in support of construction workers. Immediately after, they organized a meeting with all opposition parties present and, in response to a demand by the CGT, the Congress passed the Labour Contract Law for workers in the commerce sector. This law modified the articles of the Code of Commerce that regulated labour relations between employers and workers, reformed the severance payment system, and introduced paid vacations.

During Justo's presidency Argentina joined the League of Nations that Yrigoyen had opposed at the time of its creation. Foreign Minister Carlos Saavedra Lamas was able to significantly increase the role of Argentina and its neighbours, Brazil, Chile and Perú, in mediating between Bolivia and Paraguay to end the Chaco War. In 1936 Saavedra Lamas was the first Latin American to receive the Nobel Peace Prize for his contributions to the peace between Bolivia and Paraguay and for promoting the Anti-War Pact signed by 21 nations.

In 1937 and 1938, Justo's political confrontation with the Radical Party intensified and he decided to support the presidential candidacy of the Anti-Personalist Radical Roberto Ortiz and Conservative politician Ramón Castillo who competed with Radical candidates Marcelo T. de Alvear and Enrique Mosca. The candidates supported by Justo won at the national level, but the Radicals defeated the official candidates in the City of Buenos Aires and the provinces of Córdoba, Tucumán and La Rioja.

Roberto Ortiz, determined to end fraud and democratize the electoral system, intervened in the Province of Buenos Aires where the election of the Conservative candidate had been scandalously fraudulent. This decision pleased the Radicals who started to support Ortiz in his efforts to restore democracy but displeased many Conservative politicians, including those that Ramón Del Castillo represented on the presidential ticket.

At the start of the Second World War in 1939, President Ortiz, like former presidents Justo and Alvear, opposed the Axis powers, and was ready to support the Allies. There was, however, significant support within influential circles (including the military) for the Axis. This led Argentina to declare neutrality. At this time, President Ortiz fell ill with diabetes and went blind.

He was forced to request a leave of absence and Ramón Castillo (who harboured pro-Axis views) assumed the role of acting President.

In November 1940, Federico Pinedo who had recently been appointed Minister of the Treasury again, submitted a plan to Congress prepared by the same team that had successfully managed the economy during the Great Depression. This time the plan addressed more medium- and long-term issues related to the need to change the old strategy (based on exports to Great Britain) in light of the new developments in the world, particularly the expanding role of the USA and the war in Europe.

The plan proposed promoting industries that could diversify exports in terms of products and markets. The idea was to look for new markets, Latin America and the USA, and to create new products like food and beverages, textiles, garments and leather goods, chemicals, lime and cement, glass and ceramics and electrical appliances that until then had been produced only for the domestic market. One of the problems that the plan tried to solve was the crisis of the triangular trade that had prevailed in previous decades when a surplus in trade with Great Britain helped pay for the trade deficit with the USA. In the 1930s, and particularly during the war, Argentina would accumulate blocked pounds in London and would not have dollars to pay for imports coming from the USA. Pinedo and his team foresaw that after the war the USA would replace Great Britain as the economic leader of the world.

The tools contemplated in the plan were fiscal and financial stimulus for non-traditional exports and selective allocation of import permits and foreign exchange to ensure that the production of exportable industrial goods would not face bottlenecks from the input side. The plan put special emphasis on not stimulating industries that would not survive after the war because of a lack of competitiveness.

The Senate approved the Pinedo Plan but the plan did not get the support of the Radicals in the House of Representatives. The issue was not so much disagreement with the economic initiative but mainly because of a confrontation with the Conservative Government that had been escalating since the moment Castillo became acting President. Using the failure of the Plan as an excuse, Castillo removed Pinedo from the Treasury. This way he felt less constrained to resist the USA which had begun to pressure Argentina to abandon neutrality.

After further deterioration in his health, Ortiz finally resigned in June 1942 just a few weeks before passing away. Alvear had already died in March 1942 and Justo died a few months after Ortiz in January 1943. In the course of less than one year Argentina lost the three politicians that were the custodians of liberal republicanism and most strongly opposed to Fascism and Nazism.

Castillo suddenly found himself without any restraint on pursuing his preferred international alignment. He removed the Minister of War who had been a close associate of Justo and designated General Pedro Pablo Ramirez, a prominent member of the Group of United Officers (Grupo de Oficiales Unidos, known by its Spanish acronym GOU), a circle of nationalistic officers that supported neutrality. A few months later, when Castillo heard rumours that a group of Radicals had offered General Ramirez the candidacy for the Presidency, he tried to remove him as war minister. Rather than resigning, Ramirez organized a coup against Castillo and removed him from power on 4 June 1943.

The effect of the Great Depression on economic institutions

Table 8.1 shows the evolution of the main economic indicators to trace the effect of the Great Depression on the economic institutions.

The outflow of capital from Argentina started in 1929. This was reflected in the fall of gold reserves from 1,113 to 954 million gold pesos and a decline in foreign terms of trade of almost 10 per cent from 1928 to 1929. Since the country remained committed to the gold standard, the monetary base contracted from 1,406 to 1,247 million pesos and the price level also fell 3 per cent. The fall in reserves relative to deposits reflected the stress on the banks. The Banco de la Nación saw reserves fall from 34 per cent to 16 per cent; and, at most other banks they fell from 13 per cent to 11 per cent. The fall was larger at the Banco de la Nación because it had opened its rediscount window to support the other banks. Even though the price level was falling, because of the loss of liquidity banks raised their discount rate from 6.3 per cent in 1928 to 6.9 per cent in 1929.

In December 1929, the government decided to suspend convertibility, but in 1930 the Currency Board did not expand domestic credit and the monetary base remained almost unchanged. The suspension of convertibility accentuated the loss of bank deposits and the quality of bank assets deteriorated rapidly. The price level fell another 4 per cent and salaries that had remained almost unchanged in 1929 fell 9 per cent in 1930. There is no doubt that the fall in salaries plus the increase in unemployment generated popular unrest that, together with the violent events in the political arena, created the climate for the military coup in September 1930.

The first manifestation of the effects that the Great Depression would have on Argentina's economic institutions came when Yrigoyen was still in power and the decision was made to suspend convertibility. Contrary to what happened in other emerging economies, Argentina did not abandon its commitment to fiscal orthodoxy and did not default on its external debt. On these matters the governments of Uriburu and Justo maintained the same attitude of Avellaneda in 1876, Pellegrini in 1890, and Roque Saenz Peña and Victorino de la Plaza in 1914–1916.

In order to make up for the fall in customs revenues, the government of Uriburu increased domestic tax rates. The increase in revenue from domestic taxes was dramatic: they went from only 5 per cent of total revenue in the 1920s to 25 per cent of total revenue in 1933. Even when the devaluation of the peso increased the cost of servicing the external debt substantially and provoked an increase in the fiscal deficit in 1930, the government continued to

Table 8.1 Main economic indicators 1928–1943

Year	Monetary base	Gold stock	Domestic credit	Exchange rate (peso per dollar)	Wholesale price level	Nominal salary index	Bank discount rate (in percentage per year)	Terms of trade (1928=100)	Government deficit (in percentage of GDP)
	(in million pesos)				(1928=100)				
1928	1,406	1,113	293	2.3	100	100	6.3	100	0.3
1929	1,247	954	293	2.4	97	101	6.9	91	2.7
1930	1,261	968	293	2.7	93	92	6.9	89	3.7
1931	1,245	593	652	3.4	90	86	7.2	66	0.8
1932	1,339	584	755	3.8	91	82	7.1	69	4.9
1933	1,214	561	653	3.2	87	80	6.1	65	1.3
1934	1,172	561	610	3.9	99	77	5.5	80	1.4
1935	1,647	1,354	293	3.8	98	84	5.4	79	–1
1936	1,685	1,528	157	3.6	100	87	5.6	97	3
1937	1,679	1,422	257	3.3	114	90	5.2	111	4
1938	1,615	1,296	379	3.9	108	88	5.3	102	4.2
1939	1,796	1,396	400	4.3	109	90	5.8	90	5
1940	1,810	1,329	481	4.3	124	94	5.8	92	4.4
1941	2,200	1,571	629	4.2	128	95	5.3	101	7.6
1942	2,700	1,912	788	4.2	161	99	5.3	96	2.4
1943	3,400	2,722	678	4.1	176	105	5.3	99	1.9

Source: authors' calculations, based on material originally published in Baiocco (1973), IEERAL (1986), Della Paolera and Ortiz (1995) and Ferreres (2010) and methodology used by Della Paolera and Taylor (2001).

service the debt and made extreme efforts to reduce government spending in other areas. Because of the cuts in spending and the increases in revenue, the fiscal deficit that had been 3.7 per cent of GDP in 1930 dropped to 1.3 per cent in 1933. To finance these deficits, and particularly the very large deficit of 1930, the Treasury borrowed from the domestic markets and from the banks at the market interest rate and did not collect seigniorage.

In 1932, President Justo created a new tax on gasoline and earmarked it for the financing of new roads. This new tax had an impressive impact on the expansion of road infrastructure and was one of the keys for pulling the economy out of the recession.

On monetary matters, there was a big institutional change in 1931. Soon after taking power the government of Uriburu, advised by Raul Prebisch, decided to start using the authorization granted to the Currency Board in 1914 to create money by rediscounting commercial paper from banks' portfolios. This facility, which had rarely been used before, compensated for the monetary contraction associated with the loss of almost 400 million gold pesos of foreign reserves by having the Currency Board create an equivalent amount of domestic credit. As a result, the Banco de la Nación and the Currency Board started managing a *de facto* fiduciary currency rather than a metallic one. Although a law formally created the Central Bank in 1935, the most important change in the monetary institutions, from metallic to fiduciary money, had been in place since 1931.

The recession was softer and the recovery came sooner than it did in the USA and Canada, as shown in Figure 8.1. Great Britain suffered less than the USA, Canada and Argentina, as shown in Figure 8.2, because it used its close integration with the members of the British Commonwealth to lessen the impact of the collapse of multilateral trade on its members. Australia was the main beneficiary of the preferences Great Britain granted to the members of the Commonwealth. For its part, Argentina had to wait until the signing of the Roca–Runciman Pact to start receiving part of those benefits and Canada, despite being a member of the British Commonwealth, could not compensate for the negative impact of its having much closer trade relations with the USA.

The key to the better immediate performance of Argentina compared with the USA and Canada is clearly related to the monetary policy that helped reverse deflationary pressure. Argentina limited the fall in prices to 'only' 10 per cent over the course of the Depression whereas in the USA the fall in prices was 30 per cent. This is shown in Figure 8.3.

Such a monetary policy diverged from what had been the orthodoxy of the previous decades not only in Argentina but also in all the countries that were active participants in the global economy. The design of that policy was the outcome of the technocratic ability of Raul Prebisch and the economic ministers, particularly Federico Pinedo, and from the country's experience with the consequences of deflation, an economic disease that Argentina suffered in the 1860s and the 1890s.

In the 1890s, Silvio Gesell, a businessman and self-trained economist, had explained the negative effect of the increase in real interest rates on economic activity that resulted from deflation, anticipating the findings of Irving Fisher

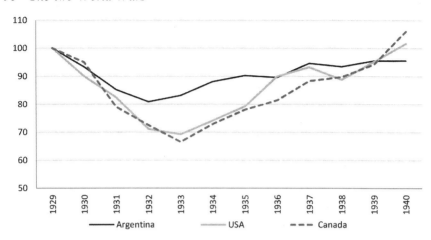

Figure 8.1 GDP per capita Argentina, USA and Canada 1929–1940 (1929=100)
Source: authors' own calculations, based on material originally published in Maddison (2006).

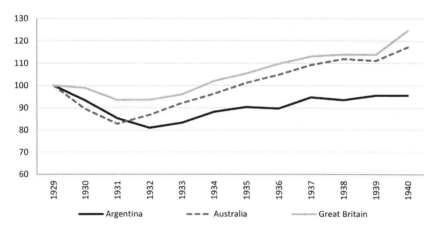

Figure 8.2 GDP per capita Argentina, Great Britain and Australia 1929–1940 (1929=100)
Source: authors' own calculations, based on material originally published in Maddison (2006).

and Keynes in the 1930s. The influential business community of Buenos Aires used this argument to support a return to the gold standard at 2.27 paper pesos per gold peso rather than the old parity of the 1870s and 1880s prior to the 1890 crisis.

At the same time, the experience of the stagflationary consequences of the extreme fiscal and monetary indiscipline of the second half of the 1880s called for a prudent fiscal policy and for an upper limit on the use of expansionary

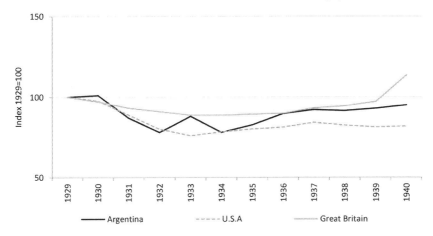

Figure 8.3 Price level Argentina, USA, Great Britain 1929–1940 (1929=100)
Source: authors' own calculations, based on material originally published in Ferreres (2010).

monetary policy. It was reasonable to use it to destroy the deflationary expectation, but not to introduce persistent inflation into the economy. Prebisch understood this concept clearly and it led him to resign from the Central Bank in 1943 in order to criticize government's attempt to continue printing money when the economy showed signs of overheating.

In 1931 the Argentine government used monetary creation to support the banks rather than to finance the Treasury. It is impossible to know if this decision was the consequence of orthodox fiscal prudence or the lobby of influential bankers and their debtors. Bailing out banks would become a recurrent practice in future crises. In this sense, what Pellegrini did in 1890 when he decided to close the insolvent banks would be unique in Argentine economic history.

Deflation could have been shorter and more limited if monetary policy had been conducted through open market operations based on treasury bills and government bonds rather than rediscounting bank assets of dubious quality. This would have meant financing the fiscal deficit of 1930 and subsequent years by seigniorage instead of creating money to bail out the banks. Of course, it is very difficult to judge if the softening of deflation and the likely lower market interest rates that would have resulted from such a policy would have been enough to prevent the sequence of bank bankruptcies that in the USA aggravated the crisis.

Rent seeking

Beginning in 1931 the rediscount windows of the Banco de la Nación and the Currency Board, together with the foreign exchange controls and the differential exchange rates imposed in 1933, induced corporations to seek rents through lobbying and sectoral pressures rather than making efforts to generate income through efficient investment and hard work.

The Banco de la Nación and the Currency Board rediscounted not only assets of banks that remained solvent but faced liquidity problems, but also institutions that were already insolvent. It repeated what had been done during the 1914 to 1918 crisis. Consequently, in 1935 the government created an institution that would set a dangerous precedent for the future: The Institute to Mobilize Bank Assets (Insituto Movilizador de Activos Bancarios). The newly created Central Bank had to use most of the profits generated by the revaluation of gold to purchase the bad assets of the banks by an amount equivalent to 7 per cent of GDP. It meant a transfer of wealth to owners of the banks and debtors – two of the most powerful pressure groups of Argentine society. There is no doubt that this political decision encouraged other sectors of the population, dispersed until that moment, to organize to defend their own sectoral interests. Even though the political system remained republican, corporatism became an economic reality that would have crucial consequences in future decades.

Foreign exchange controls had the same effect. Up to 1931, when the British pound was still convertible to gold, the Argentine authorities kept the exchange market floating without restrictions as it had during all the previous suspensions of convertibility. As soon as Great Britain decided to abandon the gold standard, the Argentine government introduced exchange controls, a new policy that, as in the case of the rediscount window, was supposed to be transitory.

Once the allocation of foreign exchange depended on government administrative decisions rather than the operation of a single foreign exchange market, economic agents whose access to foreign exchange was restricted started to lobby for getting foreign exchange in the official market.

British companies that could neither repatriate capital nor remit dividends used the negotiation of the Roca–Runciman pact to regain access to the foreign exchange market. The British government imposed this as a compensation for reopening the British meat market to Argentine exports. After granting preferences to the British Commonwealth at the Ottawa Conference of 1932, Argentina could not access the British meat market. The other conditions imposed in the Roca–Runciman Pact were authorization for the railroad companies to increase fees for their transport services and the obligation to process a large proportion of the exported meat in foreign-owned meat processing plants that had close relations to the big cattle breeders of Buenos Aires. These conditions irritated the cattle ranchers of the interior of the country whose interests Lisandro de la Torre passionately defended in the senate in 1935.

The difference between the exchange rate paid to exporters and that charged to importers that started in 1933, plus the demand constraints that emerged from the crisis abroad, generated a drastic fall in agricultural prices.

Farmers and regional producers started to lobby for the setting of minimum prices and the allocation of financial resources to purchase harvests.

Until the 1930s, markets for goods and services had operated quite freely, although not necessarily with perfect competition because in many cases there were firms that exercised monopsonistic power. The only exceptions to free operation of markets were the timid regulations that governments had established on railroads, public services' tariffs, livestock and meat markets and the market of sugar cane established by President Alvear in the 1920s.

During the 1930s, the regulatory agencies multiplied. In 1931 President Uriburu created the National Commission for Industrial Promotion, Potatoes, and Textile Fibres. President Justo, in response to corporate pressure, created the National Commissions for Tannin, Edible Oil, Viticulture, Charcoal, Cotton and Grains; the National Regulatory Junta for Yerba Mate, Milk, Grains, Wines and Meat; the Commissions for Wheat Flour, Seeds, Hydrocarbons, National Food Products and Fruit-Growing; and the Consulting Commissions for Forests. The initial purpose of these regulatory agencies was to enforce minimum prices as a way to dampen the deflationary effects of the crisis, but later they would be used to implement price controls and managed trade.

Ultimately, except for the continued commitment to fiscal discipline and to servicing the external debt, in most areas of the economic organization there were significant changes, most of them originally intended to be transitory but that, in practice, would last for many decades.

Stagnation of agriculture and slow expansion of manufacturing

The Great Depression provoked a sharp decline in foreign terms of trade, very similar to what had occurred during the First World War. But while domestic terms of trade recovered and remained above foreign terms of trade in 1917, as a consequence of the exchange controls and the differential rates of exchange applied to exports and imports, domestic terms of trade had fallen much more than the foreign terms of trade since 1930, and the gap between the two increased over time. The ratio between export and import price indices is a measure of foreign terms of trade, while the ratio between agricultural and non-agricultural wholesale price indices represents the domestic terms of trade. Domestic and foreign terms of trade are shown in Figure 8.4.

The deterioration of domestic terms of trade for agricultural exports affected the incentives to invest in agriculture. Agricultural production first declined and then recovered, but on average remained almost stagnant between 1929 and 1945. The change in terms of trade plus the restrictions on imports that increased starting with the beginning of the Second World War provided incentives for the expansion of manufacturing import substitutes. This explains the increase in industrial production in spite of the fact that agriculture and overall growth were low.

102 The two World Wars

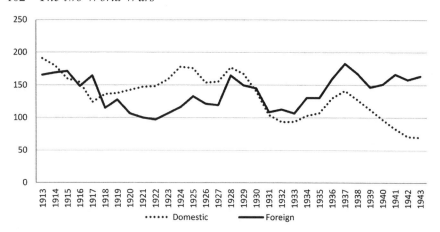

Figure 8.4 Domestic and foreign terms of trade 1913–1943
(1990=100)
Source: authors' own calculations, based on material originally published in IEERAL (1986).

Until 1914 manufacturing grew even faster than agriculture even during the period of rapid expansion of agriculture, but this growth was mainly in sectors that transformed agricultural raw materials into processed foods and fibres. It continued growing between 1914 and 1929 helped not only by the expansion of agriculture, but also by incentives generated by the First World War to produce import substitutes. The expansion of manufacturing between 1929 and 1943 happened only as the result of the incentives to substitute imports because agriculture did not expand during those 14 years. That explains why the growth of manufacturing GDP was slower than in the previous periods as shown in Table 8.2.

It is interesting to note that even though the Pinedo Plan had not been approved, the new circumstances created by the Second World War and the fact that salaries had not yet started to increase, non-traditional exports of manufactured goods expanded rapidly from only 1.9 per cent of total exports in 1937–1939 to 19.4 per cent in 1943. These figures are shown in Table 8.3. Because the encouragement of this exportable production did not come from a deliberate change in structural policies, the trend started to reverse after 1943. The government that took power after the coup promoted labour legislation that would significantly increase the cost of labour and would make the expansion of the domestic market almost the exclusive new engine of growth. Real wages remained almost constant until 1942 and started to increase after the military coup of 1943. This is shown in Figure 8.5.

The production composition of the increase in non-traditional exports of manufactured goods between 1939 and 1943 also reflects the fact that the sectoral incentives of the Pinedo Plan were in line with the natural comparative advantages of Argentina. This is shown in Table 8.4.

Table 8.2 GDP growth, total, agriculture and manufacturing 1875–1943

	Annual change 1875–1914	Annual change 1914–1929	Annual change 1929–1943
GDP (total)	5.4%	4.5%	1.5%
Agriculture	4.2%	3.5%	1.0%
Crops	10.9%	3.3%	0.3%
Livestock	1.8%	3.9%	3.0%
Manufacturing	5.9%	5.5%	2.8%

Source: authors' own calculations, based on material originally published in Ferreres (2010).

Table 8.3 Participation of exports of manufactures from 1934–1936 to 1943

Year	Exports of manufactures (in percentage of total exports)	Real wages (1943=100)
1934–1936	1.4	98
1937–1939	1.9	96
1939	2.9	96
1940	4.9	98
1941	8.2	96
1942	13	95
1943	19.4	100

Source: authors' own calculations, based on material originally published in Llach (1984) and IEERAL (1986).

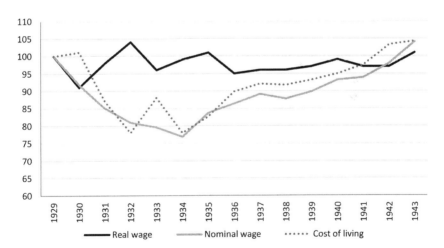

Figure 8.5 Nominal and real wages indices 1929–1943 (1929=100)
Source: authors' own calculations, based on material originally published in IEERAL (1986).

Table 8.4 Contribution of some industries to the increase in the share of non-traditional exports between 1939 and 1943
(in percentage of exports)

	1939	1943
Food and beverages	1.4	3.8
Textiles	0.3	7.6
Chemical products	0.1	2.2
Garment	0.0	1.3
Leather goods	0.0	0.8
Other	1.1	1.9

Source: authors' own calculations, based on material originally published in Llach (1984).

In terms of the planned diversification of export markets of the Pinedo Plan, actual figures show that the project was quite realistic. Comparing the periods of the years 1937–1939 with 1943–1945, the share of exports to the USA increased from 12.5 per cent to 23.2 per cent of the total exports and exports to Brazil increased from 4.9 per cent to 8.6 per cent.

References

Baiocco, Pedro J. (1973) *La economía bancaria Argentina*, Buenos Aires: Universidad de Buenos Aires.

Della Paolera, Gerardo and Ortiz, Javier (1995) *Dinero intermediación financiera y nivel de actividad en 110 años de historia económica Argentina*, Documento de trabajo, Universidad Torcuato Di Tella.

Della Paolera, Gerardo and Taylor, Alan M. (2001) *Straining at the Anchor: The Argentine Currency Board and the Search for Macroeconomic Stability, 1880-1935*, Chicago, IL and London: The University of Chicago Press.

Ferreres, Orlando (2010) *Dos Siglos de Economía Argentina*, Buenos Aires: El Ateneo.

IEERAL (Instituto de Estudios Económicos sobre la Realidad Argentina y Latinoamericana) (1986) *Revista Estudios Año IX-N39-Julio/Septiembre*, pp. 103–184.

Llach, Juan (1984) 'El plan Pinedo de 1940, su significado histórico y los orígenes de la economía política del peronismo', *Desarrollo Económico*, Número 92, Vol. 23, Jan.–Mar., pp. 515–558.

Maddison, Angus (2006) *The World Economy*, Paris: OECD Publishing.

Part IV
Four-and-a-half decades of political and economic instability

9 Inflation, stagflation and hyperinflation

After 1945 when the USA emerged from the Second World War as the undisputed leading nation of the world, that country promoted what can be safely called the second wave of globalization. After seven decades and many vicissitudes, this process continues even today. There are new strong actors challenging the economic and military power of the USA, particularly China and Russia that until 1990 were still functioning as autarchic economic systems, but they too have entered the global economy during the last 25 years.

In contrast with what happened during the first wave of globalization, Argentina waited 45 years before it engaged with the second wave of globalization. Consequently, from 1945 to 1990 the Argentine economy went through a long period of slow and unstable growth while suffering rampant inflation.

Pro-Axis, nationalistic officers supported the military coup of 1943. After being a prominent member of that military government, Juan Perón won a democratic election and became president in 1946. He defeated a broad coalition of political parties organized around the Radical Party which ranged from the Conservatives to the Socialists to the Communists.

From the beginning, Perón saw the encouragement of labour-intensive manufacturing, construction and domestic services as a way to shift the functional distribution of income away from capital- and land-intensive agriculture in favour of urban workers. The instruments to implement this strategy included multiple exchange rates, high import duties and quantitative restraints on imports, and implicit or explicit taxes on exports of agricultural goods.

In practice, Perón continued the import-substitution growth strategy that was originally imposed by the war because of the short external supply of manufactured goods. After the end of the war and even when world markets were starting to normalize and when the high demand for agricultural exports was about to reverse, Perón decided to deepen this import substitution strategy as an income redistribution policy.

In addition to the import substitution growth and redistribution strategy, Perón's government significantly increased government expenditures and fiscal deficits. In the beginning, the levies on wealth and past savings financed fiscal deficits; but, eventually the deficits were paid for with monetary expansion. Inflation became a persistent phenomenon, with the exception of 1958, a year of a drastic release of repressed inflation, inflation averaged around 30 per cent per year. The worst inflationary experience, however, was yet to come.

Even though both the price distortions and the high government expenditures and very large fiscal deficits of the late 1940s slowly reversed during the second presidency of Perón, and even more after his removal from power, Perón reinstated them in 1973.

Between 1956 and 1972, various governments tried to engage the global economy, but they failed to reduce inflation and eliminate the anti-export bias introduced after so many years of virtual economic autarchy. The pressure from trade unions and industrialists empowered under high import barriers plus the emergence of guerrilla movements brought Perón back to power after 18 years of exile.

In 1973, Perón initiated his third period as president at a time of favourable external terms of trade, not very different from those that existed during the beginning of his first presidency. In just three years his Economic Minister fully implemented policies similar to those applied in 1945: agricultural prices were heavily taxed, manufacturing, construction and domestic services were actively encouraged, public spending was sharply increased, and large fiscal deficits were financed with massive monetary expansion.

This time around, terms of trade reversed much more rapidly than they had in the late 1940s and the political power of the government declined rapidly after the death of Perón and the intensification of the war between the military and the guerrillas. In that context, an attempt by Isabel Perón to reverse the policies as Perón himself had done after 1949 generated significant social unrest and ended in an inflationary explosion in June 1975.

During the 15 years that followed the inflationary explosion of 1975 inflation was above 100 per cent per year and there were many attempts to introduce partial economic reforms that failed to reverse the climate of stagnation and high inflation. The growth performance during this period was poor. Per capita income declined at a rate of 1.5 per cent per year while the world per capita income grew at a rate of 1.6 per cent per year. By the end of this period, the Argentine economy suffered from hyperinflation. Between March 1989 and March 1990, the rate of inflation reached 11,000 per cent.

Forty-five years of slow and unstable growth

During the four and a half decades from 1945 to 1990, Argentina's per capita GDP grew only 0.9 per cent per year whereas the USA experienced 1.5 per cent per capita GDP growth, Australia 2 per cent, and Canada, Brazil and Mexico more than 2 per cent. Table 9.1 shows the big contrast in the experiences of those countries during this wave of globalization.

During the period of 1870–1913, Argentina went through two main economic crises, one that started in 1876 and another in 1890. During the years

Table 9.1 Comparative per capita GDP growth between 1870–1913 and 1945–1990

Country	1870	1913	1945	1990	Annual change 1870–1913	Annual change 1945–1990
	(in 1990 I. dollars)					
Argentina	1,311	3,797	4,356	6,436	2.5%	0.9%
USA	2,445	5,301	11,709	23,201	1.8%	1.5%
Australia	3,273	5,157	7,133	17,106	1.1%	2.0%
Canada	1,695	4,447	6,928	18,872	2.3%	2.3%
Brazil	713	811	1,390	4,923	0.3%	2.9%
Mexico	674	1,732	2,134	6,119	2.2%	2.4%
Chile	1,300	2,653	3,630	6,402	1.7%	1.3%
Great Britain	3,190	4,921	7,056	16,430	1.0%	1.9%

Source: authors' own calculations, based on material originally published in Maddison (2006).

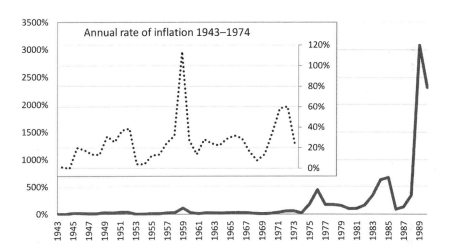

Figure 9.1 Annual rate of inflation 1943–1990
Source: authors' own calculations, based on material originally published in Ferreres (2010).

of 1945 to 1990, there were at least seven crises, including in 1949, 1958, 1962, 1975, 1981, 1985 and 1988. Therefore, growth was not only slow, but also much more unstable than in the golden age.

And since the initial year of the second wave of globalization, Argentina, which had remained mostly isolated from the world economy, suffered two-digit annual inflation during 30 years (1945–1974), three-digit annual inflation during 13 years (1975–1988), and two years of hyperinflation (1989–1990). Figure 9.1 shows this behaviour.

Long term stagnation of agriculture

In addition to the emergence of inflation as a persistent phenomenon for the entire 45-year period, the second most important change in long-term trends was the stagnation of agriculture which had been the main agent of growth since the 1870s. This change in trends was the outcome of stagnation of the cultivated area and the lag in incorporating the impressive technological change that boosted the agriculture of the USA during the 1950s and 1960s, the years of the so-called 'green revolution'.

Figure 9.2 shows that land under cultivation which had increased steadily until the early 1940s, declined in 1951 and then remained at essentially the same level of 1943 until 1990. The stagnation was not the result of the

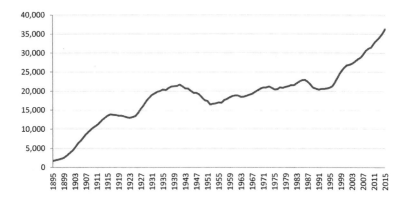

Figure 9.2 Cultivated land
(in thousand hectares)
Source: authors' own calculations, based on material originally published in Ferreres (2010).

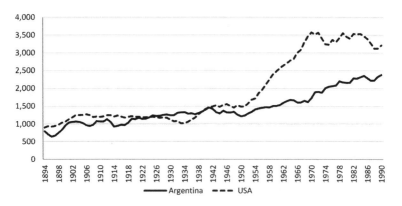

Figure 9.3 Average yield of wheat, corn and soybean
Note: the average yield is expressed in Kg/Ha.
Source: authors' own calculations, based on material originally published in US Department of Agriculture and Ferreres (2010).

exhaustion of the available land as the rapid expansion of cultivated land in the 25 years after 1990 demonstrated.

Figure 9.3 shows that the average yield of the three main crops, wheat, corn and soybeans, in Argentina increased very slowly as compared with the very rapid increase observed in the USA from the mid-1940s to the early 1970s.

To explain Argentina's terrible economic performance across 45 years requires examining the complex interactions between the politics, social conflicts, and the economic policies of the various governments that exercised power during the period.

References

Cortéz Conde, Roberto (2005) *La Economía Política de la Argentina en el Siglo XX*, Buenos Aires: Edhasa.

Diaz Alejandro, Carlos D. (1970) *Essay on the Economic History of the Argentina Republic*, New Haven, CT: Yale University Press.

Ferreres, Orlando (2010) *Dos Siglos de Economía Argentina*, Buenos Aires: El Ateneo.

Maddison, Angus (2006) *The World Economy*, Paris: OECD Publishing.

US Department of Agriculture, https://www.nass.gov/statistics_by_subject/?sector=CROPS.

10 Perón and Evita

Juan Perón initially gained power through the military coup of 1943 and went on to dominate Argentine politics from 1945 to 1955 after he was democratically elected to two presidential terms. The main sources of Perón's power were not only his charisma and that of his second wife Evita but also the support of urban workers, rural tenants and sharecroppers. Improving the welfare of their families was the main objective of his policies.

He transformed the *ad hoc* import substitution of the war years into an explicit growth strategy and expanded the interventionist and isolationist policies that had been incubating during the 1940s. Agriculture and other export activities suffered and productivity stagnated.

A significant increase in government spending and a rising fiscal deficit, together with government-induced increases in nominal wages, resulted in persistent and pervasive inflation.

Despite being democratically elected, his government was almost as authoritarian as those of the military and the conservatives during the 1930s. The citizenry was divided into two partisan groups: Peronists and anti-Peronists in a climate of extreme confrontation, particularly in Perón's second term as President.

Even though he was removed from power in 1955 by a military coup, the influence of his social and economic ideas and political praxis, for better or for worse, continues to influence Argentine politics to this day.

Politics from 1943 to 1955

After the revolution of 4 June 1943, the military of the Grupo de Oficiales Unidos (GOU) captured power. The GOU, in addition to Pedro Pablo Ramirez and Edelmiro Farrell, had a member that was a brilliant strategist with strong charisma: Colonel Juan Domingo Perón.

Perón, like many members of the military in Argentina, had been assigned to several military bases in the interior of the country, and he had also visited several Latin American and European countries which gave him a broader perspective than that of his colleagues. Between 1939 and 1941 he took courses in Mussolini's Italy and visited Germany, France, Spain, Hungary,

Yugoslavia, Albania and the Soviet Union. He had been a professor in the War College and had written several books on military strategy and history.

General Arturo Rawson initially served as the interim president but Pedro Pablo Ramirez succeeded him within a few days as the new President with Edelmiro Farrell as the new Vice-President and Minister of War. Perón was appointed the personal secretary to the Minister of War and had a strong influence on him. A few months later, after having met with important leaders of the trade unions, Perón asked to be designated the new Director of the Department of Labour, a position that until then had been unimportant.

While Ramirez struggled with the problems created by the Second World War and was under pressure from the USA to abandon neutrality, Perón transformed the Department of Labour into the Secretary of Labour and Social Welfare. He worked on getting approval of labour legislation traditionally demanded by the labour leaders and the Socialists with the trade unions. In January 1944, after suspending diplomatic relations with Germany based on reports from the USA that showed evidence of the activity of German spies in Argentina, Ramirez asked for the resignation of Farrell who he thought was plotting a coup. Farrell called for a meeting of the GOU which decided to remove Ramirez from power, designated Farrell as the new president, and appointed Perón as the Minister of War while also keeping him as Secretary of Labour and Social Welfare. In July 1944, when Perón was already popular among workers, Farrell named him vice-president. He also continued as Minister of War and Secretary of Labour. By this point, there is no doubt that Perón was the true power behind Farrell.

During his term as Secretary of Labour, Perón proposed and won approval of important pieces of labour legislation. They included the extension of severance payments and paid vacation to all workers, several professional statutes, and the law of professional associations. The law also regulated the constitution, organization, and working conditions of professional associations. It guaranteed freedom of association to all workers, but established that only one union per craft or industry could get trade union representation. The law also authorized the creation of federations and confederations of unions. Even though the law did not regulate collective bargaining, Perón promoted collective negotiations between unions and employers' associations. This led to the creation of many new trade unions in 1944 and 1945.

In 1944 the Bretton-Woods conference created what would become the International Monetary System of the post-war period. However, due to its alignment during the Second World War, Argentina was not invited to attend.

Nevertheless, this did not mean that Argentina stayed inactive in international affairs. Starting in October 1944 when it became clear that Germany and Japan were losing the war, Farrell and Perón opened negotiations with Washington about the possibility of a declaration of war against the Axis powers in exchange for Argentina being invited to participate in the Conference of San Francisco that would create the United Nations. Argentina declared war on March 1945 and was one of the 51 founding members of the

United Nations. Perón hoped that this decision would change the American view of him as fascist; but, when the new US ambassador, Spruille Braden, arrived in Buenos Aires, it became clear that he would work to destabilize Perón's military regime and, in particular, keep Perón from remaining in power.

Not everyone was happy with Perón's labour reforms. The employers' association was furious with Perón, because it believed that the new labour legislation gave too much power to the trade unions. Between May and October 1945 the employers' associations, together with most political parties and US Ambassador Braden, pushed for Perón's dismissal. A good number of Perón's colleagues who had been in conflict with him in the past and criticized his extramarital relationship with the young actress María Eva Duarte (the future Evita Perón) convinced Farrell to ask for Perón's resignation and imprisonment. Perón resigned and he was imprisoned on the Island Martín García. From there he wrote to Evita suggesting that he should retire from public life and that they could live quietly on a farm. Events, however, would take a very different course.

While Perón was on the island, trade union leaders organized a movement to request his release and return to power. On 17 October, after the CGT called for a general strike, hundreds of thousands of workers poured into Buenos Aires' Plaza de Mayo to show their support for Perón. Farrell concluded that if he tried to repress the demonstration it would trigger violence and decided instead to ask Perón to help restore order. Perón said he would accept the invitation to come to the Pink House and talk to his supporters if the government would call for free elections. Farrell agreed and Perón showed up on the balcony of the Pink House and addressed the people. He announced that the government had promised to call for an election in a few months. He asked the demonstrators to return to their homes quietly and to support his candidacy for the presidency in the next election.

In November 1945, Perón married María Eva Duarte whom from that moment everybody called Eva Perón, or, simply, 'Evita', and then moved rapidly to organize his campaign.

Cipriano Reyes, the leader of the meat processing workers trade union, had recently created the Labour Party and offered it to Perón as a political structure for his candidacy. Supporting the Labour Party was a small portion of the Radical Party called the 'Junta Renovadora', some politicians from the Conservative Party, members of FORJA, and, of course, the strong involvement of the trade union leaders of the CGT. With this Perón launched his candidacy and travelled with Evita by train to the interior of the country to campaign.

In December 1945, just two months before the election, Farrell approved the 'aguinaldo' (an obligatory annual bonus equivalent to one monthly salary to be paid at the end of each year to every worker), a benefit Perón demanded before his resignation.

Perón won the election in February 1946 campaigning on the slogan 'Braden or Perón'. The opposition to Perón was a coalition that included the

Conservatives, most of the Radical Party, and all the parties of the left, including the Socialists and the Communists. Perón's slogan suggested that those who opposed him were the candidates of the USA and did not represent the aspirations of the Argentine people.

Before leaving office Farrell promoted Perón to the rank of general so on 4 June 1946, General Juan Domingo Perón took the oath as the President of the Argentine Nation. During the next ten years, he would hold almost undisputed control of not only the executive branch, but the legislative and judicial branches, as well. More than two-thirds of the members of both the House and the Senate identified themselves as Peronists, even though many of them were members of the Labour Party and the Junta Renovadora of the Radical Party. Immediately after winning the election, Perón ordered the dissolution of the Labour Party and the Junta Renovadora and created the Justicialist Party that immediately became the Peronist Party.

Evita, young and pretty, was a passionate and fanatical follower of Perón. She was even more charismatic than he was, and workers and the poor loved her. She became an ardent orator whose style was both convincing and sincere. Her devotion to social work proved the sincerity of her words and there is no doubt that she was a formidable complement to Perón in his determination to lead the country towards the welfare of workers and against the power and wealth of the 'oligarchs'. In the political arena Perón created the typical 'friend or enemy' dichotomy of a military conflict, although it is important to note that the opposition to Perón had created anti-Peronism even before Perón had created the Peronist movement itself.

In 1947, Perón was able to appoint all the members of the Supreme Court. Congress impeached the previous members as procedure provided for in the Constitution. The House of Representatives accused them of malpractice because they had confirmed the legality of the military coups of 1930 and 1943. It was a strange double-standard since Perón had supported both of the coups in question.

In 1948 Congress called for the election of a Constitutional Assembly in order to approve a constitutional reform that recognized the social function of private property, expanded the social rights of workers, granted women the same political rights as men, and authorized the re-election of the President.

During his first term, Perón encountered no limits from the military, the opposition, or the press to restrict his ability to implement his policies. Not even the trade union leaders that had helped him to achieve power could oppose decisions they disliked. Perón was able to remove trade union leaders that he considered disloyal and consolidated complete control of the CGT that had become one of the pillars of the Peronist Party. Initially the other pillar was the political one and after granting women the right to vote, Eva Perón created the feminist pillar.

In 1951, Perón defeated a military coup that tried to remove him from power. The leader of the rebellion was General Benjamín Menendez supported by Alejandro Agustin Lanusse. Both were condemned to life in prison.

116 *Political and economic instability*

In 1952, voters re-elected Perón for another six-term. Evita, who had been sick since 1951, died a few weeks after Perón's second inauguration. She was 33 years old and her death shocked the country and changed Perón's attitude toward power. In his second term, Perón looked less joyful and more stressed by conflicts and constraints. The economic situation worsened and he faced new difficulties. These came not only from the opposition, but also from his own supporters. It was very difficult to produce the shift in attitude toward foreign capital that he desired. There was increasing opposition from members of the Catholic Church to his initiatives on divorce and banning religious education in public schools. Taken together, these new circumstances created a climate of conflict that Perón could not manage with the calm and ability that he had shown in previous years.

In 1954 and 1955, there were episodes of violence, some started by Perón's opponents but others by his followers after some of his ardent speeches. In June 1955, as part of a revolt organized by officers of the Navy, several bombs exploded in the Pink House and in the adjacent Plaza de Mayo causing the death of hundreds of innocent people. Finally, in September a more generalized rebellion of officers and soldiers from the three branches of the armed forces forced Perón's resignation.

Perón left power on 17 September 1955 and sought refuge abroad, first in Stroesner's Paraguay, then in Perez Jimenez's Venezuela, after that in Trujillo's Dominican Republic, and, finally, in Franco's Spain. He would live in exile for 18 years but come back to Argentina to take power again in 1973.

The economy from 1943 to 1955

Even though his first presidency formally started in June 1946, implementation of Perón's economic and social policies started immediately after the revolution of 1943.

The opinions of historians on the reasons for the strong commitment of Perón to the welfare of workers differ. Some say that it was sincere, others that it was opportunistic. Nevertheless, whatever the interpretation, there is no doubt that, starting in 1943, he focused on his first priority: increasing employment and real wages, no matter what other objectives were left as lower priorities.

The evolution of real wages and employment shows that Perón achieved his target. In the case of real wages, the high level reached in 1949 (60 per cent higher than in 1943) could not be sustained (see Figure 10.1). The recession that followed produced a reduction but real wages recovered again starting in 1953 and ended with an increase of 52 per cent in real terms in 1955 compared with wages in 1943. Urban employment increased 33 per cent from 1943 to 1955.

The tools Perón used to get these results were not novel. They included deepening and implementing labour legislation and supporting institutions that had started to develop in previous decades. These approaches were,

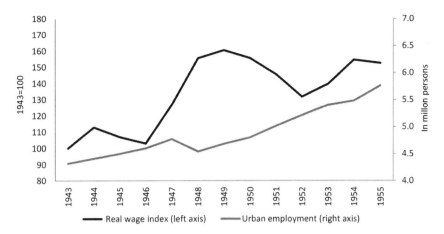

Figure 10.1 Real wage index and urban employment 1943–1955
Source: authors' own calculations, based on material originally published in IEERAL (1986).

broadly speaking, in line with the economic and social thinking that prevailed at that time not only in Argentina, but also in many other countries around the world. Some of the policies that Perón implemented had already resulted from the external circumstances that emerged after the First World War, the Great Depression and the Second World War.

Most economic historians think that Perón's policies were against the mainstream, because Perón did not realize that the world economic order was changing after the Bretton Woods Conference. Argentina did not participate in that conference because it was still neutral in the war and the US State Department considered Argentina to be sympathetic to the Axis powers. It is clear that Perón thought that a third world war was very likely because of the East–West division of the world that emerged after Yalta. In consequence, he was sceptical of the new process of globalization and decided that Argentina had to adopt an inward looking development strategy, not very different from the one viable approach that the wars had left Argentina to begin with.

However, what explains Perón's economic decisions more than scepticism on economic globalization was his commitment to increase real wages and urban employment. If this had not been the case, Perón would have been very sympathetic to the plan Federico Pinedo presented in 1940 and that, until 1943, had helped develop manufacturing. Perón was sincerely interested in Argentina's integrating with its Latin American neighbours. Therefore, the expansion of non-traditional manufacturing exports for which Pinedo had advocated and the diversification to markets other than Great Britain should have been in line with Perón's foreign policies and his desire to promote industrialization. If Perón had followed Pinedo's ideas he would not have favoured labour legislation that pushed the cost of labour for industries above their productivity levels measured at external prices. In fact, Perón's efforts to increase real wages explain the fall in non-traditional manufacturing exports after 1943 as shown in Table 10.1.

Once Perón and his advisors discarded the strategy of promoting industrialization as an export-oriented activity, the only possible way to sustain a high level of real wages was to promote activities oriented to satisfying domestic demand for goods and services – demand that expansionary macroeconomic policies were supposed to keep increasing rapidly over time. Production of manufactured goods that could be substituted for imports, construction and services were the obvious choices for promotion using the policy tools available to his government. All of these activities are much more labour-intensive than land- and capital-intensive agriculture; therefore, shifting relative prices and other incentives to favour manufacturing, construction and services should increase the demand of labour, favouring at the same time increases in wages and in urban employment. This was the growth strategy that Perón and his advisors, particularly Miguel Miranda, had in mind in 1946.

The tools and institutions used to implement this strategy were first, a monetary and banking reform with active use of rediscounts and interest rate controls; second, exchange controls complemented with governmental management of most exports and imports; third, the nationalization of the railroads and of all public utility companies; fourth, price controls including rent freezes and indefinite extensions of urban and rural lease contracts; and fifth, large initial increases in public expenditures and active use of social security savings to finance the fiscal deficit.

Monetary and banking reform

In March, 1946, while he was still President-elect Perón asked President Farrell to nationalize the Central Bank and designate Miguel Miranda President of its Board which would be comprised of the presidents of the Banco de la Nación, the Banco de Crédito Industrial Argentino, and Banco Hipotecario Nacional and nine other members.

Table 10.1 Participation of exports of manufactures in total exports and real wages from 1943 to 1947

Year	Exports of manufactures (in percentage of total exports)	Real wages (1943=100)
1943	19.4	100
1944	14.4	113
1945	13.6	108
1946	11.4	104
1947	5.5	128

Source: authors' own calculations, based on material originally published in Llach (1984) and IEERAL (1986).

One month later a presidential decree produced what was called 'the nationalization of bank deposits': the Central Bank would guarantee all bank deposits, establish the interest rate paid to depositors, and compensate banks for those payments. The banks could not use the deposits to lend to their clients but the Central Bank would rediscount past and future loans and other bank investment in amounts and conditions (destiny of the loans, interest rates and terms) that would be pre-established for each individual bank. In practice the banks would be simple executors of the Central Bank which would become the only institution able to decide the allocation of credit and credit conditions.

To complete the reform, in May 1946, another presidential decree reformed the Charter of the Central Bank. It established that the bank's objective was to promote, orient, and implement economic policy, maintain a high level of activity, maximize the employment of human and material resources, and drive the orderly expansion of the economy in order to increase national wealth for the benefit of the people's ever-increasing standard of living.

The arguments used to transform the Central Bank into a virtual development bank related to the experience of the 1930s. Miranda and his advisors believed that the use of rediscounting and fiduciary money creation during the 1930s had been oriented to help banks solve their liquidity and solvency problems but not to promoting industrial development through long-term credit. Therefore, the idea was to use the same tools, rediscounting and monetary creation, but geared toward the objectives established in the new Central Bank Charter.

This monetary and banking reform had as a precedent not only the decisions of Prebisch and Pinedo in 1930s, but also several partial reforms that started after the 1943 revolution. Those reforms had induced the resignation of Prebisch as Managing Director of the Central Bank. In August 1943, President Ramirez had created the Industrial Credit System funded through money creation. In 1944, President Farrell approved the creation of the Banco de Crédito Industrial de la Nación that made ample use of the financing facility created by the Industrial Credit System. In January 1945, a new decree authorized the Caja Nacional de Ahorro Postal (CNAP) to expand its lending and insurance activities, and, in April, another decree increased the limits that had constrained fiduciary money creation by the Central Bank since its creation in 1935.

The expansion of money supply that from 1935 to 1943 had ranged from −1.7 per cent to 14.7 per cent per year, between 1944 and 1955 ranged from 17.2 per cent to 27.3 per cent. Moreover, there was a significant increase in the velocity of money as reflected by the share of currency and sight deposits versus total money supply. It went from 56 per cent in 1943 to 73 per cent in 1955.

Miranda's Central Bank's total lack of concern about the control of money creation is clearly demonstrated by the decision made in June 1946 to rescue all the mortgage bonds (*cédulas hipotecarias* in Spanish) that were, since 1880, the most popular instrument of families to save. Mortgage bonds were long-term bonds that paid a 4 per cent interest rate. Therefore, in one day the

Central Bank issued 1,460 million pesos (equivalent to around $360 million) to rescue an equal amount of bonds. Of course, the market for mortgage bonds disappeared and the only financial instrument for people to invest accumulated wealth was bank deposits.

Interest rates paid on deposits were 2.5 per cent per year until 1951, when they were increased to 3.0 per cent per year in 1952 and remained at that level until 1955. Therefore, the real interest rate was negative and quite large in absolute values. It ranged from −0.7 per cent in 1954 to −25.7 per cent in 1952. Consequently, the real value of a deposit of 100 pesos in 1945 fell to 23 pesos by 1955. There is no doubt that the negative interest rates discouraged savings, at least savings deposited in banks.

Interest rates charged on loans were 5 per cent in 1945 and 1946, 5.2 per cent in 1947, and increased to 6 per cent in 1949 and stayed at that level until 1955. The real rates on loans ranged from 2.4 per cent (in 1954, the only year they were positive) to −29 per cent. The real value of a loan of 100 pesos in 1945 declined to only 35 pesos in 1955. Of course, borrowers were anxious to get loans from the banks because each loan meant a very large subsidy to the borrower. The banks had to ration loans. Lobbying for bank loans became one of the most common rent-seeking activities of producers and consumers and it is not surprising that this generated inefficiency and corruption.

There is no doubt that this monetary policy had a significant impact on the rate of inflation.

Foreign exchange controls and government managed foreign trade

The foreign exchange controls that had existed since 1931 created different exchange rates for exports and imports, and restricted repatriation of capital and the remittance of dividends. In 1939, the exchange rate for exports was 13.5 pesos per pound, equivalent to 3.36 pesos per dollar, and the exchange rate for imports was 17 pesos per pound, equivalent to 4.23 pesos per dollar. Financial and tourism transactions took place in a free market that was legal and that in the initial years displayed a margin of around 3 per cent above the exchange rate for imports.

In 1943, the government decided that all commercial transactions in the foreign exchange market had to go through the Central Bank and that only authorized exchange agencies could operate in the free market. The major change in 1946 was the creation of a parallel foreign exchange market that operated completely outside the control of the Central Bank. The margin between the exchange rate in the parallel market and the 'free' market was around 11 per cent in 1947 and as high as 87 per cent in 1949 and still around 85 per cent in 1955.

The exchange rate on exports and imports was adjusted up to the same amount of the adjustment of the pound/dollar exchange rate in 1949 and from 1951 to 1955, the exchange rate for exports was five pesos per dollar, the exchange rate for imports was 7.5 pesos per dollar and the 'free' exchange rate was 14 pesos per dollar. By 1955, the parallel exchange rate was around 26 pesos per dollar.

At the same time President Farrell approved the new Charter of the Central Bank he decreed the creation of the Argentine Institute for the Promotion of Trade (Instituto Argentino para la Promoción del Intercambio, known by its Spanish acronym IAPI). Miguel Miranda, the President of the Central Bank was appointed the President of IAPI and effectively centralized most decisions related to foreign trade. IAPI would purchase the harvests and decide when, how, and through whom the grains would be exported. At the same time, it would import intermediate and capital goods because the combination of exchange controls and licensing of imports by the Central Bank combined with the ability of IAPI to intermediate in every market made it almost impossible for importers to avoid using its intermediation services.

The allocation of foreign exchange, the licensing of imports, and the operation of IAPI was as arbitrary as the allocation of subsidized credit. It generated even more rent-seeking activities by producers and traders than the allocation of bank credit and, of course, plenty of inefficiency and corruption.

From 1947 to 1949, when international grain prices were high, the IAPI paid a much lower price to farmers and made a significant profit through grain exports. This facilitated an increase in real wages after 1946. In spite of the changes in labour legislation enacted in 1943, in 1946 wages were only 7 per cent higher in real terms than wages in 1939.

The effect of the exchange rate and commercial policies of the period 1943 to 1955 first enlarged and then maintained the gap between foreign and domestic terms of trade. This trend started to change after 1951, but not because of improvements in the domestic terms of trade for agriculture but more because of the fall in foreign terms of trade. Figure 10.2 shows this evolution.

Nationalization of public utilities and railroads

Beginning in 1936, the British had been proposing that the Argentine government sell the railroads. The profitability of the railroads had been declining since 1929; and, the stock prices of the railroad companies had fallen 88 per cent between 1929 and 1936. Immediately after the end of the Second World War, the British and Argentine governments initiated conversations about the possible nationalization of the railroads. In September 1946, Miranda, President of IAPI, signed a preliminary agreement on the subject and created an advisory commission to discuss the price. Initially the British demanded £375 million but Miranda offered £45 million. Argentina finally purchased the British railroads for £150 million. On the London stock market, the valuation was £120 million with a book value of £250 million.

Between 1946 and 1949, IAPI purchased the French railroads and port companies, all the telephone companies that were private, the Dodero Navigation Company, all the air navigation companies, most of the electricity

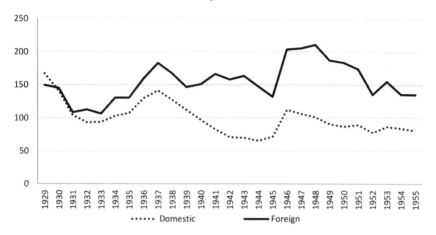

Figure 10.2 Domestic and foreign terms of trade 1929–1955 (1990=100)
Source: authors' own calculations, based on material originally published in IEERAL (1986).

companies, and created the National Reinsurance Company that had a monopoly on the reinsurance business.

All these nationalizations required the use of foreign reserves to purchase assets. The irony was that, in the following years, the government did not have the reserves necessary to purchase the capital goods that were necessary to modernize and expand the capacity of all those companies. This explains the shortages of public services that started to appear in 1949.

The state-owned companies created many new jobs; but, their efficiency declined rapidly. Additionally, the government decided to freeze most public utilities' rates or at least keep increases well below inflation. In real terms the public utility rates declined 43 per cent between 1945 and 1955, the price of gasoline declined 45 per cent, the price of electricity declined 42 per cent, urban transport tariffs fell 47 per cent, and telephone tariffs declined 23 per cent. The increase in the number of employees, the lack of replacement investment, and the decline in the real proceeds of the state owned public utilities companies generated losses that were transferred to IAPI and aggravated its deficit.

Price controls and rent freezes

In 1939, President Roberto Ortiz established maximum prices for some basic goods and services. Something similar was happening in most countries, but elsewhere, price controls were temporary measures. In Argentina, price controls covered many more products and became stricter during the years 1943 to 1948. They stayed in place every year until 1955, becoming a crucial element of the stabilization plan implemented in 1952. The punishment for violators included fines, confiscation of the merchandise, and imprisonment, depending on the gravity of the offence.

In addition to price controls, in 1943 the government declared a freeze on urban and rural rents, suspended evictions of tenants, and extended lease contracts, at the beginning for short periods of time that were continuously renewed. By 1949, all lease contracts became virtually indefinite. This had positive effects on the cost of living for tenants and benefited farmers who rented the land, but discouraged investment in construction of new houses and land improvements in the rented rural properties.

Social security savings financing the spending spree

During the years when Miranda was Perón's economic czar (1945–1948), public expenditures, including the central government, the deficit of the IAPI, and the spending of the other state-owned companies, the Social Security System, and the provinces, jumped from 23 per cent of GDP to 45 per cent. The fiscal deficit increased from 4.4 per cent of GDP in 1945 to 15.6 per cent of GDP in 1948.

This extremely expansionary fiscal policy together with the nominal wage increases promoted by labour legislation of the previous years and the extraordinary improvement in the terms of trade generated 6 per cent annual per capita GDP growth from 1946 to 1948. This is shown in Figure 10.3.

This growth performance looked impressive compared to a 0.7 per cent annual per capita GDP growth during the previous three-year period (1943–1945). However, this growth performance proved to be unsustainable and actually started to reverse in 1949. During the next three-years period, 1949–1951, annual per capita GDP growth was negative: −1.0 per cent and then negative again from 1952 to 1954 (−0.6 per cent per year). Overall, between 1945 and

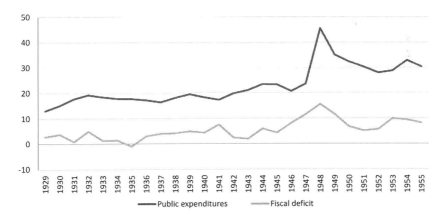

Figure 10.3 Public expenditure and fiscal deficit 1929–1955
(in percentage of GDP)
Source: authors' own calculations, based on material originally published in IEERAL (1986).

1955, during the ten years of the first two governments of Perón, annual per capita growth was only 1.8 per cent. Not impressively higher than the 1.1 per cent it had been in the previous ten-year period (1935–1945).

The main reasons for the poor growth performance after 1948 were the supply-side bottlenecks created by the distortions in relative prices originating in the multiple discretionary interventions of the state in the economy and the emergence of persistent inflation, the problem that would become a chronic disease of the Argentine economy over the next 45 years.

The onset of persistent inflation

Inflation was a recurrent problem during the 19th century, particularly from the late 1820s to the early 1890s. In those years, inflation originated in monetary expansion to finance fiscal deficits that ended up causing balance of payments crises that then forced a devaluation of the currency. Nevertheless, since the approval of the Convertibility Law during Pellegrini's government, prices in Argentina moved in line with those of Great Britain and the USA.

The suspensions and then final abandonment of convertibility happened in periods of external crises that induced deflation rather than inflation. Therefore, the introduction of exchange controls and the transformation of the peso into a fiduciary currency helped moderate deflation. By 1943 it had been more than 50 years since there had been inflation and people did not have a memory of inflation as an economic and social problem. On the contrary, since the 1890s what worried businessmen and policy makers was the risk of deflation as reflected in the writings of Silvio Gesell, the non-academic economist that prominent academics like Irving Fisher and Keynes rescued from oblivion in the 1930s.

In spite of this impressive fiscal expansion, the growth in the money supply increased from only 22 per cent per year during the period 1941–1944 to 26 per cent per year during the period 1945–1948. The explanation of this asynchrony between fiscal and monetary policies is explained by the course of foreign reserves: during the Second World War foreign reserves increased by $1.1 billion, but by 1949 foreign reserves had fallen to only $390 million. That means that the great expansion in public expenditure was in large measure financed using accumulated foreign reserves. Of course, while the level of foreign reserves declined, domestic credit creation expanded to much more than the money supply.

In spite of significant increases in nominal wages and the monetary expansion, during 1943 and 1944 the rate of inflation as measured by the cost of living was low as it had been in previous years and decades. It seems that the price freeze decreed by the government produced the desired effects, very likely because there were no inflationary expectations and inflation inertia worked in the direction of keeping inflation low. Wholesale prices as well as export and import prices increased in the range of 7.9 per cent to 18.1 per cent, even more than the increase in nominal wages which was 6.3 per cent.

During 1944, only export prices and wholesale agricultural prices increased at lower rates, but import prices continued to expand rapidly and pushed non-agricultural wholesale prices in the same direction. However, in spite of a 13.1 per cent increase in nominal wages and a 20.3 per cent expansion in the money supply, consumer price inflation was slightly negative.

The impact of all these inflationary factors finally emerged in 1945. This year was the starting point of inflation that would last for 45 years. The cost of living increased 19.7 per cent; however, since wages that year increased only 11.6 per cent the purchasing power of wages decreased 8 per cent. Something very similar happened in 1946 when wages increased 14 per cent but the cost of living inflation was 17.7 per cent. Real wages went down for a second year (by 3.7 per cent) with a total fall of almost 12 per cent in the two crucial years of the ascent of Perón to the presidency and the appointment of Miguel Miranda as his economic czar.

Perón, advised by Miranda, blamed the increase of agricultural prices for the inflation. In fact agricultural prices, pushed by export prices, had increased by 22.3 per cent in 1945 and 59 per cent in 1946. To prevent high domestic prices for food and other agricultural goods, the government fixed the prices paid by IAPI to the farmers at levels much lower that the export prices. Therefore, the gap between foreign and domestic agricultural prices increased as shown in Table 10.2.

In 1947, while export prices increased 16.7 per cent, agricultural export prices declined 0.5 per cent, a clear consequence of IAPI's price policy. The difference was so extreme that in the next year when export prices increased by only 8.1 per cent, agricultural prices increased 11.8 per cent. Taking the two years together, export prices increased almost 35 per cent, but agricultural wholesale prices increased only 11.3 per cent. This forced contraction of relative agricultural prices explains the fall of inflation. Measured by the cost of living, the inflation rate went down from 17.7 per cent in 1946 to 13.5 per cent in 1947 and then to 11.1 per cent in 1948, in spite of nominal wage increases of 38.6 per cent in 1947 and 40.3 per cent in 1948. This impressive increase in real wages is what Miranda had promised Perón. However, the movement of the external accounts started to demonstrate that these policies were not sustainable. After just two years foreign reserves were almost exhausted and, starting at the very beginning of 1949, it was clear that the economy was suffering a balance of payments crisis. Perón removed Miranda from IAPI and nominated a new economic czar, Alfredo Gomez Morales, who took the newly created post of Secretary of Finance as well as the presidency of the Central Bank.

The crisis that started in 1949

Alfredo Gomez Morales was an economist who tried to resolve the balance of payments crisis by reversing the expansionary fiscal policies of Miranda, devaluing the peso in proportion to the devaluation of the British pound with

Table 10.2 Rate of inflation 1943–1955 (in percentage per year)

Year	Rate of monetary expansion	Consumer price inflation	Wage inflation	Non-agricultural wholesale price inflation	Agricultural wholesale price	Exports price inflation	Imports price inflation
1943	19.8	1.1	6.3	7.9	8.0	18.1	14.2
1944	23.7	−0.3	13.1	1.8	0.4	1.6	12.6
1945	20.3	19.7	11.6	0.9	22.3	6.6	19.0
1946	30.7	17.7	14.0	1.4	59.0	51.7	−1.3
1947	21.1	13.5	38.6	5.5	−0.5	26.7	25.6
1948	34.4	13.1	40.3	17.7	11.8	8.1	5.4
1949	27.6	31.1	31.5	27.1	13.8	−3.8	8.2
1950	25.4	25.5	25.4	21.6	16.8	−8.6	−6.7
1951	21.3	36.7	26.9	47.9	52.3	29.1	36.2
1952	13.7	38.6	27.3	36.5	18.5	−16.5	7.2
1953	24.1	4.0	7.4	8.3	20.7	0.0	−12.8
1954	16.3	3.8	13.2	3.7	1.0	−13.5	−1.0
1955	17.6	12.3	8.6	10.1	5.3	2.8	3.0

Source: authors' own calculations, based on material originally published in IEERAL (1986).

respect to the US dollar, and increasing controls on imports. The gap between the parallel foreign exchange market and the official rate for exports was only 27 per cent in 1947, but then increased to 147 per cent in 1948, and then jumped a dramatic 265 per cent in 1949.

In 1949, even though dollar export prices declined 3.8 per cent, agricultural wholesale prices increased by 13.8 per cent thanks to the devaluation and the new pricing policy of IAPI. Nominal wages increased 31.5 per cent. The result was an inflation rate of 31.1 per cent as measured by the cost of living index and a fall in per capita GDP of 3.6 per cent.

Monetary policy was more contractionary than the growth rate of the money supply suggests. The reduction in the growth rate from 34.4 per cent in 1948 to 27.6 per cent in 1949 hides a much larger contraction in credit expansion: in 1948 sales of foreign reserves acted as an important factor in monetary absorption, something that did not exist in 1949.

The balance of payments crisis that appeared in 1949 manifested itself as a stagflationary crisis, a situation that would become very common during the next 40 years. However, it felt absolutely new to Argentines when it appeared. The last episode with these characteristics had occurred almost 60 years before, in 1891, and, of course, few remembered it.

The timid adjustments implemented by Gomez Morales did not avert the crisis, because the policies that had discouraged production and investment in agriculture for many years, plus a severe drought in 1949–1950 and 1950–1951 would have a dramatic effect on the next three years. Agricultural GDP, which had declined slightly during the 1940s, fell dramatically in the three-year period 1950–1952 as shown in Table 10.3.

The fall in production was concentrated in crops and was particularly large in exportable grains. As domestic consumption of beef increased significantly up to 1948, exports of beef had declined sharply in spite of some expansion in livestock production. In the three-year period 1950 to 1952, exports of beef had declined 23 per cent compared to 1941 to 1943 and 30 per cent compared to 1944 to 1946. The different behaviour of GDP and exports in the agriculture sector in the periods 1944–1946 and 1950–1952 is related to the sharp increase in domestic consumption of food, particularly beef. In 1944 to 1946 consumption had gone down because of high domestic prices; but, in 1950–1952,

Table 10.3 Evolution of agriculture sector GDP and exports from 1941–1943 to 1950–1952 (1941–1943=100)

Period	Agriculture sector GDP	Volume of exports
1941–1943	100	100
1944–1946	96	110
1946–1949	96	97
1950–1952	86	77

Source: authors' own calculations, based on material originally published in De Pablo (2005).

128 Political and economic instability

consumption was much higher because of the increase in real wages that had occurred in the three-year period 1946–1949. The increase in consumption had been so dramatic that in 1949 the government imposed a ban on the consumption of beef on certain days of the week, and in 1950 it imposed rationing on the consumption of flour and bread.

Per capita GDP declined 1.2 per cent in 1950, increased a meagre 1.7 per cent in 1951, and declined 5 per cent in 1952. Therefore, from its peak in 1948 to 1952, per capita GDP declined 10 per cent. Paradoxically, inflation continued to increase and peaked in 1952 when it reached a record of 38.6 per cent. The stagflation that had started in 1949 persisted until 1952, meaning that there were four consecutive years of stagflation, the longest period of stagflation that Argentina had ever seen.

The stabilization plan of 1952

Following the election of 1952, Perón authorized his ministers to design a stabilization plan to contain inflation. The plan consisted of strengthening the fiscal adjustment, limiting nominal wage increases, and emphasizing price controls. At the same time, the government made some efforts to stimulate agricultural production. The results in terms of reduced inflation were seen in 1953, when the cost of living increased by only 4 per cent followed by an increase of only 3.8 per cent in 1954. Per capita GDP growth also resumed: 3.3 per cent in 1953, 2.2 per cent in 1954, and 5.2 per cent in 1955.

On the surface, it looked like Perón and his ministers had finally been able to conquer inflation and solve the stagflation crisis of 1949 to 1952. However, it was only an illusion: in 1955 inflation jumped up again, this time to 12.3

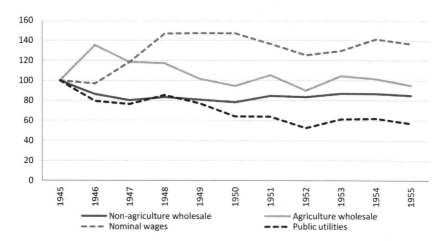

Figure 10.4 Prices relative to cost of living 1945–1955 (1945=100)
Source: authors' own calculations, based on material originally published in IEERAL (1986).

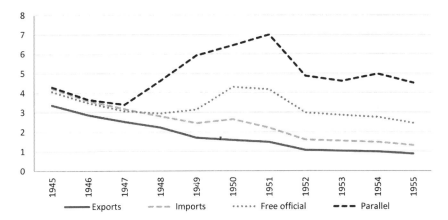

Figure 10.5 Exchange rates relative to cost of living 1945–1955 (at 1945 prices)
Source: authors' own calculations, based on material originally published in IEERAL (1986).

per cent, and now Argentina was dealing with many distortions in relative prices after more than ten years of interventionist and isolationist policies. These distortions created bottlenecks in crucial sectors of the economy due to insufficient and misallocated investment.

The behaviour of real wages on one extreme and the public utility relative to cost of living on the other extreme clearly reflect the distortions in relative prices. In addition, the trend of declining relative agricultural prices and the growing gap between the non-agriculture wholesale price index and the cost of living show the same phenomenon. Figure 10.4 shows these effects

Figure 10.5 shows another set of indicators that document significant price distortions. The exchange rates for exports and imports deteriorated almost continuously between 1945 and 1955 and the gap between the parallel market exchange rate and the export and import exchange rates widened until 1951, fell a bit in 1952, but remained large and stable throughout the rest of the period.

References

Cortés Conde, Roberto (2005) *La Economía Política de la Argentina en el Siglo XX*, Buenos Aires: Edhasa.
De Pablo, Juan Carlos (2005) *La Economía Argentina en la segunda mitad del siglo XX*, Buenos Aires: La Ley.
Diaz Alejandro, Carlos D. (1970) *Essay on the Economic History of the Argentina Republic*, New Haven, CT: Yale University Press.
IEERAL (Instituto de Estudios Económicos sobre la Realidad Argentina y Latinoamericana) (1986) *Revista Estudios Año IX-N39-Julio/Septiembre*, pp. 103–184.
Llach, Juan (1984) 'El plan Pinedo de 1940, su significado histórico y los orígenes de la economía política del peronismo', *Desarrollo Económico*, 23(92), pp. 515–558.

11 The 18 years when Peronism was outlawed

The leader of the military rebellion that removed Juan Perón from power and exiled him was retired General Eduardo Leonardi, a Catholic nationalist. He assumed the de facto presidency on 23 September 1955. Leonardi closed the Congress, replaced all the members of the Supreme Court, intervened in all of the provinces and universities, and removed the public officers, university professors, and teachers that were considered active Peronists. However, he decided to neither intervene in the CGT nor dissolve the Justicialist Party. He believed that it was necessary to maintain the social policies of Perón and the institutions for the participation of Peronism in the political arena in order to ensure social peace.

The liberal military officers and most non-Peronist political parties that made the Consulting Council created to advise the president believed that it was necessary to take control of the CGT and dissolve the Justicialist Party because they had been instruments that Perón used to exercise dictatorial powers. On 13 November 1955, the leaders of the three branches of the armed forces asked for the resignation of Leonardi and designated liberal General Pedro Eugenio Aramburu as the new *de facto* President.

The new president ordered a takeover of the CGT (federal intervention[1]), dissolved the Justicialist Party and outlawed the participation of Perón and the Peronist political organizations in elections and other political events. He revoked by decree the constitutional reform of 1949 and prohibited the display of the symbols of Peronism. Public media was forbidden to mention Perón's name but rather refer to him as a 'fugitive tyrant' or the 'deposed dictator'. Argentine society that had already split during Perón's government between Peronists and anti-Peronists became even more divided.

The Peronist versus anti-Peronist divide proved the main obstacle to governance during the years Perón was in exile. There were strikes, acts of sabotage, military revolts, and even guerrilla movements that used Perón and Peronism as the symbol of the values and goals that they were fighting to revive.

In 1956 a group of Radicals led by Arturo Frondizi, a political leader who believed it was necessary to reconcile Argentine politics with Perón, expressed disagreement with the position of Ricardo Balbín the leader of the Radical

Party which was closer to the anti-Peronist military officers. These disagreements, at the time of the election of a Constitutional Assembly, triggered a split in the Unión Cívica Radical giving rise to Unión Cívica Radical Intransigente (UCRI) led by Frondizi and Unión Cívica Radical del Pueblo (UCRP) led by Balbín.

Being outlawed, Peronists did not turn out for the election of the Constitutional Assembly in 1957, which also deliberated without the presence of the followers of Frondizi. The Assembly reinstated the National Constitution of 1853 with the reforms of 1860, 1866, and 1898, and added "article 14 bis". This article incorporated the social rights added to the civil, patrimonial and political rights of the 1853 constitution by the constitutional reform of 1949.

Aramburu called for a general election to take place on 23 February 1958. UCRI candidate Frondizi was on the ballot with UCRP candidate Balbín. No Peronists were on the ballot, but since Rogelio Frigerio had negotiated a pact with Perón in the name of Frondizi, Peronists supported Frondizi. In exchange, Frondizi secretly committed to normalizing the CGT and repealing the ban on Peronism. Arturo Frondizi won the election by a large margin and took the oath as the new president on 1 May 1958.

Frondizi took office at a difficult time. He faced opposition from not only the UCRP, but also with that of the anti-Peronist military who believed that his secret pact with Perón circumvented the ban on Peronism. He also had a conflict with his vice-president who resigned early in his administration.

Frondizi did authorize the normalization of CGT. And in 1962, during the provincial campaigns for governor, he authorized the participation of parties that identified with Peronism. In many provinces, the Peronist candidates won. The military forced Frondizi to intervene in those provinces to prevent the governors-elect from taking office. Immediately after Frondizi signed the intervention decrees a military rebellion removed him from office but the military could not appoint a de facto President. On 2 March 1962, the President of the Supreme Court acted rapidly to have the President of the Senate José María Guido who, in the absence of a vice-president, was the successor of the President, take the oath as President of the Nation to complete Frondizi's term.

President Guido called for a presidential election in 1963 and re-enacted the outlawing of Peronism. The UCRP, with Arturo Illia as candidate, won the election with 22 per cent of the vote beating Oscar Allende, the candidate of UCRI and Pedro Eugenio Aramburu of a newly created anti-Peronist Party (UDELPA, the Spanish acronym for Unión el Pueblo Argentino). Perón ordered supporters to cast blank ballots and there were more than two million blank ballots cast to the 2.4 million votes obtained by the UCRP and the 1.6 million votes obtained by UCRI. If the Popular Front advocated by Perón and Frondizi had not been banned, its candidate would have won the election. The blank ballots and those of UCRI would have added support to the Front candidate.

Arturo Illia took the presidential oath, but the Peronists and the supporters of Frondizi attacked him continuously. They argued that he lacked legitimacy because his election was the result of Peronism being outlawed. Paradoxically, as he lifted the prohibition on the Unión Popular (the new name of the Peronist Party) and the Peronists won the elections to renew Congress in 1965, the military and an important part of the press emphasized their criticism of the government. In July 1966 a new military revolt, this time led by Juan Carlos Ongania, a Catholic nationalist general who had supported Guido in his call for elections in 1963 and was considered the least anti-Peronist of the militaries, forced the resignation of President Illia and took over as de facto President on 29 June 1966.

General Ongania closed the National Congress, replaced the members of the Supreme Court, declared a federal intervention in all the provinces, universities and trade unions, and dissolved political parties and the CGT. Elected governors, university and union leaders were replaced with federally appointed authorities. He believed it was necessary to reorganize Argentine society and its political system from scratch to end the divisions and inefficiencies of the past.

Several factors gave rise to the guerrilla movements that started during Ongania's government. First, there was the turmoil created by the interventions in the universities, the exclusion of students from the university governance, and the dissolution of the student organizations that had existed since the University Reform of 1918. Perón also encouraged resistance to the new military government. Second, it was the active support for guerrilla groups across Latin America by the Cuban regime of Fidel Castro and Ernesto 'Che' Guevara. Finally there was general worldwide student unrest as demonstrated by university riots in Paris and elsewhere from 1968 on. In this climate, a large number of middle-class and well-educated youth organized several guerrilla armies. The two most important were the Montoneros, who defined themselves as the armed branch of the Peronist resistance, and the People's Revolutionary Army or ERP (from the Spanish Ejército Revolucionario del Pueblo), which defined itself as Marxist or Castro Communist.

The ERP operated in the mountains of Tucumán and had a strong influence on the northern part of the country, while the Montoneros were active in Córdoba. In May 1969, the Montoneros carried out its first attack in La Calera, a small town close to military units in the suburbs of Córdoba. One year later, the Montoneros showed up in Buenos Aires and kidnapped General Aramburu from his home and after a mock people's trial condemned him to death.

In May 1969 there were serious riots in Córdoba that become known as the '*Cordobazo*'. The activity of the Montoneros and riots in Córdoba and other parts of the country gave the military, led by liberal General Alejandro Agustín Lanusse, the justification to remove Ongania from power and replace him with an almost unknown general, Roberto Levingston. This occurred on 8 June 1970, though this would prove to be short lived. After new riots in Córdoba and a general strike declared by the CGT, Lanusse asked for the resignation of Levingston and assumed the presidency on 23 March 1971.

Lanusse had been an early anti-Peronist and participated in all the revolts against Perón since 1951. After assuming the presidency, however, he was concerned about the guerrilla movements that claimed to be fighting for the return of unrestricted democracy. Therefore, he decided it was time to legalize all political activity and negotiate Peron's return to Argentina.

Former President Aramburu had left a sealed letter with the order that after his death the letter should go to the hands of the incumbent President. Immediately after confirming the death of Aramburu, Lanusse received the letter. It contained information on the location in Italy of Evita's embalmed body that had mysteriously disappeared after the dismissal of Perón in 1955. As a gesture of good faith, Lanusse ordered the return of Evita's mortal remains to Perón. He also authorized the return of Perón to Argentina and lifted the ban on Peronism.

Perón did not accept some of the conditions that Lanusse required before approving Perón's candidacy for the presidency. So, he nominated Hector Cámpora, his representative in Buenos Aires, as the candidate to run in the next presidential election. The slogan of Cámpora's campaign was 'Cámpora to Government, Perón to Power'. Cámpora won the presidential election with 49.5 per cent of the vote. Peronism was back in after 18 years of Perón in exile.

The economy from 1956 to 1972

Soon after the fall of Perón in 1955, the new military government (advised by the politicians of the opposition that made up the Consultation Council) invited Raúl Prebisch, by then the Secretary General of the Economic Commission for Latin America of the United Nations, to prepare a diagnosis of the economic situation in 1955 and to propose future economic policies. Prebisch prepared a report with recommendations for immediate actions to solve the crisis and offered the support of the Economic Commission for Latin America (ECLA) for a long-term development plan. The government approved the report with a short-term recommendation in April 1956 and accepted the offer of technical support for the preparation of a development Plan. ECLA published its study on the economic development of Argentina together with a long-term policy proposal in 1958, the year Frondizi took office.

Prebisch began his report by stating that:

> Argentina is suffering the deepest crisis of its economic development; worse than those faced by Avellaneda in 1876 and Carlos Pellegrini in 1890 and even worse that the crisis that originated in the Great Depression of the 1930s. The difference is that in those circumstances the country had its productive forces intact. This is not the case in 1955: the dynamic factors of the economy are seriously compromised and an intense and persistent effort will be necessary to restore its vigorous rhythm of development.

Why has it happened? For three reasons: the efficiency of agriculture production has gone down; the government has not followed an appropriate and far-sighted import substitution policy; and there has been no strong stimulus for the local production of oil. The excessive and disorderly state intervention has seriously disturbed the economic system at the expense of its efficiency and, together with inflation, has generated extraordinary benefits to rent seekers but not to creative entrepreneurs and efficient producers. Only a small number of good technicians remain working. The number of hours needed to construct a square meter is twice that which was necessary in the past. There are 25 years of delay in the renovation of the railroads. The development of the road system has stagnated. The ports are in precarious condition.

(De Pablo 2005: 388–389, authors' translation)

Based on this crude analysis Prebisch proposed a series of recommendations, some of which were implemented immediately and others that were delayed or never seriously applied.

Exchange rate, commercial policy and stimulus to agriculture

The foreign exchange system changed in October 1955, less than two months after the fall of Perón. In the official market, the reunified exchange rate was set at 18 pesos per dollar. Therefore, the adjustment in the exchange rate paid to exporters increased 260 per cent (it had been 5 pesos per dollar since September 1950). The exchange rate paid by importers increased 140 per cent (up from 7.50 pesos per dollar). The so called free exchange rate that applied to authorized financial transactions in foreign currency (which had been 14 pesos per dollar since 1950) increased 29 per cent. This official rate remained unchanged until the end of 1958. The new exchange system kept the exchange controls; but, all transactions banned in the official market could go to a legal free market. The parallel market disappeared and in the free market the dollar traded at 30 pesos per dollar in October 1955 (a gap of 66 per cent with respect to the official exchange rate). It jumped up to 40 pesos per dollar in 1956 and 42 pesos per dollar in April 1958, the month before Frondizi assumed the Presidency.

At the same time as the reorganization of the foreign exchange market, the government imposed export taxes on agricultural products (*retenciones* in Spanish) of up to 25 per cent of the value of exports. With this in place the effective exchange rate for exporters of agricultural products was 13.5 per cent, which meant a 170 per cent increase with respect to the exchange rate previously paid to exporters. In fact, since IAPI had been paying farmers higher prices than those it had received for exports the actual increase of agricultural prices was not 170 per cent, but rather 40 per cent. Therefore, a good part of the devaluation helped to eliminate losses in the official sales of agricultural products and only partially went to increases in proceeds for farmers. Taxes on agricultural exports went down during 1956 and 1957 and almost disappeared by 1958.

The new government liquidated the IAPI in 1955 and the private sector started to export most agricultural products. In 1957 only exports of wheat remained in official hands. In May 1956 the National Meat Council (Junta Nacional de Carnes) and in October 1956 the National Grain Council (Junta Nacional de Granos) were re-created not so much to work in the export business as to support prices whenever they did not reach the levels set as minimum prices.

On the import side, the government established import duties for the goods bought at the free market price. The import duties were lower than during the years of Perón, but higher than those in the 1930s.

In the case of cars imports, the duties ranged from 125 per cent to 340 per cent depending on the weight and dollar value of the vehicle. In spite of these very high import duties car imports doubled between 1955 and 1957, auto parts' imports increased three times, and truck and bus imports increased eight times. Since the cost of imported oil increased significantly after the closing of the Suez Canal, truck and bus imports were suspended in August 1957. From January 1958 on, imports of goods other than oil, newspaper and machinery for industrial modernization were required to pay a deposit of 20 per cent or 100 per cent of the import value 120 days in advance, depending on whether the import was done in the official or the free segment of the exchange market.

In spite of the significant adjustment of the price of the dollar, imports of goods considered non-essential were still severely restricted. The import substitution strategy imposed during the wars and accentuated by Perón remained in place, although the new government introduced more explicit prioritization of imports of crucial inputs and machinery.

Figure 11.1 shows the effect of the new exchange rate and commercial policies on the relationship between domestic and foreign terms of trade. The gap between the two terms of trade was not as large as in the years of Perón but it did not disappear. The gap that remained, increased again after 1960 and, particularly after 1965, was related not only to the taxation of exports but also to the high protection given to domestic industrial production that came in the form of high import duties and other import restrictions on most imported goods.

As Prebisch proposed, in 1956 the government created the National Institute for Agricultural Technology (Instituto Nacional de Tecnología Agropecuaria, known by its Spanish acronym INTA) that would play an important role in promoting research and development of more advanced technologies and then disseminating them among the farmers.

The relationship with international institutions

Another important recommendation by Prebisch was related to Argentina's external debt and its self-exclusion from the Bretton Woods financial and trade institutions.

136 *Political and economic instability*

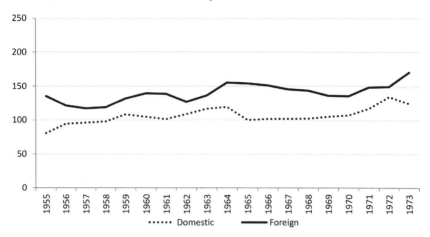

Figure 11.1 Domestic and foreign terms of trade 1955–1973 (1990=100)
Source: authors' own calculations, based on material originally published in IEERAL (1986).

In his report, Prebisch stated,

> If Argentina is to rapidly overcome the current development crisis, it will need loans and private investments from abroad... as well as the return of the large amount of Argentinean funds that flow abroad ... These days there is a movement away from bilateral agreements. Brazil has worked with the United Kingdom and Holland on arrangements that allow it to go from a bilateral to a multilateral regime. This way Latin America starts to benefit from some advantages of the European Payments Union... Argentina must enter the International Monetary Fund and the World as to prevent exclusion from two very convenient sources of international financing that promote economic development and monetary stability.
> (De Pablo 2005: 390–391, authors' translation)

By 1955, Argentina's external debt that originated in bilateral agreements with 11 countries amounted to US $757 million of which $260 million became due on 1956. Argentina did not have reserves nor did it generate a trade surplus so as to make these payments on time. The government decided to send the undersecretary of finance, Roberto Verrier, to negotiate the restructuring of its debt with official creditors and reach an agreement that Argentina could honour. In May 1956, Verrier signed a preliminary agreement with 60 representatives of 11 Western European countries. The procedure used to reach this multilateral agreement, whose details in terms of maturity and interest would be negotiated country by country, came to be known as the 'Paris Club' and since then it has become one of the international financial institutions used by emerging economies to arrange their debts with official creditors.

In September 1956, Argentina formally joined the International Monetary Fund (IMF) and the World Bank. The IMF requested the elimination of exchange controls and the system of multiple exchange rates, a gradual process of fiscal consolidation, organization of foreign trade under the rules of the General Agreement on Tariffs and Trade (GATT), reform of the Central Bank and the financial system, and the compilation of reliable statistics. The World Bank requested well thought investment project proposals and evaluated a policy that would allow private capital to participate in the development of the energy sector.

In April 1957, Argentina made its first purchase of foreign reserves (US $75 million) with Argentine pesos. Argentina could repurchase the pesos with gold or foreign exchange in five years. By 1956 Argentina already had $60 million of financing at 5 per cent over 20 years for SOMISA (from the name Sociedad Mixta Siderúrgica Argentina) and in 1957, the USA's EXIN Bank granted another loan of $100 million over 14 years at 5 per cent to finance the renovation of the transportation system. In short, during 1956 and 1957 the country obtained around $500 million in financing.

Foreign investment increased from around US $12 million in the two last years of Perón to $38 million in 1956 and 1957. It was important but an even more significant increase in foreign direct investment would come after 1958 because of the aggressive policies of President Frondizi.

The monetary and banking reforms

In his report, Prebisch had recommended 'returning to the banks the deposits that in 1946 had been transferred to the Central bank as to give them back technical and administrative autonomy'. In October 1957, the Government enacted monetary and banking reform and implementation started on 1 December 1957.

The reform of the charter of the Central Bank eliminated the provision that had transformed the Central Bank into a development bank, but maintained the suspension of the articles that required 25 per cent of its monetary base to be backed by gold and foreign reserves.

After balancing deposits and rediscounts, commercial banks would be able to resume lending with their own resources. The Central Bank would set the interest rates on deposits and loans. It would also set the minimum reserve requirements banks should keep in relation to their deposits. The reserve requirement could differ by type of deposit and region where the bank was located. At the beginning of the new regime the Central Bank set the maximum passive interest rate to be paid on deposits at 5 per cent per year (it had been 3 per cent per year until that time) and the maximum active rate that borrowers could be charged was set at 10 per cent per year (up from the 9 per cent that had been applied before). At the same time, the reserve requirement on saving accounts and time deposits was set at 10 per cent. The on demand deposits reserves requirement was set at 20 per cent on the stock on 30 November

1957, and at 30 per cent on the increment after that date. These rates and reserve requirements remained fixed until May 1958.

The Treasury issued a long-term bond to replace the debt of IAPI and other public entities with the Central Bank, the Banco de la Nación, the Banco Industrial de la República Argentina, the Banco de la Provincia de Buenos Aires and other banks. The capital of the Central Bank and of the Banco Hipotecario Nacional were multiplied by 10, that of the Banco Industrial de la República Argentina by 20, that of the Banco de la Nación by 20.

In 1956 and 1957 the rhythm of money creation slowed a bit in comparison to the last years of Perón, but not enough as real interest rates continued to be negative, even more than they had been in the last years of Perón because the inflation rate had more than doubled since.

Salaries, prices and rents

Price controls continued, rental contracts were extended and rents remained frozen, and public utilities prices increased below the rate of inflation. As a result, in general, the distortions in relative prices created during the years of Perón remained unchanged and in some cases were aggravated.

Public sector salaries went down in real terms during 1956 and 1957 because of the decision to reduce public spending. Real wages for the rest of the workers remained at levels similar to those of 1955. However, there was increasing social unrest because of the intervention of the CGT and the persecution of Peronist trade union leaders.

Fiscal policy

The new government tried to achieve some reduction in public expenditures and to increase tax revenue. It succeeded in reducing public expenditures and the fiscal deficit in 1956 and 1957; but, in 1958, during the transition from the military government to Frondizi's given the initial decisions of the new president, public expenditures and the deficit jumped up again to levels as high as those in the last year of Perón.

In fiscal policy as in many other aspects of economic policies, the big change would come as a consequence of the Stabilization and Development Plan announced by Frondizi in December 1958. This is shown in Figure 11.2.

Inflation and the disclosure of the latent crisis in 1958

In 1956 and 1957 inflation continued at rates that were not much different from the Perón years, but repressed inflation continued to accumulate. The gap between the exchange rate in the free and the official markets as well as the fall in real terms of public utility rates and urban and rural rentals, together with the scarcity of goods subject to price controls, were clear signals of how much prices were being repressed. Even though the nominal interest rates

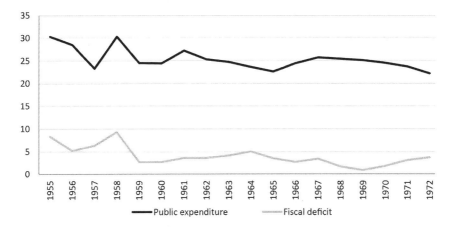

Figure 11.2 Public expenditure and fiscal deficit 1955–1972
(in percentage of GDP)
Source: authors' own calculations, based on material originally published in IEERAL (1986).

on bank deposits and loans looked low and were largely negative in real terms, banks rationed credit and almost 7 per cent of the financial needs of the private sector came from informal sources that charged high interest rates significantly above inflation. Long-term financing was almost non-existent except for limited amounts offered by official banks to privileged borrowers.

Immediately after taking office Frondizi in May 1958 decreed a 60 per cent increase in nominal wages for all workers. This wage hike had to absorb all the increases that had occurred since 1 February 1956. Frigerio estimated that the actual increase was 20 per cent. This wage increase, the normalization of the CGT, and the repeal of all legislation that had imposed sanctions and restrictions on the union activity of Peronist trade union leaders were commitments that Frondizi had made in his pact with Perón. To facilitate the payment of the increased salaries the Central Bank decided to reduce the reserve requirement on the future increase in demand deposits from 30 per cent to 15 per cent. The money supply, which in 1956 and 1957 expanded at rates between 12 per cent and 16 per cent per year, increased to more than 40 per cent in 1958 with inflation starting to accelerate, particularly after November 1958. The inflation rate for the calendar year 1958 was almost 34 per cent compared with 24 per cent in 1957.

Even though the exchange rate in the official market remained fixed at 18 pesos per dollar, price controls were not relaxed, and rental rates were kept frozen. By November, the exchange rate in the free market had increased to 70 pesos per dollar from 42 pesos per dollar in May. The gap between the free and the official exchange rates was close to 300 per cent. Frondizi was convinced that drastic steps were needed: on 28 December 1958, he announced the Stabilization and Development Plan that would be implemented over the next three years.

Frondizi's Stabilization and Development Plan

Stabilization became necessary as inflation started accelerating at the end of 1958. However, the main goal for Frondizi continued to be the development of Argentina. Frigerio had convinced him that to develop the economy it was necessary to open the country to foreign direct investment, but remain closed to competition from foreign imports. So, as soon as Frondizi had assumed the presidency Frigerio started to negotiate contracts with investors that were ready to explore and exploit oil reserves and other mineral resources, and to invest in manufacturing, particularly in the automobile industry, to produce manufactured goods for the protected domestic market. Argentinean law would grant foreign investors treatment equal to local investors, investment tax credits in the income tax for everybody, and special tax incentives for those investing in sectors prioritized by the government, that is, capital-intensive industries and the production of cars. Frondizi set a clear quantitative goal: to reach self-sufficiency in oil before the end of his presidential term. By October 1958, even before the launch of the Stabilization and Development Plan, Frondizi's government had negotiated and signed 13 contracts with foreign oil companies.

From 1959 to 1961, Frondizi's government authorized foreign investment of US $454 million dollars, 35 times the amount authorized by Perón during his last three years and eight times the amount of the three previous years.

In his speech presenting the Stabilization and Development Plan in December 1958 Frondizi explained that having put his development strategy in place it was imperative to stabilize the economy and eliminate inflation after 'introducing sincerity' into the Argentinean economy. That meant in order to reach stability it was first necessary to let the markets operate without controls of any kind. The IMF supported the plan with the first standby loan that Argentina received after engaging fully with the international financial system.

The government decided to eliminate exchange controls and to merge the exchange markets immediately. The exchange rate fluctuated from 66 pesos per dollar in January 1959 to 90 pesos per dollar in June 1959. As inflation measured by the cost of living index had been 90 per cent and measured by the wholesale price index 105 per cent in eight months, the government decided to fix the exchange rate at 83 pesos per dollar and kept it at that level until the fall of the government in March 1962. It was the first time that Argentina had liberalized and then fixed the exchange rate without any restriction on the purchase or sale of dollars in a unified free market. That brought the inflation rate down rapidly and kept inflation expectations low in spite of a sharp increase in prices in 1959. Frondizi and Frigerio referred to the inflation spike as the result of 'introducing sincerity' and eliminating distortions from the markets. Repressed inflation had been a reality for 16 years, but became unsustainable and the main constraint on Argentina's economic development.

The year 1959 was a typical one with inflation as high as 114 per cent and a fall in per capita GDP of 8 per cent, but it was followed by two years of declining inflation and rapid growth. Inflation fell to 27 per cent in 1960 and 14 per cent in 1961 with per capita GDP growth rates of 6.1 per cent and 5.4 per cent respectively in those two years. The rate of monetary expansion had been 46 per cent in 1958 and 44 per cent in 1959, and import prices in pesos increased 342 per cent and agricultural prices by 127 per cent. No doubt these price increases were due to the devaluation of the peso for imports and exports rather than a consequence of the increase in money supply. This is shown in Table 11.1.

Investment drove growth from 1958 to 1962. By 1962, investment had increased 36 per cent in comparison to 1958, because of Frigerio's growth strategy combined with the stabilization policies conducted by Alvaro Alsogaray and Roberto Aleman that kept consumption under control. In 1961, consumption was still at the same level as in 1958 after falling substantially during 1959. The combination of these two components of the Stabilization and Development Plan produced simultaneous disinflation and rapid growth after the spurt of both inflation and recession in 1959.

The stabilization efforts required significant fiscal restraint and a significant fall in real wages, particularly during 1959. That explains the numerous strikes and the social unrest that occurred between 1959 and 1963. The changes in relative prices are shown in Figure 11.3.

The fall of Frondizi's government in March 1962 and the uncertainty that resulted from the political events generated a new crisis that lasted almost two years. The peso was devalued in 1962 and again in 1963: the average exchange rate in 1962 was 116 pesos per dollar and in 1963 jumped to 139 pesos per dollar. Inflation was 28 per cent in 1962 and 24 per cent in 1963, with per capita GDP falling 3.1 per cent and 3.9 per cent respectively in those two years.

The recession of 1962 and 1963 was aggravated by investment's falling to a level below that of 1958; consumption did not decline more than between 1958 and 1961. The increase in exports in 1962 and 1963 helped somewhat to dampen the fall in GDP. In 1963, GDP was 4 per cent below the level of 1958, but it would be a mistake to think that Frondizi's growth strategy was a total failure. The recovery after 1963 and the growth up to 1972 would not have happened without the investment efforts of 1962 and 1963, and the consequent modernization of the productive capacity of the economy. This is shown in Table 11.2.

Moderate inflation and consumer driven growth during Illia's presidency

Inflation would remain in the range of 25 to 30 per cent per year during the three years of Arturo Illia's administration and the first year and a half of the *de facto* presidency of Juan Carlos Onganía with the exchange rate adjusting gradually in a free and reunified market. These were the years when the economic authorities reintroduced exchange controls and managed the exchange rate through gradual and periodical adjustment (what came to be known as the 'crawling peg' in the economic literature). The Illia administration took the

Table 11.1 Rate of inflation and rate of per capita growth 1956–1972 (in percentage per year)

Year	Rate of monetary expansion	Consumer price inflation	Wage inflation	Non agriculture wholesale price	Agriculture wholesale price	Free exchange rate	Import price inflation	Per capita GDP growth
1956	14	13	24	21	42	17	79	0.9
1957	12	25	23	24	26	12	1	3.3
1958	46	32	38	30	33	27	−10	4.3
1959	44	114	61	127	151	59	342	−8
1960	26	27	31	17	13	4	4	6.1
1961	15	14	25	9	6	0	−2	5.4
1962	7	28	24	28	37	40	42	−3.1
1963	29	24	29	26	35	20	17	−3.9
1964	40	22	32	25	29	12	1	8.6
1965	26	29	38	30	10	55	22	7.5
1966	35	32	32	20	21	−1	25	−0.8
1967	30	29	28	26	26	40	59	1.2
1968	27	16	9	9	10	−1	4	2.8
1969	11	8	12	5	8	5	6	7
1970	20	14	17	13	16	10	17	3.8
1971	38	35	41	36	49	59	18	3.2
1972	44	59	48	69	93	88	19	1.4

Source: authors' own calculations, based on material originally published in IEERAL (1986).

When Peronism was outlawed 143

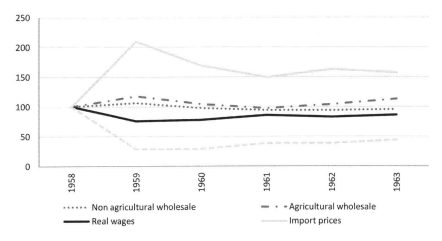

Figure 11.3 Relative price indices 1958–1963
(1958=100)
Source: authors' own calculations, based on material originally published in IEERAL (1986).

Table 11.2 Investment the driver of growth from 1958 until 1962
(indices at constant prices of 1960 in base 1958=100)

Year	GDP	Consumption	Investment	Exports
1958	100	100	100	100
1959	92	91	87	102
1960	98	92	126	102
1961	103	100	136	92
1962	100	94	123	122
1963	96	92	99	122

Source: authors' own calculations, based on material originally published in IEERAL (1986).

IMF's suggestions to produce a large initial adjustment in the exchange rate. This happened because it believed that the drastic adjustments of 1959 and 1962 had provoked large falls in real wages and consumption that generated social unrest.

Monetary policy was first actively used to facilitate recovery in consumption and then it became 'passive' to accommodate the rate of inflation determined by inertia and the fiscal deficit. The fiscal deficit increased in 1964. Money supply increased almost 40 per cent that year and thereafter it ranged from 25 per cent to 35 per cent per year. GDP growth was high in 1964, driven this time by consumption as the economy recovered from the recession of 1962 and 1963. Per capita GDP increased 8.6 per cent in 1964 and 7.5 per cent in 1964. The growth rate turned slightly negative in 1966, because of the fall in agricultural production that followed the deterioration of relative agriculture prices in 1965. This was the year of the military coup against Illia and his replacement by General Onganía. Per capita growth was positive but low in 1967 when a new economic minister Adalbert Krieger Vasena launched a novel stabilization and growth plan.

Krieger Vasena's Stabilization and Growth Plan

Minister Krieger Vasena designed his plan after a diagnosis similar to the one that Prebisch presented in 1955. As the gap between the black market exchange rate and the exchange rate in the controlled official market increased from 3 per cent in 1964 up to more than 20 per cent in 1966, Krieger Vasena recognized that to remove exchange controls he needed to allow a step devaluation of the peso. However, in order to avoid the distributional effect of the devaluations of 1959 and 1962, he decided to implement a devaluation compensated on the export side by the introduction of taxes on traditional exports and on the import side by reducing the level and the dispersion of ad valorem import duties.

This partially compensated devaluation also had the purpose of opening the economy to foreign trade and investment in a way that would promote efficient development of industrial production. The reduction in import duties would introduce foreign competition to the local producers, and given that industrial exporters would not pay taxes but instead receive drawbacks and other tax incentives, it was hoped that it would encourage industrialization for export, as Federico Pinedo had proposed in his thwarted 1940 plan.

On 13 March 1967, the new economic team eliminated exchange controls, liberalized the foreign exchange market, and set the exchange rate at 350 pesos per dollar, an increase of 37 per cent from the exchange rate in the official market at that time. The government announced that there would be no further devaluations in the future; the nominal exchange rate would be the anchor of the system. Krieger Vasena stated that Mexico had done the same in 1954 and that Spain and France had done the same in 1958, and that the strategy had successfully stabilized those three economies. A standby agreement with the IMF supported the programme.

Over the course of slightly more than three years – and for the first time since the 1930s – a team of professional economists who were convinced that fiscal prudence, monetary discipline, and integration with the world economy would pave the road to stability and growth, conducted Argentina's economic policies.

The main political advisors of Onganía did not share the liberal ideas of the economic team. They were, in most cases, Catholic nationalists, closer in ideology to that of the corporatist state of the 1940s and 1950s than to the economic liberalism of Krieger Vasena and his team. For at least two years, the government of Onganía was stable, but serious problems started to emerge after the '*Cordobazo*', in May 1969. Onganía decided to appoint a new Economic Minister, José María Dagnino Pastore who provided continuity to his predecessor's programme. Until July 1970, when the military junta removed Onganía from power, the economy continued to be managed within the framework announced in March 1967.

Both economic ministers favoured opening the economy, attracting foreign direct investment, developing infrastructure, and a functional financial system. They reformed the social security system, suspended the collective bargaining agreement between workers and employers until the end of 1970, and granted moderate wage increases by decree in line with the target inflation. At the same time, most medium and large sized private firms participated in a voluntary programme of price moderation that replaced the price controls that had prevailed in the past.

The fiscal deficit was 3.4 per cent of GDP in 1967, declining to 1.7 per cent of GDP in 1968 and 0.9 per cent of GDP in 1969 (see Table 11.3). It increased to 1.8 per cent in 1970, but was still much lower than the deficits that existed from 1936 to 1967. Monetary expansion was 27 per cent in 1968, 11 per cent in 1969 and 20 per cent in 1970. The bulk of monetary expansion came from credit creation for the private sector. This credit expansion helped the recovery of the economy on the supply side because it offered credit to rebuild working capital for firms, removing a constraint that had prevented the expansion of activity by small and medium sized firms in previous years.

Inflation declined from 16 per cent in 1968 to 8 per cent in 1969, but bounced back up to 14 per cent in 1970. In response to social unrest that followed the 'Cordobazo', the government decided to grant a 17 per cent wage increase in 1970. Per capita GDP growth was 2.8 per cent in 1968, 7 per cent in 1969 and 3.8 per cent in 1970, much higher than for any consecutive three-year-period during the previous two decades.

After the replacement of Onganía, first by Levingston and then by Lanusse, the guerrilla movements and a transition to democracy became the government's primary concern. The economy returned to its traditional course of increasing fiscal deficits, aggressive monetary expansion, and nominal wage

Table 11.3 Macroeconomic indicators from 1967 to 1972

Year	Fiscal deficit (in percentage of GDP)	Monetary expansion	Nominal wage increase	Rate of inflation	Per capita GDP growth
		(in percentage per year)
1967	3.4	30	28	29	1.2
1968	1.7	27	9	16	2.8
1969	0.9	11	12	8	7
1970	1.8	20	17	14	3.8
1971	3.1	38	41	35	3.2
1972	3.7	44	48	59	1.4

Source: authors' own calculations, based on material originally published in IEERAL (1986).

increases decided in collective bargaining agreements conducted in a context of accelerated inflation. The economy continued to grow, although at a slower pace, but inflation returned, increasing to 35 per cent in 1971 and 59 per cent in 1972.

The course of events in the world of those years did not support viable political and economic reforms for Argentina. The USA still suffered from its post-Vietnam War trauma. The Bretton Woods' system that had helped to reorganize and develop the economies of Western Europe and Japan under the leadership of the USA was in crisis. US President Richard Nixon declared the inconvertibility of the dollar to gold and to fight inflation, he imposed a price freeze, a wartime economic measure never before used in peacetime. In Chile, the winner of the presidential election of 1971 was Salvador Allende, the first socialist president in the Americas. And, the guerrilla movements supported by Castro-led Cuba spread across Latin America.

Note

1 The concept of 'intervention' is particular to the Argentine experience. It is both a political and an economic federal intervention. It is an executive order, by the president to take political and economic control of a province, a federal agency or even a non-governmental entity such as, in this case, a labour union.

References

Cortés Conde, Roberto (2005) *La Economía Política de la Argentina en el Siglo XX*, Buenos Aires: Edhasa.

De Pablo, Juan Carlos (2005) *La Economía Argentina en la segunda mitad del siglo XX*, Buenos Aires: La Ley.

Diaz Alejandro, Carlos D. (1970) *Essay on the Economic History of the Argentina Republic*, New Haven, CT: Yale University Press.

IEERAL (Instituto de Estudios Económicos sobre la Realidad Argentina y Latinoamericana) (1986) *Revista Estudios Año IX-N39-Julio/Septiembre*, pp. 103–184.

12 The return of Perón and the military

Former president Juan Perón returned to power on 25 May 1973 in a tumultuous way. Hector Cámpora had won the election in March of that year and then taken the oath of office on 25 May. His first decision was to pardon all the guerrilla leaders and soldiers sentenced to prison by a court that had been specially appointed to judge the crimes they had committed. Even though Montoneros and the Peronists that now demanded a socialist homeland instead of a Peronist homeland (*Patria Socialista* instead of *Patria Peronista*) applauded this decision, it displeased the old right wing of Peronism, including the trade union leaders that were said to reflect the deep feelings of Perón.

On the day Perón returned to Argentina from Spain a deadly gun battle erupted between the two wings of Peronism in the middle of a two-million-person crowd near the international airport to welcome Perón. The battle took more than 300 lives. The jet that transported Perón and Cámpora had to divert to a military airport and it became clear that Cámpora was not leading the country in a way that Perón considered appropriate. Cámpora resigned on 13 July to allow for a new election.

The interim president was Raúl Lastiri, the son-in-law of José Lopez Rega, a sort of Rasputin character who was very close to Perón's wife María Estela Martínez de Perón (nicknamed "Isabelita") who in practice led the right wing of Peronism. President Lastiri called for a new election in September. The Juan Perón–Isabel Perón ticket defeated the Ricardo Balbín–Fernando De la Rúa ticket with 62 per cent of the votes.

Perón took the oath as president on 12 October 1973 and governed until 1 July 1974, the day of his death. His wife succeeded him and on 24 March 1976, a military coup removed her from power initiating a new de facto regime.

The conflicts between the left and the right wings of Peronism did not end with the election of Perón. On the contrary, the fight became more violent. Just two days after his election, Montoneros assassinated José Ignacio Rucci who was the top trade union leader and had been one of the main architects of the Perón's return to Argentina. He had also been instrumental in assembling the Social Pact, the framework of economic policies that the government was implementing. In October, José Lopez Rega, the Minister of Social Affairs organized a paramilitary force (called Triple A from the Spanish Alianza Anticomunista Argentina) to fight the guerrillas. In January 1974, the People's Revolutionary Army (Ejército Revolucionario del Pueblo, known by its Spanish acronym ERP) attacked an important military unit in Azul, province of Buenos Aires, and there were several deaths on both sides. Perón condemned the guerrilla movements and suggested that the leftist governor of the Province of Buenos Aires, Oscar Bidegain, was responsible for the attack. Bidegain resigned and Vittorio Calabró, a trade union leader linked to the right wing side of Peronism, replaced him. Perón also asked Congress to approve a modification to the Criminal Code to increase the penalties for the crimes committed by the guerrillas. But 13 representatives that belonged to the Montoneros group expressed opposition to Perón's initiative. In response, Perón expelled them from the Peronist movement.

On 1 May 1974, when a crowd went to the Plaza de Mayo in Buenos Aires to commemorate Worker's Day, some of the people attending attacked Isabel Perón and started to shout '*qué pasa General que está lleno de gorilas el gobierno popular*' ('What is happening, General, is that the people's government is full of gorilas', the anti-Peronists were called 'gorilas' by the Peronists). Perón expelled those that were shouting and one-third of the crowd left the Plaza. Eight leftist representatives resigned from the Peronist Caucus in the House of Representatives, including several that would return to official positions in Nestor Kirchner's government 30 years later.

On 12 June 1974, Perón delivered his last speech from the balcony of the Pink House to a crowd gathered in the Plaza de Mayo in a show of support organized by the CGT. A few days later, on 1 July, Perón passed away and his widow Isabel Perón succeeded him.

The fight between the Triple A and the guerrillas intensified, the economic crisis erupted into an inflationary explosion, José Lopez Rega fell in disgrace after taking on the trade unions, and a few months later the military decided to put an end to Isabel Peron's government in the face of widespread chaos.

The economy from 1973 to 1976

The economic policies applied by José Ber Gelbard, the economic minister that Perón chose and Cámpora appointed, were exact copies of those that Miguel Miranda, the first economic czar of the first Peronist Government, had applied in 1946 and 1948. Gelbard, like Miranda was not a professional economist. Moreover, the policy shift that Alfredo Gomez Morales attempted after the resignation of Gelbard in September 1974 was very similar to the policies he had applied between 1949 and 1952.

As in 1946, in 1973 foreign terms of trade had turned favourable to Argentina due to the high demand for agricultural products after the Second World War and now due to the commodity boom associated with the decline of the dollar that preceded and accompanied the first oil shock. However, in 1973 the high prices for agricultural exports continued only until 1974 and, in

1975, the terms of trade began to deteriorate. In the 1940s the terms of trade remained favourable for almost four years.

The big difference between the two experiences is related to the duration of the policy experiments: that of Miranda lasted almost three years while that of Gelbard only a year and a half. The attempt to cope with the consequences of the preceding policies lasted four years in the first Gomez Morales's period as the economic fixer under Juan Perón, but it only lasted eight months in his second period under Isabel Perón. After 1974 the Peronist Government could not muddle through the disequilibria accumulated in the previous years as Perón and the military government that succeeded him had been able to do in the 1950s.

Inflation, which after the first Peronist period took three years to explode, showed up with great force in 1975 during the second Peronist period. The episode is recorded in history as the 'Rodrigazo', named after Celestino Rodrigo, the friend of José López Rega who, advised by a group of liberal economists, assumed responsibility for managing the economy after the resignation of Gomez Morales in June 1975.

The essence of the Gelbard Plan, like that of Miranda, was a social pact that increased nominal wages at the beginning at the same time as it fixed the exchange rate, froze public utility prices, and controlled the prices of most goods and services supplied by the private sector. On top of these wage and price freezes, the government significantly increased government expenditures and the fiscal deficit. Monetary expansion financed a high proportion of the deficit. Government expenditures that in 1972 had been 22 per cent of GDP went up to 25 per cent in 1973, 28 per cent in 1974, and 30 per cent in 1975. The fiscal deficit doubled in 1973 compared to 1972 and doubled again in 1975 compared to 1974. At its peak, the fiscal deficit represented 16 per cent of GDP, a record figure for Argentina until that moment.

Monetary expansion increased 96 per cent in 1973 compared to 44 per cent the previous year and remained high in 1974 in spite of the frozen prices and exchange rate. Inflation was 60 per cent for calendar year 1973 and 24 per cent for 1974 only to jump up to 194 per cent in calendar year 1975. All these figures are shown in Table 12.1.

To understand the dynamic of short-term inflation it is necessary to look at the annualized rate of inflation of each quarter. This is shown in Figure 12.1. Inflation went down from 124 per cent in the first quarter of 1973 to 21 per cent in the second quarter and to only 5.4 per cent in the third quarter when the full effect of the exchange rate, prices and wage freezes were in full operation. It remained relatively low in the fourth quarter of 1973 and in the first quarter of 1974; but, in the second and third quarters of 1974, it was already above 38 per cent per year. It reached the three-digit level in the last quarter of 1974 and remained high in the first quarter of 1975. In the second quarter of 1975, when the Rodrigazo started to have its effect, inflation jumped up to 263 per cent per year and by third quarter of 1974 had reached its peak of 1,017 per cent per year.

Table 12.1 Macroeconomic indicators from 1972 to 1976

Year	Government expenditures	Fiscal deficit	Monetary expansion	Nominal wage increase	Rate of inflation	Rate of devaluation in the official market	Rate of devaluation in the parallel market	Per capita GDP growth	Gap between parallel-official exchange rate (in percentage)
	(in percentage of GDP)			(in percentage increase per year)					
1972	22	4	44	48	58	11	88	1.4	129
1973	25	8	96	76	60	0	-2	4.3	126
1974	28	8	59	60	24	0	44	4.7	225
1975	30	16	194	170	183	719	369	-2.5	174
1976	28	14	256	249	444	326	238	-1.8	72

Source: authors' own calculations, based on material originally published in IEERAL (1986).

The return of Perón and the military 151

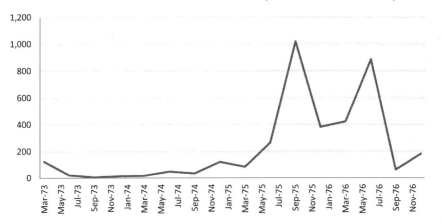

Figure 12.1 Annualized rate of quarterly inflation I-73 to IV-76
(percentage per year)
Source: authors' own calculations, based on material originally published in Ferreres (2010).

The extraordinary fiscal and monetary expansion on top of the wage, price and exchange rate freezes produced per capita GDP growth in 1973 and 1974; but, during the inflationary explosion of 1975 per capita GDP went down 2.5 per cent in 1975 and 1.8 per cent in 1976.

The economic policies implemented by Gelbard were similar to those of Miranda not only in relation to the macroeconomic policies, the management of prices, and the exchange controls but also in terms of the structural policy decisions that accompanied them. The Plan included heavy taxes on agricultural exports and quantitative restrictions on imports. Under the plan, Gelbard also nationalized several companies and maintained a strict system of price controls for a year and a half. The same thing happened with foreign exchange controls, but a large black market premium showed the magnitude of the price and exchange rate repression: in 1973, the gap between the parallel and official exchange rate was 126 per cent of the official rate and jumped to 226 per cent in 1974. In 1975 the gap averaged 174 per cent in spite of a large devaluation of the peso in the official market in June.

After replacing Gelbard, Gomez Morales attempted to implement a gradual fiscal adjustment and monetary contraction. The measures he adopted did not produce a perceptible result given the magnitude of the accumulated imbalances. Gomez Morales resigned in May and Celestino Rodrigo, that until then had been undersecretary in the Ministry of Social Affairs, was appointed minister. Ricardo Zinn and other liberal economists advised him to apply a shock adjustment strategy traditionally recommended by the IMF. Rodrigo decided on a large increase in public utility rates to reduce the fiscal deficit and at the same time increased the official price of the dollar by 150 per cent.

Rodrigo thought that the collective bargaining process had already agreed to limited nominal wage increases for the next 12 months, but the trade unions did not accept that view and declared an indefinite general strike asking for an additional wage adjustment of up to 100 per cent. Isabel Perón had to satisfy the workers' requests to end the strike so Rodrigo resigned after only 50 days as economic minister. But inflation had already exploded. The new economic Minister, Pedro Bonanni, and his successor, Antonio Cafiero, could not fix the economic chaos that followed and the economic crisis added one more element to the argument made by the military that they needed to force the resignation of Isabel Perón and usher in a new military government.

The 'National Reorganization Process'

The military government that deposed Isabel Perón, which called itself the Proceso de Reorganización Nacional (National Reorganization Process), designated General Jorge Rafael Videla as de facto President for a five-year term. It set as it main goal the extermination of the guerrilla movements, a mission that the government of Isabel Perón had given to the armed forces after Lopez Rega fell in disgrace and the Triple A started to be seen as more of a problem than a solution. Tragically, the armed forces did not use an approach that was much different from that of the Triple A. The armed forces exterminated the guerrilla movement, but the so-called 'dirty war' left several thousand *desaparecidos* (disappeared), detainees who were murdered and never seen again.

In addition to the war against Montoneros and the ERP, the military government began to prepare for a war with Chile after declaring that Britain giving Chile sovereignty over three islands in the Beagle Channel at the tip of Cape Horn null. The Pope sent Cardinal Antonio Samoré to intermediate between the two military governments and offered the Vatican as a site for a new arbitration. The Pope's intervention prevented a war at the last minute.

In 1981, after the completion of his five-year term General Roberto Viola replaced General Videla. Because of the economic crisis that deepened in 1981 and arguing that the President was suffering from heart problems, the military junta decided to remove General Viola and replace him with General Leopoldo Galtieri in December 1981.

In April, 1982 the military junta under General Galtieri's leadership decided to take the Islas Malvinas by force. The British government reacted by sending an expeditionary force to reclaim the islands.

Argentina and the United Kingdom engaged in a war that lasted until June 1982 when Argentine troops on the islands surrendered. Galtieri was dismissed by the military junta and General Reinaldo Bignone was appointed president with a mandate to organize the return of democracy. Bignone called for general elections in March 1983 when Raúl Alfonsín, the leader of the Radical Party, won against Italo Argentino Luder, the candidate of the Peronist Party.

The years of stagflation

On 2 April 1976, five days after his appointment as economic minister, José Alfredo Martínez de Hoz announced the new economic programme approved by the military junta. The diagnosis and the main ideas of the economic policy reform were similar to those espoused by Prebisch in 1955, by Alsogaray in 1959, and by Krieger Vasena in 1967 although adapted to the much larger initial imbalances and restrictions that the military had imposed as a consequence of the war that it was fighting with Montoneros and ERP. The military wanted to avoid a decline in investment and public expenditures, to increase military expenditures, and avoid unemployment and significant deterioration of real wages in order to preserve social peace. There is no doubt that restoring the basic economic balances under those restrictions was not an easy job.

Instead of adopting a shock treatment to restore price stability, Martínez de Hoz chose gradualism on almost every front. (There was one exception: following the advice of Adolfo Diz, the newly appointed President of the Central Bank, Martínez de Hoz decided to move quickly in liberalizing the financial system.) The policy was particularly gradual on the fiscal front. The reduction of the deficit did not come from a reduction in public expenditures as a proportion of GDP, but mainly from increased tax revenues. In 1978 government expenditures as a proportion of GDP were even higher than they had been in 1975. The slow pace of fiscal adjustment is shown in Table 12.2.

The large increase in the fiscal deficit that appeared from 1981 to 1983 originated in interest payments on the growing public debt. Public debt in turn increased rapidly because in previous years fiscal deficits were financed by borrowing rather than printing money. Therefore, it related more to the financial management of the economy than to a lack of effort to control the primary expenditures of the government (primary expenditures exclude interest payments on the public debt).

In commercial policy the government moved fast to reduce and eventually eliminate the export taxes that had been high under the Peronist government; but on the import side, the effective lowering of import duties and easing of quantitative restrictions was much slower. The import duties reform of 1977 did not reduce the effective protection for the domestic industries much because in practice it only eliminated redundant nominal tariffs, those that were not reflected in differentials between domestic prices and border priced competing imported goods. Consequently, the gap between the domestic and foreign terms of trade went down in 1976 but increased as the peso appreciated in real terms following the financial opening in 1978. After 1981, the closing of the gap related more to the deterioration in foreign terms of trade rather than to the effects of commercial policies which continued to discriminate against exports in general, and more specifically agricultural exports.

The exchange rate represents the incentive to produce tradable goods (both exportable and importable goods) relative to non-tradable goods. It initially peaked in 1977 and then fell to low levels until 1980 when it increased sharply

Table 12.2 Slow pace of fiscal adjustment 1975–1989 (in percentage GDP)

Year	Government expenditures	Fiscal deficit
1975	30	16
1976	28	14
1977	28	8
1978	31	10
1979	28	8
1980	30	9
1981	31	17
1982	27	20
1983	31	21
1984	30	10
1985	29	7
1986	32	5
1987	36	7
1988	35	8
1989	38	8

Source: authors' own calculations, based on material originally published in IEERAL (1986).

with the large devaluations of the peso after 1981. The much larger variations of the real exchange rate compared to the effects of commercial policies represented by the gap between domestic and foreign terms of trade is also indicative that the changes in the financial management of the economy were much more relevant to explain the real events than the commercial policies themselves (see Figure 12.2).

Martinez de Hoz's financial reform and monetary policy

Martínez de Hoz and Adolfo Diz moved quickly to liberalize and unify the foreign exchange market. By 1977 the exchange market gap disappeared, exchange controls were removed, and foreign direct investment encouraged. Two years later financial flows from abroad were also authorized to come into the economy without restriction.

At the same time, the government also implemented a financial reform that deregulated interest rates and the allocation of credit by the banks. The Central Bank would only control expansion of bank credit by setting uniform reserve rate requirements on deposits. Since initially the reserve requirement was set at 45 per cent (a relatively high requirement) to avoid an undesired initial jump in the stock of credit, the Central Bank decided to remunerate the reserves at the same average rate that the banks paid on deposits. This way the banks would not need to set large spreads between deposits and interest rates on loans.

The return of Perón and the military 155

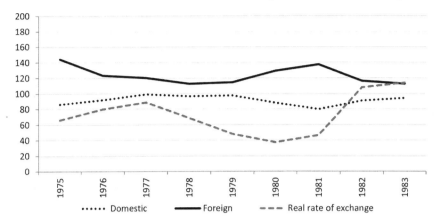

Figure 12.2 Real exchange rate and domestic and foreign terms of trade 1975–1983 (1990=100)
Source: authors' own calculations, based on material originally published in IEERAL (1986) and Ferreres (2010).

In practice, the remuneration of reserve requirements meant an interest cost for the treasury of the monetary financing of past fiscal deficits.

Until the financial reform of 1977, the Central Bank only guaranteed bank deposits in the regulated portion of the market. The non-regulated portion of the market had expanded rapidly in the few years before the reform, but did not have a Central Bank guarantee. The reform guaranteed that deposits would pay interest rates set freely by the banks. This encouraged irresponsible behaviour by insolvent banks that tried to generate liquidity by paying high interest rates on deposits that the Central Bank would have to reimburse after the bank went bankrupt.

During the long period of persistent inflation in Argentina negative real interest rates, sometimes with a large absolute value, had discouraged savings, and even more, had discouraged the channelling of savings into formal financial intermediation. Bank credit had been scarce and rationed. When deposits were nationalized, the Central Bank decided how to allocate credit among private banks' clients. When the banks regained the ability to lend the money of their depositors, they made their own credit allocation decisions once they met the reserve requirement.

When the banks, or the Central Bank, gave credit to a private firm in practice they were granting a subsidy that would likely increase the solvency of the beneficiary. Therefore, the allocation of credit made a careful appraisal of insolvency risk unnecessary. The only thing that the bankers had to care about was the willingness of the borrower to continue with its business and in case of losses that the loss be not larger than the amount of the subsidy that the borrower was receiving from the bank. In most cases, inflation would facilitate the payments of the debts and the amount of bad debt would be almost insignificant. Since the allocation of credit was effectively an allocation of subsidies, the system created many opportunities for corruption, not only by officials of the Central Bank and the government, but also by those in public and private banks.

Bank credit became increasingly scarce. Private firms and consumers had to look for financing in the informal market that operated with free interest rates, but lacked transparency and was highly fragmented. In practice, private firms invested only when they were able to generate their own surplus funds or were lucky enough to access bank credit at negative real interest rates. This explains why, in the discussion of how to reactivate the economy after a recession or how to promote investment, the main tool that policy makers considered was bank credit expansion, even if it could only be created through monetary expansion.

Martínez de Hoz and Diz were right in identifying negative real interest rates as an important feeder of inflation and one of the main determinants of the misallocation of resources in the economy. Financial disintermediation meant that savings would very often finance investment of low productivity activities because there was no mechanism available to compare the opportunity with a large set of investment alternatives. In response to this, families would typically invest their savings in urban or rural land, cars and appliances, or would purchase construction material to build the family house during a construction process that could take years. Mortgages were a privilege that only a few families could obtain and these people were normally connected with the government or the lending bank.

The shift from negative to positive real interest rates and the elimination of financial repression proved to be neither easy nor safe. On the contrary, four years later the policy of trying to fight inflation by deregulating interest rates and promoting financial re-intermediation of savings produced a financial crisis that resulted in inflation rates almost as high as those that followed the Rodrigazo of 1975. Tables 12.3 and 12.4 explain why and how it happened.

In 1977, because of the deregulation of interest rates and the decision to fully guarantee bank deposits regardless of the interest rate paid by the recipient bank and the application of monetary rather than fiscal restraint as the main anti-inflationary tool, there was a significant increase in the interest rates banks charged for loans.

The average 1977 inflation rate was 175 per cent per year with inflation at 144 per cent as measured by the non-agricultural wholesale price index and 164 per cent as measured by the agricultural wholesale price index. The resulting real interest rates ranged from 4.3 per cent per year in the agricultural sector to 12.7 per cent for the average non-agriculture firm. As small- and medium-sized firms normally paid interest rates 10 percentage points higher than the average, their real interest rate was probably as high as 22.7 per cent per year.

The interest cost of a dollar loan from abroad was still 7.5 per cent higher than the domestic bank loan for a non-agricultural firm but by the second

Table 12.3 Real interest rates after financial liberalization 1977–1981 (in percentage per year)

Year	Nominal interest rate charged on loans	Rate of non-agricultural wholesale inflation	Rate of agricultural wholesale inflation	Rate of increase in the peso price of a dollar	Real rate of interest for non-agricultural producers	Real rate of interest for agricultural producers	Real rate of interest for small- and medium-sized firms	Difference between peso and dollar interest rates
1977	175	144	164	179	13	4	23	−8
1978	172	148	142	94	10	13	20	32
1979	135	149	151	65	−6	−6	4	33
1980	100	80	63	38	11	22	21	24
1981	205	114	94	143	43	57	53	6

Source: authors' own calculations, based on material originally published in De Pablo (2005) and IEERAL (1986).

Table 12.4 Per capita GDP growth by main sectors 1976–1981 (in percentage per year)

Year	Per capita GDP	Agriculture	Industry	Construction	Commerce	Finance and insurance	Government and personal services
1976	−1.5	3.2	−4.5	13.5	−4.9	−5.6	−1.2
1977	4.9	0.9	6.3	10.7	6.5	12.3	−0.8
1978	−4.7	1.3	−11.9	−6.4	−7.7	5.1	−0.6
1979	5.5	1.4	8.2	−2	11.9	6.5	0.5
1980	0	−6.9	−5.1	−0.4	6.6	10.8	0.5
1981	−8.1	0.3	−17.2	−14.4	−10.6	−6.9	0.8
1976–1981 (average)	−0.8	0	−4.4	−0.3	0	3.4	−0.1

Source: authors' own calculations, based on material originally published in IEERAL (1986).

half of 1977 as the rate of devaluation slowed the interest cost of external borrowing started to decline rapidly. This explains why in 1977 there was already an inflow of US $1.2 billion of foreign capital when in 1976 there had been an outflow of $500 million. Foreign reserves increased by $2.5 billion during the year because the current account of the balance of payments was positive by $1.3 billion. The growth rate of the money supply declined, but not as fast as the creation of domestic credit because the Central Bank had to issue money to purchase the foreign exchange. Inflation decelerated but not as much as the authorities had expected.

In 1978, the picture was not much different from 1977, except that real interest rates had risen significantly for agriculture as the much slower pace of devaluation started to reduce the rate of agricultural price inflation and the interest cost of external financing in dollars went down significantly. The interest cost rate for a firm or a bank that got a foreign loan was 32.2 per cent per year cheaper than the domestic loan for a non-agricultural firm. Of course, this difference encouraged foreign financing and the inflow of capital increased to $1.4 billion. The big jump in the inflow of foreign capital would occur in 1979 after the authorities pre-announced a much lower pace of depreciation for the peso, a system to try to induce a reduction of inflationary expectations that came to be known as '*la tablita*' (the little tablet).

In 1979, it became even clearer that the interest cost of foreign financing would become much lower than the cost of domestic financing. This explains the big jump in the inflow of foreign capital. This inflow amounted to US $4.9 billion in 1979. As the peso started to appreciate significantly in real terms, the current account of the balance of payments turned negative. In 1979, the inflow of foreign capital created abundant liquidity. The economy had been depressed in the previous year due to the large increase in the real interest rate, particularly for the agriculture sector. The banks adjusted down the nominal rate of interest they charged on loans and as a result, 1979 was the only time during this four-year period that real interest rates turned slightly negative. Per capita GDP recovered but not for long.

In 1980, real interest rates would jump again to high positive levels, particularly for agriculture which was continuing to suffer the effect of the strong real appreciation of the peso. The current account deficit became large, and the flow of capital started to decline as several banks declared bankruptcy when interest rates in the USA increased rapidly because of Paul Volcker's stabilization plan. Due to the large current account deficit, foreign reserves that had been growing until the year before went down by $2.5 billion.

In 1981, after the transfer of presidential powers from Videla to Viola and the resignation of Martínez de Hoz, the crisis began to impact almost every corner of the economy. The peso suffered several large devaluations starting with a 10 per cent devaluation decreed by Martínez de Hoz before his resignation. Real interest rates skyrocketed and more banks became insolvent. Even for the firms that had received foreign financing in previous years, financial costs increased significantly in 1981. They were only 5.5 basis points

Table 12.5 Financial indicators 1976–1982

Year	Demand for money M3/GDP (monthly average figures)	Black or free market margin (in percentage of the official rate)	Rate of increase of the official peso price of the dollar	Rate of cost of living inflation	Rate of growth M1	Real exchange rate (1975=100)	Current account of the balance of payment	Capital account of the balance of payment	Change in international reserves
			(annual percentage increase)					(billion US$)	
1976	13	72	468	444	288	100	0.6	-0.5	0.1
1977	17	1	179	176	151	111	1.3	1.2	2.5
1978	20	0	94	176	158	86	1.8	1.4	3.2
1979	21	0	65	160	145	60	-0.5	4.9	4.4
1980	23	0	38	101	103	47	-4.8	2.3	-2.5
1981	22	36	143	104	81	58	-4.7	1.3	-3.4
1982	17	35	496	165	216	135	-2.4	-2.7	-5.1

Source: authors' own calculations, based on material originally published in IEERAL (1986).

below the cost of credit for domestic non-agriculture borrowers that were paying 42.5 per cent per year. The amount of bad loans increased rapidly and the loss of foreign reserves intensified as the deficit in the current account of the balance of payments remained very large and the inflow of foreign capital continued to decline.

The only sector of the real economy that experienced a significant expansion during the period 1976–1981 was finance and insurance. Agriculture was stagnant and industry declined 4.4 per cent in per capita terms. All the efforts made during this period to increase investment and productivity did not produce sustainable effects due to high real interest rates and the extreme appreciation of the peso that discouraged the production of tradable goods, particularly in the manufacturing industry, but also in agriculture which was supposed to be the beneficiary of trade liberalization.

By the end of 1981, the military junta decided to remove Viola and designated General Galtieri as the new president. Roberto Aleman the highly regarded former minister under President Frondizi replaced Lorenzo Sigaut who had been the economic minister during the Viola presidency. His mission was to restore confidence; but the approach that the military junta was secretly planning would make that impossible. The course of events after 1981 is shown in Table 12.5.

The decision of the military junta to invade the Malvinas Islands and the war with the United Kingdom drastically reversed the direction of the capital flows: there was an outflow of US $2.5 billion and the loss of reserves peaked at $5.1 billion.

During the South Atlantic War, the government introduced exchange controls and continued servicing the external financial debt, but went into arrears in external commercial debt. At the same time, the banking system's situation worsened as bad debts skyrocketed and many debtors declared bankruptcy.

When the Argentinean troops surrendered and Galtieri resigned, the military government had lost any possibility of reestablishing its authority and decided to appoint Reinaldo Bignone as the president who would lead the transition to democracy.

References

Cortés Conde, Roberto (2005) *La Economía Política de la Argentina en el Siglo XX*, Buenos Aires: Edhasa.
De Pablo, Juan Carlos (2005) *La Economía Argentina en la segunda mitad del siglo XX*, Buenos Aires: La Ley.
Ferreres, Orlando (2010) *Dos Siglos de Economía Argentina*, Buenos Aires: El Ateneo.
IEERAL (Instituto de Estudios Económicos sobre la Realidad Argentina y Latinoamericana) (1986) *Revista Estudios Año IX-N39-Julio/Septiembre*, pp. 103–184.

13 Transition to democracy and Alfonsín's presidency

Immediately after the defeat of Argentine forces in the South Atlantic War in June 1982, the political parties demanded a return to democracy. As soon as General Bignone took office on 1 July, he announced that the mission of his government would be a transition to democracy.

General Bignone did try to solve the financial crisis, but the focus of his government was on establishing an electoral process that would allow a return to civilian power.

In the second half of 1982 and the first quarter of 1983, the political parties organized themselves to participate in the elections and chose their candidates. In the Radical Party, the two pre-candidates were Raúl Alfonsín and Fernando De la Rúa. Alfonsín was the leader of a movement call Renovación y Cambio (Renewal and Change) that in the past had disputed leadership with the traditional leader Ricardo Balbín who had passed away in 1981. De la Rúa had been a candidate for vice-president with Ricardo Balbín in 1973, running against the Perón–Perón ticket, and was the leader of the Línea Nacional (National Line), more centrist than the centre-left space occupied by Alfonsín. Alfonsín won the primaries and became the candidate of the Radical Party sharing the ticket with Victor Martínez who ran for vice-president.

Italo Luder and Antonio Cafiero competed on the right to run as the nominee of the Peronist Party. Luder had been president of the senate from 1973 to 1976 and had actually replaced Isabel Perón as the president of the country for several weeks before the military coup of 1976. Cafiero had served as a minister under Juan Perón in the 1950s and under Isabel Perón after the Rodrigazo from 1975 until March 1976. Luder won the nomination with Deolindo Bittel as the candidate for vice-president.

During the campaign the Peronists were unable to demonstrate that they had overcome the internal divisions and conflicts of interest that had erupted between 1973 and 1976, particularly between the Peronist labour unions and the political leaders. In contrast, Radicalism presented itself as united and committed to reinstating the principles of the national constitution to pacify and democratize Argentine society.

While the Peronists did not blame the military for human right violations, probably feeling responsible for the violence during the years preceding the military coup, Raúl Alfonsín strongly condemned the human rights violations during the 'Dirty War' and promised to punish those responsible. One month before the election, he denounced a pact between Peronism and the military that committed them to a general amnesty.

There were not major differences in how the candidates talked about the economy. On the contrary, the language of both parties continued to be populist as it had been since the mid-1940s. Both candidates blamed what they called 'the liberal policies of Martínez de Hoz' for the economic problems of the country, refusing to assign any responsibility to the populist policies that had preceded the inflationary explosion of 1975 and that, in many respects, the military had continued.

Alfonsín won the election and took the presidential oath on 10 December 1983. As president he was successful in restoring good diplomatic relations with most countries and followed a prudent judicial strategy to punish human right violations by the military and the guerrillas by prosecuting the members of the military junta and the leaders of the Montoneros and the ERP. He settled the dispute with Chile over three islands in the Beagle Channel by accepting the decision of the Pope and started negotiations with Brazil to revive economic integration.

Alfonsín also had to deal with the consequences of the fight between the military and the left-wing terrorists that organized mutinies and uprisings. As a result of overcoming these attacks, the opposition parties supported him and successfully defeated attempts at destabilization from both sides of the dirty war.

Alfonsín is widely recognized as the main architect of recreating Argentina's democratic institutions; but his relationship with the labour movement was highly conflictive and various economic crises he had to confront cast a shadow over his leadership. Hyperinflation forced his resignation five months before the end of his term.

From an economic point of view, the break with some of the economic policies of the military government began in General Bignone's transition period; therefore, this chapter begins with his government. Unfortunately, that break did not mean a successful redefinition of the rules of the game to defeat stagflation, the main problem that had plagued the economy for eight consecutive years.

Bignone's government focus on the financial crisis

President Rafael Bignone designated Jose María Dagnino Pastore as new economic minister and Domingo Cavallo as the new president of the Central Bank. Cavallo and his associates in the economic research institute of the Fundación Mediterránea had warned of the pitfalls of the financial reform and had a plan to prevent widespread bankruptcy of families and small- and medium-size companies that had suffered from extremely high real interest rates on peso-denominated loans.

The plan combined partial regulation of interest rates with the legalization of a free-floating foreign exchange market that would coexist with the commercial foreign exchange market that was subject to exchange controls. The nominal interest rate on short-term deposits and on outstanding peso-denominated debts would be regulated and, for some time, set below the expected rate of inflation. Most of those debts would be adjusted according to a financial adjustment index that compounded the monthly interest rate paid on bank deposits. Therefore, the plan consisted of keeping the financial adjustment index below the price indices for enough time (probably months) to produce the reduction of debt (in real terms) to levels that debtors could afford to pay.

The interest rates would continue to be freely set for bank deposits with a six-month minimum term of maturity and the principal of those deposits would adjust according to a price index. The same would be applied to loans financed with those deposits.

The foreign exchange rate for commercial transactions would also track to a price index and the financial foreign exchange rate would be determined by the operation of the market without any intervention by the Central Bank.

The margin between the two foreign exchange markets would have a negative impact on the solvency of firms that had to service dollar-denominated debts during the two years that the dual exchange market was expected to last. In order to prevent bankruptcy, the Central Bank offered those firms exchange insurance to pay for services at the commercial foreign exchange rate if they were able to postpone those payments for two years. At the same time, they could value the outstanding dollar debts at the commercial exchange rate which allowed them to avoid declaring the effect of the temporary margin between the financial exchange rate and the commercial exchange rate as a current loss.

The regulated rate was set at 6 per cent per month while monthly inflation was around 10 per cent so, after some months, the plan produced the desired reduction in real terms of the peso-denominated debts helping to rescue many families and small- and medium-sized firms from bankruptcy. Unfortunately, because of the lobbying of the large firms that had dollar debts, a change in the leadership of the Central Bank opened the door for the transformation of the exchange insurance into the nationalization of the dollar debts of the private sector. Cavallo had resisted the demands of the dollar debtors to adjust the cost of the exchange insurance by the regulated interest rate rather than by a price index. However, Julio García Del Solar, who replaced Cavallo 52 days after the launch of the plan, authorized that very change and announced the nationalization of private dollar debts. After that public external debt increased by the amount of the outstanding private dollar debt and the assets that the Central Bank acquired in compensation suffered the same reduction in real terms as the peso-denominated debt of the private sector.

The dual foreign exchange system lasted four years, until the launch of the Plan Austral. The acceleration of inflation combined with the regulated interest rate (set at 6 per cent) transformed what should have been a controlled process of realigning debt to the real capacity of debtors to pay, into a complete wipe out of debts. Of course the dollar debt, now a liability of the Central Bank, did not disappear. On the contrary, it became a heavy burden on future fiscal accounts. Table 13.1 shows the financial indicators for the period 1982–1989.

Wehbe and Grinspun

Jorge Wehbe was the last economic minister of the military government. Julio Gonzalez Del Solar served at the same time as president of the Central Bank. Bernardo Grinspun was the first economic minister of the democratically elected government of Alfonsín. Enrique García Vazquez accompanied him as president of the Central Bank. All of these people were admirers of Raúl Prebisch and had had experience with economic policy making in the 1960s and 1970s, but they had never dealt with a stagflationary experience like the one that Argentina had endured since 1975.

They tried to implement policies similar to those that the economic ministers under Arturo Illia had applied in the 1960s based on the gradual adjustment of all the economic variables accompanied by an accommodating monetary policy. In the 1960s most of those adjustments were done once a year, but the exchange rate adjustments started to be done every month in order to avoid a large devaluation. In the 1970s, only a small proportion of prices and salaries adjusted annually. More recently, prices adjusted twice a year or quarterly. As inflation accelerated, however, an increasing proportion of prices started to adjust monthly or even more frequently. In the first half of 1985, the exchange rate adjusted almost every day.

With the demand for money falling rapidly in real terms from 23 per cent in 1980 down to only 11 per cent in 1984, the outcome could not be other than dangerously accelerating inflation. The rate of inflation went from 165 per cent in 1982 to 344 per cent in 1983 and 627 per cent in 1984. In January 1985, in spite of the standby programme approved by the IMF in December 1984, the monthly inflation rate jumped to 25 per cent from an average of 18 per cent per month in 1984.

In February 1985, President Alfonsín replaced Grinspun with Juan Vital Sourrouille and García Vazquez with Alfredo Concepción. The new economic team prepared to launch a new stabilization plan in June, but from April to June worked out a realignment of relative prices that would allow the introduction of a price and wage freeze as an ingredient of the new plan. This explains why in the first half of 1985 the annualized rate of inflation reached almost hyper-inflationary levels at 1,500 per cent.

Sourrouille's Plan Austral

A group of professional economists that combined practical experience in policy making with academic research on applied economics staffed the economic team. They realized that 40 years of inflation had introduced strong

Table 13.1 Financial indicators 1982–1989

Year	Demand for money (monthly average figures)	Black or free market margins (in percentage of the official rate)	Rate of increase of the official peso price of a dollar	Rate of cost of living inflation	Rate of growth of M1	Real exchange rate (1975=100)	Current account of the balance of payments	Capital and financial accounts	Change in foreign reserves
			(annual percentage increase)				(billion US$)		
1982	17	35	496	165	216	135	-2.4	-2.7	-5.1
1983	12	40	321	344	355	143	-2.5	-1.7	-4.2
1984	11	30	563	627	492	132	-2.4	0.5	-1.9
1985	13	15	735	672	800	150	-1.0	0.4	-0.6
1986	17	0	54	90	65	125	-2.9	0.8	-2.1
1987	15	0	157	131	92	128	-4.2	0.1	-4.1
1988	14	0	357	343	364	130	-1.6	0.2	-1.4
1989	12	15	4084	3079	4368	213	-1.3	-5.5	-6.8

Source: authors' own calculations, based on material originally published in Ferreres (2010).

inertia for two reasons: at any moment in time there were a large number of prices that had pending adjustments; and, at the same time, financial contracts such as loans and deposits reflected a *de facto* agreement to pay the nominal amount plus inflation at some future date. The nominal interest rates were the vehicle that incorporated expected inflation into financial contracts. Even if they found an effective mechanism to limit the pending adjustments and to drastically reduce the rate of inflation, the successful stabilization would produce large wealth redistribution from debtors to creditors and widespread insolvency problems since increases in debtors' real interest rates would closely track the decline in inflation.

The most obvious and commonly used coordination mechanism to reduce and even eliminate inflation expectations was the nominal exchange rate. Many times in the previous 40 years, policy makers relied on a nominal exchange rate anchor, normally following a nominal devaluation of the local currency, to create a sort of buffer stock to absorb the pending adjustment of the prices that had lagged behind the most recently adjusted ones. Plan Austral was going to use that coordination mechanism once more, supplemented with wage and price controls; but in order to prevent the wealth redistribution from debtors to creditors and curb inertial inflation more effectively it included an innovative monetary reform mechanism.

A new monetary unit, austral, would immediately replace the peso: 1,000 pesos would become one austral for all current prices and spot transactions. But for future contracts the peso would convert into australes deducting from peso-denominated future nominal figures the impact of inflation that was expected before the introduction of the austral. The average nominal interest rate that prevailed in the market prior to the announcement of Plan Austral indicated the rate of expected inflation. The operation of deducting expected inflation from future nominal figures consisted of the application of a downward percentage adjustment for each contractual term indicated by a table published as part of the plan.

The fixing of the exchange rate, the wage and price controls, and the correction table were the heterodox component of the stabilization plan. There was also an orthodox component: the commitment to a reduction in the fiscal deficit. As the economic team expected a significant increase in the demand for money in real terms (a reduction in the velocity of money), monetary policy would not need to be restrictive.

The immediate impact of Plan Austral was impressive. Monthly inflation that had ranged between 20 and 30 per cent per month leading up its implementation in June 1985, dropped to around 2 per cent per month between August 1985 and February 1986, the period when the exchange rate remained fixed at the rate 0.80 australes per dollar (see Figure 13.1). Another promising impact of the Plan Austral was the recovery in the level of economic activity. Economic activity had fallen dramatically from the last quarter of 1984 until the second quarter of 1985, but by just the third quarter, immediately after

Democracy and Alfonsín's presidency 167

the launching of the Plan, economic activity started to recover and by the fourth quarter, the recovery was picking up momentum.

The initial success of Plan Austral helped the Radical Party win the election to renew one-third of the House of Representatives. However, the political team of Alfonsín's government did not give the economic team the support necessary to deepen the fiscal adjustment on the expenditure side. The evolution of fiscal accounts is shown in Table 13.2.

The fiscal deficit remained high in spite of increased taxes. Due to the need to preserve the increase in tax revenue it was not possible to remove export taxes as a way to recover competitiveness. In April 1986, the economic team decided to introduce gradual adjustments in the nominal exchange rate to

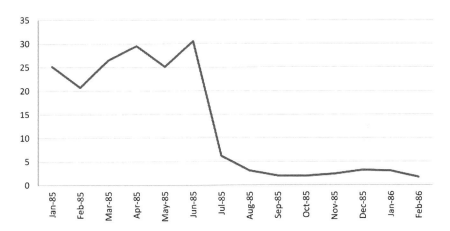

Figure 13.1 The initial success of Plan Austral: monthly inflation (percentage by month)
Source: authors' own calculations, based on material originally published in Ferreres (2010).

Table 13.2 Government expenditure and fiscal deficit 1982–1989 (in percentage of GDP)

Year	Government expenditure	Fiscal deficit
1982	27	19.6
1983	31	21
1984	30	10
1985	29	7
1986	32	5
1987	30	5.8
1988	29	6.7
1989	31	6.4

Source: authors' own calculations, based on material originally published in IEERAL (1986) and Ferreres (2010).

avoid further reductions in competiveness. The real exchange rate had gone down by 23 per cent since June 1985.

At the same time Sourrouille announced that the exchange rate would crawl. Trying to avoid the real appreciation of the austral, he announced that all economic variables would adjust gradually in small steps as had happened in the 1960s during Illia's administration. Sourrouille thought this system had failed during Whebe and Grispun's ministries due to the high inertial inflation. Therefore, this time, as inertial inflation was removed, gradual adjustments would not accelerate inflation.

By July 1986, monthly inflation jumped up to 6.8 per cent from an average of 3 per cent in the initial months of the implementation of the Plan Austral. The economic team reached the conclusion that monetary policy had been too expansionary and decided to add some doses of orthodoxy to the stabilization plan. Juan Luis Machinea replaced Concepción as president of the Central Bank. He restricted monetary expansion and the government adopted some fiscal consolidation. Monthly inflation, that in August had been 8.8 per cent, went down to 5 per cent in December but increased again to 7.6 per cent in January 1987.

Disillusioned with the poor results of the turn to orthodoxy, the economic team decided to impose a price freeze on 26 February 1987. As the inflation rate did not fall as far as expected and the electoral season was approaching, the government decided to appoint as minister of labour a union leader from a group of trade unions that appeared to be less antagonistic than the CGT. As expected, the new labour minister pushed for wage increases and the government had to allow prices and the exchange rate to shift accordingly.

By August, the month preceding the election, monthly inflation was 13.7 per cent and in September the electoral results were disastrous for the Radical Party. Only two provinces, Córdoba and Río Negro, would remain governed by Radicals. The Peronists increased the number of provinces under their control from 12 to 17 and in the House of Representatives, the government lost 12 seats. Consequently, in the next two years, it did not have a majority in either the Senate or the House.

In October 1987, the month after the election, inflation as measured by the cost of living index was 19.6 per cent and 30.4 per cent as measured by the wholesale price index, almost as high as in the months preceding the launching of the Plan Austral.

In mid-October 1987, Sourrouille and Machinea announced a new plan based on splitting the foreign exchange market. The official market would channel exports, imports, and debt services of public debt and the registered foreign debt of the private sector. In this market, the Central Bank would set the exchange rate. The free market would absorb all other exchange transactions at a rate determined by supply and demand. In the official market the exchange rate jumped 12.1 per cent and in the free market 26.5 per cent. The official exchange rate remained unchanged until December, but the free market exchange rate increased rapidly without any pause. In January 1988, the official exchange rate was trying to catch up with the free market rate. As a result, from October 1987 to August 1988 the official exchange rate increased 207 per cent and the free market exchange rate 218 per cent. Inflation, which had just fallen for two consecutive months after October 1987, accelerated during the period of January to August. In August 1988, the monthly inflation rate as measured by the cost of living was 27.6 per cent, almost as high as in the months preceding the launch of the Plan Austral.

In light of the frustrating results of the stabilization plan and with the economy again in recession by mid-1988, the economic team resumed negotiations with the IMF, the Paris Club and the World Bank. The World Bank was the only institution that decided to make a loan and lent US $1.25 billion to support the new commercial policy that would be the core of Plan Primavera. It disbursed an initial tranche of US $350 million in October 1988.

The IMF believed that Argentina had failed to comply with the conditions of the previous standby loans and did not find evidence of sufficient monetary restraint and fiscal consolidation to justify support for the proposed plan.

Plan Primavera maintained the split in the foreign exchange market implemented in October 1987. It also established that while exporters of primary goods were obliged to sell their proceeds in the official market (an obligation reduced to 50 per cent in the case of exports of manufactured goods and services), importers and all other demanders of foreign exchange had to purchase foreign currencies on the free market. The Central Bank, which would purchase dollars on the official market at the same time, would sell foreign exchange in the free market through pre-announced auctions. Foreign financing was important because the Central Bank needed to absorb part of the money created to finance the deficit by selling more dollars on the free market than were purchased on the official market.

In practice, the foreign exchange regime of the Plan Primavera was equivalent to a system of a unique exchange market with taxes on exports at rates of 50 per cent and 25 per cent for primary and non-primary goods, respectively. The revenue for the government accrued not to the Treasury but to the Central Bank, though for all intents and purposes the macroeconomic effect was equivalent.

Accompanied by a new price and wage freeze, the plan produced a significant reduction in the monthly inflation rate in just three months, but in December 1988 the rate of inflation started to rise again. It was 6.7 per cent in December and jumped to close to 10 per cent in February 1989.

The commitment to the World Bank to open up a closed economy just ahead of a general election in May 1989 turned out to be a poor decision. In February 1989, when the World Bank was supposed to disburse a second tranche of US $350 million, the Bank decided to suspend the programme because Argentina was not complying with this condition.

Immediately after the World Bank's announcement, Machinea decided that the Central Bank would cease selling foreign exchange on the free market. The free market exchange rate immediately jumped 23 per cent and the official exchange rate increased only 2.6 per cent. By the end of February, the

170 *Political and economic instability*

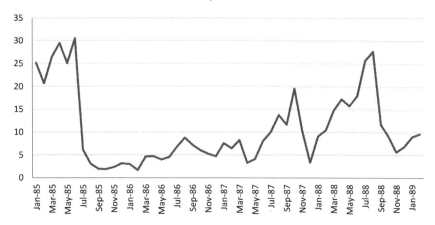

Figure 13.2 The melting down of Plan Austral: monthly inflation (percentage by month)
Source: authors' own calculations, based on material originally published in Ferreres (2010).

margin between the official and the free market exchange rates was 90 per cent and by the end of March the margin had increased to 215 per cent. Holders of australes had desperately already started to exchange them for dollars in the free market. The demand for australes collapsed and hyperinflation was around the corner.

Hyperinflation during the transition from Alfonsín to Menem

In the middle of the 1989 presidential campaign, the Argentine economy had all the ingredients for hyperinflation similar to Bolivia during the transition from Hernán Siles Suazo to Victor Paz Estensoro in 1985.[1] At the end of March 1989 Eduardo Angeloz, the presidential candidate of Alfonsín's Radical Party, requested the resignation of the economic team. His advisors, all orthodox economists, blamed the lack of fiscal discipline for the country's economic situation. They were right, but removing the economic team would have simply aggravated the situation because it was impossible to implement a fiscal adjustment in the middle of an election year. Furthermore, the politicians that would replace the economic team were those that had prevented Sourrouille and his team from complementing the Plan Austral with fiscal consolidation in 1987. The appointment of Juan Carlos Pugliese for a few weeks and of Jesús Rodriguez immediately after only increased the uncertainty. Carlos Menem, the candidate of the Peronist Party, was vague in his proposals for the economy and the economists that served as his advisors did not share a common diagnosis of the country's economic problems.

Therefore, at the moment of the election, uncertainty about the future course of the economy was at its peak and Argentineans were desperately purchasing dollars on the black market to protect their savings. Even the most modest informal workers and retirees who received the minimum pension converted their salaries and pensions into dollar bills in an effort to protect the purchasing power of their income. Prices increased every hour. In May 1989, the monthly inflation rate was 78 per cent; which means that prices increased almost 2 per cent per day. In July 1989, when President Alfonsín transferred power to President Menem, monthly inflation was 200 per cent or 3.6 per cent per day.

Under hyperinflation, the price of the dollar in the black market led the price dynamic. The price of the dollar in the restricted free market followed it with a short lag. The government was obliged to authorize periodic adjustments to the price of the dollar in the controlled portion of the exchange market, in salaries, and in public utility rates. Of course, the frequency of the adjustments went from monthly to weekly at first and then ended up being daily.

Even if the rate of increase in the price of the dollar slowed after announcements that were meant to reduce uncertainty, as happened in August 1989 when the new government received support in Congress for the Reform of the State and Economic Emergency laws, the deceleration did not reassure Argentines that hyperinflation was over. As soon as new events provoked an acceleration of inflation, hyperinflation revived because the economy was highly dollarized and sensitive to the changes in the price of the dollar on the black market. This explains the two bursts of hyperinflation after the peak of July 1989, one in December 1989 and the second one in January 1991 (see Figure 13.3).

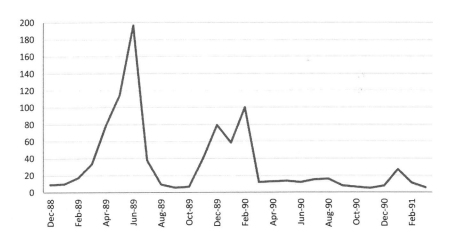

Figure 13.3 Monthly inflation rate during the hyperinflation (percentage by month)
Source: authors' own calculations, based on material originally published in Ferreres (2010).

The Argentine economy in 1990

By 1990, Argentina had been a stagnant economy for many years and the rules of the game that governed relationships among the different economic agents were both highly complex and unstable. The economy was so complicated that not even specialists could understand what went on. Each day they discovered a new hidden subsidy, a new regulation that hindered private initiatives in one area or another, all of which resulted in a resource redistribution of which only the beneficiary was aware.

The public budget had steadily accumulated an ever larger number of activities, including the production of goods and services that were clearly for private benefit and that should have been paid for at market prices rather than with taxes. Simultaneously transparency and order had steadily disappeared resulting in disorderly decisions and insufficient information.

Excessive government intervention in the activities of the private sector delayed necessary adjustments to correct erroneous business strategies and the economy lost its ability to correct disequilibria between supply and demand. Low productivity activities kept using productive resources, bottlenecks became more persistent, and sectors experiencing greater demand could not get enough resources to produce enough supply to meet demand. Government intervention had transformed private goods into public goods.

Easy solutions that appealed to politicians even if they defied basic economic laws characterized the highly distorted and complicated Argentine economy. This resulted in a continuous expansion of administrative intervention by the government in economic decisions. The government implemented policies that, even from the outset, it knew were impossible to enforce. The final effect of this 'irrational voluntarism' was Argentines' loss of respect for the capacity of the government to implement and control its decisions and consequently to comply with its role as organizer of the overall economy.

This had serious effects on political credibility: no one believed the announcements that were made about the future unless they were reasonable, and there were measures taken rapidly in order to support the announcement and ensure its implementation.

Each important economic agent, or group of economic agents with common interests, had proposals about nearly every economic decision. This was a distinctive characteristic of the public debate over economic issues. It was as if the society as a whole had a say in deciding what economic agents could do regardless of their assent or interest.

Because of this type of public debate of economic issues the economic rules of the game became unclear and unstable. They were unclear due to inattention to defining the frameworks for assigning responsibilities for decision making, information, and risk taking. They were unstable because they were not sufficiently understood and accepted; and, because experience had taught each economic agent or pressure group that it was more profitable to dedicate their efforts to changing the rules in their favour than doing things better within the existing framework.

Many economic advisors also fell into 'irrational voluntarism'. They often knew very little about the dilemmas that business faced, but nonetheless they tried to instruct entrepreneurs about areas in which to invest. Advisors believed that they were able to choose the most appropriate technology for an entrepreneur or to identify the most promising markets. This led to bad policies and, even worse, to a poor economic structure.

Inflation was one of the worst examples of 'irrational voluntarism'. It had prevailed during 45 years because governments wanted to spend more than they were capable of collecting through legally mandated taxes. They wanted to obtain something for nothing. Since that was impossible, the result was a tax that lacked legal legitimacy, namely, inflation.

This form of economic organization imposed a surcharge on economic activity, either in the form of its organization or the resulting effects. This surcharge blocked the realization of potential development in two ways: it impeded the development of activities and, in the case of productive activities already under way, imposed an unproductive allocation of resources since resource allocation adjusts to the existing economic structure. Given the inefficiency in resource utilization and the resulting low level of productivity, a vicious circle ensued in which investment was discouraged, leading to stagnation, or worse, economic backwardness.

Note

1 In April 1989, Domingo Cavallo wrote the prologue of a book entitled *Economía en tiempos de crisis* (Economics in Times of Crisis). Editorial Sudamericana published it in Spanish in May 1989. The second paragraph of the prologue reads: 'In a short time the Government will face the challenge of reversing a phenomenon that has been unknown in Argentina until now: hyperinflation. Bolivia went through this traumatic process in the transition from the Government of Hernán Siles Suazo to that of President Víctor Paz Estensoro.'

References

Cortés Conde, Roberto (2005) *La Economía Política de la Argentina en el Siglo XX*, Buenos Aires: Edhasa.
De Pablo, Juan Carlos (2005) *La Economía Argentina en la segunda mitad del siglo XX*, Buenos Aires: La Ley.
Ferreres, Orlando (2010) *Dos Siglos de Economía Argentina*, Buenos Aires: El Ateneo.
IEERAL (Instituto de Estudios Económicos sobre la Realidad Argentina y Latinoamericana) (1986) *Revista Estudios Año IX-N39-Julio/Septiembre*, pp. 103–184.

Part V
Reform and counter-reform

14 The Latin American consensus of the 1990s

The hyperinflation in Argentina at the time of the change in government from Raúl Alfonsín to Carlos Menem (1989) marked the beginning of the sharpest shift in Argentina's economic policy and its relationship with the world since the end of the Second World War.

A Peronist government made the biggest change that reversed most of the economic practices that had been introduced by Perón in the mid-1940s and remained in place, with minor modifications, for 45 years.

Until 1988, Menem was typical of the populist political leaders of the traditional parties in Argentina. The metamorphosis of his views stemmed from his ability to observe reality along with the broader evolution of economic ideology in Latin America over the preceding decades. There is no doubt that stagflation and hyperinflation opened the eyes and minds not only of Menem, but also of many other political leaders in the region.

Menem's evolution in thinking was just one of the many breakthroughs that by the end of the 1980s and the beginning of the 1990s gave rise to what I like to call 'The Latin American consensus of the 1990s'. Different from the so-called 'Washington Consensus,' it did not originate in Washington, but in the political and economic centres of the countries that suffered from stagflation and hyperinflation.

An exploration of the way in which Latin American politicians and academics participated in the ideological discussions between East and West and absorbed the lessons of their respective countries' histories helps to explain why so many Latin American leaders reached a political consensus that was very different from their earlier views.

The ideological discussion in post-war Latin America

In the aftermath of the Second World War ideological discussions in the world focused on the dichotomy of socialism versus capitalism. Naturally, this dichotomy embodied the economic aspect of the East–West confrontation that characterized the Cold War.

Latin American countries initially tried to avoid this confrontation by adopting 'The Third Position' (La Tercera Posición in Spanish) of Juan

Perón. This set of ideas would be the seed of the later Non-Aligned Countries movement, which several developing countries joined.

At the same time, in Latin America academic economic thinking moved into so-called 'structuralism' which was opposed to the 'orthodoxy' that had prevailed in previous decades.

'Structuralism' provided the intellectual support for the import substitution industrialization growth strategy (ISI) and the populist macroeconomic policies implemented by most Latin American governments from the mid-1940s through the 1980s with varying intensity.

Structuralist economic organization and policies were convenient to the political regimes that prevailed in most Latin American countries in those years: either civilian governments in corporate-state democracies or military dictatorships. For them, 'statism' was a way to accumulate and preserve political power.

In Mexico and Brazil, it was not until the eruption of the debt crisis in 1982 that strong criticism of the ISI growth strategy gained momentum. Overall, the ISI growth strategy had delivered rapid growth in both countries from 1945 to 1982. These good results were indisputable until the first oil crisis in 1973; however, the commodity crisis of the 1970s created difficulties that went unnoticed because of the availability of cheap foreign financing.

By the mid-1980s, criticism of the ISI growth strategy that began with the debt crisis became more acceptable. A comparison of Southeast Asia's and Latin America's economic performance during the period from 1965 to 1980 showed the superiority of an export-led growth strategy.[1]

In Argentina, evidence against structuralist policies were even more evident because it came from its own history. Until 1930, Argentina had maintained a standard of living that was relatively close to that of the most advanced countries in the world. Argentina reached this standard of living through vigorous international trade, infrastructure development, and an inclusive education system. However, the implementation of an ISI growth strategy coupled with populist macroeconomic policies produced a disappointing outcome. This set of policies, unlike those in Brazil and Mexico, generated a stagnant economy with persistent high levels of inflation.

Argentine think tanks such as the Instituto Torcuato Di Tella (ITDT) and the Fundación de Estudios Latinoamericanos (FIEL), and the Departments of Economics of the universities of Buenos Aires, Córdoba, Tucumán, La Plata and Mendoza, questioned the adequacy of an ISI growth strategy and populist macroeconomic policies as early as the mid-1960s. However, these views were not able to achieve a political impact until the 1980s when the Fundación Mediterránea synthesized and operationalized these views.

Supported by the Fundación Mediterránea, Yair Mundlak and I led a group of researchers who studied the Argentine case in comparison with countries with similar human and natural resource endowments such as Canada and Australia.[2] There was an obvious divergence in the economic performance of those countries after the Second World War. We concluded that a certain distortion of institutional roles that was a consequence of the trade and macroeconomic policies implemented since 1945 was responsible for Argentina's disappointing performance.

In a well-organized economy the efficient allocation of resources for the production of private goods comes from relative prices determined in competitive markets. The budget is used for financing public goods and as a tool for redistributive policies.

In Argentina, in contrast, those mechanisms of economic policy switched roles. Instead of encouraging efficient allocation of resources through market prices, the government manipulated relative prices expecting to achieve income redistribution. Conversely, the government budget instead of being a tool for income redistribution guided investment and the allocation of human capital, that is, employment.[3]

The research that we did laid the foundation for the approach of the economic team that would lead the economy in the 1990s. Borrowing an expression from Adolfo Sturzenegger (1984), I explained that Argentina's problem was neither too much capitalism as the proponents of structuralism argued nor was it too much socialism as the orthodox economists argued. The real problem was a failed combination of capitalism and socialism. We described Argentina's economy as 'capitalism without markets and socialism without plans'.

This diagnosis led us to propose a different approach to achieve sustained economic growth – a complete reorganization of the economy. In political debates we would talk about establishing 'new rules of the game'. In 1985 I published *Volver a Crecer* (Returning to Growth), as a way to spread IEERAL's and IFPRI's analysis of Argentina's maladies and their proposed possible solutions. The book's subtitle was 'Proposing new economic rules of the game for Argentina'.[4] Latin American economists and political leaders, including myself, came up with our own ideas about how to unlock investment opportunities, mobilize domestic savings, and stop perennial high inflation. We did not base our proposal on theoretical universal guidelines generated in a distant city. Rather we reached our conclusions based on research and observations of reality in our respective countries.

Even though Latin American economies had dissimilar starting points a common element was the 'the debt trap'. To get out from the debt trap Latin America needed help and most Latin American leaders looked to Washington for that assistance.

We argued that in order for help to be effective, the USA needed to support the change in the rules of the game that we proposed using mechanisms similar to those applied to rebuilding Japan and Western Europe in the aftermath of the Second World War. We also argued that, just like in the postwar period, the benefits would spread from our countries to the global economy. We believed that only through new stimuli would the world achieve higher levels of growth without unleashing inflationary pressures. The new stimuli should not stem from ever greater expansion of consumption in the

USA where saving rates were already very low, but from increased investment in Latin America.[5]

Stagflation and hyperinflation as signals of lack of 'stateness'

In an article entitled 'Market Reforms', Javier Corrales (2003) synthesizes the state of the economy before the reforms using the expression, 'increasing statism, declining stateness' and characterizes the reforms as more 'markets as a recipe for more stateness'.

Inflation, a phenomenon that in most Latin American countries evolved into stagflation and in some cases hyperinflation, has been the most obvious sign of the state's inability to run economic policy. That is the lack of 'stateness', to use Corrales' term.

To a greater or lesser extent, until the 1980s almost all economies in Latin America suffered from persistent inflation. Every time they tried to stop it, inflation reappeared but even stronger. In the 1950s and 1960s, Keynesian and Structuralist economists believed inflation resulted from an adjustment of relative prices in a context where nominal prices and wages were downwardly inflexible.

However, in the 1970s and 1980s the economic thinking began to change. Economists postulated that the main cause of persistent and accelerating inflation was fiscal deficits and distributive tensions in the economy.

By that time, Latin American economies faced two kinds of abnormalities. On the one hand, economies in Latin America functioned in such a way that expenditures and investments, which in a normal economy were private, became the responsibility of the government and were included in the budget. On the other hand, governments were unable to increase tax collections to fund the increase in spending. To make matters worse, tax systems grew more complex and included discriminatory levies that were often difficult to control.

The consequence of this double-problem was increasing budget deficits which in turn tested the capacity of the state to finance them whether through taxes or debt. When the tax collection approach proved unable to fund all the spending, and governments were unable to raise more debt, printing money was the answer. Printing money is a subtle way to collect a kind of tax that does not need approval by the legislature – the inflation tax. In short, 'socialism without a plan' does not find a way to fund its disequilibria other than by imposing a tax on people's monetary holdings, including savings and wages.

The ensuing distributive tension in the economy that originated in the absence of markets prompted the government to intervene on a case-by-case basis, deciding the level of the most important prices in the economy such as wages, public utilities' prices, and the rate of exchange. When one sector's income lagged behind, the government tried to compensate by granting subsidized credit, which in turn required printing more money.

Inflation was higher not only due to the printing of money, but also due to abrupt currency devaluations. Usually, a fixed exchange rate accompanied by expansionary fiscal and monetary policies ends in an abrupt devaluation. At the later stages of this process, the inflationary tax becomes the main source of state financing given private sector disequilibria. This occurs when an economy operates as 'capitalism without markets' as was the case in Latin America in the 1970s and 1980s.

During those years, special circumstances made credit abundant. Fiscal disequilibria and private sector financial needs were satisfied with increasing debt. Regional economies could avoid resorting to printing money to meet their obligations for a while. Nonetheless, eventually distributive tension between debtors and creditors is unleashed and inflation reappears, in this case reducing the value of monetary assets and debts, thus causing a massive wealth transfer from creditors to debtors.

Besides causing an arbitrary redistribution of income and wealth, inflation also discourages voluntary savings and financial investment within the country's borders. When inflation turned erratic and hyperinflation loomed, governments were unable to handle not only the public budget, but also relative prices. None of the usual economic tools resulted in the desired outcome. Hyperinflation is the most dramatic expression of a state's inability to run an economy. When hyperinflation appears 'stateness' has vanished.

Persistent and erratic high inflation hinders economic performance because it negatively affects investment and the productivity of the factors of production. Therefore, in Latin America, the usual outcome is not a combination of economic expansion and accelerating inflation as is very commonly the case in mature economies. On the contrary, the phenomenon that spread across the region was so-called 'stagflation' which is the simultaneous presence of recession and inflation.

In the face of stagflation and hyperinflation, Latin American leaders were finally convinced that deep economic reforms were necessary. Economists advising these political leaders envisioned a set of reforms aimed at reorganizing the economy, introducing competition through properly functioning markets, and improving the state's control over the economy via fiscal balance and transparency. This was the source of the 1990s reforms in every Latin American country in response to stagflation or, worse, hyperinflationary chaos.

In the mid-1970s Chile stopped stagflation (after Salvador Allende's failed socialist experiment) with a programme of economic reforms that became a model for the rest of Latin America. Chile implemented its reforms under the authoritarian government of General Pinochet. Bolivia was the first country that fought hyperinflation with a plan decided upon and implemented by a democratic regime. Hyperinflation exploded in 1985 when former President Hernán Siles Suazo was about to end his term in office. Victor Paz Estenssoro's administration with Gonzalo Sánchez de Lozada as its minister of planning, decided to implement a set of economic reforms that sought to stabilize the Bolivian economy once and for all.

Chile as a model

By the mid-1980s, countries in Latin America suffering from stagflation or on the verge of hyperinflation considered Chile an emerging regional model. Scholars have studied the Chilean experiment extensively during the last quarter of the 20th century and evaluated the merits and costs of the Chilean experience. Today there are numerous books and papers that analyse, describe, and explain Chile's economic process in that period in great detail. No other period and country in Latin America has drawn the attention of academia more than Chile in the late 20th century with the possible exception of Argentina from 1870 to 1913.

Chile during the last 40 years and Argentina at the turn of the 19th century have attracted scholars' attention for the same reason. First Argentina and then Chile were rare economic and social development success stories in Latin America. And there is one distinctive factor that these two success stories share.

In Argentina by the end of the 19th century and in Chile by the end of the 20th century, what stands out is the ability of the state to properly organize and govern the economy.

The main reason for Argentina's success by the turn of the 19th century was not just the adoption of an export-led growth strategy. Almost every country in Latin America adopted that model at the same time. The success came because, in addition to supporting export-led growth, the state implemented and sustained a particular set of social policies that had a direct impact on economic growth. The policies affected every aspect of economic life in the country: from immigration policies aimed at attracting people and capital to the country to the development of transport and communication infrastructure to the creation of an education system. These policies were a true milestone in Argentina's development process. Through these policies Argentina took full advantage of the opportunities that globalization offered at that time.

Similarly, Chile opened its economy and implemented free-market reforms removing government obstruction in markets to allow prices to be set freely and under competitive conditions. However, these policy changes alone do not explain Chile's success. Chile's success is better explained by the state's ability not only to establish new rules of the game but more importantly to credibly sustain them using a crucial feedback loop. After the reforms of the late 1970s, Chileans only introduced marginal changes that improved the new rules of the game, they never tried to go back to the old economic 'dis-order'.

From 1964 to 1990, according to Martínez and Díaz (1996), three different political elites led Chile, each of which developed its own programme of radical reforms. The 'Revolution in Liberty' led by Eduardo Frei, the 'Peaceful Road to Socialism' led by Salvador Allende, and the 'Neo-liberal Revolution' led by Augusto Pinochet were each aimed at radically changing the system.

The authors explain that these three elites ended up losing in the political arena. The socialists defeated the Christian democrats, the military defeated the socialists, and a new democratic consensus defeated the military. However, the combined actions of the three streams brought about a real capitalist revolution.

Most interestingly, the democratic administration that took over after the military dictatorship did not try to undo this revolution. On the contrary, it allowed the new rules of the game to stay in place. As a result, the economy could sustain high growth rates and society could achieve progress and enjoy higher standards of living.

Andrés Velazco (1994) explains that groups protected by the elites that had ruled the country – conservatives, Christian democrats and socialists – exerted power in a discretionary fashion. This use of power deeply affected property rights, freedom and security of the groups that were occasionally opposed to that extreme discretion. This way of doing politics led to an insurmountable crisis leading up to the military coup of 1973. Every sector that had benefited from the state's arbitrary use of power also suffered significant losses when they lost power. Therefore, when the technocrats that advised the military proposed a complete overhaul of the economy and set 'rules' which in turn would significantly reduce the arbitrary use of power in economic policy, every sector ended up endorsing the proposal. By accepting the new strategy these groups and elites would forego the benefits of the arbitrary use of power; but, by the same token they were protected against losses following abrupt changes in government leadership.

Economists across Latin America interested in public policy followed the Chilean reform and compared it with the situation in their own countries. Several of these economists were already involved in public policy discussions and policy making. Others would enter that arena soon. To many Argentinean economists the Chilean experience became a crucial model for economic reform. These economists understood the importance of 'rules versus discretion' as the cornerstone of proper economic organization. In Europe and the USA academics discussed this topic with regards to monetary policy and inflation.

The Chilean experience showed Latin America that clear rules of the game were the foundation of good economic organization. These rules should minimize the opportunities for discretion and arbitrariness. Such an organization is important not only in monetary policy but also in fiscal and trade policy and, more generally, it is important for the smooth functioning of every aspect of the economy and society.

The course of reforms in other Latin American economies

Most Latin American leaders became convinced that the region should seek macroeconomic stability and trade openness after the 1982 Mexican debt crisis fuelled a long and painful stagflation process in that country.

Mexican President De la Madrid took office in December 1982. His administration made big efforts to cut government spending and to open up the economy. Even so, in the period 1982–1987 Mexican inflation remained high and exports did not increase enough to become an engine of growth. In order to be able to generate large current account surpluses in its balance of payments, Mexico kept the domestic currency deeply undervalued, which in turn led to a very low investment rate. The continuous devaluation of the domestic currency fuelled inflation which remained persistently high. A high exchange rate of pesos per dollar would supposedly foster exports; however, the low investment rate along with insufficient productivity increase limited that upside. At that point, the cause behind the persistent stagflation process seemed clear. Since 1982, Mexico had been transferring as much as 5 per cent of its GDP abroad (in net terms).

Carlos Salinas succeeded De la Madrid in December 1987 and announced a stabilization plan called 'The Solidarity Pact'. It was not the standard IMF stabilization guideline. In fact, initially the IMF did not support it. On the contrary, it was a heterodox plan along the lines of those implemented in Argentina and Brazil in 1985 which by 1987 had failed to curb inflationary inertia.

There were two crucial differences that explain the Mexican Solidarity Pact success versus the Argentine Austral Plan and the Brazilian Cruzado Plan. Mexico implemented those heterodox economic policies along with prudent macroeconomic policies and far freer and more open trade policies. Lessons learned from Chile's and Bolivia's experiences indicated that those two ingredients were fundamental to the sustainability of stabilization policies. But those elements were absent from Argentina's and Brazil's plans.

As part of the programme, Mexico began a process of privatizing state-owned enterprises which would help it obtain the necessary resources to meet its domestic debt obligations. However, this commitment was insufficient to reverse the net transfer of resources abroad which was critical to strengthening the currency and increasing the rate of investment.

By 1985, Victor Paz Estenssoro's administration in Bolivia had to accompany its reform programme with the suspension of debt payments as recommended by Jeffrey Sachs and scholars from the indebted nations in Latin America.

By that time, both Wall Street and Washington favoured debt-equity-swap schemes to rapidly and simultaneously cut external debt and foster private investment in indebted countries. Yet Mexico rejected the idea because it would fuel inflation since the Mexican Central Bank would have to issue domestic currency to swap for foreign debt.

Mexico looked for an alternative solution. It proposed a debt restructuring scheme based on external support. In 1989, the Bush administration accepted the proposal. This is the origin of the Brady Plan.

The Brady Plan produced two positive effects on the Mexican economy. First, it allowed Mexico to significantly reduce its debt burden. Second,

Mexico was able to attract foreign savings and significantly reduce net capital outflows. Thus, the transfer of resources abroad dropped from the equivalent of 5.7 per cent of GDP in 1988 to close to zero in 1989.

This trend strengthened over the following years and by 1994 inflows of foreign savings had reached 8 per cent of GDP. Opening the economy to foreign trade and prudent macroeconomic policies during the De la Madrid Administration along with successful debt restructuring during Salinas' first year in office were key contributors to restoring confidence in the Mexican economy. Consequently, the foreign currency drain stopped and Mexican authorities could curb the stagflation inertia that had predominated during the period 1982–1987.

Salinas' initial success against stagflation made it possible to amass the political and public support required to undertake the economic reform agenda pursued later on. His initial success drew the attention of the USA which began to see Mexico as a potential crucial economic and trade partner, a vision that some years later resulted in the historic North Atlantic Free Trade Agreement (NAFTA).

The Latin American consensus and US leadership

US leadership at the end of the 1980s and early 1990s was clear in three key decisions by the George H. W. Bush administration. First, the joint work of the USTR (the United States Trade Representative) and the Cairns Group to include agriculture in the Uruguay Round of the GATT negotiations; second, the Brady Plan, which allowed Latin American countries an orderly way to restructure their debts with a haircut on principal and reduction in interest; and third, the Initiative for the Americas, which ultimately led to NAFTA.

Most Latin American leaders, even those from different political parties, welcomed this change of Washington policy towards Latin America. They even drew a parallel between this new approach to Latin America and the Marshall Plan, which the USA launched after the Second World War to rebuild Europe. They also thought that it was a smart way to coordinate with Japan's initiative called the 'Miyasawa Plan'.

None of the Latin American leaders in power interpreted these US initiatives as a way to impose any particular economic 'recipe' suggested by Washington. On the contrary, most of these leaders were proud to have designed and implemented the economic reforms themselves and rightly so. Reforms were a clear and eloquent response to stagflation and hyperinflation problems that had marred the economies of their respective countries.

Carlos Salinas de Gortari in Mexico, Carlos Menem in Argentina, Fernando Color de Mello and Fernando Henrique Cardoso in Brazil, Alberto Fujimori in Perú, Gonzalo Sánchez de Lozada and Jaime Paz Zamora in Bolivia, César Gaviria in Colombia, Patricio Aylwin in Chile, Luis Alberto Lacalle and Julio Sanguinetti in Uruguay, Andrés Rodríguez and Juan Carlos Wasmosy in Paraguay, Carlos Andrés Pérez in Venezuela and Sixto Durán

Ballén and Alberto Dahik in Ecuador, all adhered to the 'Latin American Consensus' of the 1990s.

The George H. W. Bush and Clinton administrations' support for the economic reforms undertaken in Latin America helped facilitate commercial and financial integration of Latin American economies into the global economy. Most Latin American leaders, even in the aftermath of the Mexican and Brazilian crises of 1995 and 1999, continued to think of these policies in very positive terms up until the Argentine crisis of 2001–2002.

After the Argentine crisis, several Latin American countries engaged in policies inspired in the 'Foro do São Paulo' that were denominated by President Hugo Chávez of Venezuela as 'twenty-first-century Socialism'. Mexico, Chile, Colombia, Peru, Uruguay and Paraguay continued to support the economic policies of the Latin American Consensus. Venezuela and Argentina abandoned the consensus. Brazil, Ecuador and Bolivia went back to highly interventionist policies, while keeping some macroeconomic discipline.

Notes

1 See Table 1.2 in Edwards (1995), chapter 1, page 4. See also, Cavallo and Serebrisky (2016), Chapter 2, page 28.
2 We conducted the research in the Research Institute of Fundación Mediterránea (Instituto de Estudios Económicos sobre la Realidad Argentina y Latinoamericana—IEERAL) located in Córdoba, Argentina, and the International Food Policy Research Institute (IFPRI) located in Washington DC.
3 The article entitled 'The Argentina that Could Have Been', authored by Domingo Cavallo, Roberto Domenech and Yair Mundlak presents a synthesis of findings of the research group led by Yair Mundlak in IEERAL and IFPRI.
4 There is no English translation; however, a very short synthesis of my thesis appears in the chapter 'Three Views on Restoring Growth', from the book *Inflation Stabilization: The Experience of Israel, Argentina, Brazil, Bolivia and Mexico*, edited by Bruno et al. (1988).
5 Our views did draw on conventional Macroeconomic Theory and the recent developed Open Economy Macroeconomics, but these were simply tools for the analysis.

References

Aspe Armella, Pedro (1993) *Economic Transformation, the Mexican Way*, Cambridge, MA and London: MIT Press, Chapter 1, pp. 1–60.

Bosworth, Barry P., Dornbusch, Rudiger and Laban, Raul (eds) (1994) *The Chilean Economy: Policy Lessons and Challenges*, Washington, DC: The Brookings Institution, Chapter 8, pp. 379–429.

Bruno, Michael, Di Tella, Guido, Dornbusch, Rudiger and Fischer, Stanley (eds) (1988) *Inflation Stabilization: The Experience of Israel, Argentina, Brazil, Bolivia and Mexico*, Cambridge, MA and London: MIT Press, Part VI, pp. 395–407.

Cavallo, Domingo, F. (1984) *Volver a Crecer*, Buenos Aires: Planeta Argentina.

Cavallo, Domingo F. (1992) 'Economic Reorganization as a Prerequisite to Growth', in *Policies for Long Run Economic Growth*, A Symposium Sponsored by the Federal Reserve Bank of Kansas City, Jackson Hole, Wyoming, 27–29 August.

Cavallo, Domingo (1996) 'Lessons from the Stabilization Process in Argentina, 1990–1996', in *Achieving Price Stability*, A Symposium Sponsored by the Federal Reserve Bank of Kansas City, Jackson Hole, Wyoming, 29–31 August.

Cavallo, Domingo F. (2003) *Argentina and the IMF during the two Bush Administrations*, Robert F. Kennedy Lecture Series, David Rockefeller Center for Latin American Studies, Harvard University, 5 November.

Cavallo, Domingo and Cottani, Joaquin (1998) 'Argentina's Convertibility Plan and the IMF', *AEA Papers and Proceeding*, 87(2).

Cavallo, Domingo F., Domenech, Roberto and Mundlak, Yair (1992) *The Argentina that Could Have Been. The Costs of Economic Repression*, San Francisco, CA: International Center for Economic Growth.

Cavallo, Eduardo and Serebrisky, Tomás (eds) (2016) *Saving for Development: How Latin America and the Caribbean Can Save More and Better*, Washington, DC: Inter-American Development Bank.

Corrales, Javier (2002) 'The Politics of Argentina's Meltdown', *World Policy Journal*, 19(3), 29–42.

Corrales, Javier (2003) 'Market Reforms', published as Chapter 4 in Jorge I. Dominguez and Michael Shifter (eds), *Constructing Democratic Governance in Latin America*, Baltimore, MD and London: The John Hopkins University Press, 2nd edn.

Dornbusch, Rudiger and Werner, Alejandro (1994) 'Mexico: Stabilization, Reform and No Growth', *Brooking Papers on Economic Activity*, 1, pp. 253, 303.

Edwards, Sebastian (1995) *Crisis and Reform in Latin America, from Despair to Hope*, New York: Published for the World Bank by Oxford University Press.

Martínez, Javier and Díaz, Álvaro (1996) *Chile: The Great Transformation*, Washington DC and Geneva: The Brookings Institution and the UN Research Institute for Social Development, Chapter 5, pp. 130–141.

Naim, Moises (1999) 'Fads and Fashion in Economic Reforms: Washington Consensus or Washington Confusion?' International Monetary Fund, Conference on Second Generation Reforms, Washington, DC, 8–9 November.

Rodrik, Dani (2002) 'Feasible Globalization', NBER Working Paper, No. 9129. http://www.nber.org/papers/w9129.pdf.

Rubin, Robert E. and Weisberg, Jacob (2003) *In an Uncertain World: From Wall Street to Washington*, New York: Random House; Chapters 1, 9 and 10, pp. 1–38 and 243–297.

Sturzenegger, Adolfo (1984) 'Mercado, plan, crecimiento, estabilización en Argentina', *Ensayos Económicos*, No. 31, Septiembre, Banco Central de la República Argentina.

Velazco, Andrés (1994) 'The State and Economic Policy: Chile 1952–1992' in B. Bosworth, R. Dornbusch and R. Labin (eds) *The Chilean Economy: Performance and Prospects*, Washington, DC: The Brookings Institution.

Williamson, John (ed.) (1990) *Latin American Adjustment: How Much Has Happened?* Washington, DC: Institute for International Economics.

Yerguin, Daniel and Stanislaw, Joseph (1998) *The Commanding Heights: The Battle between Government and the Marketplace that is Remaking the Modern World*, New York: Simon & Schuster.

15 Menem and De la Rúa

In 1988 Carlos Saul Menem, then governor of Province of La Rioja, competed as a pre-candidate for the presidency in the open presidential primaries of the Peronist Party, with Antonio Cafiero, then governor of the Province of Buenos Aires. La Rioja is a tiny province in the foothills of the Andes Mountains with fewer than 300,000 inhabitants, while Buenos Aires is the largest province with more than 11 million inhabitants that surrounds the capital city of Buenos Aires.

At that time, Cafiero was the leader of the Peronist Party and had served as a minister under Perón twice (in the 1950s and in the 1970s), and had the support of 17 of the 19 Peronist governors and most of the labour leaders. Argentina's economic and intellectual establishment, not exactly sympathetic to Peronism, saw Cafiero as an acceptable candidate for the presidency, but they were scared by Menem who liked to dress and act like Facundo Quiroga, the traditional federal strongman from La Rioja in the times of Rosas.

On economic matters, Cafiero advocated the traditional import substitution and populist macroeconomic policies that were not that different from those that Alfonsín continued to apply in spite of the efforts of Sourrouille's economic team to introduce reforms. As governor of the Province of Buenos Aires, Cafiero tried to support Alfonsín's policies even more than the governor of the Province of Córdoba, Eduardo Angeloz, who was the natural candidate for the presidency from the Radical Party.

Angeloz had already started to campaign with language that was quite critical of Alfonsín's policies and not much different from that of Alvaro Alsogaray, the natural candidate of the economically liberal UCeDé (the acronym for the Unión del Centro Democrático). Angeloz had announced that Roberto Aleman, who like Alsogaray had been one of the economic ministers of President Frondizi, would be his economic minister if he won the presidency.

At the beginning of Alfonsín's government, Menem was the only Peronist that supported Alfonsín in accepting the Pope's decision over the conflict with Chile in the Beagle Channel. Since 1987, however, he had strongly opposed Alfonsín's economic policies in line with the arguments Guido De Tella and I made in the House of Representatives. Cafiero, a close friend of Di Tella, did not feel comfortable with our opinion. He believed that we were implicitly criticizing the traditional Peronist economic policies. Menem, however, did not care. His intuition was in line with our criticism.

In a few conversations I had with Menem before the primaries, I realized that not only was he paying attention to our criticism of Alfonsín's economic policies, but that he was also listening to Alsogaray's proposal for a more liberal economic order. Menem was not explicit in describing the economic ideas that would inspire his future government. He just promised a big change that would improve people's happiness.

Even though I frequently spoke at events attended by members of the economic and intellectual establishment and was consulted on what could happen if Menem were elected, I realized that my arguments rarely convinced the audience.

Menem's simplicity, common sense and charisma convinced most of the people that he would sincerely try to do well. Through that approach he won the Peronist Party's nomination in the primaries and then the presidency in the general election.

Differently from Perón, Frondizi, Illia and Alfonsín (and, of course, all the presidents during the military regimes), Menem reached power without the strong support of any established political structure, economic, labour or military entity. There is no doubt that he was the spontaneous choice of the people.

Peronism, while the ruling philosophy from 1946 to 1955 and again from 1973 to 1976, had introduced the isolationist and interventionist policies that had brought about Argentina's long-lasting inflationary problem. Political analysts find it difficult to explain how Carlos Menem, who presented himself as a Peronist, became the leader that transformed Argentina's relationship with the world, eliminated inflation, and reorganized its economy as one of the most open and liberal among developing countries.

His critics, within and outside of Peronism, argue that Menem changed his original ideology to please the government of the USA. This interpretation is wrong. In the specific case of Menem, to understand his transformation it is necessary to realize that Menem, and perhaps like only Perón and Frondizi among the presidents of the previous six decades, was a conscientious observer of what was going on in the rest of the world and particularly Latin America. The rest of the presidents that governed Argentina between 1930 and 1989 were inward-looking military leaders or politicians that did not pay much attention to world events.

Moreover, in the late 1940s Perón had not predicted the re-emergence of a global economic order after Bretton Woods, but Menem did predict that by the end of the 1980s the revitalization of globalization would offer opportunities to Argentina. Frondizi had also understood the international situation of his time and had made the right predictions about the future course of events; but, domestic military conflicts prevented him from completely implementing his plan. Menem was lucky and able enough not only to decide upon, but also implement his strategy during more than ten years.

Politics from 1989 to 2001

Menem took the oath as president in July 1989, completed the term of Alfonsín who had resigned five months before the end of his term, and then governed his own six-year term. In 1993, at the peak of his popularity, Menem convinced Alfonsín to support his call for a Constitutional Assembly that should discuss constitutional reform. The Constitutional Assembly approved the reform in 1994 and it shortened the term of the Presidency to four years but allowed for two consecutive terms. This meant that Menem could run in 1995 for a second term of four years.

In spite of the fact that the election took place in the middle of the recession caused by the Tequila Crisis he won a second presidential election in 1995.

In 1997, Menem's closest friends started to lobby for a decision of the Supreme Court that would allow Menem to run for a third term because the first six-year term corresponded to the constitution before the reform. In fact, Eduardo Angeloz, the governor of Córdoba, won a similar ruling from the Superior Tribunal of Córdoba that allowed him to serve as governor for three consecutive terms. In 1997 and 1998, there was a wild competition between Menem and Eduardo Duhalde, the governor of the Province of Buenos Aires, for the nomination for the 1999 election. The competition ended when the Supreme Court ruled that Menem could not run for a third term.

For a while, it seemed that there would be a competition between Duhalde and Senator Ramón 'Palito' Ortega, a very popular former governor of Tucumán. Ortega had been a firmer supporter of the Convertibility Plan than Duhalde. However, as in the earlier times, rather than having open primaries, the Peronist Party decided to present a joint ticket: Duhalde for the presidency and Ortega for the vice-presidency.

Duhalde started the campaign by saying that 'the economic model was exhausted'. He did not suggest abandoning convertibility; but, he did suggest that there should be a moratorium on the debt and a return to an ISI growth strategy.

The Radical Party entered into an alliance with the FREPASO (the Spanish acronym for Frente País Solidario), an offshoot of the Peronist Party that had distanced itself from Menem when, in 1990, Menem pardoned the military leaders that had been condemned for human rights violations. The Radical Party chose Fernando De la Rúa, the leader of the centre right fraction of the party and governor of the City of Buenos Aires, to compete in the primaries with Graciela Fernández Meijide, a human rights activist who had been co-founder of FREPASO. De la Rúa won the primaries and was at the top of the ticket with Carlos Alvarez, the co-leader of FREPASO, as candidate for vice-president. Fernández Meijide was the candidate for governor of the Province of Buenos Aires.

In his campaign, De la Rúa supported Menem's economic policies but distanced himself from him on social and human rights policies. The main television spot of his campaign was '*Conmigo, un peso-un dólar*' ('With me, one peso-one dollar') to reaffirm that if he were elected President, convertibility would not be at risk. His campaign advisors realized that if he attached himself to convertibility more than Duhalde, whose language created doubts, he would benefit from the popularity of the monetary regime that had defeated hyperinflation.

After leaving Menem's government, I created a new political party called Acción por la República ('Action for the Republic' in English) and was elected as a representative by the people of the City of Buenos Aires. I was convinced that neither the Peronist Party nor the Radical Party would continue to reform Argentina's society and political system towards the federal and republican values of the Constitution, the only values consistent with the economic reforms that had been introduced during Menem's tenure. The vices of traditional populist policies had infected the Peronist and the Radical parties and they were not ready to respect the principles that had inspired Juan Bautista Alberdi, the father of the National Constitution of 1853.

I decided to run as a candidate for president to have the opportunity to continue to spread my ideas and to plant the seeds for a new political space in Argentina. I chose Armando Caro Figueroa, the former Minister of Labour who had worked hard to reform the archaic labor laws as my running mate.

Polls said that I had a positive image, even higher than that of the other candidates, but voters intentionally disfavoured my candidacy because I was seen as lacking the support of an existing political structure. At the same time, the other candidates, most clearly De la Rúa, campaigned under the flag of what people saw as my main contribution to their welfare, removing the main reason that people might have voted for me. Furthermore, I felt that I had to tell people the truth and I was explicit about the efforts that the provinces and the federal government would be compelled to make in order to eliminate the fiscal deficit. I also insisted that it was necessary to continue with the reforms, especially in terms of labour laws and the system used to distribute social benefits.

I knew that I would not be elected president at this time, but I was happy with gaining a space in the House of Representatives that would be crucial for whomever won the election to assemble the necessary majority for the approval of important laws.

A few weeks before the first round of the election, the polls reported that De la Rúa was capturing more votes than Duhalde. Nestor Kirchner, who had been a strong supporter of the economic reforms while I was the economic minister and was now a sort of campaign manager for Duhalde, proposed that Peronism and Acción por la República should form an alliance to support a joint ticket, Duhalde for the presidency and me as vice-president. He tried to recreate in the collective imagination the Menem–Cavallo team that had successfully defeated hyperinflation. I rejected the proposal because it was clear that my ideas were not compatible with those of Duhalde. I was sure that the people would find De la Rúa's commitment to economic reform that I had inspired more convincing than a last minute association between Duhalde and me.

De la Rúa ultimately won the election and took the oath as the new President of Argentina in December 1999. He would have to govern with an economy in recession and facing the risk of dangerous deflation. De la Rúa exhausted his political capital in 2001 trying to fight off deflation. I exhausted mine when I accepted the role of economic minister in the middle of the crisis. Convertibility, which had been the key for Menem and me to defeat hyperinflation ten years before, was blamed for the failure to defeat deflation. After De la Rúa resigned, Eduardo Duhalde, the candidate who had lost the election in 1999, took office.

The first 18 months of Menem's government

Even though in 1989 the economic situation was horrible, with hyperinflation at its peak and a deep recession, the first strategic decision Menem made after his inauguration was not in the realm of the economy but in the foreign policy arena. Menem decided that Argentina should become a trustworthy nation to its neighbours, to the USA, to Europe, Japan, and to the extent possible, to every nation in the world.

This line of action may seem obvious but it was not. It was a profound change in Argentine politics. Argentina had had a distant and sometimes contentious relationship with the USA ever since the first Pan-American meeting in 1890. The relationship with Europe had deteriorated due to the South Atlantic War which was still unsolved because Argentina and the United Kingdom had still not signed a peace accord. As a result, we did not have diplomatic relations with the United Kingdom.

Close to home, Argentina had been on the brink of fighting a war against Chile in 1978 and still had several unresolved border disputes with that neighbour. Furthermore, Argentina and Brazil had embarked on a very expensive nuclear race with neither country having ratified the Tlatelolco Treaty that sought to prevent nuclear weapons in Latin America. On top of that, Israel's secret service disclosed that Argentina's Air Force was secretly developing a middle-range missile for export to Iraq. And, Argentine state-owned companies, after signing partnerships with Japanese investors, had stopped projects without notice or explanation.

Di Tella and I had noticed that Argentina's international situation was Menem's primary concern. Although we were both influential economists and Argentina's economy faced collapse, Menem still sought our insights on foreign policy rather than economic matters. In 1989, Menem was convinced that the changes that were taking place in the world would open a window of opportunity for progress to those nations ready to seize them. To take advantage of the opportunities he foresaw, nations would need to actively seek to be part of the globalization process.

Menem knew that at the turn of the 20th century, Argentina had enjoyed one of the ten highest per capita incomes in the world. This achievement had been possible because the country took advantage of the opportunities offered by the first wave of globalization. Naturally, we shared his vision.

Poorly advised by his first three economic ministers, Menem's decision-making process did not follow a clear order and produced limited results. By the beginning of 1991 stagflation was rampant and hyperinflation was a constant threat. Meanwhile, Menem's favourable ratings had fallen to a low 15 per cent.

Nonetheless, Argentina had made progress in international affairs. We were able to establish good relations with our neighbours Chile and Brazil and had improved our relationships with the USA, Europe and Japan. Our navy had also been involved in the Gulf War as a member of the International Task Force sponsored by the United Nations which in turn helped Menem establish a close personal relationship with George H. W. Bush.

In 1991, Menem restructured his cabinet. I was appointed minister of economy and Di Tella became minister of foreign affairs. Up to that moment, Di Tella had been Argentina's ambassador to the USA and I had served as minister of foreign affairs. At the same time Menem made the decision to lead a complete overhaul of the economy. He grasped how important it was to provide the economy with clear and foreseeable 'rules of the game' instead of decision-making processes based on discretion and in response to emergencies. We had had long talks about these issues when we travelled together while I was his foreign minister.

The diagnosis and the plan I discussed with Menem

I convinced President Menem that a reorganization of the economy was the basic prerequisite for the recovery of economic growth. A comprehensive economic and social reorganization would ensure greater transparency and better planning in the public sector and greater competition and improved performance in the private sector.

Therefore, it was necessary that the entire private sector of the economy accept the rules of the market while the public sector accepted the rules of planning and budgeting.

Argentina had to advance towards an economy of clear and simple rules that were as automated as possible in order to create a situation where private initiative and entrepreneurial capacity could fully emerge. In order to reach this objective, a reorganization of the public sector, a reallocation of business activities to the private sector, and a more efficient tax administration were indispensable.

When I explained my ideas to Menem and outlined the plan of reforms, I drew heavily from the experiences of Chile, Bolivia and Mexico. Chile was an excellent example of openness, privatization and deregulation. Bolivia, in turn, was a very good case study for monetary policy because, like Argentina,

194 Reform and counter-reform

the country had suffered from hyperinflation that ended up in a *de facto* dollarization of the economy. Finally, Mexico received support from the USA to restructure its external debt at a 35 per cent discount.

After our conversations and the experience of the first year and a half in office, Menem became convinced that the policies needed to restore sustainable growth and improve the standard of living were:

- Trade liberalization, including the elimination of taxes on exports, the reduction and simplification of import duties, the elimination of non-tariff barriers on imports, the simplification of related paperwork requirements, the elimination of restrictions and discriminatory treatment of foreign investment, and the encouragement of advanced technology transfer.
- Reform of the state and recreation of a market economy based on a substantial reduction in public expenditure and the fiscal deficit. Rapid and effective progress in the privatization of state companies; the elimination of controls on prices, wages, interest rates and foreign exchange transactions; and the elimination of a complex network of subsidies and hidden taxes that distorted the operations of a market economy.
- Reform of fiscal and tax policies to simplify the tax system, reorganize tax administration, and substantially reduce non-social expenditure by the federal government.
- Reaching agreements with the IMF to pave the way towards accession to a Brady Plan restructuring of the debt with commercial banks.

Menem's intuition and Argentine economic history suggested that these reforms would be politically difficult. Rogelio Frigerio, Alvaro Alsogaray, and Roberto Aleman as ministers of President Frondizi; Adalbert Krieger Vasena and Jose María Dagnino Pastore as ministers of President Onganía; Alfredo Martínez de Hoz as a minister of President Videla; and Sourrouille as a minister of President Alfonsín had attempted to implement some of these reforms, but all of them encountered strong opposition and ultimately insurmountable obstacles.

Even the timid and partial reforms that Menem had attempted during his first year and a half in office had encountered similar opposition and demonstrated that the reforms would become impossible unless the government found a way to convince the people that they were essential to improving their own well-being.

Ultimately, the key was the monetary reform that would defeat hyperinflation and deliver sustainable price stability. An immediate success against hyperinflation would secure the support of the public and the political leaders that the government needed. We would then need to use this support wisely and quickly to bring about the reforms that would offer Argentina a long period of sustained economic growth.

The Convertibility Plan

I assumed office as the economic minister on 31 January 1991 with responsibility not only for finance but also for trade, agriculture, industry, mining, energy, transportation and communications. Menem accepted the view that the government needed a team prepared to work in a coherent way and with clear leadership. The first year and a half year in power had convinced him that the appointment of people that had never worked together in positions that required teamwork was a recipe for failure. I could appoint secretaries and undersecretaries that had already worked with me either in research or in the government.

Inflation had accelerated in January and was projected to be even higher by February as the price of the dollar had jumped from 5,000 australes to close to 10,000 in just a few days. People feared that the economy was again on the brink of hyperinflation.

I decided to let the peso float after paying cash for all the short-term debt of the treasury with resources provided by the Central Bank. The exchange rate stabilized at 10,000 australes per dollar and, by coincidence, the monetary base was quite close to 10,000 times the dollar amount of foreign reserves in the Central Bank. I concluded that we were ready to implement a new monetary regime.

On 14 March, Menem submitted to Congress the draft of the Convertibility Law. On 28 March the House and the Senate approved the law. It took effect on 1 April 1991.

The Convertibility Law created a new monetary system based on the peso which was now convertible to dollars on a one-to-one basis and was fully backed by foreign reserves. The new monetary system was similar to that of the initial decades of the 20th century, but, in addition to making the peso convertible into dollars, it secured a right that Argentines had demanded: the right to use foreign currency, in particular the US dollar, to protect their savings and as the currency for medium- and long-term contracts.

The Convertibility Law originated as Common Law in a country with a Napoleonic Law tradition. Indeed, the law owed its initial popularity[1] to the fact that it ruled according to already established customs of the people.

The inflation rate went down immediately. In April 1991 inflation fell to 2.9 per cent per month as compared to 27 per cent in January. It continued to go down and stabilized at less than 0.5 per cent per month for more than ten years. Figure 15.1 shows the evolution of the monthly rate of inflation from a year before the Convertibility Plan launched until December 2001.

All the previous stabilization plans, starting with that of Perón and Gómez Morales in 1952 and up until the Plan Austral of Alfonsín and Sourrouille in 1985, had failed to reach and maintain inflation rates below 25 per cent per year. Table 15.1 shows that only in the case of the Frondizi–Alsogaray Stabilization and Development Plan of 1959 did the inflation rate during the 10 years after the start of the plan stay below the initial one, but even in this case the inflation continued to be around 25 per cent per year.

196 *Reform and counter-reform*

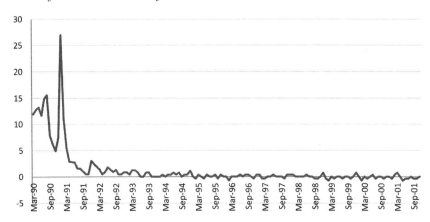

Figure 15.1 Monthly inflation rate from March 1990 to December 2001 (percentage by month)
Source: authors' own calculations, based on material originally published in Ferreres (2010).

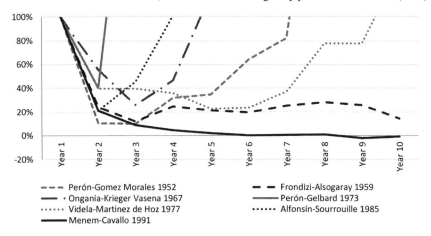

Figure 15.2 Course of the inflation rate after launching of the stabilization
Note: equalizing all rates at 100% the initial year of plan.
Source: authors' own calculations, based on material originally published in Ferreres (2010).

Figure 15.2 shows that in the case of the plan launched by Videla and Martinez de Hoz in 1977, the inflation rate surpassed the initial rate in the ninth year and in none of the eight previous years did the annual inflation rate fall below 100 per cent. In the case of the plan that Perón and Gomez Morales launched in 1952, the rate of inflation surpassed the initial rate in year seven. The plan launched by Onganía and his Minister Krieger Vasena maintained the inflation rate below the initial rate for only four years, the Plan Austral launched by Alfonsín and Sourrouille in 1985 for three years, and the plan of Perón and Gelbard in 1973 maintained an inflation rate below the initial one for only two years.

Table 15.1 Course of annual inflation rate in the years after launching the stabilization plans (in percentage per year)

Period	Perón–Gomez Morales 1952	Frondizi–Alsogaray 1959	Onganía–Krieger Vasena 1967	Perón–Gelbard 1973	Videla–Martínez de Hoz 1977	Alfonsín–Sourrouille 1985	Menem–Cavallo 1991
Year 0	37	32	32	59	183	688	1,344
Year 1	39	114	29	60	444	385	84
Year 2	4	27	16	24	176	82	18
Year 3	4	14	8	183	176	175	7
Year 4	12	28	14		160	388	4
Year 5	13	24	35		101	4,924	2
Year 6	25	22			105		0
Year 7	32	29			165		0
Year 8	114	32			344		1
Year 9		29			344		-2
Year 10		16			627		-1

Source: authors' own calculations, based on material originally published in Ferreres (2010).

Several differences between the Convertibility Plan and its predecessors explain why inflation almost disappeared as a problem during the 1990s while it had been so persistent during the previous 45 years. The main difference was that the Convertibility Plan did not simply peg the peso to the dollar as had been the case in all the previous stabilization plans. Instead, it introduced a comprehensive monetary reform. The reform consisted of the creation of a convertible peso and the legalization of the use of the dollar and any other convertible currency in any kind of transaction or contract.

Another important difference is that the Convertibility Plan let all prices be set freely in competitive markets, eliminating all previous price controls and liberalizing foreign trade. The drastic disinflation came from a complete elimination of inflationary expectations which was the consequence of reassuring the public that there would be no money printed to finance any government budget deficit. The obligatory backing of the peso by an equivalent amount of dollars and the competition of the peso with the dollar as a means of exchange and a store of value reassured the people that the Central Bank could not print money to create credit for the government and the private sector.

Many scholars think of the Convertibility Law that fixed the peso to the dollar as a 'Currency Board'. I explained on several occasions that the peg was only temporary.[2] The Convertibility Law set a cap on the exchange rate of pesos per dollars but it did not set a floor. Consequently, the peso could have floated and appreciated at times of strong capital inflows. This characteristic created a natural exit mechanism from the fixed exchange rate regime without abandoning the convertibility system and, at the same time, maintained the enforceability of contracts made in foreign currencies.

To summarize, convertibility rather than the fixed exchange rate was the permanent rule the Argentinean economy was in need of. What was important for the correct functioning of the economy was the freedom to choose a currency. During the initial phase, the Currency Board that backed all pesos with dollars at a fixed exchange rate was necessary to restore people's confidence in the peso. However, when capital inflows became large the Currency Board became unnecessary because the peso would have become a trusted currency due to responsible management of an independent Central Bank. Unfortunately, the opportunity of having convertibility without a fixed exchange rate was lost in 1997, and after the Russian and Brazilian crises it was no longer an option.

Convertibility and the IMF during the 1990s

In April 1991, the IMF still had not given its support to the Convertibility Plan and had not granted Argentina a standby loan. Three months later, it changed its position and gave significant support, which incidentally, was a key factor in implementing the Brady Plan on Argentinean debt. Japan followed suit and gave Argentina its support by means of granting another loan.

In 1994, Argentina decided to decline the use of the last two disbursements of the extended facilities loan that the IMF had granted to help finance the country's Brady Plan. Even so, in 1995 the IMF was willing to make those disbursements and provide additional financing to offset the consequences of the Tequila effect on our economy. Hence, we were able to demonstrate that a country can achieve a significant adjustment in the current account of the balance of payments and, at the same time, maintain the value of the domestic currency. From 1994 and 1995, the current account deficit went down by 3 per cent of GDP.

Even though Argentina had a rigid monetary system, its economy was flexible enough to adjust to external shocks. In the face of this evidence, the IMF came up with its theory of 'two corners' with respect to the exchange rate system. The argument says that either a clean floating exchange rate system or a strong peg will work, but that intermediate exchange rate systems are crisis prone.

Export performance

Simultaneous with the implementation of the Convertibility Law, we eliminated taxes on agriculture exports, reduced import duties, and removed quantitative restrictions on imports.

These changes in commercial policies were meant to offer local producers domestic terms of trade that were even more favourable than foreign terms of trade, particularly in the years around 1991 and after 1998 when export prices deteriorated. In this way the commercial policy reform consolidated the trend towards the elimination of the anti-export bias that had started with the Plan Austral in 1985 and in some years actually gave extra incentives to export activities to compensate for adverse effects in the exports markets. The anti-export bias reflected in the significantly lower domestic terms of trade compared with the foreign terms of trade between 1973 and 1984 had discouraged exports throughout the 1980s. In addition, in the years when the bias disappeared the macroeconomic instability discouraged investment. During the 1990s, when the commercial policy reform accentuated the incentive to produce exportable goods the convertibility plan provided macroeconomic stability and encouraged investment. Therefore, the joint effects of commercial policy and monetary reforms helped increase exportable agricultural and industrial production. Figure 15.3 shows the evolution of domestic and foreign terms of trade.

The comparison of export performance shown in Figure 15.4 clearly demonstrates that the rate of growth of exports increased significantly more in the 1990s than in the 1980s. The most impressive increase happened in exports of primary products, but the increase was also important for industrial products.

Figure 15.5 shows that during the 1990s export performance in Argentina was similar to that of Chile and almost 30 per cent greater than that of Brazil.

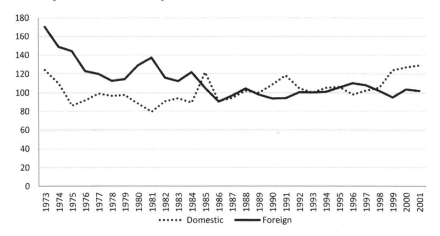

Figure 15.3 Domestic and foreign terms of trade 1973–2001 (1990=100)
Source: authors' own calculations, based on material originally published in Ferreres (2010).

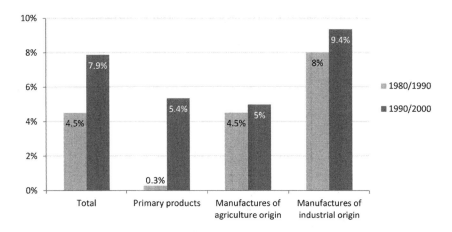

Figure 15.4 Comparative export performance, 1980/1990 and 1990/2000
Note: annual rate of growth of value of exports in current dollars.
Source: authors' own calculations, based on material originally published in Ferreres (2010).

Investment

The most important effect of the Convertibility Law besides eliminating inflation was fostering investment. For the first time in many years, national savings were channelled towards investment through the financial system. This had not happened before because saving and lending in foreign currencies was forbidden or severely restricted.

Latin American consensus of the 1990s 201

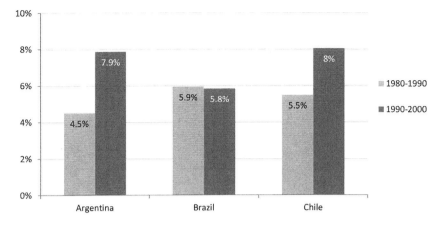

Figure 15.5 Comparative exports performance, Argentina, Brazil and Chile
Note: annual growth of value of exports 1980–1990 and 1990–2000.
Source: authors' own calculations, based on material originally published in World Development Indicators, World Bank.

When foreign investors realized that Argentineans were investing in their own country they started to evaluate direct and financial investments that they had not previously considered. This process was encouraged by a deep deregulation of the economy and the privatization of inefficient state-owned corporations. The deregulation and the privatization process created investment opportunities for the private sector that until that moment had not existed.

The largest investments went into the energy, transportation, communications, storage and commercialization, financial services, mining, agriculture and manufacturing sectors. This would not have happened if the Convertibility Law had not protected property rights.

The comparison between the average annual per capita investment in constant 1995 US dollars in Argentina and Brazil demonstrates that the increase in investment was higher in Argentina (see Table 15.2). In spite of the Plan Real in Brazil, financial intermediation continued along the lines that it had in previous decades and as a result there was not a significant increase in the availability of domestic and foreign financing for investment.

Table 15.2 Rate of growth of per capita investment in constant local prices (in percentage per year)

Country	1981 to 1990	1991 to 1998	Increase between the two periods
Argentina	−3.3	5.2	8.5
Brazil	−0.4	0.8	1.1
Chile	2.0	6.4	4.4

Source: authors' own calculations, based on material originally published in World Development Indicators, World Bank.

Productivity and growth

Over and above achieving stability in the early 1990s, Argentina also enjoyed four consecutive years of rapid growth, as shown in Figure 15.6. In 1995, a sudden halt in capital inflows occurred as a result of the crisis in Mexico and caused a recession, but the IMF and other financial institutions, including international private banks, provided lending of last resort and the country recovered in one year without any alteration to the rules of the game. Argentina enjoyed rapid growth again from 1996 until 1998.

GDP growth was higher in Argentina in the 1990s than in the 1980s not only because investment was higher, but also because productivity increased much more than in previous decades. This difference came from the fact that the new investment took place in a context of opening the economy to international trade, deregulation, and privatizations.

A comparison of yields for the three main crops, wheat, corn and soybeans, eith the yield for the same crops in the USA documents the improvement of productivity in agriculture. Figure 15.7 extends to 2001 the comparison already presented in Figure 9.3.

It is not easy to find similar clear indicators of productivity increase for the other sectors of the economy. Nevertheless, it is possible to calculate the increase in total factor productivity using aggregate GDP, capital, and labour data. Table 15.3, which reports this kind of computation, shows that during the 1990s productivity growth turned positive and, in Argentina, significantly so. On the other hand, in Brazil, during the 1990s productivity growth was lower than the average of the previous decades. These figures suggest that the key to explaining economic growth in Argentina during the 1990s is the growth in total factor productivity.

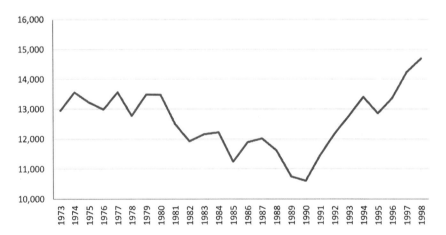

Figure 15.6 Per capita GDP 1973–1998
Note: at 1990 I. dollars converted to 2014 prices.
Source: authors' own calculations, based on material originally published in Ferreres (2010).

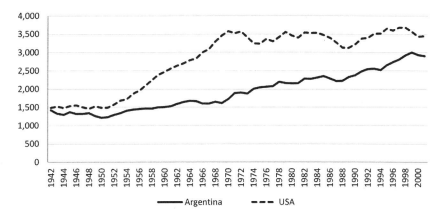

Figure 15.7 Average yield of wheat, corn and soybean 1942–2001
Note: the average yield is expressed in Kg/Ha.
Source: authors' own calculations, based on material originally published in US Department of Agriculture and Ferreres (2010).

Table 15.3 Factor productivity growth in Argentina and Brazil in the 1980s and 1990s (average annual growth in percentage)

	Argentina		Brazil	
	1980–1990	*1990–1998*	*1980–1990*	*1990–1998*
GDP	0.7	6.3	4.9	2.7
Capital stock	0.9	0.6	1.9	0.8
Labour force	0.9	1.4	2.2	1.3
Total factor productivity	−1.1	4.3	0.8	0.6

Note: Factor productivity growth calculated by subtracting from GDP growth, the growth is of capital multiplied by ⅓ and the growth of labor multiplied by ⅔.
Source: data from World Development Indicators, World Bank.

The opening up of the economy would not have been possible without the credit expansion allowed by the Convertibility Plan. Without such a credit increase the agricultural and manufacturing sectors could not have invested in new capital and technology and, without these investments, competition with foreign economies would have been impossible.

Privatization was possible because the Convertibility Law authorized medium- and long-term contracts in foreign currency. With Argentina's long history with inflation and with so many distortions created by the combination of indexing and price controls it would have been impossible to sign concession contracts with 30-year terms without the Convertibility Law. The deregulation that eliminated restrictions to competition was possible only in a context of price stability. Under high inflation, the competition would have been worse than imperfect and many markets would not have even existed.

Social security normalization and reform

During the last years of Alfonsín's administration, the social security system almost collapsed because of the accumulation of unpaid debts to pensioners that the Supreme Court recognized but which ANSES (Administración Nacional de la Seguridad Social, the Argentine social security agency) did not have resources to pay out. For many years, ANSES paid pension benefits significantly below those established in the various social security laws. A large number of retirees sued ANSES in court and after years of litigation the Supreme Court ruled that ANSES was obliged to increase the monthly benefit to comply with the law and that it also had to pay a compensation to make up for past underpayments. The annual cost of the implied adjustments represented more than 1 per cent of GDP and the debt to the retirees amounted to about US $18 billion.

After the approval of the Convertibility Law, we started to work together with the Labour and Social Security Ministries to find a solution. The Debt Consolidation Law of 1991 permitted cancelling the debt with BOCONs (Bonos de Consolidación de Deudas, debt consolidation bonds), ten-year bonds that paid a six per cent interest rate.

In September 1992, we decided to adjust the pensions of all those retirees underpaid in previous years to comply with the law and as mandated by the Supreme Court. Table 15.4 shows the effects of this decision. The number of retirees that received the minimum pension went down from 2,730,000 in December 1991 to 730,000 in December 2002 and the average pension increased from 192 pesos to 266 pesos in the same period. Of course, this decision had a fiscal cost. The social security outlays that in 1991 represented 4.1 per cent of GDP went up to 5.2 per cent of GDP in 1993 when retirees received the full benefits required by law.

Immediately after normalizing the social security system, the Ministry of Labour and Social Security submitted to Congress a draft law to reform the social security system. After a year and a half of discussion, Congress passed the reform which gave workers two alternatives: continue contributing to the old pay-as-you-go system or enter into a new capitalization system. If they chose to enter into the new pension fund system their contributions would be directed to the pension fund administrator of their choice and upon retirement they would benefit from the annuity paid for with the capitalized contributions. Most workers 50 years old and younger chose to enter in the new capitalization system.

Since the pay-as-you-go system which was responsible for the payments to the existing retirees suffered a reduction in their monthly revenues, the Treasury had to figure out how to fill the gap. The government received the necessary resources by negotiating an agreement with the provinces to earmark 15

Table 15.4 Evolution of the number of retirees and of pension benefits 1989–2001

December 31 of the year	Number of retirees	Of which receive the minimum pension	Minimum pension	Average pension	Minimum pension	Average pension	Minimum pension	Average pension
	(in thousand persons)		(in current pesos)		(in constant pesos at prices of December 2015)		(In constant dollars at the official exchange rate)	
1990	3,220	2,700	80	107	2,528	3,424	256	343
1991	3,260	2,730	150	192	2,607	3,341	261	334
1992	3,272	730	150	266	2,218	3,936	254	450
2001	3,301	725	150	280	2,018	5,240	204	559

Source: authors' own calculations, based on material originally published in Secretaría de Seguridad Social.

per cent of the revenue base of the tax sharing system for the financing of the pay-as-you-go social security system. Therefore, up until 1993, 82 per cent of the revenue for the pay-as-you-go system came from social security contributions; in 1995, once the reform was complete, the contributions provided only 70 per cent of the revenue.

No doubt, the normalization and reform of the social security system influenced both, fiscal policy and debt management after convertibility.

Fiscal Policy and debt management from 1989 to 1996

Government expenditures that had represented 31 per cent of GDP in 1989 went down to 25 per cent in 1990. Part of that reduction in government spending was the result of hyperinflation that reduced salaries and other expenses in real terms. The initial reforms by Menem's government even before launching the Convertibility Plan also contributed to fiscal consolidation. By the last months of 1989, Menem's government had already started to implement reforms authorized by the Economic Emergency Law and the Reform of the State Law, both of which were approved by Congress in August 1989 with the support of the Radical Party. When President Alfonsín decided to resign and asked Menem to replace him as president five months before his term ended, Menem conditioned his acceptance on the approval of these two laws. President Alfonsín accepted and his legislators delivered.

Fiscal consolidation could be implemented more efficiently and with less cost after the launching of convertibility because the population, happy with the sudden stabilization, understood that reform of the state and privatizations were essential to making disinflation sustainable. During the gubernatorial campaigns in the second half of 2001, the candidates of the Peronist Party, Eduardo Duhalde and Nestor Kirchner among them, promised to support the stabilization programme and to implement the reform of the state in their respective provinces. Peronism won the election in most of the provinces with a programme that was very different from what had been its traditional economic prescription.

Government expenditure went down to 23 per cent of GDP in 1991, remained at that level in 1992 and went down to 20 per cent of GDP in 1993, increased to 21 per cent in 1994 and to 22 per cent in 1995. In 1996 when I resigned as economic minister, government spending represented 21 per cent of GDP. The primary deficit disappeared and in 1992 and 1993 the primary surplus was around 2 per cent of GDP. The largest fiscal deficit showed up in 1996, but it was still half the deficit of 1990 and less than one-third of the deficit of 1989. Furthermore, the fiscal deficit in 1996 was not the result of increased spending, but a decline in revenue that originated in the recession of the previous year and the reduction in tax rates, particularly payroll tax rates designed to fight unemployment. Of course, the social security reform contributed around 1 per cent of GDP to the fiscal deficit beginning in 1995. Table 15.5 reports these fiscal figures.

Orderly debt management started in 1991 after launching the Convertibility Plan which prohibited monetary financing of the fiscal deficit. Argentina had defaulted on most of its debt in 1987 and stopped registering the arrears and the debt with suppliers, retirees, and other creditors that had or were in the process of getting judicial decisions ordering the government to pay. The amount of unregistered debt was US $25.7 billion at the end of 1989 and the total debt amounted to $89.4 billion.

The drastic reduction of the fiscal deficit plus the debt reduction obtained thanks to the restructuring under the Brady Plan and the debt consolidation scheme approved by law in 1991, allowed Argentina to keep total public debt constant in current dollars. The public debt that at the end of Alfonsín's government had been US $89.4 billion declined until 1994 thanks to the debt reductions and the fiscal surpluses. By the end of 1995 the debt was still nine billion dollars below the level of December 1989 in spite of the fiscal deficit of 1995 that resulted from the impact of the Mexican crisis. New debt financed the fiscal deficit of 1996, as had happened with all the deficits after launching convertibility, but in spite of that, total debt at the end of 1996 was the same as in December 1989 (see Table 15.6).

Bonds in circulation went up from US $8 billion in 1989 to $58.2 billion in 1996 (see Table 15.7), but most of those bonds were the consequence of the Brady Plan and the Debt Consolidation Law. The Brady Plan transformed $38.7 billion of debt with the banks at the end of 1989 into $24.1 billion of Brady Bonds. The Debt Consolidation Law had transformed $25.7 billion dollars of non-registered debt into $15.6 billion of Consolidation Bonds. The remaining bonds in circulation, $7.1 billion in the domestic market and $11.2 billion in foreign markets, represented an increase of $10.3 billion compared to the $8 billion in bonds that circulated at the end of 1989.

Table 15.5 Fiscal accounts for the consolidated public sector, 1989–1996 (in percentage of GDP)

Year	Primary expenditure	Total expenditure	Total revenue	Primary deficit (−)	Interest bill	Total deficit (−)
1989	30	31	25	−4.9	1.5	−6.4
1990	24	25	22	−2.4	1.5	−3.9
1991	21	23	22	0.6	1.8	−1.2
1992	21	23	23	1.9	2.3	−0.4
1993	18	20	20	2	1.7	0.3
1994	19	21	20	1.1	1.8	−0.7
1995	20	22	21	0.7	2.2	−1.5
1996	19	21	19	0.2	2.2	−2.01

Source: authors' own calculations, based on material originally published in Ministerio de Economía, Secretaria de Hacienda and Dirección Nacional de Coordinación Fiscal con las Provincias.

Table 15.6 Evolution of the public debt between 1989 and 1996 (in billion dollars)

	1989	1995	1996
Bilateral	7.4	11.6	10.2
Multilateral	8	15.4	16.4
Suppliers	1.5	0.4	0
Banks	38.7	1.3	1.5
Bonds	8	58.2	68.5
Non-registered	25.7	0	0
Total public debt	89.4	80.6	89.6

Source: authors' own calculations, based on material originally published in Melconian and Santángelo (1996) and Ministerio de Economía.

Table 15.7 Bonds and treasuries in circulation, 1989 and 1996 (in billion dollars)

	1989	1996	Increase
Bonds and treasuries	8	58.2	50.1
In pesos	1.9	5.9	4
Consolidation bonds	0	5.8	5.8
Others	1.9	0.1	1.8
In foreign currencies	6.2	52.3	46.1
Brady bonds	0	24.2	24.4
Consolidation bonds	0	9.8	9.8
Other bonds and treasuries	6.2	18.3	12.2
Domestic law	6.2	7.1	1
Foreign law	0	11.2	11.2

Source: authors' own calculations, based on material originally published in Melconian and Santángelo (1996) and Ministerio de Economía.

Until 1996, the issuance of new debt in the international markets had been very limited for two reasons. First, because only after the implementation of the Brady Plan at the beginning of 1993 Argentina left default behind and regained access to the international capital markets. Second, because the Tequila crisis in 1995 closed the markets for all emerging economies. Only in the second half of 1996 did investment banks start to visit Buenos Aires with offers to issue global bonds in significant amounts.

Post-Cavallo economy on automatic pilot

After being the most important minister in Menem's administration for seven years, I resigned in July 1996. After leaving, I continued to support the

Latin American consensus of the 1990s 209

reforms, but I also continued to denounce the mafias that I had fought against while in the ministry because somehow they remained protected and able to operate and interact with those in power.[3]

When I was invited to give talks or speeches the establishment's business people and intellectuals did not welcome my comments as I was considered too critical of Menem's administration. They said that I had become an ambitious politician and, for the same reason, they saw my successor at the ministry, Roque Fernandez, as a more orthodox and less politicized economist.

Roque Fernandez decided that no further reforms were necessary and as Argentina had full access to the international capital markets, he thought it was time to put the economy on 'automatic pilot'. He and Pedro Pou, the new president of the Central Bank, started to discuss going from convertibility to full dollarization of the economy.

It was the wrong idea. In fact, in 1997, when Argentina overcame the Tequila Crisis and was growing vigorously, the peso should have begun to float. At that time, the outcome would have been an appreciation of the domestic currency, and Congress could have eliminated the ceiling (one to one) without concerns. To the astonishment of all of those who confused convertibility with a fixed exchange rate system, Argentina would have had convertibility with a floating exchange rate as they have in most advanced economies including the Euro zone, Canada, Australia, Great Britain, and Singapore. The case of Singapore is particularly interesting because it dropped the fixed exchange rate without eliminating convertibility precisely through floating the currency at a time that the Singaporean currency needed to appreciate with respect to the British pound.

Why did Argentina not let the peso float in 1997 when that would have eliminated the 'sword of Damocles' of a traumatic devaluation? The reason is political. By 1997 the rivalry between Menem and Duhalde for the presidential candidacy of the Peronist Party in 1999 had intensified. Both decided to use the provincial public expenditures as a tool to win the candidacy. The appreciation of the peso would have stopped the inflow of short-term capital and, therefore, financing growing provincial expenditures would have become more difficult. Instead of focusing on consolidating the monetary system that Argentineans had regained trust in, the government facilitated the financing of increasing fiscal deficits in the provinces. This created a problem of excessive debt which made the fixed exchange rate unsustainable and, at the end, destroyed convertibility.

In spite of some critical comments of Teresa Ter-Minassian, the IMF staff member who was following Argentina, Washington was not aware of the new developments in Argentina's economy.[4] On the contrary, by the second half of 1998, Washington considered Argentina the most successful economy amongst those that had restructured their debt under the umbrella of the Brady Plan. By that time, no Washington Consensus sponsor would acknowledge that Argentina's economic reform package differed in several aspects from the ten policy recommendations that constituted the core of the so-called Washington

Consensus. On the contrary, the IMF, the World Bank and the US government pointed to Argentina as the 'best student'.

President Bill Clinton invited Menem to join him at the podium at the IMF–World Bank annual meeting that took place in Washington in October 1998 and to offer an address about his successful experience. Argentine economists would very often tell Argentina's success story in international conferences and seminars. Everyone praised Argentina's performance.

The causes of the recession that started in mid-1998

Inflation disappeared and the Argentine economy grew quickly during the 1990s. However, the economy entered into a recession in mid-1998 (see Figure 15.8).

This recession had its origin in the significant expansion of provincial expenditures financed by local banks. This policy characterized the 1997–1998 period when Eduardo Duhalde, then governor of the Province of Buenos Aires, competed with President Menem for the nomination of the Peronist Party for the next presidential election. The huge assistance provided by the banks to the provinces crowded out credit for the private sector. This phenomenon intensified after the Russian crisis when the influx of capital to the emerging economies started to decrease.

The recession became more severe and less manageable because of the devaluation of the Brazilian real in February 1999, and the sustained depreciation of the euro between 1999 and the middle of 2001. The exchange rate being pegged to the dollar did not allow the peso to depreciate as would have

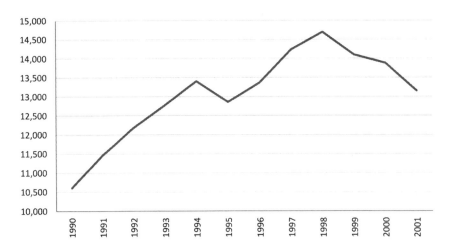

Figure 15.8 Per capita GDP 1990–2001
Note: In 1990 I. dollars converted to 2014 prices.
Source: authors' own calculations, based on material originally published in Ferreres (2010)

happened in a floating exchange rate system. Consequently, deflation was the only way for the system to re-establish long-term equilibrium of relative prices between exportable and non-tradable goods and it aggravated the recession.

An alternative to soften the deflationary impact of the depreciation of the euro and the real would have been to adopt in 1999 the dollar–euro standard instead of the original dollar standard created under convertibility. The authority ignored this possibility at that time similar to the way in which it ignored the possibility of floating in 1997. In March 2001, when I returned to the Ministry of the Economy under President De La Rúa I proposed and obtained the approval from Congress to change from the dollar standard to the dollar–euro standard. However, it was too late in the sense that the economy had already suffered the deflationary effects of the strong devaluation of the real and the depreciation of the euro.

The recession turns into a financial crisis

Since 1996, government expenditure had increased as a proportion of GDP because of increases in both primary expenses and interest on debt. Total public expenditures rose from 21.5 per cent of GDP in 1996 to 24.8 per cent of GDP in 1999. In addition to the increase in primary expenses typical of an election year, there was an increase in interest costs on the public debt (particularly that of the provinces owed to the local banking system) and lower tax revenue due to the recession. In 1999 the increase in total revenue came not from increased tax revenue, but from the sale of the shares of Yacimientos Petrolíferos Fiscales (YPF) that were still owned by the State.

In 2000, the first year of the De la Rúa government, primary spending declined from 21.6 per cent to 20.8 per cent of GDP, but the fiscal deficit increased from 2.6 per cent to 2.9 per cent of GDP because the interest bill increased from 3.2 per cent to 3.8 per cent of GDP and total revenue declined from 22.2 per cent to 21.6 per cent of GDP (see Table 15.8). Economic minister José Luis Machinea attempted to increase tax revenue by increasing the income tax rate on middle-income wage earners, but it was not enough to compensate for the one-time extraordinary revenue obtained in 1999 from the sale of YPF shares.

To understand what happened in 2001 it is necessary to look at not only the expenditure and deficit figures as a proportion of GDP (reported in Table 15.8) but also at the figures in current dollars reported in Table 15.9. The De la Rúa government continued reducing primary expenditures from US $74 billion in 1999 to $71 billion in 2000 and to $69 billion in 2001. To achieve those reductions, it had to adopt unpopular measures such as reducing public salaries and pensions. In spite of this fiscal effort, total expenditures did not go down in the same proportion because the interest bill exploded. It went from $11 billion in 1999 to $13 billion in 2000 and $14 billion in 2001.

212 *Reform and counter-reform*

Table 15.8 Fiscal accounts for the consolidated public sector, 1996–2001 (in percentage of GDP)

Year	Primary expenditure	Total expenditure	Total revenue	Primary deficit (−)	Interest bill	Total deficit (−)
1996	19.3	21.5	19.4	0.1	2.1	−2.0
1997	19.6	22.1	20.9	1.3	2.5	−1.2
1998	20.1	22.6	20.9	0.8	2.5	−1.7
1999	21.6	24.8	22.2	0.6	3.2	−2.6
2000	20.8	24.5	21.6	0.8	3.8	−2.9
2001	21.3	25.6	20.9	−0.3	4.3	−4.6

Source: authors' own calculations, based on material originally published in Ministerio de Economía.

Table 15.9 Fiscal accounts for the consolidated public sector, 1996–2001 (in billion dollars)

Year	GDP at current prices	Primary expenditure	Total expenditure	Total revenue	Primary deficit (−)	Interest bill	Total deficit (−)
1996	330	64	71	64	0	7	−7
1997	355	69	78	74	5	9	−4
1998	362	73	82	76	3	9	−6
1999	343	74	85	76	2	11	−9
2000	344	71	84	74	3	13	−10
2001	325	69	83	68	−1	14	−15

Source: authors' own calculations, based on material originally published in Ministerio de Economía.

There is no doubt that the public debt and its increasing interest cost had become the main problem of the Argentine economy. This happened because during the years 1997 to 1999, Argentina flooded the international capital markets with global bonds and treasury notes. The investment banks brought to the attention of the government many opportunities to float new bonds or implement bond exchanges that would free the collateral of the Brady bonds. In 1999, the markets were increasingly open for Argentina in spite of the Asian crisis of 1997. After the Russian crisis of 1998, the markets did not close, but the interest rate spreads went up. In spite of these unfavourable developments, Menem's government, in the middle of the 1999 electoral campaign, continued to issue bonds and implement swaps to finance the increasing fiscal deficit.

Total public debt, which had not increased between 1989 and 1996, went up from US $90 billion in 1996 to $111 billion in 1999 (see Table 15.10). The bulk of that increase came from issuing new bonds and treasuries and new bank loans, particularly to the provinces. The increase was particularly large in bonds and treasuries other than Brady and consolidated bonds. As Brady bonds went down from $24 billion to $17 billion and consolidation bonds from $11 billion to $6 billion, the new bonds and treasuries in circulation increased from $19 billion to $46 billion. Most of those bonds were issued under foreign law as the main buyers operated in the international markets.

Foreign capital started to leave the country in the last quarter of 2000. In 2001, a sudden stop in capital inflows produced illiquidity in the banking system. As the banks had lent to the provinces and the provinces had difficulty in continuing to service their debts, several banks became insolvent and neither the Central Bank nor the government had the resources to help them.

The crisis of 2001

I accepted the challenge to become the economic minister under De la Rúa in the middle of the 2001 crisis. Rumours of default were already circulating. These began the previous October after the resignation of Vice-President Carlos Alvarez and they had caused a draining of deposits from the banking system of over 789 million pesos in October 2000 and over 1 billion pesos in November 2000.

Table 15.10 Evolution of the public debt between 1996 and 2001 (in billion dollars)

	1996	1999	2001
Bilateral	10	6	4
Multilateral	16	20	32
Banks and suppliers	1	6	4
Bonds and treasuries	62	79	52
In pesos	8	11	8
Bocones	7	5	1
Others	1	5	7
In foreign currency	53	68	44
Brady	24	17	6
Consolidation bonds	11	6	2
Other bonds and treasuries	19	46	35
Domestic law	8	13	6
Foreign law	11	33	29
Guaranteed loans	0	0	42
Net public debt	90	111	135

Source: authors' own calculations, based on material originally published in Ministerio de Economía.

214 *Reform and counter-reform*

The then-Economy Minister José Luis Machinea and the Secretary of Finance Daniel Marx had managed to reverse the initial draining of deposits with the 'Blindaje' (armour in English), a financial assistance package from the World Bank and the IMF in late 2000. This package consisted of an economic programme for 2001 supported by the IMF, the International Development Bank, the World Bank and the main commercial banks.

The Blindaje programme foresaw disbursing the financial support through 2001 and 2002 under a set of conditions. To avoid default, in addition to receiving these disbursements, it would be necessary for a) the commercial banks to roll over the US $10 billion of treasury notes due in 2001 and for b) the market to provide fresh funds to pay for the capital amortization produced in 2001, an amount estimated at $7 billion.

The Blindaje reversed the deposit withdrawal until March 2001. At the beginning of that month, several signals made it clear that Argentina would not be able to meet the public spending and fiscal deficit targets that were conditions of the Blindaje. Consequently, the international financial organizations would likely withhold the disbursements scheduled for April.

Rumours of a default reappeared, which triggered a new outflow of deposits. In this context, José Luis Machinea resigned and Ricardo López Murphy moved from the Defence Ministry to the Economic Ministry. When the new minister announced his programme consisting of a fiscal reduction of 2 billion pesos for the rest of the year, there were large street protests and several members of the national cabinet, including key members of the already weakened alliance between the FREPASO and the Radical Party, resigned. All these events emphasized the negative prognosis, both political and economic.

In this context, I agreed to become the new economy minister on 20 March 2001. I was convinced that it was possible to produce the needed fiscal reduction with an orderly restructuring of the debt and, at the same time it was possible to reactivate the economy through the application of a competitiveness plan.

While all these political changes occurred, Argentina suffered the largest monthly deposit drain in its history: 5.5 billion pesos in March 2001. Until then, the biggest deposit outflow had occurred in March 1995 during the Tequila crisis when the deposit outflow had been 4.6 billion pesos.

Reversing expectations of default and avoiding the continuous draining of deposits was the toughest duty I had to face; and I confronted the challenge based on our successful handling of the Tequila crisis. At that time, in 1995, from the Economy Ministry and with the collaboration of Roque Maccarone, then Secretary of Finance, we were able to create an economic programme that won the support of international financial organizations and commercial banks and allowed us to meet the financial crisis in a sustainable way.

I also had in mind the traumatic experiences of Mexico in December 1994 and Brazil in February 1999 when their decision to devalue generated or aggravated a financial crisis. I was convinced that to avoid aggravating the financial crisis we had to avoid the devaluation of the peso. Only after eliminating the fiscal deficit and restructuring the debt to push back large dollar-denominated debt repayments three or four years, could we think of letting the peso float and accept its devaluation. In addition, restructuring of the debt would avoid a disorderly debt default.

The De la Rúa–Cavallo attempt to avoid a disorderly debt default

Default means the suspension of payments on public sector debt. There is no doubt that it leads to great economic damage to creditors. Some political leaders argued that default was good for the country because it made the country's debt servicing lighter. However, this is not true for four fundamental reasons.

First, a large segment of the government's creditors is made up of Argentine savers. In their role as financial intermediaries, banks lend the deposits of the Argentine people to the public sector in the form of bonds and loans for the national and provincial governments. Therefore, when rumours about default spread, some depositors become scared and withdraw their money from the banks. Furthermore, the social security system keeps a high proportion of workers' contributions invested in government bonds. Finally, many Argentine savers hold bonds from the national government or provincial governments.

Second, external creditors do not accept the suspension of payments in a passive way and creditors take actions that restrain the recovery of credit while a state of default remains in place. It is important to bear in mind that since the 1990s the makeup of external bondholders had moved away from the traditional small number of commercial banks to a larger number of private pension funds, investment funds, and individual investors that refuse to buy bonds from a country that stops payments on its debt.

Third, the suspension of payments of the public sector causes the default of many private companies, leading to the stagnation of the productive system.

Finally, the suspension of payments raises the expectations of a depreciation of every asset of the country which leads to expectations of devaluation of the national currency. These expectations exacerbate recessive tendencies and cause a fall in tax revenue further weakening the fiscal situation and the negative expectations.

Summing up, default often ends up in devaluation and both of these create real economic and social chaos recovering from which requires considerable time.

Therefore, it was imperative to attempt to avoid default. And this is what I did as economy minister.

Throughout the nine months I was in that position, I led three negotiations with the IMF to avoid default and reverse the deposit outflow. Two of the negotiations were successful, and the last one remained unfinished when I was forced to resign. The governments that came after President De la Rúa formally declared default and devalued the currency.

First attempt: agreement with the IMF in May

As soon as I took office at the Economy Ministry, I sought to restore the Blindaje to avoid the interruption of the agreed disbursements.

As the targets on public expenditure and fiscal deficit for the first quarter of 2001 had not been fulfilled, it was necessary to take strong measures to control spending as well as to increase tax resources so that by the end of the first half we could meet the agreed upon targets. That is to say, we could reverse the negative performance of the first third of the year by improving performance in the second one. In addition, it was necessary to take those measures in the second quarter so that we could fulfil the original goals for the third and fourth quarters of 2001. Moreover, we were again required to demonstrate to the international community that we would be able to obtain the financing to pay capital amortizations on the public debt that would come due in 2001 and beyond.

The National Constitution states that at time of a national emergency Congress can delegate to the President part of its legislative powers for a limited period.

The National Congress passed these special powers with only one important limitation: it did not authorize the Executive to use tax collections as a guarantee of the public debt, although Congress did enact the creation of a Public Credit Trust Fund that would receive the revenue from the new financial transactions tax. In any case, Congress created the new tax and the revenue it generated helped to fulfil the fiscal targets.

The special powers allowed us to take measures that encouraged investments and the recovery of competitiveness, both of which became structural ingredients of the economic programme. We could also take some steps to reform the state apparatus and reorganize the tax administration which were also central to the fulfilment of the fiscal targets.

The decision to restructure the public debt, including the debt of the provinces, to reduce capital amortization for the next years, and to reduce interest payments was central to the Competitiveness Plan that I presented when I took office. However, the limitations imposed by Congress prevented the use of taxes as a guarantee which impeded the inclusion of provincial debt in the swap offering and made it impossible to get voluntary reductions of the interest rate paid on public debt.

Provincial public debt could not be included in the proposed swap because taxes from the Federal Revenue Sharing Agreement ('Coparticipation Federal de Impuestos') already guaranteed that debt and its holders would not accept non-collateralized national bonds in exchange.

We could not expect to reduce the interest rate because without special guarantees we had to offer market rates to convince bondholders to participate in the exchange. Thus, the so-called Global Bond Exchange excluded provincial public debt and become a market rate-based operation not very different from the several bond exchanges implemented in the previous years.

Even though provincial debt would not be included and we could not expect interest cost reduction, it was imperative to go ahead with this limited operation so that the IMF would consider the economic plan we presented to restore the Blindaje.

Argentina would not have received the approval of IMF on 21 May 2001 if we had not carried out the Global Bond Exchange (known as the Megacanje). Moreover, the official report of the IMF executive committee meeting of 21 May 2001 stated:

> The managers praised the efforts of the (Argentine) authorities to interest creditors in a voluntary swap operation directed to reduce the financial requirements of the government during the next three or four years. They emphasized the need to finish this voluntary operation quickly to reduce uncertainties and move towards a sustainable financial scenario in average terms.
>
> (IMF 2001)

The road shows, designed to convince bondholders to take part in the Global Bond Exchange, were an opportunity to make the government's Competitiveness Plan known and to show the world that Argentina still had enough political cohesion to find solutions to its crisis. Not only did officials from the Economy Ministry, agents from underwriting banks, and officials from the IMF take part in the road shows, but so did Peronist governors José Manuel de la Sota and Carlos Reutemann, as did Governor Angel Rozas, an important Radical leader who took part as a show of support and consensus. Governor Carlos Ruckauf had visited the Economic Ministry a couple of days before and asked for a press conference to offer his implicit support for the Global Bond Exchange.

The Competitiveness Plan, including the Global Bond Exchange, was successful in reversing the bank deposit outflow and it even allowed a significant fiscal recovery during April, May and June of 2001 (see Table 15.11). In this way, the severe deposit outflow in March was followed by an increase in deposits that rose to 184 million pesos in April, 828 million in May and 562 million in June. The fiscal deficit of the national public sector, which had registered US $3 billion in the first quarter, fell to US $2.2 billion in the second quarter.

Second attempt: agreement with the IMF in August

In the first week of July, the province of Buenos Aires and other provinces that had gone deeply into debt declared that they needed no less than US $3 billion to meet their needs for the second quarter and they requested support from the national government to obtain US $300 million that week. Despite the support offered by the Economy Ministry and the Chief of Cabinet, it was impossible to obtain that amount in the market and the Banco de la Nación extended a loan without true fund backup.

218 Reform and counter-reform

Table 15.11 Bank deposit's monthly variation

Month	Variation in million pesos
January	910
February	771
March	−5,543
April	184
May	828
June	562
July	−5,268
August	−2,091
September	−69
October	6
November	−2,917
December	−2,546

Source: authors' own calculations, based on material originally published in BCRA.

The following week, the government sold 180-day treasury notes at an average annual rate set at 16 per cent. These two facts convinced us that we could not count on new credit for either the provinces or the nation. This left us with only one choice, to press ahead with the zero deficit regulation established in the Fiscal Responsibility Law. This law set the zero deficit for 2003. The disappearance of credit obliged us to set that target beginning in the second half of 2001.

The instrument to ensure the new zero deficit target was a modification of the Financial Administration Law that authorized the executive to reduce primary expenditures, including public sector salaries and pensions. Despite the announcement of the policy and its approval in Congress after the unanimous support of the provincial governors, doubts about Argentina's capacity for paying capital amortization of the provincial debt, as well as the non-deferred national debt appeared again. These doubts, along with a great number of unfavourable comments about the interruption of the service of the debt and the abandonment of convertibility, caused a new draining of bank deposits that climbed to 5.3 billion pesos in July and 2.1 billion pesos in August.

The new confidence crisis in July required a new negotiation with the IMF to get external support that would allow us to stop draining reserves from the Central Bank and the financial system. This negotiation would include not only the Zero Deficit programme, but also the completion of the debt restructuring of the national and provincial debt. The debt restructuring would allow us to lower the interest costs from the US $13 billion we paid in 2000 ($9 billion at the federal level and $4 billion from the provinces) to no more than US $7.5 billion ($5.5 billion at the federal level and $2 billion from the provinces).

These negotiations were complex and resulted in the approval of a new IMF loan of US $8 billion. The IMF disbursed US $5 billion on 10 September to strengthen the Central Bank and the financial system's liquidity, and $3 billion were reserved for disbursement between November 2001 and March 2002 to support the on-going debt restructuring. On top of these additional funds, the quarterly disbursements of the Blindaje were pending.

The new agreement with the IMF stopped deposits from draining during September and October, but we had to postpone the presentation of the debt restructuring until November, due to the mid-term congressional election on 14 October in which many candidates were recklessly campaigning in favour of default. We needed the authorization to use taxes, especially the Public Credit Fund, as guarantees of payment to go ahead with the debt restructuring.

After the elections in October, President De la Rúa determined that the conditions were such that he could decree a national and provincial public debt restructuring with the inclusion of tax guarantees using the power granted to the president in the national constitution. Thus, on 1 November De la Rúa signed Executive Order 1387 which allowed us to immediately carry out the swap of national and provincial public debt for loans guaranteed by federal taxes. This was going to be Phase 1 of a total swap of the national and provincial public debt. With the IMF and other multilateral credit organizations' consent, and the domestic swap complete, we could then carry out Phase 2 and exchange every bond held outside the country.

We carried out Phase 1 of the orderly debt restructuring between 1 November and 15 December. By 30 November, bondholders and other creditors had exchanged a total of US $42 billion for a guaranteed loan that paid a 7 per cent annual interest rate. For the nation, this successful transaction meant a reduction of more than US $2 billion in annual interest costs and the deferral of all amortization payments until after 2005. The creditors of the provinces, including the banks, had 15 more days to submit their credits to the exchange for guaranteed loans and when they did, the provinces also got a reduction of around US $2 billion in annual interest costs and a deferral of amortizations for three years.

Six months after the Global Bond Exchange was completed, it became clear that the tax guarantee was the mechanism capable of producing a voluntary interest reduction.

Bondholders from the Global Bond Exchange decided to exchange them for collateralized loans with a 7 per cent annual interest rate and three additional years of amortization deferral. That showed that the high market rate demanded during the Global Bond Exchange auction reflected the market's distrust which had been generated by so many demands for default and the refusal of the National Congress to offer taxes as a guarantee.

Third attempt: negotiation with the IMF to launch Phase 2 of the orderly debt restructuring

When we launched Phase 1 of the orderly debt restructuring, local banks began to point out that the illiquid collateralized loans could create cash problems for them. Analysts indicated that banks that had extended loans to the provinces would be prone to difficulties and this fact caused a new flight of deposits from the banking system.

While in September and October, the level of deposits had been stable, during November there was an outflow of almost US $3 billion, mainly during the last week of November, the moment when rumours of more draining became louder and banks had to decide if they would participate or not in Phase 1 of the Global Bond Exchange.

It was also unfortunate that the political leaders who wanted to 'change the economic model' and the economists and entrepreneurs who favoured devaluation allied to work against the restructuring. Some of the major media groups subscribed to the ideas of this virtual 'tactical alliance', since they thought that abandoning convertibility through devaluation would be a way of reducing their excessive indebtedness. This strategic coalition tried to gather support from both public and private debtors. After all, they would all end up in simultaneous and generalized default, which would lead to a substantial reduction in the real value of their debts.

Many discouraging signals also came from abroad. The IMF delayed sending an assessment team that would determine whether Argentina had fulfilled the fiscal target for the third quarter of 2001 which had been set in August's programme. The IMF did not publicly support the debt-restructuring scheme announced by the government on 1 November. Some staff members of the IMF informally commented that bondholders abroad would not receive the same treatment as domestic bondholders. Former IMF and IDB (Inter-American Development Bank) officials went public with their opinion supporting devaluation and advocating peso-ification.

All these signs startled deposit holders and fuelled the bank run. And, heavily indebted companies and provincial governments took such signs as 'Washington's' acknowledgement that Argentina's debt problem could only be resolved through significant 'haircuts' that domestic and international bondholders would have to accept. Had the message not been clear enough for Argentine leaders, Allan Meltzer mentioned this idea in interviews with the Argentine press.[5] Moreover, during a trip to Buenos Aires he told national senators that the restructuring process announced by the Argentine Government would not generate enough of a 'haircut' so the country should simply default on all of its debts.

In November, Hurst Kohler, the Managing Director of the IMF, started to show doubts about the possibility of continued support for Argentina and delayed the disbursement of US $1.3 billion that were due in November in spite of clear evidence that Argentina had complied with the fiscal target for the third quarter. He believed that the unwillingness of the US government to help Argentina deal with its crisis, in contrast to the pressure it had put on European governments to help Turkey, forced the IMF to take disproportionate risks. Understandably, the attention of the US government after the 11 September 2001 terrorist attacks had shifted toward the region that hosted Al Qaeda. Even though in August the US Secretary of the Treasury had insisted on the need to help Argentina restructure its debt, after the attack on the World Trade Center towers in New York, the US Government would not provide any specific help.

The last day of November while we announced that Phase 1 of the debt restructuring was progressing satisfactorily, we had to impose restrictions on the amount of cash depositors would be able take from their banks. We were also compelled to impose temporary exchange controls on financial transfers abroad, as Ann Krueger had effectively requested in her speech on the Sovereign Debt Restructuring Mechanism, on 23 November. Paradoxically, Hurst Kohler also announced the suspension of the Argentine IMF programme.

To stop a new draining of deposits we had no choice, but to finish the national and provincial public debt restructuring as soon as possible. In this context, I flew immediately to Washington and started new negotiations with the IMF to obtain the payments from the Blindaje and the US $3 billion that had already been approved in August, to support the debt restructuring.

Conscious of her responsibility in the imposition of the exchange controls and the restrictions to cash bank deposits, Ann Krueger facilitated my discussion with Hurst Kohler and we reached an agreement. The IMF would resume its support for Argentina. The only requirement from the IMF was that Congress approve the national budget bill for 2002 and the Senate should begin discussing a new federal tax revenue sharing plan for approval before September 2002.

In a meeting with the governors summoned by Senator Ramón Puerta, we settled on an agreement that the bill regarding Federal Tax Revenue Sharing would be put before Congress before the end of the year.

In the draft budget bill presented by the Executive, a US $5.5 billion financial allotment had been included to cover interest payments (exactly half the amount budgeted for 2001) because of the interest cost reduction we expected from the debt-restructuring programme. After completing Phase 2 through the swap of the US $52 billion in bonds not included in Phase 1, the interest cost for year 2002 would not be greater than US $5.5 billion.

The House of Representatives was due to form the new Budget Committee on 10 December after the new deputies had been sworn in, so that the Committee could discuss the draft budget law on 19 December, with the participation of the Secretary of Finance, Jorge Baldrich. With the budget approved, the IMF would support Phase 2 of the restructuring. We had planned to launch Phase 2 on 15 January 2002 and complete it in one month.

We were only two months away from reassuring the complete fiscal equilibrium and the restoration of financial trust through a transaction that would reduce by half the annual interest cost of the national and provincial public debt and would relieve the government of capital maturities for the following three years.

The restoration of financial confidence was crucial to eliminate the restrictions on withdrawing cash from the banks and making financial transfers abroad that had been imposed on 1 December to stop the run on the banks. These restrictions had forced most payments using bank money, but they had not prevented payments with money deposited in the banks, nor had they changed in any sense the original currency of the deposit. Therefore, once banks recovered liquidity for their assets, which would have happened after the completion of the debt restructuring, we could have removed the restrictions. The so-called 'corralito' would have lasted only 90 days, as originally promised.

Unfortunately, the restriction on cashing out bank deposits and the discussion in the legislature of Province of Buenos Aires on cutting expenditures had generated riots that became increasingly violent on 19 December, precisely the day the Budget Committee was supposed to discuss the draft of the budget law.

The institutional coup of 19 December to 30 December of 2001

The institutional coup that transpired from 19 December to 30 December 2001 prevented us from accomplishing these important objectives. Instead, it paved the way for an institutional rupture without precedent in Argentine history. Default and devaluation, long praised by the coup conspirators and their allies, was brought about and chaos fell upon the Argentine economy.

De la Rúa's government had to resign on 20 December. After a short interim presidency by the President of the Senate, Ramón Puerta, Congress designated Adolfo Rodriguez Saá as new president and called for a new election in two months. Rodriguez Saá declared a moratorium of foreign debt, but decided to maintain convertibility. As this decision displeased the promoters of the institutional coup, the riots continued and Rodriguez Saá resigned on 30 December.

Eduardo Duhalde, the former Peronist candidate, and Ignacio de Mendiguren, then head of the UIA (Unión Industrial Argentina, an organization which represents Argentine industrialists), realized that an institutional coup would give them the opportunity to wipe out all debts, public and private, held at home and abroad. It was to their benefit that the coup appeared to be sponsored by the Radical Party of the Province of Buenos Aires and against their own political peer, President De La Rúa. There was no doubt that the purpose of the coup was to put an end to the so-called 'Neoliberalism of the 1990s'.

Notes

1 The popularity of this law was ratified in every election after its promulgation, including the last one in October 2001. In a debate about this issue, all candidates to Senator for the City of Buenos Aires backed and pledged to maintain the Convertibility Law.
2 See Cavallo, Domingo in collaboration with Cavallo, Sonia (1996); also Cavallo (1999), and Cavallo and De Pablo (2001)

3 See Cavallo (1997).
4 Vito Tanzi (2007) provides very entertaining and accurate descriptions of how Argentina was seen by the IMF during the years in which he was the Director of the Fiscal Affairs Department of the IMF.
5 See *Revista 3 Puntos*, año 4, # 231, Interview with Allan Meltzer by Pablo Rosendo González, www.3puntos.com/seccion.php3?numero=231&seccion=protagonista.

References

BCRA (Banco Central de la República Argentina) http://www.bcra.gob.ar/PublicacionesEstadisticas/Descarga_paquetes_estandarizados_series_estadisticas_1.asp.

Boletín Estadístico de la Seguridad Social (2012) Buenos Aires: Ministerio de Trabajo, Empleo y Formación de Recursos Humanos, http://www.trabajo.gov.ar/left/estadisticas/descargas/bess/boletin2trim_2012.pdf.

Cavallo, Domingo F. in collaboration with Cavallo, Sonia (1996) 'Lessons from the Stabilization Process in Argentina, 1990–1996', in *Achieving Price Stability*, a Symposium Sponsored by the Federal Reserve Bank of Kansas City, Jackson Hole, Wyoming, 27–29 August.

Cavallo, Domingo F. (1997) *El Peso de La Verdad*, Buenos Aires: Editorial Sudamericana.

Cavallo, Domingo F. (1999) 'La Qualite de la Monnaie', *Economie Internationale*, No. 80, 4 trim., Paris.

Cavallo, Domingo Felipe and De Pablo, Juan Carlos (2001) *Pasión Por Crear*, Buenos Aires: Editorial Sudamericana.

De Pablo, Juan Carlos (2005) *La Economía Argentina en la segunda mitad del siglo XX*, Buenos Aires: La Ley.

Ferreres, Orlando (2010) *Dos Siglos de Economía Argentina*, Buenos Aires: El Ateneo.

IMF (International Monetary Fund) (2001) News Brief: IMF Completes Third Argentina Review, News Brief No. 01/44, 21 May 2001, Washington DC, https://www.imf.org/external/np/sec/nb/2001/nb0144.htm.

Melconian, Carlos and Santángelo, Rodolfo (1996) *El endeudamiento del sector público argentino en el periodo 1989–1995*, Buenos Aires: United Nation Development Programme, Proyecto Arg. 91-03.

Ministerio de Economía, Dirección Nacional de Coordinación Fiscal con las Provincias www2.mecon.gov.ar/hacienda/dncfp/provincial/info_presupuestaria/esq_total_serie_APNF.php.

Ministerio de Economía, Secretaria de Hacienda, http://www.economia.gob.ar/secretarias/hacienda/.

Ministerio de Economía, Secretaria de Seguridad Social del Ministerio de Trabajo, *Panorama de la Seguridad Social, Serie Histórica 1971–2000*, Buenos Aires: Ministerio de Trabajo, Empleo y Formación de Recursos Humanos, http://www.trabajo.gov.ar/downloads/biblioteca_estadisticas/pss71-00.pdf.

Tanzi, Vito (2007) *Argentina: An Economic Chronicle*, New York: Jorge Pinto Books Inc.

US Department of Agriculture, www.nass.gov/statistic_by_subject/?sector=CROPS.

World Bank, *World Development Indicators*, Washington, DC: World Bank, http://data.worldbank.org/data-catalog/world-development-indicators.

16 The origin of Duhalde's decisions and Kirchner's metamorphosis

In the middle of the political chaos, after Congress appointed Eduardo Duhalde as the new president with the support of the Radicals, Duhalde decided to abandon convertibility and to transform all dollar-denominated financial obligations, including bank deposits, into obligations in inconvertible pesos. This triggered a large devaluation of the peso. The price of the dollar jumped from 1 to 3.8 pesos between January and September 2002. And inflation re-emerged, in 2002, the consumer price index increased 42 per cent.

The destruction of convertibility through the combination of devaluation, generalized reprogramming of deposits in the financial system, peso-ification of contracts, and default of the internal but already restructured debt, and later, floating of the peso, implied the demolition of the contractual base of the economy and a violation of property rights.

Prices of export goods went up, relative prices reversed, and the exchange rate misalignment was larger than before, but now in the opposite direction. The credit crunch and the difficulties of importing goods prevented a positive export response. Import substitution was encouraged by the large devaluation, but it would turn out to be inefficient and unsustainable under normal conditions. Simultaneously, the fall of domestic demand had been so large that the outcome was a deepening of the recession never seen before in Argentina.

Contrary to what the proponents of the abandonment of convertibility expected, these decisions generated a further rise in unemployment and poverty.

Were all these terrible effects predictable? They certainly were. Because they were so predictable, those of us who were in charge of governing the country spent 2001 struggling to avoid defaulting the debt and devaluing the peso. However, once exchange controls and restrictions for cashing dollar deposits were established, was there really a better alternative than the one chosen by Duhalde?

Even though I resigned on 19 December, the interim President, Adolfo Rodriguez Saá and the Governor of Santa Cruz, Nestor Kirchner, consulted me on what could be done to overcome the crisis.

I told them that the best alternative was to continue eliminating the fiscal deficit by forcing the provinces to reduce salaries in the same way that the federal government had done in July 2001, cut interest payments on the public debt, and defer capital maturity dates. This alternative certainly implied there would be some degree of compulsion and rescheduling to achieve the reduction of financial outlays. It was necessary, however, to minimize the negative impact on the property rights of savers, investors and workers.

To halt the run on the financial system, on 1 December we had implemented some temporary restrictions on cash withdrawals of deposits – popularly known as a 'corralito' Spanish for 'little fence'. This implied a temporary control on transactions in foreign currencies, similar to those imposed by several countries between 1870 and 1930 via a measure called 'suspension of convertibility'. The corralito was only a curb on cash withdrawals and financial transfers abroad. Deposits did not lose their value and savers could use their funds to make payments within the country using debit cards, cheques, and inter-account bank transfers. Furthermore, these methods of payment improved tax administration. Far from aiming at a default on the debt or the termination of convertibility, the corralito focused on preserving the value and availability of savings while the government implemented the debt restructuring process and national and provincial fiscal consolidation.

Interim president Rodriguez Saá announced that he would maintain convertibility, but declared a moratorium on external debt. In practice, the moratorium meant the pre-announcement of Phase II of the orderly debt restructuring that began on 1 November 2001. It did not affect the consolidated loans that had replaced the debt restructured in Phase I. It was precisely this announcement that he would maintain convertibility that convinced the politicians and business lobbyists who wanted to 'change the model' to remove Rodriguez Saá from power only seven days after his appointment.

After becoming President, Duhalde offered Néstor Kirchner the office of Chief of Cabinet. Kirchner rejected the offer when he learned that Duhalde intended to abandon convertibility. I interpreted this to mean that Kirchner, like Rodriguez Saá, had been persuaded by my opinion about how to overcome the crisis. I was not surprised, because they had been strong supporters of the reforms in the 1990s.

Beginning in May 2003 Kirchner, however, unexpectedly not only provided continuity to Duhalde's economic policies, but also went further. The result being: a complete reversal of the reforms of the 1990s. He also pursued a significant shift in foreign policy, particularly after the Conference of Mar del Plata in 2005, when he boycotted President Bush's proposal to create a free trade zone throughout the Americas, and authorized, a parallel anti-American conference financed by then-President Hugo Chávez of Venezuela. Understanding Kirchner's metamorphosis into the ideological opposite of Menem is the key to explaining the sea change between the economy of the 1990s and that of the 12 years of the Kirchners.

To understand Kirchner's metamorphosis it is necessary to explain why Eduardo Duhalde, backed by Raúl Alfonsín, took such a wrong path. The political discussions on unemployment and poverty, the professional discussions among the economists about public debt and the currency regime, and the various interpretations of the origin of the crisis misled them to such an extent that they truly believed that they were implementing 'the change' that would immediately ease poverty and unemployment.

The political discussions on unemployment and poverty

In the years following the implementation of the convertibility system GDP grew quickly. Initially, statistics showed a reduction in the unemployment rate (see Figure 16.1). And the significant fall in the inflation rate contributed to a sharp decline in poverty. However, the downward trend in unemployment started to change in 1993 (see Figure 16.2) and a similar phenomenon affected the poverty rate starting in 1994. Since then, both problems have shown a firm tendency to grow worse.

The question about how to design a strategy to address these problems continued throughout the 1990s. One camp of economists believed that opening and deregulating the economy, privatization of publicly owned industries, and the protection of property rights were the best instruments to ensure sustainable economic growth. These individuals also insisted that labour, tax and welfare system reforms were necessary to reduce unemployment and poverty. I was one of those economists, of course.

As far as labour deregulation is concerned, we insisted on having more flexible employment contracts. In terms of taxation, we proposed and started to eliminate payroll taxes and other distorting taxes. Regarding the welfare system, we demanded that provincial governments conduct social policies in a

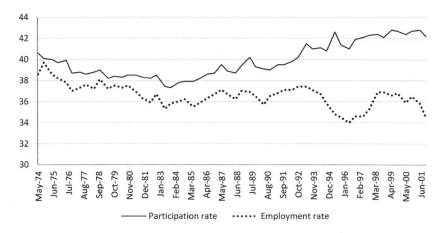

Figure 16.1 Participation and employment rates 1974–2001
(as a proportion of total population)
Source: authors' own calculations, based on information original published in INDEC.

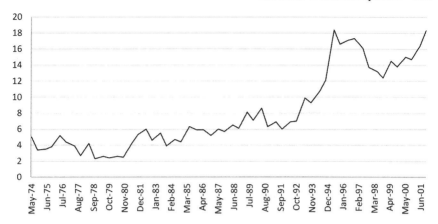

Figure 16.2 Unemployment rate 1974–2001
(as a proportion of active population)
Source: authors' own calculations, based on information original published in INDEC.

less biased and more efficient way, especially in the fields of education, health care and social aid.

There was an opposing camp. Other national leaders lobbied for a 'change of rules' referring to the economic reforms implemented in Argentina throughout the 1990s as 'the neo-liberal model'. According to them, the neo-liberal policies triggered the rise in unemployment and poverty. Consequently, in their minds only 'changing the neo-liberal model' could possibly reverse the negative trends of the last half of 1990s. That meant reversing the economic reforms and revoking the Convertibility Law which was viewed by them as the epitome of the so-called neo-liberal policy.

The strongest advocates of this idea were Eduardo Duhalde (Peronist Party) and Raúl Alfonsín (Radical Party). Neither Alfonsín nor Duhalde had won an election by promising to abandon convertibility. On the intellectual side, they were influenced by a group of economists that proposed the so-called Phoenix Plan. This plan was a revival of the old ISI growth strategy combined with a modified version of the populist macroeconomic policies of the past. The only change was that they now shifted away from advice to overvalue the peso and advocated a long period of undervaluation. On the business side, the influence came from the industrialists that until the 1990s had profited from strong protection and negative interest rates.

They even thought that the evolution of economic and social events of 2001 proved them right. Therefore, when Duhalde came into office with Alfonsín's support, he was convinced that his mission was to repeal the Convertibility Law and to change the neo-liberal model. They both expected that this would bring down unemployment and poverty rates.

The professional discussion on public debt and the currency regime

While the political arena showed different standpoints regarding the diagnosis of the problem and the strategy to fight unemployment and poverty, professional economists discussed about the sustainability of the public debt and the currency board system.

The people who held these strongly opposing views coalesced into two groups. On the one hand, there were those who supported dollarization who argued that adopting the US dollar as the only currency would produce enough fiscal discipline to ensure the payment of the debt. On the other hand, there were those who recommended floating the currency; most of them thought that Argentina should default on its debt and restructure it compulsorily. The former group emphasized that by maintaining monetary stability and servicing the debt this would help confidence return and interest rates would go down enabling the economy to recover. The latter group believed that unless relative prices of tradable goods increased the economy would continue to be stagnant and the country would no longer be able to service its debt.

I shared most of the views held by those who wanted to float the peso. However, I was also persuaded, as were the supporters of dollarization, that if the property rights of those who had trusted in the country and saved locally were severely affected by a devaluation, economic growth would not resume, no matter how rapidly and firmly relative prices were adjusted in favour of exports. For that reason, I tried to find a balance between both positions. I sought to apply all possible non-monetary resources to correct relative prices without violating convertibility. In terms of the exchange rate policy, the plan was to move towards a more flexible system once the reduction of interest rates obtained after restructuring the debt in an ordered manner had balanced the budget.

Instead of forcing a change in the currency of contracts, towards either dollarization or peso-ification, the government I served wanted to preserve people's freedom to choose between the Argentine peso and the US dollar for their transactions. Unfortunately, this idea lacked adequate professional support, possibly because both peso-ification and dollarization advocates were focused mainly on a debate about the exchange rate regime – currency board system versus floating exchange rate system – rather than on the monetary regime and protection of property rights. The Convertibility Law provided the monetary system that people demanded and, under the proper fiscal conditions, it was perfectly compatible with the two different exchange rate regimes or another intermediate alternative.

Those who pointed out the recessive effects caused by the divergence of the prices of tradable goods and non-tradable ones recommended the replacement of the currency board with a free-floating exchange system. They thought that by setting correct prices the economy would recover through an increase in the production of exportable goods and the substitution of imports. However, they did not realize that the adjustment of relative prices via the destruction of the convertibility system would affect property rights in such a way that medium and long-term contracts would become highly difficult and savings as well as investment inside the country would almost disappear.

At the same time, those who supported the defence of savers and financial investors' property rights were critical of any government action tending to correct relative prices without abandoning convertibility.

In this context, it is understandable that national leaders such as Duhalde and Alfonsín, who had always favoured a 'change of the neo-liberal economic model', believed that this was an opportune moment to reverse the economic reforms of the 1990s.

The discussion abroad on the factors that triggered the crisis

This discussion was very lively in the second half of 2001.

The senior management and most of the staff of the International Monetary Fund argued that the determining factor of the crisis was the federal government's and provincial administrations' reluctance to cut back public expenditures and stop borrowing to finance their fiscal deficits. The advocates of the currency-board system and supporters of the forced-dollarization policy blamed it on the plan to broaden the dollar–peso peg (which would eventually become a basket peg) and on the Competitiveness Plan launched in 2001. Some economists believed that the crisis was due to the stagnation of exports caused by an overvalued peso. Others blamed President De la Rúa's decision to preserve the convertibility policy and to avoid resorting to devaluation as an instrument for financing fiscal deficit. Finally, there were those who claimed that it took too long to propose an orderly debt-restructuring programme.

Most of these opinions were misleading, but they contributed to the confusion. However, the position that the IMF finally adopted in November and December of 2001 goes perhaps the longest way towards explaining why Duhalde and Alfonsín decided to destroy the rules of the game.

The government's reluctance to cut back expenditures

Michael Mussa (2002), a former chief economist of the IMF, argued that the factor that triggered the crisis was the US $2 billion fiscal adjustment that the central government failed to support in March 2001, when Ricardo López Murphy was the Economic Minister. Mussa's argument is mistaken because shortly after López Murphy's resignation, I took over as Economy Minister and, together with President De la Rúa, succeeded in getting parliamentary support for a $3 billion fiscal tightening package. This measure along with the Competitiveness Plan helped to improve the relative prices of internationally tradable goods without abandoning convertibility and allowed us to avert a bank run in March 2001.

In the same line as Mussa, in July 2001 IMF Managing Director Horst Köhler took notice of Argentine political leaders' criticism of the fiscal adjustments. He threatened that the IMF might discontinue support to Argentina and not approve the financial extension programme that the country needed to contain the bank run that restarted early that month. In August we reached an agreement with the provincial governors and Congress passed the Zero Deficit Law. This demonstrated that the central government was working hard to build the necessary internal political support. Köhler reconsidered his previous statement and the board of the IMF finally approved the new loan in August 2001.

Fiscal statistics do not support the idea that Argentina refused to cut back expenditures. Federal primary outlays decreased by US $1.5 billion in 2000 and by $3.5 billion in 2001. These cuts included a 13 per cent reduction in public sector wages and pensions over $500 per month. Furthermore, in the second half of 2001, the provinces, whose primary expenditures in 2000 and the first half of 2001 were the same as 1999, took pains to balance their budgets to achieve a $2 billion adjustment. Even without any further tightening by 2002 primary public expenses would have been $7 billion less than in 1999.

Almost all the governors and, needless to say, President De la Rúa, knew that abandoning the economic rules of the 1990s would mean a tighter and costlier adjustment than if the expenditure cuts were voluntarily applied. Naturally, they also knew that without this, public expenditure in real terms would end up being cut even more through inflation. For that reason, to assume that they refused to make the necessary adjustments only to stir up the crisis and undermine the economic policies of the 1990s is to believe they were on the verge of political irrationality.

The Government's decision not to force dollarization on the economy and the implementation of the Competitiveness Plan

Steve Hanke (1999), the world's main proponent of currency boards, and other think tanks like the Argentine CEMA (Centro de Estudios Macroeconómicos de Argentina) and the US-based Cato Institute, argued that the economic rules of the 1990s were in crisis because I opposed the plan to dollarize the economy and launched the Competitiveness Plan instead. According to them, this raised doubts about whether the country would continue to uphold the Convertibility Law.

I did not want to force a dollarization policy because I always believed that introducing the dollar as Argentina's only legal currency was not appropriate for our economy. In 2001, in particular, I thought that if the central government believed it was constitutional to enforce the currency conversion of contracts from pesos to dollars then the reverse should also be true. In other words, enforcing a dollarization process would have set a constitutional precedent for the compulsory peso-ification of contracts. Under the Convertibility Law, dollarization and even peso-ification (provided that it was a voluntary decision and not a forced one) was possible. The Convertibility Law clearly allowed multiple currencies.

By promoting a forced dollarization of the economy, President De la Rúa's government would have accelerated the crisis that eventually subverted the economic order of the 1990s. A dollarization process would have added to the real cause of the crisis and therefore triggered a collapse much earlier in 2001. This would have provided more powerful political and judicial arguments than the ones used in January 2002 to support forced conversion of dollars into pesos. Hence, the decision not to force dollarization was not the cause of the crisis.

Neither was the Competitiveness Plan. The Plan consisted of a series of measures intended to correctly set relative prices to favour tradable goods without undermining the convertibility rule. Indirect taxes and subsidies served as the instruments of this plan which also eliminated regulations that discouraged investment and productivity. The Competitiveness Plan could not have contributed to sparking the economic crisis because it aimed to correct the misalignment of relative prices that discouraged the production of tradable goods. The purpose of the plan was to correct the so-called misalignment of the real exchange rate without modifying the nominal exchange rate present in all the contracts in force. In any case, what raised doubts about the fixed dollar–peso parity was the misalignment of the real exchange rate rather than attempts to redress the imbalance.

The stagnation of exports

Most of the technical papers on the Argentine Crisis, especially those produced abroad, said that the stagnation in exports that resulted from an overvalued dollar-pegged peso was the main cause of the crisis. However, those who write on Argentina and attribute the crisis to the dollar–peso parity seem to have overlooked the factual data available on the Argentine case. US Secretary of the Treasury Paul O'Neill made this mistake when, in July 2001, he told *The Economist* that, 'Argentines have been off and on in trouble for 70 years or more. They do not have any export industry to speak of at all. They like it that way. Nobody forced them to be what they are.'[1]

After O'Neil made this statement, I pointed out that he might have been misinformed. I explained to him that during the 1990s Argentina's export performance had been similar to that of Chile and had been 50 per cent higher than Brazil's, not as Mr O'Neill seemed to believe. After this gaffe, he asked the IMF to grant Argentina US $8 billion to support an orderly debt-restructuring programme to reduce the country's interest bill. The IMF Board approved the monetary aid by the end of August 2001. The IMF's $5 billion disbursement contributed to strengthening the financial system and contained the bank run that started in July and August.

President De la Rúa's decision to support convertibility instead of devaluing the peso to finance the fiscal deficit

According to Joseph Stiglitz, it was President De la Rúa's determination to support the convertibility plan that actually triggered the crisis. Some economists claimed that the economic collapse stemmed from the government's decision not to implement Keynesian policies to spur economic recovery when it became clear that the country had entered a recession. They shared Stiglitz's view.

In fact, had President De la Rúa's administration decided to abandon convertibility and applied Keynesian policies, the economic order of the 1990s would have been subverted two years earlier. This approach ran the serious risk of an eventual hyperinflationary process because devaluation with no fiscal austerity and large monetary issuances could have caused the peso to depreciate so severely that dollar-indebted individuals and institutions would have demanded their contractual obligations be peso-ified to prevent bankruptcy.

Having knowledge of and experience with the negative consequences of such policies in Argentina in previous decades meant that no Argentine political leader or economist seriously proposed such an alternative.

The lack of decision to restructure the public debt

Adam Lerrik and Allan Meltzer (2001) among others have argued that Argentina showed no willingness to restructure its public debt. But, the restructuring proposal that they proposed in April 2001 was unfeasible in practice. Their proposal assigned the IMF the role of lender of last resort. However, the IMF showed no disposition at all to allocate the financing necessary to support a last resort lending scheme. The factor that actually triggered the crisis had already started by the time we launched the orderly debt restructuring option and after the IMF had accepted to support it through the US $8 billion provision that it approved in August 2001.

By 30 November 2001, Argentina had successfully completed the first phase of the restructuring scheme, which covered US $42 billion of debt principal (more than 40 per cent of the expected restructured value).

With the second phase of the debt swap scheme, we expected to bring the interest bill down by the necessary amount to guarantee a zero deficit for 2002. Ultimately, though, this was not enough to prevent the crisis.

Why then did the crisis occur?

Influential Argentine leaders' perception that there was external support peso-ification of dollar contracts

As explained in Chapter 15, the signals coming from the international financial organizations and some very influential economists like Alan Meltzer convinced Eduardo Duhalde, and Ignacio de Mendiguren, the head of the industrialists, that an institutional coup would provide them with the opportunity to wipe out all debts, public and private, at home and abroad. This would be achieved through what the 'new' Washington Consensus seemed to suggest: devaluing the Argentine currency after compulsorily peso-ifying all of the economy's contracts.

Kirchner's metamorphosis

The disastrous exit from convertibility Duhalde decided on in 2002 convinced many people that it was necessary to resume the main approaches to economic organization from the 1990s. This was the position, with differences in other aspects, of three of the main candidates that participated in the presidential election of 2003, namely former presidents Menem and Rodriguez Saá and former Defence and Economic Minister Ricardo López Murphy. In the first round of the election, Menem got 24 per cent of the votes, López Murphy 18 per cent, and Rodriguez Saá 16 per cent. Therefore, by extrapolating from these results it is fair to say that 58 per cent of the population still supported the economic rules of the 1990s.

Only Néstor Kirchner campaigned on softening his criticism of Duhalde and being ambiguous on his appraisal of the 1990s. He was so ambiguous that he chose Daniel Scioli as his vice-president. Scioli had been a strong supporter of convertibility until the end of 2001. In the election of October 2001, he won a seat in the House of Representatives as a candidate of an alliance between Peronism and Acción por la República, the political party that I had created. As a campaigner, he was the strongest supporter of the policies I applied as economic minister under De la Rúa. Kirchner obtained 22 per cent of the votes but since Menem declined to participate in the second round Kirchner became president.

Already in government, Kirchner not only provided continuity for the worst features of Duhalde's policies, but he also worked to complete the reversal of the policies of the 1990s with an increasingly statist and isolationist ideology that was in sharp contrast to the economic ideology he had strongly supported for the previous 12 years.

What explains Kirchner's metamorphosis? I am convinced that the answer is political opportunism combined with an extreme ambition for economic and political power. After the conflict with the farmers and the world crisis of 2008, he turned again towards policies closer to those of the convertibility period, but he died and his widow, already president, transformed his pragmatic change into an extreme ideological turn towards Chávez's 21st century socialism.

I knew Néstor Kirchner very well. He was one of the governors who was elected thanks to convertibility's success in defeating hyperinflation and renewing growth. In the electoral campaign of 1991, at his request, I visited his province to support his candidacy. Once elected, he adopted drastic measures to eliminate the fiscal deficit of his province and implemented all the reforms I recommended to the governors as accompanying policies to convertibility.

He was an enthusiastic supporter of convertibility, privatization and deregulation. In 1992, he convinced the governors of oil-producing provinces to support the restructuring and privatization of YPF. He also privatized the provincial bank and public utility companies in his jurisdiction.

I campaigned for him again in 1995. He supported my attack on the mafias that controlled the postal services and that had created a virtual parallel customs and migration service to help criminal activities even after I resigned as economic minister as a result of a disagreement with the way Menem's government acted on these matters.

In the 1999 presidential campaign, Kirchner proposed a Duhalde–Cavallo ticket instead of a Duhalde–Ortega ticket as a way to increase the chances of defeating De la Rúa. In 2000, he supported my candidacy to serve in the government of the City of Buenos Aires.

By the second half of 2002, Duhalde decided that he would shorten his term and called for an early presidential election to take place in March 2003. By then, Kirchner and Duhalde realized that if the Peronist Party held primary elections, Menem would win and become the only candidate of the Peronist Party since he was still very popular among the Peronists. However, Menem did not have a good chance of winning the general election because the polls indicated that more than 50 per cent of voters said that they would never vote for him. Duhalde, who disliked Menem, knew that the alternative to Menem was López Murphy who had been building support among the Radicals and Liberals who were disillusioned with Menem's final years in power.

The idea that Menem or López Murphy would succeed him in power was completely unacceptable to Duhalde. They had been strong critics of abandoning convertibility and the interventionist economic policies that he had pursued. Kirchner saw the opportunity to run as president with the support of Duhalde if, instead of selecting a single candidate through a primary, the Peronist Party decided to allow several candidacies.

Under this scenario, the idea was to have a second round with two Peronist candidates, presumably Menem and Kirchner, in which case Kirchner would prevail given the high negatives Menem had in the polls. The bet was that López Murphy would not get enough votes to be a contender in the second round. Duhalde liked the idea and, being the president he had the key to the Peronist Party and cancelled the primaries.

To minimize López Murphy's chances, Duhalde decided that the election of representatives and senators would be held at the same time as that of the governors. The main provinces planned elections separately from the presidential one. This way the presidential candidates of new political parties, including López Murphy, would not be able to pull representatives for their parties.

Kirchner's virtual alliance with Duhalde was purely opportunistic. Until that moment, his opinion of Duhalde's policies was not very different from Menem's, López Murphy's and Rodriguez Saá's. But, if Duhalde were to accept this electoral strategy, Kirchner would have to campaign promising continuity for Duhalde's policies even though this was contrary to his previous positions and ideology.

Duhalde proposed Roberto Lavagna, his economic minister, as candidate for the vice presidency to ensure continuity of his policies, but Kirchner preferred Scioli, a close associate of Menem, as a way to draw votes from Menem and the liberals that remained sympathetic to Peronism. To please Duhalde, Kirchner announced that, if he reached the presidency, Lavagna would continue as economic minister.

Kirchner's electoral strategy delivered the outcome he pursued and there is no doubt that he was a very astute politician. Duhalde, motivated by his antipathy for Menem and his distaste for López Murphy's liberalism, helped Kirchner reach power only to suffer Kirchner's betrayal two years later. Néstor Kirchner was the last and only winner of a Machiavellian political fight.

When Kirchner took the oath as president on 25 May 2003, inflation, the biggest immediate problem created by Duhalde's policies, was already receding. Alfonso Prat-Gay, the president of the Central Bank who had replaced Mario Blejer after the turbulent months that followed the decision to forcefully convert dollar deposits into peso deposits, started to implement monetary policy that targeted inflation and succeeded in bringing inflation down below 0.5 per cent per month. Foreign terms of trade, which had been dramatically unfavourable in 2001 and early 2002, began to improve and the almighty dollar that had been as strong as 82 dollar cents per euro in mid-2001, had weakened to 1.12 dollars per euro. All these were very favourable trends.

However, many problems, originating in the peso-ification and the accompanying policies Duhalde had implemented in 2002, created growing distortions in the structure of investment incentives. The peso-ification and freeze in public utility rates, particularly for natural gas and electricity, not only provoked the virtual expropriation of the assets that investors in privatized companies had created during the 1990s, but also generated operational losses in most of those companies.

The trend towards appreciation of the peso that the monetary policy of Prat-Gay had achieved created a good opportunity to reverse the distortions, at least those created by the low prices paid to local producers of natural gas. Everybody expected that Kirchner would use the opportunity to adjust the price of gas up to return to the levels compatible with the operation of the energy sector as a free market integrated into the global economy.

In his first trip to New York, Vice-President Scioli conceded that the natural gas price freeze was a problem that needed to be resolved for American companies that had invested in Argentina. However, as soon as he was back from the USA, President Kirchner rejected the adjustment of the price of natural gas and deprived the vice-president of authority in the areas of the government that he still controlled. This was the first indication that Kirchner was not willing to return to the earlier rules of the game for the energy sector that he had helped to create.

Why did he change his mind on this crucial matter? Foreign and local investors had already invested their money to create abundant capacity in the energy sector so he decided that Argentina did not need new investment and, if it did, the government would be able to generate the funds needed for financing whenever new investment became necessary. He turned from being a privatizer to again promoting nationalization of investment as had happened in the pre-Menem times. In practice, he began to confiscate and spend the savings of those that had trusted Argentina's reforms. Furthermore, keeping public utility rates frozen helped him to keep inflation under control with greater room for increasing public salaries and pensions and allocating public resources toward social policies and public works.

Something similar happened with the export taxes that Duhalde had introduced in 2002. They were supposed to be temporary measures to capture part of the benefits exporters got from the extreme devaluation of the peso and to dampen the impact of the devaluation on food prices. However, as permanent ingredients of a tax structure they created the same distortions that until 1991 discouraged export activities. Everybody expected that Kirchner, a strong supporter of opening up the economy during the 1990s, would start removing the export taxes. On the inflation side, circumstances were favourable for this action because the peso was appreciating and, therefore, the increase in food prices would have had a negligible impact on the cost of living.

However, Kirchner did the opposite. He increased export taxes, because this time export taxes were used to strengthen the political power of the presidency with respect to the provincial governors. Exports taxes and import duties are the only taxes not shared with the provinces. Therefore, the president could distribute them as a reward to some governors and punish others, depending on what served his political ambitions.

In terms of public salaries and pensions, Duhalde authorized minimal increases as a way to avoid inflation spiralling out of control in line with the freeze he had imposed on public utility rates. Wages for workers in the private sectors suffered a significant reduction in real terms and due to the high unemployment rate trade unions were unable to increase nominal wages enough for a recovery in real terms. Kirchner authorized gradual increases of public salaries and pensions above the inflation rate but with a populist bias.

In the case of pensions, between 2003 and 2007 Kirchner authorized rapid increases for the minimum pension only and kept the pensions above 1,000 pesos per month frozen. This freeze contradicted the Constitution and the social security laws and created a debt problem similar to that which had emerged during the years of high inflation prior to 1991. The retirees who saw their rights violated, made claims in the courts, which ruled in their favour. Those court decisions, amounting to billions of pesos, were ignored. In this matter, Kirchner's policies also diverged from those of the 1990s and a problem that had been solved in those years re-emerged with force during his presidency. The populist policies that he helped eradicate earlier his government brought back in 2003.

During the 1990s the private companies that had invested in the privatized areas of the economy, like energy and transport, provided financing for and were contracted to provide new investment projects. After the decision to nationalize these new investments, the financing and the contracts became the responsibility of the government as in the decades preceding the reforms that Kirchner had previously strongly supported. The allocation of contracts and their conditions brought back the vices of favouritism and corruption that had blocked the contracts of public works and services before the privatizations. In 2005, Roberto Lavagna resigned as minister of economy denouncing what he called the 'construction companies' friends of the government club' behaving like a cartel. The regional distribution of public works was characterized by the same arbitrary allocation as the financial resources generated by the export taxes.

On matters such as the management of debt and monetary policy, Kirchner also reversed the earlier reforms. Instead of conducting an orderly restructuring of the defaulted debt, he preferred to impose large haircuts without first negotiating them and imposed the repudiation of the debt of those creditors that would not accept the pre-established haircuts by law. He decided to cancel all of Argentina's debt with the IMF and issued bonds using the intermediation of Chávez's Venezuela at a much higher interest rate. He did this to disengage from the international financial institutions and in order to avoid their audits and conditions.

In monetary policy matters, in 2003 he decided to interrupt the appreciation of the peso and, in practice, imposed a quasi-fixed exchange rate of three pesos per dollar which resembled convertibility but lacked the obligation to maintain full backing of the monetary base. Therefore, when the fiscal surplus that helped to finance the purchase of reserves disappeared, the Central Bank resorted to printing money to continue purchasing dollars and prevent appreciation of the peso.

In those years many economists believed that Kirchner was convinced of the advantages of keeping the peso undervalued to promote exports and import substitution, as predicated by the theorists of Plan Fénix.[2] However, that belief proved to be wrong in 2007, after the peso had appreciated too much in real terms and financial capital started to flee the country. Instead of letting the peso depreciate, Kirchner decided that the Central Bank should keep the nominal value of the peso unchanged. He authorized a strategy to cheat the markets, that had been invented by the president of the Central Bank Martín Redrado, that forced an additional appreciation of the peso to discourage dollarization of assets by local holders of peso-denominated assets.

As in all other matters, his decisions on debt and money were not ideological, but pragmatic and more oriented to his own political benefit than to the stability and growth of the economy.

So far, I have described Kirchner's metamorphosis with respect to his four years as president. However, the story is different for the two periods of his wife Cristina Fernández de Kirchner. The turn she made was much more ideological and was inspired by Chávez's 21st century socialism. It is not clear if in her case it was a turn at all. She expanded the arbitrary interventions in markets, the nationalization of companies, imposed widespread price and exchange controls, and, of course, did not solve any of the disequilibria created by Duhalde's and her husband's governments. On the contrary, they all grew worse.

Notes

1 See *The Economist*. 19 July 2001 (http://www.economist.com/node/702434). See also interview with CNN, 17 August 2001, quoted in several Argentina mass media. For an example, refer to *La Nación*, 18 August 2001, Buenos Aires, Argentina, page 7 (www.lanacion.com.ar/328392-eeuu-se-mostro-cauto-con-respecto-a-la-posible-ayuda-financiera).
2 In September 2001, a group of professors of the Universidad Nacional de Buenos Aires published the first draft of the so called 'Plan Fenix' that proposed a return to the economic policies that had prevailed during the 1970s and 1980s. The best known member of the group was Aldo Ferrer. See http://www.econ.uba.ar/planfenix/index2.htm

References

Hanke, Steve and Shuler, Kurt (1999) *A Dollarization Blueprint for Argentina*, Washington, DC: Foreign Policy Briefing No 52, Cato Institute.
INDEC (Instituto Nacional de Estadísticas y Censos) http://www.indec.gov.ar/.
Lerrik, Adam and Meltzer, Allan H. (2001) *Beyond IMF Bailouts: Default without Disruption*, Carnegie Mellon Gailliot Center for Public Affairs Quarterly International Economics Report, May 2001.
Mussa, Michael (2002) *Argentina and the Fund: from Triumph to Tragedy*, Washington, DC: Institute for International Economics, July.

17 Duhalde and the Kirchners

During the 1990s, Argentina defeated hyperinflation with strict monetary rule and inaugurated a period of stability and growth with its economy well integrated into the global economy. At the time of a sharp deterioration in terms of trade, between 1999 and 2001, this strategy did not help to prevent a recession turning into debt-deflation. This crisis was fatal for De la Rúa's presidency. He had to resign in the midst of riots after working to avoid default and devaluation.

As explained in Chapter 16, initially Eduardo Duhalde and after him Néstor and Cristina Kirchner reversed most of the reforms that were introduced during Menem's governments and prevailed under De la Rúa's.

During the 2000s, Chile, Mexico, Colombia, Perú, Uruguay, Paraguay and most Central American countries deepened the reforms that started in the 1990s, while Argentina, Brazil, Bolivia, Ecuador, Nicaragua, and Venezuela embraced what Venezuela's president Hugo Chávez christened 'the socialism of the 21st century'. That trend, in realty, was no more than a return to the statism and isolationism that prevailed in most Latin American countries before the market-oriented reforms of the 1990s.

After 13 years of regression to policies similar to those that prevailed between 1945 and 1990, Argentineans voted in 2015 for a return to foreign and economic policies more in line with what had been the Latin American Consensus of the 1990s. Mauricio Macri, the candidate of the coalition 'Cambiemos' ('Let's change' in English) was elected President.

Macri's initial declarations and actions show clearly that Venezuela is no longer a role model for Argentina. It may be that over time the other countries under Venezuela's influence will follow suit.

Politics between 2002 and 2015

After the resignation of De la Rúa in December 2001 and the interim two-day presidency of the Senate's President Ramón Puerta, the provincial governors proposed designating Adolfo Rodriguez Saá as president with a mandate to call for a new election within two months. The riots that had forced the resignation of De la Rúa continued and after seven days the organizers of the institutional coup forced the resignation of Rodriguez Saá, as well. This time, with the support of the Radicals led by former president Raúl Alfonsín, Congress designated Eduardo Duhalde as the new president to complete De la Rúa's term. He was supposed to transfer power to his successor on 10 December 2003 after a presidential election that would take place in October of that year.

Instead of fixing the debt problem in an orderly way and changing the monetary rule to allow for more flexible inflation targeting, Eduardo Duhalde opted for a disorderly debt default and a change in the monetary regime. The new monetary regime led to the destruction of the contractual base of the economy by forcing the conversion of all dollar contracts into pesos.

The default and the forced conversion of contracts provoked a significant devaluation of the peso and opened the door for a damaging freeze in public utility rates, price controls, distortionary taxes, and administrative interventions thought to be substitutes for an inflation targeting monetary rule.

Initially Duhalde's government froze wages, pensions and public utility rates, and introduced taxes on agricultural exports and price controls on beef and other items in the consumer basket to try to avoid the spiralling inflation that had jumped from −1 per cent to 41 per cent per year.

By the end of 2002, worried by the possibility of new riots, Duhalde decided to shorten his term and called for an election in March to transfer power on 25 May 2003. Néstor Kirchner won the election and became the new president for the 2003 to 2007 term.

At the end of 2002, an expansionary fiscal policy was initially useful in spurring economic growth, even without significant investment in key sectors of the economy that were still well capitalized as a result of the reforms of the previous decade.

In 2003, as foreign terms of trade recovered and the dollar weakened in world markets, the Argentine economy, which between 1998 and 2002 had suffered a 25 per cent decline in GDP, started to recover rapidly and the peso to strengthen. Inflation also started to decline.

The new government led by Néstor Kirchner allowed wages to increase gradually in 2003 and more rapidly after 2005. Government expenditure also started to increase rapidly and by 2006 represented the same proportion of GDP as in 2001, in spite of a sharp reduction in the interest cost of the public debt achieved after the compulsory debt restructuring of 2005.

As monetary policy targeted growth rather than inflation, the Central Bank intervened to stop the appreciation of the peso. After 2005, as wages started to recover, government expenditures increased rapidly and, since monetary expansion was committed to preventing the appreciation of the peso, inflation began to creep up.

Inflation increased to 6 per cent in 2004, 12 per cent in 2005, and then declined slightly to 10 per cent in 2006, when price controls produced a temporary reduction. However, it rose again to 18 per cent in 2007 and to 24 per cent in 2008. The government, beginning in 2007, instead of using monetary policy as an anti-inflationary tool, decided to cheat by fixing the official measurement of inflation at around 8 per cent through data manipulation.

In 2007, Kirchner decided not to seek a second term. Instead, he encouraged his wife, Senator Cristina Fernández, to run. It was a strategy to create a Kirchner dynasty with Néstor planning to run again in 2011. This continuous switching from one to the other would avoid the constitutional restriction of only two successive terms. Cristina won the election with Julio Cobos, the former governor of Mendoza and a member of the Radical Party as his running mate. Cristina did not compete against candidates that represented the policies of the 1990s, but against Roberto Lavagna, the former economic minister to both, Duhalde and Kirchner and whose candidacy was supported by Duhalde and the Radicals.

During Cristina's first presidential term, the economy continued to grow quickly, except during 2009, when the global recession and a conflict with farmers produced a recession. Favourable external terms of trade and large fiscal and monetary stimulus to support domestic demand boosted growth.

The intervention of the government in the markets, the restrictions on foreign trade, the freezing of public utility rates, the renationalization of public utility companies, and the large increase in government expenditures and tax pressure constituted a de facto counter-reform of the economy that was a sharp contrast with the reforms of the 1990s.

In October 2010, Néstor Kirchner died and the apparent economic success plus the emotional impact of Néstor's death increased Cristina's popularity. She ran for re-election in 2011 competing against numerous opposition candidates, Eduardo Duhalde and Ricardo Alfonsín, the son of former President Raúl Alfonsín, among them. She won with 54 per cent of the vote, well ahead of the second-largest vote getter, Hermes Binner, the former Governor of Santa Fe and the Socialist Party's candidate.

In her second term, Cristina became more ideological and clearly supported the ideas of Chávez's 21st century socialism. During this period, she came to rely upon a group of young economists, politicians, and some members of the government who were close to the leftist Peronist groups that Perón had expelled from Plaza de Mayo in his last public appearance in the 1970s. These individuals filled the role that her husband, Néstor, had played until his death. She appointed Axel Kicillof as economic minister and embraced his views on economic history and economic policies.

Immediately after the election, she intensified the interventionist measures from the previous years and established exchange controls. The economy entered a new period of stagflation that made the unsustainability of the policies of the last 12 years increasingly apparent. She persisted and did not make any decision to soften the problems that whoever succeeded her would inherit. On the contrary, she gave her support to the only candidate of her party that had any chance of winning the election, former Vice-President and twice Governor of Buenos Aires Daniel Scioli. He had to commit himself to continuing her policies and based his campaign on the same narrative she had

242 *Reform and counter-reform*

espoused during the last four years which was, as mentioned above, based on Kicillof's interpretation of history.

Daniel Scioli lost the election in the runoffs and Mauricio Macri, an engineer and entrepreneur, who had been twice governor of the City of Buenos Aires became the new president. He took office on 10 December 2015.

Duhalde's economy

The forceful conversion of all dollar contracts, including bank deposits and loans, was the most important and, at the same time, the most damaging economic policy decision Duhalde made in 2002. He did it in spite of an explicit promise during his inaugural speech to Congress that 'those that deposited dollars in the banks will be returned dollars'.

A strong lobby of industrialists and bankers that wanted to solve their debt problems convinced Duhalde not to comply with his promise. This would then pass the costs on to the people that had deposited dollars in the banks. With just one magic touch, they wanted to recreate the conditions that for 45 years, between 1945 and 1990, had helped to wipe out debts by producing an unexpected inflationary explosion, well above the contractual nominal interest rate, which would reduce the real burden of debt.

The consequences of this decision were terrible. First, the devaluation of the peso, (which nobody expected) that would bring the exchange rate above 1.4 pesos per dollar, was extremely large. By July 2002, the exchange rate was 3.8 pesos per dollar in spite of the sale of US $5 billion of reserves by the Central Bank. Some economists believed that the forced conversion of dollar contracts was inevitable after Congress modified the Convertibility Law to allow the peso to float freely, because otherwise most debtors would have become insolvent. If that were the case, the Central Bank would have had to regulate mechanisms to spread the effect of the devaluation on dollar debts or encouraged private negotiations between debtors and the banks to restructure bad debts over time.

In the interval between the reform of the Convertibility Law by Congress on 11 January and 2 February, the day that the government announced the forced total conversion of dollars into pesos on a one-to-one for loans and one-to-1.4 for deposits, the exchange rate in the free market was below 2 pesos per dollar. There was a clear overshooting because there were only 12 billion pesos circulating and the foreign reserves in the Central Bank were only US $15 billion. Even counting the 8 billion pesos of quasi-monies that the provinces had issued to pay salaries in the previous years, the relationship between the stock of pesos and quasi-monies was 20 to 14. Therefore, the Central Bank could have exchanged all the pesos and quasi-monies per dollars at a rate of 1.42 pesos per dollar.

Before the forced conversion from dollars into pesos, the composition of private sector assets included 16 billion pesos and US $44 billion. The monetary base was 12 billion pesos. After the conversion, the private sector lost all its dollars and suddenly became the holder of 77 billion pesos. During the first month, depositors were able to withdraw 6 billion pesos so by the end of January their assets in the banking system were 71 billion pesos. The monetary base started to increase rapidly. By June it had increased 78 per cent and by December 143 per cent. The depositors that during January had withdrawn 6 billion pesos continued withdrawing pesos and at the end of June the total assets of the private sector in the banking system had fallen to 62 billion pesos.

The 15 billion pesos that disappeared from the banking system purchased dollars at an average price of three pesos per dollar. That explains why from December 2001 to June 2002 the Central Bank sold foreign reserves of US $5 billion. By selling dollars the Central Bank reduced the amount that the monetary base expanded, but even still, the monetary base expanded 193 per cent by June and 241 per cent by December 2002.

There is no doubt that this flood of pesos explains the extreme depreciation of the peso that in June 2002 brought the peso to a price of 3.5 pesos to the dollar. People did not want to keep those pesos in their portfolios and ran to exchange them for dollars. That would not have happened if the government had kept people's assets in dollars rather than forcefully peso-ifying them.

If the peso had devalued from one to 1.4 pesos per dollar, as had been the original intention of Jorge Remes Lenicov, the first economic minister under Duhalde, the contractual base of the economy would not have been affected and many of the problems that the large devaluation created could have been avoided. The strong lobby for the forced conversion convinced Duhalde to take the wrong way.

As shown in Figure 17.1, the immediate consequence of the large devaluation was a 60 per cent increase in the prices of tradable goods relative to the consumer price index (CPI) while most of the prices of non-tradable goods, including wages, salaries, and pensions, remained almost constant. Therefore, there was a sharp deterioration of wages, salaries and pensions in real terms. Average real wages and salaries declined 18 per cent, real wages for workers in the informal sector declined 34 per cent, and pensions declined 32 per cent.

The number living below the poverty line, already high in 2001, jumped from 38.9 per cent of the population in October 2001 to 53 per cent in May 2002 and to 57.5 per cent in October 2002. In May 2003, at the time of the change of government, it was still 54.7 per cent. Table 17.1 shows these numbers.

The result of the peso-ification was a transfer of billions of dollars of wealth from depositors to debtors through the banking system and a large transfer of real income from workers and pensioners to producers of tradable goods. It is impossible to imagine a more inequitable redistribution of wealth and income than that which was engineered by the forced conversion of dollars into pesos.

Worried by the inflationary impact of devaluation, Duhalde decided to freeze public utility rates, particularly those of energy, transportation and

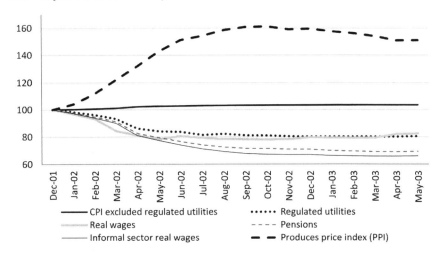

Figure 17.1 Evolution of relative prices after peso-ification
(December 01=100)
Source: authors' own calculations, based on material originally published in INDEC, Índices de precios.

Table 17.1 Evolution of poverty rate 2001–2003
(percentage below poverty line)

Date	Households	Persons
May 2001	26.2	35.9
Oct. 2002	28.0	38.3
May 2002	41.4	53.0
Oct. 2002	45.7	57.5
May 2003	42.6	54.7

Source: authors' own calculations, based on material originally published in INDEC, Bases de datos.

communications. Therefore, on average and in real terms, rates declined 20 per cent, but the price of natural gas, electricity, and urban transport services relative to the CPI declined 32 per cent. In practice, the freeze of public utility prices constituted a virtual confiscation of the assets of the companies that had invested in privatizations during the 1990s. Of course, investment in these sectors stopped and production continued based on existing capacity alone.

The peso-ification had a significant fiscal cost in spite of the relief it meant for the service of public debt, because the government had to compensate the banks for the difference between the conversion rate of deposits (1.4 pesos per dollar) and the conversion rate of loans (one peso per dollar). The government had to issue new bonds in the amount of US $35 billion increasing total public debt from US$135 billion at the end of 2001 to US$170 billion at the end of 2002.

As soon as Duhalde realized that in addition to the benefits debtors obtained from the peso-ification, exporters also got a significant increase in their export proceeds, he decided to introduce taxes on agriculture and oil exports like those that had been imposed in the 1970s and 1980s. Therefore, the export taxes that had disappeared during the reforms of the 1990s again became an important source of government revenue.

Thanks to the nearly 50 per cent drop in the interest bill and the reduction of primary expenditures in real terms that resulted from the fall of salaries paid to public employees, fiscal accounts improved by 3 per cent of GDP. The fiscal deficit that had been 4.6 per cent in 2001 fell to 1.6 per cent. The bulk of the improvement was the reduction in the interest bill that declined from 4.3 per cent to 2.1 per cent of GDP. In spite of the introduction of export taxes, total revenue as a percentage of GDP went down slightly. Table 17.2 reports these numbers. The effect of exports taxes started to show up in the following years. Thanks to the increase in tax revenues starting in 2003, the fiscal accounts generated a surplus for the first time in many years.

The economy during the governments of Néstor and Cristina Kirchner

When Néstor Kirchner took the oath as the new president on 25 May 2003, he inherited many distortions in relative prices, but he was happy with two key events that would allow him to build power: the fiscal surplus generated by the export taxes and the increase in the foreign terms of trade. Of course, export taxes would reinstate the gap between domestic and foreign terms of trade that had been endemic to the Argentine economy until the mid-1980s and this ran the risk of discouraging investment and productivity in agriculture as had happened in the past. However, Néstor Kirchner was not worried about investment and productivity. Export taxes would give him not only additional revenue but also an instrument to build political power. Since export taxes were not automatically shared with the provinces he could allocate them at his own discretion.

Figure 17.2 shows the improving foreign terms of trade and the increasing gap with domestic terms of trade produced by the export taxes.

Table 17.2 Fiscal account for the consolidated public sector, 2001–2003 (in percentage of GDP)

Year	Primary expenditure	Total expenditure	Total revenue	Primary deficit (-)	Interest bill	Total deficit (-)
2001	21.3	25.6	20.9	−0.3	4.3	−4.6
2002	19.8	21.9	20.2	0.5	2.1	−1.6
2003	20	21.8	22.5	2.5	1.8	0.8

Source: authors' own calculations, based on material originally published in Ministerio de Economía.

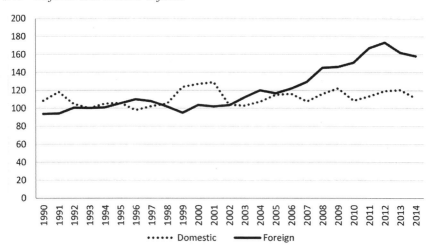

Figure 17.2 Domestic and foreign terms of trade 1990–2014 (1990=100)
Source: authors' own calculations, based on material originally published in Ferreres (2010).

The economists that gave intellectual support to the commercial policies adopted by Duhalde and, for some years, by the Kirchners, argued that exports taxes would not discourage exports because the undervalued peso was stimulating production of exportable goods. This was one of the main assertions of the so-called Plan Fénix and, at the same time, the main criticism of the commercial policies of the 1990s. Figure 17.3 shows the different exchange rate policies before abandoning convertibility. There is no doubt that between 2002 and 2015 the average real value of the peso was much lower than between 1991 and 2001.

The relative export performance between the two periods contradicts the assertion that the undervaluation of the peso compensated for the disincentive created by the export taxes. Figure 17.4 shows that the value of exports in current dollars increased more during the 1990s than during the 2000s. Total exports increased 9 per cent per year during the period of 1989 to 2001 and only 6 per cent per year in the period of 2001 to 2015 in spite of the much higher export prices during the second period. Manufactured goods of agricultural origin are the only item where exports were higher during the period of 2001 to 2015 and this was purely a price effect.

Figure 17.5 compares export performance based on constant prices figures. The contrast is striking. While exports at constant prices increased 10 per cent between 1989 and 2001, between 2001 and 2015 they increased only 1 per cent. At constant prices, the exports of manufactured goods of agricultural origin increased 6 per cent in the first period compared with only 2 per cent between 2001 and 2015. And, in spite of the insistence of Néstor and Cristina

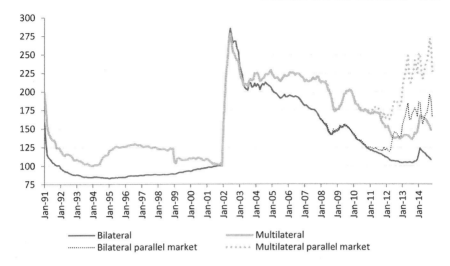

Figure 17.3 Bilateral and multilateral real exchange rate (December 2001=100)
Source: authors' own calculations, based on material originally published in Ferreres (2010).

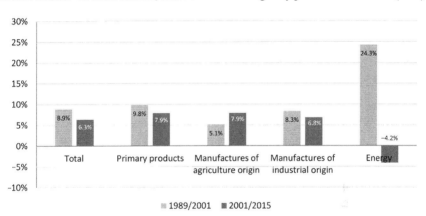

Figure 17.4 Comparative export performance, 1989/2001 and 2001/2015
Note: annual rate of growth of exports at current prices.
Source: authors' own calculations, based on material originally published in INDEC, Comercio Exterior.

Kirchner that their priority was to re-industrialize the country, exports of industrial origin at constant prices, which in the period 1989–2001 had expanded at 8 per cent per year, during the period 2001–2015 expanded only 2 per cent per year. Of course, the extreme contrast relates to exports of energy. While energy exports expanded at 21 per cent per year during the 1990s, over the past 15 years they declined 9 per cent per year.

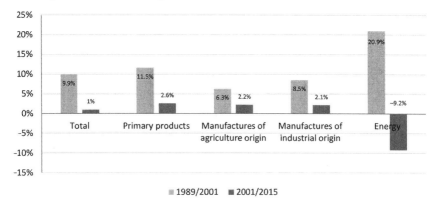

Figure 17.5 Comparative export performance 1989/2001 and 2001/2015
Note: Annual rate of growth of exports at constant prices.
Source: authors' own calculations, based on material originally published in INDEC, Comercio Exterior.

The poor performance of exports during the period 2002–2015 happened because productivity lost the dynamism that it had had in the 1990s. The comparison between crop yield in Argentina and the USA provides again a clear indication of the stagnation of productivity. In spite of favourable external terms of trade for agriculture between 2002 and 2015, crop yield for wheat, corn and soybeans interrupted the rapid expansion that had existed until 2001. Therefore, the gap between yields in the USA and Argentina widened as had happened previously. Figure 17.6 extends the information already presented in Figure 9.3 and Figure 15.7 until 2015 and shows the stagnation of productivity in agriculture.

The allocative and fiscal effects of price distortions

In addition to the wide changes in relative prices that resulted from the peso-ification, the most distinctive characteristic of economic policy after 2002 was widespread interventions by the state in affecting the structure of relative prices using taxes, quantity regulations, and exchange and price controls. These interventions affected relative prices, sometimes in the opposite direction from those that arose from peso-ification, but in some crucial cases, accentuating the disequilibria created by the initial shock.

Salaries in real terms that at the beginning suffered a significant drop, recovered after a few years. However, the recovery was not uniform. Figure 17.7 shows the evolution of different categories of salaries.

While salaries in the public sector never recovered in real terms, salaries paid by private employers not only recovered rapidly, but also exceeded the levels of 2001 by 37 per cent in 2013 and were still 28 per cent above in 2014

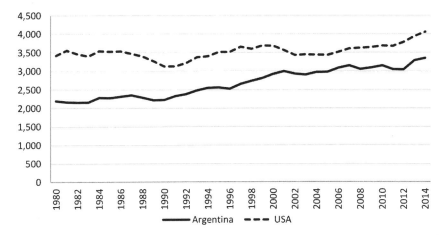

Figure 17.6 Average yield of wheat, corn and soybean, 1980–2014
Note: average yield is measured in Kg/Ha.
Source: authors' own calculations, based on material originally published in US Department of Agriculture and Ferreres (2010).

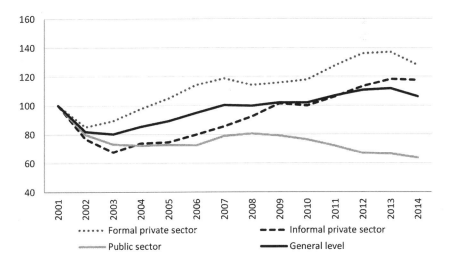

Figure 17.7 Evolution of salaries in real terms, 2001–2004
(fourth quarter 2001=100)
Source: authors' own calculations, based on material originally published in Ferreres (2010).

despite devaluation of the peso in February of that year. Even the salaries paid in the informal sectors of the economy which in 2002 had virtually collapsed were close to 20 per cent above the level of 2001 by 2014. The average salary for the economy as a whole was only 9 per cent above the 2001 level; however, that was the consequence of the increased weight of public sector employment as part of total employment.

250 Reform and counter-reform

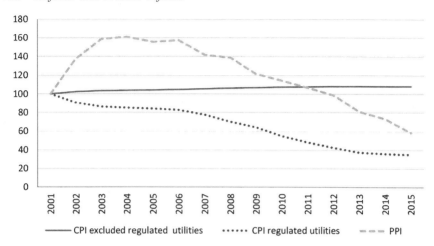

Figure 17.8 Prices relative to CPI index, 2001–2015
(December 2001=100)
Source: authors' own calculations, based on material originally published in Ferreres (2010).

Figure 17.8 shows the evolution of prices charged by the producers of goods and by the public utilities. Here also there is an extreme divergence at the beginning but a convergence afterwards. Producers' prices increased 60 per cent in 2002 above the level of consumer prices, but after 2011 they went down and by 2015 they were 30 per cent below the level of 2001. The decline in public utilities prices that began in 2002 continued, and by 2015, they were 65 per cent below the level of 2001.

The sustained deterioration of public utility prices explains the deterioration of the quality of the services, the shortages, and, especially the transformation of a surplus of foreign trade in energy into a large deficit.

The decline in prices received by producers of goods combined with the significant increase in salaries paid by the private sector explains the loss of competitiveness and the decline in exports of industrial origin. It resembles the phenomena that followed the expansion of Argentine industrial exports during the Second World War. The policies of import substitution and encouragement of salary increases during the first years of Perón's government made it impossible for manufacturing companies to continue exporting so their production was exclusively oriented to the domestic market. Peronist interventions in the market to increase salaries in real terms ended up destroying the capacity of local industry to export their production. That means that industrialization would become domestic market-dependent and require permanent protection from import competition.

In addition to the allocation effects of relative price distortions, they also produced fiscal effects that were damaging. In order to sustain the provision of public utilities, as the authorized prices did not cover the variable costs of production, the government was obliged to pay subsidies to the public utility companies. These subsidies became an increasingly important part of government expenditures and contributed to the complete reversal of the fiscal surpluses of the initial years after convertibility. Table 17.3 shows the fiscal accounts from 2003 to 2015.

From fiscal conservatism to reckless spending

Fiscal discipline was something I respected from Kirchner's governance of the Province of Santa Cruz in the 1990s. Until 2007 he stood for fiscal discipline although he emphasized revenue increases rather than expenditure restraint. Primary expenditures as a proportion of GDP reached the same level of 2001 in 2004, 21.3 per cent, and continued to increase up to 24.4 per cent in 2007. Revenue increased from 22.5 per cent in 2003 to 26.9 per cent in 2007 thanks to export taxes and an income tax on salaries that in the past did not reach the minimum taxable income, but became taxable due to lack of inflation adjustment for that minimum. However, whatever the origin, in 2007 there was still a fiscal surplus.

The fiscal surpluses from 2003 to 2005 helped the government rebuild foreign reserves without printing money and, using those reserves, repay all the debt to the IMF in 2005. Kirchner preferred to pre-pay payments to the IMF rather than use the reserves to facilitate the restructuring of the debt to non-official creditors because he wanted to shed all IMF conditions that might restrict his manoeuvring room on economic policy.

Table 17.3 Fiscal accounts for the consolidated public sector, 2003–2015 (in percentage of GDP)

Year	Primary expenditure	Total expenditure	Total revenue	Primary deficit (-)	Interest bill	Total deficit (-)
2003	20	21.8	22.5	2.5	1.8	0.8
2004	21.3	22.5	25.6	4.3	1.2	3.1
2005	22.3	24	25.8	3.5	1.7	1.8
2006	22.8	24.3	25.8	3	1.5	1.5
2007	24.4	26.2	26.9	2.5	1.7	0.7
2008	26	27.5	27.9	1.8	1.5	0.3
2009	29.8	31.6	28.7	−1	1.9	−2.9
2010	30.3	31.6	30.4	0.1	1.3	−1.2
2011	31.7	33.4	30.3	−1.4	1.7	−3
2012	33.4	35.4	31.9	−1.5	2	−3.5
2013	36	37.4	33.5	−2.6	1.3	−3.9
2014	39.5	41.2	35.9	−3.6	1.7	−5.3
2015	40.8	42.8	35.7	−5.1	2	−7.1

Source: authors' own calculations, based on material originally published in Ministerio de Economía.

With the decline of the fiscal surplus after 2005, the purchase of foreign reserves by the Central Bank to prevent the appreciation of the peso required increasing the monetary supply that triggered inflation. Throughout the year 2007, when Cristina campaigned for the presidency, Néstor looked for new sources of revenue as a way to neutralize the inflationary pressure. After the election, he decided that the additional revenue would again come from export taxes. The price of soybeans continued to increase in the international market. Therefore, Néstor advised Cristina to increase the export tax rate on agriculture. That decision created the first major popular opposition to the Kirchners. Farmers reacted against the decision, there were three months of conflict, and finally Congress revoked the decision of the president. The vice-president, having to break a tie in the Senate, voted against the initiative of the president, which distanced Julio Cobos from the Kirchners for the remainder of the presidential term.

After the failure to increase the tax rate on agricultural exports, Amado Boudou, the new economic minister who had been president of the Social Security Agency (ANSES) presented the idea of dissolving the private pension fund system that had been created in the 1990s. This way the government could take the monthly withholding on salaries that went to a worker's private individual account and the cash would become part of general tax revenue. At the same time, the government would take over the administration of the portfolio that was supposed to guarantee future pension benefits from the private pension fund managers. Both the Kirchners liked the idea and they submitted to Congress a bill to 're-nationalize the Social Security System'. They did not present this idea as the appropriation of the funds of the future retirees by the government, but as a modification of the Social Security System to return to the solidarity concept. They used the opportunity created by the depreciation of assets caused by the global financial crisis to demonstrate the supposed incompetence and corruption of private pension fund administrators when it came to managing the savings of future retirees.

The political propaganda convinced most of Congress to pass the law with a large majority. So, beginning in 2009, the 2 per cent of GDP that workers were saving from their monthly pay were transformed into taxes to finance the government. Formally, this money would enter into ANSES, but in fact ANSES would become another window for non-pension government outlays. Even the returns on the assets transferred to ANSES would become government revenue.

This sort of tax creativity also showed up in the provinces. They increased tax rates on rural and urban land and recreated taxes such as the stamp tax and the gross income tax on agriculture and manufacturing which had disappeared in the 1990s. Tax pressure continued to grow and reached 35.7 per cent of GDP in 2015, 70 per cent higher than in 2001.

In spite of the significant rise in government revenue, the picture for government expenditure remained grim. Primary expenditures as a proportion of GDP doubled from 2001 to 2015 and total expenditures reached the second highest proportion to GDP in economic history in 2015, surpassed only in 1948, the year Perón spent most of the country's gold reserves that had accumulated during the Second World War. Primary expenditures grew from 25.6 per cent in 2001 to 42.8 per cent in 2015.

The increase in government expenditures resulted mainly from two sources: subsidies that were paid to the public utility companies affected by the rate freeze and the losses of and investments in the renationalized companies like Aerolíneas Argentinas and newly created state companies like ARSAT (the acronym for Argentina Satelital, a telecommunication company). In addition, the number of public employees and retirees almost doubled from 2001 to 2015. In spite of the deterioration of public salaries in real terms, the total salary outlays and social security benefits as a proportion of GDP increased significantly. And, of course, there were plenty of expenses associated with publicity, financing the public media system and the media of friends of the government, and contracts for the overpriced provision of goods and services.

Therefore, in spite of the extraordinarily high tax pressure, the fiscal deficit was 7.1 per cent of GDP in 2015. Of course, a completely different fiscal picture showed Néstor Kirchner as a fiscally conservative governor during the 1990s.

Social security counter-reform

During the government of the Kirchners, social security policy underwent numerous changes when compared to the 1990s. Table 17.4 shows the numbers that help to explain the changes.

These changes came at a time when the number of retirees almost doubled from 3.3 million in 2001 to 5.8 million in 2015. The decision in 2005 to offer the possibility of a moratorium to those who had never contributed, but would still allow them to get the minimum pension meant an increase of 2.5 million beneficiaries. The transfer of the retirees from the capitalized system that disappeared in 2008 and influx of new retirees explains the rest of the increase in the number of beneficiaries.

From 2002 to 2007, the government kept pensions higher than 1,000 pesos per month frozen and increased the minimum pension at a rate higher than inflation starting in 2003. This way, by 2008, the number of retirees that had benefits above the minimum had fallen from 2.6 million to only 1.4 million. This is why the number of retirees receiving the minimum pension increased by 3.2 million of which 2.5 million were those that entered in the moratorium and 680,000 were retirees that, until 2001, had received a pension higher than the minimum but that during the years their pensions were frozen fell into the minimum pension category.

Clearly, the Kirchners' policy was meant to increase the number of beneficiaries and raise the minimum pension at the cost of reducing the benefits of those retirees that had been receiving benefits above the minimum since 1992. The retirees whose benefits were frozen from 2002 to 2007 sued ANSES in

Table 17.4 Evolution of the number of retirees and of pensions 2001–2015

December 31 of year	Number of retirees	Of which receive the minimum pension	Minimum pension	Average pension	Minimum pension	Average pension	Minimum pension	Average pension
	(in thousand persons)		(in current pesos)		(in constant pesos at the prices of December 2015)		(in constant dollars at the parallel exchange rate)	
2001	3,301	725	150	412	2,018	5,240	204	559
2002	3,268	720	150	421	1,432	4,032	56	159
2008	5,301	3,900	690	840	3,346	4,207	228	286
2015	5,787	4,100	4,229	7,662	4,222	7,650	297	538

Source: authors' own calculations, based on material originally published in *Boletín Estadístico de la Seguridad Social* (2012).

court and the Supreme Court ruled that ANSES was obliged to increase their benefits by 88 per cent and pay the difference between the adjusted and unadjusted benefits for the period 2002–2007. From 2008, ANSES adjusted the pensions and paid the compensation to a limited number of retirees each year. This resulted in the average pension in 2008 exceeding the minimum pension by only 25 per cent, while in 2001 it had been 75 per cent higher. In spite of the decision by the Supreme Court, a large number of beneficiaries have not yet received their adjusted pensions nor have they received the compensation for their frozen pensions. The Kirchner administrations transferred this hidden debt to Macri's government. Experts estimate this debt to be around US $20 billion and the annual cost of the complete adjustment of pensions that remained frozen between 2002 and 2007 represents 0.5 per cent of GDP.

In social security matters the Kirchners extended the benefits to reach more people, but at high current and future fiscal costs and without any consideration for inter-temporal solvency. The liquidation of the capitalized pension system introduced in the 1990s meant an additional blow for the future solvency of the system because even when ANSES argues that it is creating a 'sustainability fund' with part of the social security contributions of workers, the returns on those funds are not capitalized but transferred to the treasury. Consequently, inflation quickly erodes the sustainability of the fund.

Debt management

Even though the promoters of peso-ification thought of it as an instrument for reducing debts in real terms, in practice it had a boomerang effect. The peso-ification increased the stock of defaulted debt from the US $52 billion affected by Rodriguez Saá's moratorium to US $92 billion with the reversal of the majority of the guaranteed loan. In addition, Duhalde had to issue new bonds worth US $35 billion to compensate for the losses that resulted from the asymmetric treatment of deposits and loans meant for banks. Therefore, despite defaulting, in 2002 public debt increased from US $135 billion to $170 billion.

From 2002 until 2005, the government did not pay any interest on the defaulted debt, but continued paying interest to the multilateral institutions and the creditors that purchased the newly issued bonds. In 2005, Kirchner decided to make an offer to the holders of defaulted debt that comprised a 60 per cent haircut on the principal and a 100 per cent haircut on past due interest. To convince the bondholders to accept the offer he decided to get Congressional approval for the so-called locked law, a law that prohibited any future payment to the holdouts. Some 75 per cent of the holders of defaulted bonds accepted the offer in 2005 and 17 per cent more accepted in 2010 when the government reopened the exchange. Therefore, Kirchner and his economic minister could claim great success in reducing the debt in an amount that was similar to the amount of new bonds issued by Duhalde. In reality, public debt was still very close to the amount outstanding at the end of 2001; but, it had the advantage of a significant extension of terms and a reduction in interest rates. To confirm his policy of debt reduction and to get rid of any conditionality imposed by the IMF, Kirchner decided to use the reserves of the Central Bank to cancel US $4 billion of obligations to the IMF. Total debt did not go down by that amount because Kirchner started to issue bonds marketed through the intermediation of Venezuela. This debt had a cost that was twice as high as the loans from the IMF, but Kirchner preferred it because it lacked conditionality.

In 2005 and 2006, the government could also issue domestic bonds adjustable by the CPI with a relatively low real interest rate. However, the market for these bonds disappeared after 2007 because INDEC (the Spanish acronym for the Instituto Nacional de Estadística y Censos, the Argentine statistical bureau) started to lie about the CPI index. Therefore, the Argentine economy had to function without access to public credit at precisely the moment when the fiscal surpluses were disappearing and fiscal deficits started to demand increasing amounts of financing. From 2007 until 2015, the Central Bank and ANSES started to accumulate long-term non-liquid government bonds issued to finance the fiscal deficits. ANSES received the resources from the appropriation of the accumulated savings of workers who chose to send their contribution to the capitalization pension system and from that part of the workers' contribution that until 2008 had gone to the pension funds. The Central Bank issued new money and whenever it decided to reabsorb part of it, borrowed from the banks through LEBACs (acronym for Letras del Banco Central). In this way, fiscal policy dominated monetary policy that had become mostly accommodating.

Even though the government had lost access not only to foreign capital markets, but also to the domestic capital market, the debt, although hidden, continued to increase at a rapid pace. On the one hand, there were the debts that emerged from the decisions of the Supreme Court in favour of the retirees with frozen pensions from 2002 to 2007. On the other hand, there were the claims of the holdouts and the foreign investors that sued the government in foreign courts and the arbitration mechanisms contemplated in the investment treaties signed by Argentina during the 1990s. Those claims, most of them with final decisions of legitimate foreign courts represent more than US $10 billion of hidden debt. The registered debt as of December 2015 is US $239 billion, adding the US$25 billion of hidden debts raises it to US $264 billion or 50 per cent of GDP, a proportion similar to the one in December 2001.

Monetary policy

During the 1990s monetary policy was committed to keeping the parity between the convertible peso and the dollar and, in 2002, it became endogenous as the forced conversion of dollar deposits into pesos implied an unbounded monetary expansion. From 2003 until 2008 monetary policy was committed to avoiding the nominal appreciation of the peso. Kirchner, still a believer in the theory that growth would come from an undervalued peso, instructed the Central Bank not to let the price of the dollar fall from three pesos per dollar. Table 17.5 reports the main indicators of monetary policy for the period 2001 to 2015.

During 2002 and part of 2003, as a result of the extraordinary monetary expansion that resulted from peso-ification, and as reflected in the 143 per cent increase of the monetary base (M0) in 2002, there was a large outflow of dollars through the capital account of the balance of payments (US $13 billion in 2002 and US $5 billion in 2003). Consequently, money supply (M1) increased only 61 per cent as depositors withdrew cash from banks to purchase foreign exchange. However, in 2003, as people realized that the devaluation had been excessive, the peso started to appreciate. The price of the dollar, which had jumped up 227 per cent in 2002, went down 9 per cent in 2003. In the second half of 2003 and more intensely during 2004, the current account surplus of the balance of payments started to exceed the outflow through the capital account. In 2004, the capital account turned positive and the abundance of dollars accelerated the pace of the appreciation of the peso.

It was at that point that Kirchner ordered the Central Bank to prevent the price of the dollar falling from three pesos and the new president of the Central Bank, Martín Redrado did what the former president, Alfonso Prat-Gay, had resisted. The Central Bank could not control the rate of growth of money supply to prevent the nominal appreciation of the peso because it had to print as much money as necessary to purchase the net inflow of dollars. This way, from 2003 to 2008, the monetary base increased at a pace inconsistent with low inflation and the result was the appreciation of the peso in real terms, even though the Central Bank tried to avoid the nominal appreciation. The real exchange rate went down from 247 in 2002 to 150 in 2008. Of course, the other side of the coin was that annual inflation that had been only 3.7 per cent in 2003 went up to 21.9 per cent in 2008.

The rate of monetary expansion eased in 2008 and 2009, because capital flight started again due to evidence that the peso again looked overvalued in real terms, and inflation seemed not to be slowing.

Because of the 2009 recession caused by the global crisis and some reduction in the prices of exports, the Central Bank started to use monetary policy to promote growth without any concern for inflation. Kirchner decided that the fight against inflation was the responsibility of the secretary of commerce (who should rely on price controls) and was not the main objective of the Central Bank. The new president of the Central Bank, Mercedes Marcó Del Pont, enthusiastically followed the instruction that Martín Redrado had accepted only reluctantly. She managed the Central Bank as if it were a development bank rather than the monetary authority. Consequently, the inflation rate, which due to the global recession had gone down to 16.9 per cent in 2009 increased to 24.9 per cent in 2010 and remained above 20 per cent per year after that.

Table 17.5 Monetary policy indicators 2001–2015

Year	Convertability relationship FXR/M1	Convertability relationship FXR/M3	Demand for money M0	Demand for money M3	Rate of increase M0	Rate of increase M1	Rate of increase The official peso price of the dollar	Black market margin above the official rate (as a percentage)	Real rate of exchange pesos per dollar (2001=100)	Balance of payments Current account	Balance of payments Capital account	Balance of payments Change in foreign reserves
	(in percentage of MS)		(in percentage of GDP)		(annual percentage increase)					(billions of dollars)		
2001	127	21	6	26	−20	−15	0	0	100	−4	−6	−12
2002	121	42	7	21	143	61	227	0	247	9	−12	−5
2003	89	35	9	23	59	58	−10	0	213	8	−3	4
2004	112	40	10	25	13	30	0	0	208	3	2	5
2005	156	48	11	25	4	27	−1	0	195	5	4	9
2006	123	44	11	24	46	20	5	0	191	8	−5	4
2007	147	54	10	24	24	26	1	0	175	7	6	13
2008	146	52	10	23	10	17	2	0	150	7	−8	0
2009	149	52	10	23	12	13	18	0	150	8	−7	1
2010	129	43	10	23	31	36	5	2	131	−2	7	4
2011	89	32	10	25	39	29	6	6	117	−4	−2	−6
2012	72	26	13	26	31	48	10	26	107	−1	−1	−3
2013	53	19	14	27	23	24	22	58	105	−12	3	−12
2014	60	21	14	26	22	31	45	61	106	−8	9	1
2015	47	17	13	26	41	33	12	54	113	−16	14	−5

Source: authors' own calculations, based on material originally published in INDEC, Balance de pagos, BCRA and Ferreres (2010).

In the years that followed, as the government imposed exchange controls to prevent a rapid devaluation of the peso and stop capital flight, monetary policy remained unconcerned with the exchange rate, but fiscal policy started to dominate monetary policy. Money expanded at the rhythm demanded by the increasing fiscal deficit. The exchange controls prevented a more rapid devaluation of the peso, but only in the official market. The increasing margin between the parallel market and the official exchange rates reflected the excess demand for dollars and consequently, repressed inflation.

Therefore, during 13 years, the Argentine economy functioned without any monetary anchor. Not surprisingly, inflation returned and was a widespread and persistent phenomenon just like it had been in the 45 years before convertibility.

Growth and inflation

In addition to the dramatic redistribution effect of peso-ification, the generalized debt default and the large devaluation of the peso, the year 2002 transformed the debt-deflation into an inflationary explosion associated with an additional recession, at least during the first part of the year (see Table 17.6). Consumer prices increased close to 41 per cent and producer prices increased 124 per cent. GDP declined an additional 5 per cent in the first half with most of that drop in the first quarter. In spite of a thin recovery in the second

Table 17.6 Growth and inflation 2001–2015 (in percentage per year)

Year	GDP growth	Rate of inflation
2001	−5.4	−1.6
2002	−11.8	40.8
2003	7.7	3.7
2004	5.2	6.1
2005	8.1	12.3
2006	7.2	9.8
2007	6.9	19
2008	2	21.9
2009	−1	16.3
2010	8	24.9
2011	7.4	21.2
2012	−0.3	23.9
2013	1.7	26.5
2014	−3.6	40.6
2015	−1.2	26

Source: authors' own calculations, based on material originally published in Ferreres (2010).

half, 2002 still ended with a drop of 11.8 per cent in per capita GDP compared to the previous year.

After the second half of 2002, export prices started to increase above import prices and the dollar started to weaken in relation to the Euro and other currencies. Therefore, the main external drivers of the depression of the previous years were reversed. In addition, thanks to court decisions, the depositors that had not accepted the conversion into pesos started to recover their dollars and the government decided to offer new dollarized bonds in exchange for the deposits of those people who had not accepted the peso-ification.

Individuals who held dollars realized that there had been an overshooting in the price of the peso to the dollar and started, little by little, to demand domestic assets that although non-liquid could offer capital gains because they were clearly underpriced. Those assets included properties and cars among others. The price of the dollar stopped rising and the peso started to appreciate, slowly at first, but at a more rapid pace at the beginning of 2003.

The high price of the dollar forced a drastic reduction of imports and import-competing manufacturers started to see increasing domestic demand. Therefore, both export demand at better dollar prices and demand for import substitutes pushed up industrial production which used existing productive capacity. Recovery of manufacturing and construction began in the second half of 2002 and gained strength in 2003 and 2004. Of course, it was a recovery using existing capacity because total GDP matched the level of 1998 in 2005 and per capita GDP in 2006. Because of the appreciation of the peso in 2003, in parallel with a similar appreciation of the real in Brazil after Lula took office as president, the rate of inflation went down rapidly and 2003 ended with only 3.7 per cent inflation. The prices that in dollar terms remained below market equilibrium started to rise more than the increase in peso terms. Therefore, the appreciation of the peso helped move towards rebalancing the structure of relative prices which were distorted by the initial large devaluation.

By mid-2003, when the price of the dollar went down to 2.8 pesos, economists and businessmen who subscribed to the theory of the advantages of a permanently undervalued currency started to argue that the peso was once again overvalued. Kirchner who had already decided to transform export taxes into the main instrument with which to build his political power ordered Prat-Gay, the president of the Central Bank, to intervene in the exchange market to prevent further appreciation and to stabilize the price of the dollar at around three pesos. From then on, the Central Bank would use pesos to purchase foreign reserves whenever necessary.

The strategy of preventing further nominal appreciation of the peso even at the cost of monetary expansion became the rule when Redrado replaced Prat-Gay as president of the Central Bank.

It was the decision to prevent the nominal appreciation of the peso that triggered the increase in the inflation rate beginning in 2004. As the real rate of exchange sought its equilibrium, even against the will of the government and the advocates of undervaluation of the peso, the peso appreciated in real terms through inflation.

Inflation went up to 6.1 per cent in 2004 and 12.3 per cent in 2005. In 2006, after firing Lavagna as economic minister, Kirchner decided to fight inflation by strengthening price controls and quantitative restrictions on exports, particularly of wheat and beef. Guillermo Moreno, the price-control advocate secretary of commerce, became the inflation fighter. But inflation proved persistent and was still 9.8 per cent in 2006. As already mentioned, at the beginning of 2007, following the advice of Moreno, Néstor Kirchner removed the technical staff at INDEC and ordered the new appointees to start lying about the rate of inflation. Beginning in January 2007, the official rate of inflation remained steady at around 9 per cent per year, while true inflation went up to 19 per cent in 2007 and 21.9 per cent in 2008. In the second half of 2007 for the first time after 2003, the capital account of the balance of payments registered capital flight, albeit still moderate. This phenomenon would continue and grow in the next years, indicating that holders of peso-denominated assets believed that the undervaluation of the peso had disappeared and depreciation became more probable.

In 2009, the global recession affected the Argentine economy as it did most emerging economies. Per capita GDP went down by 1 per cent and inflation slowed to 16.3 per cent because of the fall of world commodity prices. The Argentine government intensified the already strong fiscal stimulus of the previous years, sold foreign reserves to avoid depreciation with the result that the economy recovered rapidly in 2010. Per capita GDP went up 8 per cent in that year, but the expanding demand proved excessive and inflation revived at 24.9 per cent per year.

In 2011, when Néstor Kirchner had died and Cristina was campaigning for re-election, the government intensified both the fiscal stimulus and the price controls. Per capita GDP increased 7.4 per cent, but stubborn inflation was 21.2 per cent. Cristina Kirchner won the election, but capital flight began to intensify over time and accumulated more than US $50 billion by November 2011. The new economic minister Axel Kicillof advised her to enact strict exchange controls in response.

Four years of stagflation

The imposition of exchange controls and additional quantitative restrictions on imports and exports created a gap between the official exchange rate and the exchange rate in the parallel market that, even though illegal, was as active as it had been in the years preceding convertibility. The gap was unstable but the trend was clearly up as shown in Figure 17.3. The exchange and price controls did not help to reduce inflation. On the contrary, they created additional repressed inflation and, at the same time, increased the number of bottlenecks on the supply side of the economy. Not only did the economy suffer from a shortage of public utilities affected by the disinvestment following the price freeze, but the controls impeded normal importation of key inputs of the production processes.

The combination of excessive monetary and fiscal expansion combined with supply side bottlenecks and disincentives for investment generated simultaneously stagnating production and accelerating inflation. This phenomenon was not dissimilar from the stagflation of between 1975 and 1998.

If the distorting control of the official exchange rate, the price controls, and the restrictions on exports had not repressed inflation, the open inflation rate would have been above 40 per cent per year. Therefore, the inflationary problem that Macri's administration actually inherited was more accurately described as being around 40 per cent per year rather than the 26 per cent unofficially registered in 2015.

Unemployment and poverty

The stated objective of the governments of Néstor and Cristina Kirchner was to increase employment. Figure 17.9 shows the official figures published by INDEC and an adjustment to take into account that part of employment that was created by the state to hide virtual unemployment. According to official figures employment increased from 36 per cent of the population in May 2003 to 41.8 per cent in May 2011, the government's goal. However, after this date, employment went down to 40.1 per cent in May 2015. Therefore, the official employment figures are consistent with describing rapid growth in the economy after 2011 and stagnation afterwards.

Throughout the 12 Kirchner years, the proportion of public employees in the population increased from 5 per cent, a proportion that was stable from

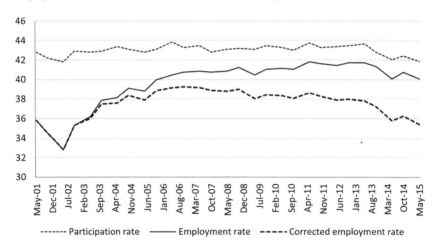

Figure 17.9 Participation and employment rate 2001–2016
 (as a proportion of total population)
Source: authors' own calculations, based on material originally published in INDEC.

1993 to 2003, to 9.4 per cent in 2015. If marginal public employment is subtracted from the official employment figures the adjusted numbers show that at the peak in 2008 it was only 39 per cent of the population and by May 2015 it had gone down to 35.4 per cent, a proportion similar to that of May 2001 and slightly lower than that of May 2003. Therefore, it is clear that the Kirchners were able to increase employment not through private sector employment opportunities, but because the public sector doubled employment during their administrations.

Another indicator that the economy did not really gain in employment during the Kirchner years is the rate of participation of population in the labour force shown also in Figure 17.9. It reached a peak of 48.3 per cent in May 2006, but by May 2015, it was only 41.9 per cent, lower than the 42.8 per cent of May 2001 and similar to the lowest point in the middle of the crisis, May 2002, when the participation rate was 41.9 per cent. Therefore, the number of discouraged workers, that is people who do not look for a job because they are convinced they will not get one and decide to withdraw from the labour force, was as high in 2015 as it was in the worst moments of the crisis from 2001 to 2002.

The description of the evolution of the participation rate and the official and adjusted employment rates helps to explain the misleading message of the unemployment rate that was reported by INDEC. Figure 17.10 shows the official and the corrected unemployment rates. The corrected rate includes the unemployed and the proportion of public sector employees above 5 per cent of the population. It is clear that the true unemployment rate did not go down as the official figures report. In May 2015, the corrected

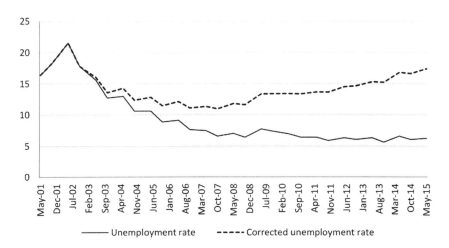

Figure 17.10 Unemployment rate 2001–2016
(as a proportion of active population)
Source: authors' own calculations, based on material originally published in INDEC.

unemployment rate is 17.4 per cent, as high as it was in May 2001 and May 2003.

To complete the picture of results of the policies that the Kirchners declared had the objective of reducing unemployment and poverty, Figure 17.11 presents the official and the true estimates of the proportion of persons living below the poverty line. Of course, they differ since in 2007 INDEC started to lie about the inflation rate. The estimates prepared by the Social Observatory of the Catholic University of Argentina (Universidad Católica Argentina–UCA) show a proportion of persons below the poverty line of 27.4 per cent of the total population in the second half of 2012 while INDEC estimated the same rate as 4.7 per cent. That was the last time INDEC published the official figures on poverty, because the Economic Minister believed that counting the number of poor people was discriminatory. The estimate of the Catholic University for the first half of 2015 was 29 per cent, as high as it was in 2000, immediately before the depression and in 1988, immediately before hyperinflation.

This social picture of Argentina at the end of 2015 demonstrates that a large amount of subsidies together with the increase in the number of public employees increased government expenditures to levels never seen before, and were completely ineffective in changing the picture of unemployment and poverty at the end of the convertibility period. This happened in spite of the favourable external conditions the country enjoyed for 10 of the 12 years of Kirchner governments.

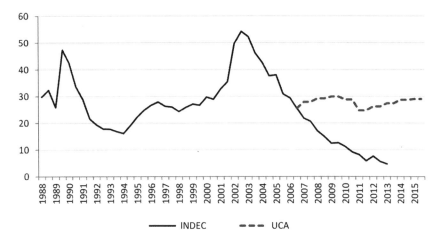

Figure 17.11 Poverty rate 1988–2015
Note: percentage of people under poverty line.
Source: authors' own calculations, based on material originally published in INDEC and UCA.

References

BCRA (Banco Central de la República Argentina) http://www.bcra.gov.ar/Publicacio nesEstadisticas/Monetarias_financieras.asp.

Boletín Estadístico de la Seguridad Social (2012) Buenos Aires: Ministerio de Trabajo, Empleo y Formación de Recursos Humanos, http://www.trabajo.gov.ar/left/estadis ticas/descargas/bess/boletin2trim_2012.pdf.

Cavallo, Domingo F. (2014) *Camino a la Establidad*, Buenos Aires: Sudamericana.

EDSA-Bicentenario (2010–2016) INDEC http://www.indec.gov.ar/bases-de-datos.asp.

Encuesta Permanente de Hogares Continua. EDSA (2007–2009) INDEC http://www.indec.gov.ar/bases-de-datos.asp.

Ferreres, Orlando (2010) *Dos Siglos de Economía Argentina*, Buenos Aires: El Ateneo.

INDEC (Instituto Nacional de Estadísticas y Censos) Balance de pagos, http://www.indec.gov.ar/nivel4_default.asp?id_tema_1=3&id_tema_2=35&id_tema_3=45.

INDEC (Instituto Nacional de Estadísticas y Censos) Bases de datos, http://www.indec.gov.ar/bases-de-datos.asp.

INDEC (Instituto Nacional de Estadísticas y Censos) Comercio Exterior, http://www.indec.gov.ar/nivel3_default.asp?id_tema_1=3&id_tema_2=2.

INDEC (Instituto Nacional de Estadísticas y Censos) Índices de precios http://www.indec.gov.ar/nivel3_default.asp?id_tema_1=3&id_tema_2=5.

INDEC (Instituto Nacional de Estadísticas y Censos) http://www.indec.gov.ar/.

Ministerio de Economía, Secretaria de Hacienda http://www.economia.gob.ar/secreta rias/hacienda/.

US Department of Agriculture, www.nass.usda.gov/statistics_by_subject/?sector=CROPS.

UCA (Universidad Católica Argentina) Observatorio de la Deuda Social Argentina http://www.uca.edu.ar/index.php/site/index/es/uca/observatorio-de-la-deuda-social-a rgentina/deuda-social-argentina/informes-anuales-de-la-deuda-social-argentina/.

Part VI
Conclusions

18 Conclusions

This book had an ambitious objective: to cover Argentina's economic history from colonial times to 1990 and for one of the authors, Domingo Cavallo, to contribute a more detailed account of the last 25 years for the benefit of future historians. Throughout the period Cavallo was an influencer and a major protagonist.

In the first 13 chapters of this book, 400 years of history were reviewed. Historical events were included to the extent that they were considered relevant to understanding the recurring economic and social problems of Argentina. We strategically selected political and economic episodes and their impact on Argentina's history. We concentrated on those that could not be left out when trying to explain the recurring crises and crisis responses. Political events are often overlooked in other economic history books. We have given them particular attention. The dilemmas faced by political leaders in the past are not very different from those faced by present and future generations of leaders.

Chapters 14 to 17 covered a quarter of a century in depth and in Cavallo's own voice. Having occupied multiple important positions allowed him to analyse policies, events and politics far beyond the scope of what a scholar can do because, as an implementer, he experienced first hand the dilemmas, debate and socio-political environment in real time.

This final chapter summarizes the book's main conclusions on foreign policy; fiscal account management, debt management and the role of money; domestic and foreign savings; investment, productivity and long term growth; crisis management and stabilizations plans; and, last but not least, unemployment and poverty.

Foreign policy

More often than not, restrictions on external trade, capital movement, and access to more advanced technologies, whether self-imposed or imposed by circumstances, end up being costly in terms of economic growth and well-being of the population.

Argentina's history sadly provides multiple examples of this dangerous mix of policy and circumstances. When Argentina was part of the Viceroyalty of

Perú, trade restrictions imposed by the Spanish mercantile monopoly severely limited human development in regions that were distant from the mines of Alto Perú. The prohibition on trading with other nations paved the way for smuggling by Portuguese, British, French and Dutch vessels through the port of Buenos Aires. Ironically, Buenos Aires became the capital of the Viceroyalty of Río de la Plata not so much because Spain needed to defend its territory from the Portuguese, but mainly due to the strength of the illegal trade passing through its port.

With the creation of the Viceroyalty of Río de la Plata, external trade, both legal and illegal, expanded. Breaking ties with Spain further opened up trade in the port of Buenos Aires. In spite of the war of independence, the civil wars, and wars with neighbouring nations, trading with the rest of the world was the principal engine of growth and the country's most important source of revenue. The impressive expansion of exports of livestock was a source of wealth for merchants and landowners alike.

Trade was beneficial from an economic standpoint, but it also generated much political tension. After ridding itself of the Spanish mercantile monopoly, Buenos Aires' self-imposed restrictions caused tensions. Initially only Buenos Aires got benefits from freer external trade. For the rest of provinces, the political and commercial order remained as centralized as it was at the time of the Viceroyalty. This situation created constant confrontations and ultimately led to the separation of Bolivia, Paraguay and Uruguay from the United Provinces of Río de la Plata.

Beyond trade relations, foreign relations were, in many aspects, limited. For example, Argentina remained financially isolated for a long period after defaulting on its first foreign loan. As a result, for more than four decades Argentina could not finance the infrastructure and technologies that were at the time reshaping the USA, Canada, Australia and other resource-rich developing economies.

Buenos Aires held on for as long as it could to its control of the Río de la Plata waterways enjoying the monopoly rents from its port. But the ambitions of Buenos Aires alienated the provinces that were part of the Confederation. In the end strongmen from the provinces formerly allied to Juan Manuel de Rosas, revolted against him and forced the approval of a constitution that organized the country as a federal representative republic. Only then would the benefits of free trade reach all of Argentina and bring with it widespread sustainable growth.

The six decades of impressive economic development that followed adoption of the 1853 Constitution came about not only from peace and immigration, but also from trade liberalization. The removal of the restrictions on external trade, on capital movements, and on access to advanced technologies allowed Argentina to take full advantage of the opportunities offered by the first wave of globalization. The country grew faster than the USA, Canada and Australia, and tripled the growth performance of the rest of Latin America. Remarkable social and human development followed.

The expansion of economic and social infrastructure, in particular the educational system inspired by Sarmiento was a tremendous boost to the nation's human capital and enhanced the productivity of locals and immigrants alike.

It was also a period of political and institutional development. Argentina's political system, initially fraudulent, oligarchic, and dominated by landowners, evolved through a series of incremental changes into a democratic system. The cap stone was the Roque Saenz Peña Law that made voting mandatory and established the secrecy of the ballot.

During those seven decades Argentina tried to abide by the rules of international trade and engage in the financial system led by the United Kingdom. But relations with the new emerging economic leader of the world, the United States of America were not as smooth.

In the years between the Great Depression and the beginning of the Second World War, external events led to a series of restrictions on trade and on capital flows. At the same time, the United Kingdom gave trade preference to the countries in the British Commonwealth. Many Argentine elites distrusted the USA and this made it difficult to adapt to the emerging structure of production and trade.

The Second World War and the context immediately post-war had an expansionary effect on production of agricultural and industrial exports while curbing imports of capital goods and non-domestically produced inputs. The traditional ideological clash between liberals and nationalists merged with the confrontation between the pro-Allies and pro-Axis political and military leaders. In the aftermath of the deaths of Agustín P. Justo, Marcelo T. de Alvear and Roberto Ortiz, the discord within the armed forces and the political parties deepened. These confrontations neutralized any positive economic impacts from the war. Furthermore, the clash between domestic interest groups intensified and invited corporatism into the political organization of the country. It was this socio-political environment in the post-Second World War period that prevented Argentina's full integration into the second wave of globalization.

General Juan Perón's statist and isolationist policies initially succeeded in redistributing income in favour of the working class, but had a negative effect on investment and productivity. These policies diverted resources from the more productive sectors of the economy. They promoted activities that could only survive as long as they were highly protected from import competition which required fiscally costly subsidies. Trade restrictions and capital controls aggravated by inflationary financing of fiscal deficits discouraged efficient investment and restricted implementation of technological advances in economic sectors that could have benefited from international trade. Economic growth was thus constrained by the limited expansion of domestic markets. To make matters worse, whenever excessive fiscal and monetary expansion accelerated inflation a large devaluation of the currency and a recession would follow.

Isolationism was Argentina's foreign policy for too long. Argentina did not participate in the Bretton Woods Conference and did not become a member of the International Financial Institutions and the GATT until 1957. Even when it finally joined, Argentina was not effective in negotiating the dismantling of trade restrictions. The timid attempt after 1960 to facilitate regional integration through the Latin American Free Trade Association failed to expand regional trade because the case-by-case bilateral negotiations prevented the removal of tariff and non-tariff barriers. It would be only decades later, in the 1990s, simultaneous with the negotiations of GATT's Uruguay Round and the creation of the World Trade Organization, that the Argentine government would proactively seek to increase access to foreign markets.

The reform of the 1990s, in addition to purging the economy of inflation, reversed the isolationist policies of the previous 45 years. Trade was liberalized by eliminating export taxes, removing all quantitative restrictions on imports and exports, and reducing and simplifying import duties. At the same time, capital controls were eliminated and bilateral investment agreements were signed with most countries of the world. Even though export prices relative to import prices were stable and terms of trade were not any better than they had been in the past, export performance in every sector of the economy outpaced that of the previous decades. In addition, Argentina's export performance was better than that of Brazil during the same period and similar to that of Chile, Latin America's best export performer.

The reforms of the 1990s not only eliminated distortions from the structure of relative prices but incentivized investment in energy, transportation and telecommunication infrastructure which, in turn, eased supply side bottlenecks and lessened inefficiencies that in the past had impeded competitiveness and depressed the production of goods for export.

If the counter-reform that began in 2002 did not have an initial negative effect on exports, it was because the large devaluation of 2002 compensated for all the distortive anti-export measures reintroduced by Duhalde and the Kirchners. However, once the overvaluation of the peso began to weaken, the export taxes, the quantitative restrictions on imports and exports, the exchange controls, and the supply bottlenecks discouraged not only agricultural exports but also manufacturing and service exports. Consequently, in spite of extremely favourable terms of trade from 2003 to 2012, the export performance of Argentina was significantly inferior to that of Argentina in the 1990s and, of course, inferior to that of Brazil and Chile during the same period.

Not all trade agreements produce the desired results. MERCOSUR, at its inception in the 1990s facilitated freer intra-regional trade. Later, the ambition to turn MERCOSUR into a customs union prevented the bilateral free trade negotiations of its members with third countries, severely weakening it. Other countries such as Chile, Mexico, Peru, Colombia and Panama were able to pursue bilateral free trade agreements and fared far better. It is encouraging to see that in both countries, Brazil and Argentina, government officials now recognize this weakness and seem determined to reinitiate efforts to establish freer trade conditions not only within MERCOSUR, but also with other important nations of the world, following the example of the countries of the Pacific Alliance.

In sum, the economic history of Argentina reinforces the importance of removing obstacles to external trade and capital movements in order to resume and sustain rapid growth. This claim is most obvious when, as we have done in earlier chapters, one compares the periods 1870–1913 to 1945–1990 and more recently, by contrasting the reform of the 1990s with the counterreform that began in 2002.

Fiscal accounts

There is no doubt that the inability of governments to balance the budget has been the central and most tragic characteristic of 200 years of Argentine economic history.

During the Viceroyalty of Río de la Plata fiscal accounts depended on transfers from Potosí's coffers. During the years of the United Provinces of Río de la Plata and the Argentine Confederation, when transfers ceased, the fiscal accounts of the provinces (including the Province of Buenos Aires which controlled the Customs) ran permanent fiscal deficits. Up until 1822, the provinces financed those deficits by issuing debt documented with bearer bonds or simply delaying payments to suppliers and civil servants.

In 1822, Argentina began to issue paper currency. The Banco de la Provincia de Buenos Aires first issued paper pesos. Those paper bills eventually were devalued in relation to the peso fuerte whose value was fixed to the value of precious metals. A poor store of value, paper pesos were used for spot transactions, but not for saving. Several inflationary spikes in the first half of the 19th century taught merchants and landowners to invest their savings in precious metals, land or cattle.

Elites tied to export products adapted to the inflationary environment. Printing paper currency and the periodic devaluations benefited exporters by reducing the cost of labour and taxes in real terms. Tax pressure also went down when the government financed its expenses through printing money instead of taxation. The net losers in this inflationary environment were labourers who endured increases in the cost of living. To appease them, after each inflationary spike, Juan Manuel de Rosas, the governor of the province of Buenos Aires, attempted to restore stability by imposing fiscal discipline that only lasted until the next war also required financing.

Once Argentina became a constitutional republic, federal governments looked abroad for monetary policy prescriptions. Governments often tried to fix the convertibility of the peso to gold at a fixed parity, imitating the monetary system that prevailed in other nations that participated in the international trade and financial system until 1930. Oftentimes gold parity ended in a financial crisis that resulted in the suspension of convertibility. The suspension would be temporary because successive governments eventually returned to a fixed parity with gold. The commitment to convertibility did not ensure financial stability, but it was effective in maintaining stable price levels during periods of rapid growth and integration into the global economy.

Financial instability sometimes resulted from external events but more often than not it was the consequence of large fiscal deficits financed with external debt coupled with low or non-existent domestic savings. One of the most important differences between Argentina's economy and that of the USA, Australia and Canada during those decades was its underdeveloped domestic financial sector. In those years Argentina was dependent on foreign financing to cover its fiscal deficits and for much-needed infrastructure. The government issued debt to finance deficits and corporations issued debt to finance infrastructure, but there were no domestic financial institutions or domestic savings available to absorb much of that debt.

Between 1862 and 1929, government expenditure as a proportion of GDP reached peak levels of 14 per cent in 1910 and again in 1929 but most of the time stayed below 10 per cent of GDP. Government expenditures increased significantly during the war with Paraguay, the Desert Campaign, and when foreign inflows of capital permitted expansion of public investment in infrastructure. The expenditures in education, public health and administration increased gradually, but there is no evidence of an expansion of bureaucratic or patronage expenditures. The fiscal deficits increased whenever tax and custom revenues fell, generally at times of crises. Foreign debt increased to finance investment in infrastructure or war not to finance current expenditures.

The level and composition of government expenditures changed significantly after 1930. During the 1930s and the early 1940s, government expenditures soared to 20 per cent of GDP and remained around that level. The increased tax revenues generated from the newly introduced income tax financed government policies seeking to dampen the recessionary effect of the Great Depression. Printing money to cover fiscal deficits helped reverse deflation and inflation did not appear as a persistent phenomenon until 1945.

Beginning in 1944 and continuing under Perón, expenditures as a percentage of GDP almost doubled by 1948 with extremely favourable foreign terms of trade. Furthermore, Perón decided to nationalize most public utility companies. Such levels of government expenditure soon became unsustainable. The deterioration of the terms of trade and the acceleration of inflation forced Argentina to cut government expenditures; but, even after the cuts, government expenditure remained around 30 per cent of GDP and the fiscal deficit (though declining) averaged a damaging 10 per cent of GDP.

The governments that succeeded Perón's after 1955 introduced several stabilization plans all of which attempted to reduce government expenditure and fiscal deficits. By 1972 government expenditures were only 22 per cent of GDP, not far from the level in the 1930s and early 1940s. The fiscal deficit as a proportion of the GDP was halved at one point but was never completely eliminated. From 1973 to 1975, encouraged by another sudden improvement in foreign terms of trade and inspired by the policies of his previous government, Perón once again increased government expenditure to 30 per cent of GDP. For the next 15 years, government expenditures would remain at that level, but there were important changes in the spending composition. The fiscal deficit exceeded 10 per cent of GDP for most of this period.

The reforms introduced during the 1990s were able to drastically reduce government expenditures through the privatization of public utilities and investment in infrastructure. Initially, government expenditures dropped to 23 per cent of GDP, but increased up to 26 per cent in 2001 when, after 1997, interest payments on the public debt increased significantly. In the aftermath of the 2001 to 2002 crisis, government expenditures dropped again to 23 per cent of GDP when the debt default drastically reduced the interest bill and the devaluation reduced public salaries and pensions in real terms. This effect, however, was short lived.

Beginning in 2003, faced with a rapid improvement in foreign terms of trade and inspired by the traditional populist Peronist policies, President Néstor Kirchner gradually increased government expenditures. The pace would later accelerate in the two successive governments of his wife, Cristina Kirchner.

Fiscal deficits returned around 2007 in spite of a significant increase in tax collection. In 2015, the fiscal deficit as a percentage of GDP was over 7 per cent of GDP, almost as high as in the years of hyperinflation.

Debt management and the role of money

From 1853 to 1930, governments around the world tried to finance fiscal deficits by issuing and placing debt in both domestic and foreign markets while keeping their local currency convertible to gold. Argentina was no different. Whenever the deficits became too large, financing vanished, or there was a sudden stop of foreign capital inflows, the economy endured recession and devaluation. In order to restore confidence governments would consistently adopt strict fiscal and monetary policies and if possible return to convertibility. During the 1930s, most countries of the world introduced exchange controls and so did Argentina. Unlike in the rest of the world post-1945, exchange controls in Argentina were not temporary. They became an almost permanent fixture of the economy.

Exchange controls, multiple exchange rate systems, printing of money to finance fiscal deficits, and providing bank credit to the private sector at negative real interest rates transformed the local currency into the base of an inflationary tax. Local currency completely lost its role as store of value. Its role diminished to a mere means of exchange for spot transactions. People increasingly saved by investing in real estate and durable goods. When attempting to preserve value but maintain liquidity, Argentines would purchase foreign currency, such as US dollars on the black market, or illegally send those savings abroad.

When inflation spanned between 10 and 60 per cent per year, only high- and middle-income households could dollarize their liquid savings. Low-income earners, not sufficiently financially sophisticated or geographically isolated from black markets, would keep their meagre savings in pesos and suffer the erosion caused by inflation.

However, after 1975, when inflation broke the three-digit annual threshold, ever more people found ways to dollarize their savings. Black markets for foreign currency proliferated. During the 1989 to 1990 hyperinflation, every household, even the most modest, rushed to exchange their income in local currency for US dollars on the black market. Despite being illegal, inflation had pushed the economy to an *ad hoc* dollar standard. Local currency was only used for everyday on the spot commercial transactions.

Naturally, the ad hoc dollarization caused an acceleration in the velocity with which the local currency circulated. As the revenue the government collected through the printing of money depreciated in real terms, the rate of monetary emission and the consequent rate of devaluation and inflation needed to finance a given fiscal deficit increased. This led inevitably to hyperinflation.

Once an economy reaches this pre-hyperinflation stage, the only way to stop hyperinflation is through monetary reforms that convince citizens that the government will refrain from printing money to finance the government or the private sector. That is what Latin American countries suffering hyperinflation did in the late 1980s and the early 1990s.

In Argentina, the monetary reform had two main features. First, it introduced a currency board that made the peso convertible. Second, and even more importantly, it legalized the use of the US dollar for all commercial and financial transactions. Sceptics were free to use US dollars in their transactions and contracts. Inflation disappeared almost instantaneously as people realized that the convertible peso had fully recovered its role as a store of value.

Such monetary reform is contingent on either the elimination of fiscal deficits or the recreation of domestic and foreign credit capable of absorbing all the public and private debt at moderate interest rates.

At the turn of the new century, following the forced conversion of all dollar contracts to pesos in 2002, Argentina's economy opened the door to inflation. Argentina's citizens realized that the government had decided to wipe out public and private dollar denominated debts. Everybody anticipated that the printing of money and inflation would once again finance government deficits. In other words, the Argentine economy relapsed to the disease that over 45 years had left Argentina as one of the highest inflationary economies in the world.

This has been a hard and costly lesson for Argentina and for other countries with high inflation.

As of 2016, Argentina's new government seems determined to fight inflation. It has no choice but to recreate a monetary regime that reassures people inflation will no longer be used to wipe out debts and finance fiscal deficits.

Domestic and foreign savings

In Argentine history, domestic savings were frequently insufficient to finance real investment. Foreign savings filled the gap. Moreover, more often than not, this financing has often been in the form of foreign financial investment rather than foreign direct investment. Foreign financial investment is more crisis prone than foreign direct investment. Most of the debt crises that plagued Argentina originated from this weakness. It happened in the post-Second World War period, but also in the decades during which Argentina grew rapidly and was fully integrated in the world economy.

High inflation and persistent fiscal deficits always produce a negative effect on domestic savings. Price stability and fiscal prudence, on the other hand, may not be enough to increase the share of investment that is financed by domestic savings and minimizes the need for foreign financing. Such was the lesson from the ten years of stability in the 1990s. Taxation and social security reform are necessary instruments to lower consumption rates and increase savings rates.

Removing tax incentives that in most countries, including Argentina, encourage debt financing rather than equity financing may reduce the risk factors associated with foreign financing. Economists suggest that the pay-as-you-go social security system hides the risk of default and depresses domestic saving. If this were the case, replacing a pay-as-you-go social security system with a capitalization one, would help boost domestic savings. This happened in Chile. Unfortunately, in Argentina, social security reform was short lived and reversed too soon to show any positive effect on saving rates.

Some cultural trait in Latin America seems to favour consumption to the detriment of precautionary savings. This is seen not only in Argentina but also in most other Latin American countries, at least when compared to Asian countries. One possible explanation is that this behaviour is the outcome of many years of demagogy and paternalism by authoritarian business and political leaders. However, it is not easy to explain this shortsightedness and naiveté after so many frustrating experiences. This subject requires further research not only by economists, but also by sociologists and psychologists.

Investment, productivity and long-term growth

The factor that best explains the difference in the growth performance of the Argentine economy in the period 1870 to 1913 compared to the period 1945 to 1990 is not the investment rate but the productivity rate.

During the period 1870 to 1913, investment in physical capital created productive capacity in sectors and activities that faced strong external demand. The country could take advantage of its richness in natural resources

278   *Conclusions*

by importing labour services. Temporary foreign workers eventually turned into resident immigrants that, thanks to investment in education, allowed for a quick accumulation of human capital.

During this period in Argentina's history, relative domestic prices favoured production of tradable goods. The domestic market expanded alongside an increased per capita income. Construction and manufacturing also expanded rapidly without any import substitution protection. The investment opportunities that came from the demand generated an expanding export-led manufacturing sector and a strong domestic demand for non-tradable goods and services. Restrictions on imports were the outcome of financial crises or wars, not a protectionist strategy to induce development and growth. On the contrary, those restrictions were de facto constraints on the production of tradable and non-tradable goods.

Thanks to foreign direct investment, Argentina had early access to advanced technologies in the transportation, energy, communications, agriculture and manufacturing sectors. Technology, capital goods, and human resources were not limiting factors. Local industrialists could easily import capital goods and hire trained workers to operate them.

The experience of the period 1945 to 1990 was completely different. Investment in export activities and export-related infrastructure almost disappeared. The lack of investment prevented the absorption of all the technological change taking place abroad. Argentina's productivity started to lag, most markedly in the agricultural sector. Staple crop yields remained stagnant while in countries like the USA, Canada and Australia they increased at a rapid pace.

Manufacturing production in this period increased only as the result of import substitution policies in the form of import restrictions and exchange controls. Exchange rate manipulation more than doubled labour costs, making local production of tradable goods completely uncompetitive. Growth of the export-oriented manufacturing that had started during the Second World War ceased.

Manufacturing remained almost stagnant. The domestic market remained small. Low efficiency in production translated into higher prices for goods. Just as in agriculture, industrialists were also often constrained by limited access to technologically advanced imported capital goods. Foreign exchange needed to pay for imports became very scarce at times of balance of payment crises. As a result, the increase in per capita manufacturing growth was lower in the period 1945 to 1990 than in 1870 to 1913.

Moreover, the higher inflation between 1945 and 1990 as compared to 1870 and 1913 inevitably diverted resources to the kinds of unproductive speculative activities that thrive in unstable environments.

The superior long-term growth performance achieved by the export-led growth strategy of the earlier period when compared to the import substitution strategy of the latter period is consistent with the most recent historical experience. The 1991 to 2001 period was export-led growth followed by a period of import substitution beginning in 2002. Neither period was long enough to make relevant comparisons of per capita GDP growth. However, by observing exporters' behaviour, and taking into consideration the favourable exchange rate policy of the latter period, it can be argued that export-led growth performs better than import substitution as a long-term growth strategy.

Crisis management and stabilization plans

Some crises can be blamed on unforeseen external circumstances, but most have their origins in domestic mismanagement. Examples of the latter are the crises of 1876, 1890, 1952, 1958, 1967, 1975, 1985 and 1989. All of them, without exception, were caused or were preceded by large devaluation of the local currency. The crisis of 2001 like those of 1914 and 1930 happened after years of low inflation and imported deflation.

All successful stabilization programmes, including those of 1877, 1891, 1914, 1930 and 1991, involved a commitment to a monetary regime that assured stability in the value of money. The programmes of 1877, 1891 and 1914 were based on a commitment to return to the gold standard. In the 1930s, the judicious use of exchange controls to soften deflation was critical. Likewise, in 1991 success came from the introduction of convertibility.

In the 200-year history of the Argentine Republic, all the stabilization plans that included some mix of exchange and price controls, public utility rates freeze, and monetary contraction, always failed. They failed either because they produced immediate stagflationary effects or because the social costs of the recessions they caused generated political instability. Of this entire set of stabilization plans, only one, the Plan Austral, included a commitment to monetary reform. In the absence of fiscal discipline and openness to trade, this commitment lost credibility within two years.

The Convertibility Plan of 1991 was part of a comprehensive reform of the economy. The new rules of the game tried to emulate the organization of the economy between 1870 and 1913 that delivered several decades of sustained growth while integrating Argentina into the global economy. The breadth of the Convertibility Plan of 1991 was far larger than the Plan Austral and other previous stability programmes. Its complete overhaul of the prevailing rules was central to its success in delivering eight years of sustainable growth and ten years of price stability.

The crisis of 2001 was similar in nature to that of 1914 or 1930. Aside from political turmoil, the economic crisis management at the beginning of 2002 was very different from that of Roque Saenz Peña and Victorino de la Plaza in 1914 and that of Raúl Prebisch and Federico Pinedo in 1930. Prebisch introduced exchange controls to soften deflation while he was well aware of the inflationary risks. That explains why he did not rely on extreme currency depreciation and did not breach financial contracts as a response to the private and public debt crises.

When in 2002 the Duhalde government forced the conversion of dollar contracts and all deposits into pesos, it exacerbated the effects of the crisis it was meant to solve. That very decision produced a regressive redistribution of income and wealth that subsequently opened the door for interventionist policies and a complete reversal of the open market reforms of the preceding decade. That explains why 14 years later inflation remains around 40 per cent per year and many relative price distortions and supply bottlenecks persist.

Unemployment and poverty

In the early days of Argentina and during the prosperous decades of growth and immigration, unemployment was never an issue. On the contrary, there was a permanent scarcity of labour that opened the door to the large influx of European immigrants. At times of crisis, immigration would temporarily halt, but there were no significant episodes of high unemployment.

Nevertheless, social unrest, particularly during the 1890s, but also during the first 13 years of the new century, indicates that many families lived in poor conditions even at times when the country was growing rapidly. Poverty mobilized an increasing number of urban workers to organize labour unions during the 1920s and 1930s. Widespread poverty in both rural and urban settings caused social tensions and led to President Perón's income redistribution policies between 1945 and 1955.

Even if well intentioned, Perón's redistribution policies were ill conceived. Redistribution was not pursued through national and provincial budgetary allocations with an adequate combination of tax and expenditures. Instead, redistribution was pursued through market interventions, nationalization of companies, and the closing of the economy to foreign trade. Those policies created many relative price distortions and deterred efficient investment. The impact on productive investment translated into stagnant productivity that in turn negatively affected income distribution.

Inflation further eroded and reversed the progressive income redistribution attempts and resulted in further social unrest. Most new jobs were in protected sectors with low productivity. Low productivity growth in addition to frequent balance of payments crises severely limited the expansion of the domestic market. An inflationary hike in 1975 caused unemployment to rise by 1976, inaugurating a period of 15 years of stagflation that ended in the hyperinflation of 1989 and 1990.

Populist governments reacted to unemployment by creating new jobs in the public sector. This artificial growth of unproductive public employment generated a 25 per cent reduction in labour productivity over the course of the 15 years after the crisis of 1975.

In the 1990s, a shift in policy tools sought to reconcile an efficient allocation of resources with a progressive redistribution of income. Growth was expected to absorb unemployment. GDP grew at an average rate of 6 per cent per year but employment did not increase as rapidly as GDP because it took several years to make up for the fall in labour productivity of the previous 15 years. In addition, the Mexican crisis of 1995 hit just as the export-led sector was taking off and ready to create new jobs. Next came the dampening effects of the Brazilian crisis, the strong US dollar, and finally the deterioration of export prices after 1998.

Measures like those implemented by Prebisch and Pinedo in the 1930s would have been appropriate to reduce the impact of foreign shocks on employment and income. Policymakers at the time, however, equated convertibility with full dollarization and this confusion prevented the introduction of some flexibility in the fixed exchange rate system. When the government attempted to introduce that flexibility in May 2001, expectations of default were already too strong to prevent the crisis that followed.

After 2002, the forced conversion of dollars to pesos generated an extremely large devaluation of the peso causing a massive fall in real wages and a dramatic increase in unemployment and poverty. In the aftermath, very low real wages allowed employment and income to increase over time. However, once real wages reached their pre-devaluation levels, job creation in the private sector stalled. Only the federal government, the provinces and the municipalities created new, public sector jobs. However, these were low productivity jobs generated at a high fiscal cost.

Eventually such a strategy became unsustainable. The adjustments needed to balance the budget imply that 'hidden' unemployment will become 'open' unemployment. Once more, the experience of the period 2001 to 2015, just like that of the period 1945 to 1990 demonstrates that interventionist and isolationist policies are not a durable remedy for unemployment and poverty. On the contrary, these policies planted the seeds for difficult fiscal and social crises.

The use of tax and expenditure policies as redistribution instruments is the only viable way of reconciling good resource allocation incentives with progressive redistribution policies. The use of fiscal tools for redistribution minimizes distortions and favours job creation in high productivity sectors. There is no experience to prove this fact in the 200 years of economic history of Argentina, because of the shortcomings of its tax system and tax administration. Value added taxes and income taxes do not produce extreme distortions in resource allocation. However, an ineffective tax administration system has kept enough tax revenue from being generated from such taxes. Instead, taxes that are easier to collect but more distortive have been used and abused. Development of electronic payments and information systems applied to tax administration could reduce tax evasion and improve the prospects for the future.

When the state engages in interventionist and statist economic policies instead of concentrating on the efficient provision of public goods like education, security and justice it discourages the creation of productive jobs and limits human capital accumulation. Therefore, unemployment and poverty may not only be the result of failed economic policies but also of a state that fails its responsibility to provide its citizens with quality education, adequate health services, security and justice.

Are these lessons relevant for other nations?

Many countries at some point in time succeed in creating a stable macroeconomic environment and maintaining good commercial and financial relations with the world. However, no economy is crisis-proof. Crises will present decision junctions and how leaders react to those crises makes all the difference. The lesson from the Argentine historical experience is that leaders should be wary of the temptation to rely on inflation, distortive state interventions, and international isolation as ways to overcome crises. We hope that others will avoid making the mistakes that Argentina has made so many times over its 200 years of independence.

Argentina's experience is also relevant for countries that still suffer from high inflation, are largely isolated from the rest of the world, have a high degree of legal or illegal dollarization, or are suffering a debt crisis that is generating an economic depression. These are certainly the cases of Venezuela and Ecuador in Latin America; of Greece, Portugal, Italy and Spain in Europe; Turkey, Iran, Russia, the nations of the Commonwealth of Independent States in Eurasia such as Kazakhstan; and the countries of Africa that have not yet reached an economic organization that delivers stability, growth, and social progress. Those countries would do well to draw lessons from the Argentine experience.

The comparison between the experience of Argentina during the first and the second waves of globalization demonstrates the importance of building constructive relationships with the rest of the world. This lesson is particularly important for Venezuela and Iran that have isolated themselves from the rest of the world. It is also relevant for the members of the European Union that occasionally feel uncomfortable with the constraints imposed by the EU's rules; it is also relevant to Turkey, Russia, and the former members of the Soviet Union that have not yet developed fluid and trusting relations with the USA and the European Union.

The superior long-term growth performance of Argentina during the decades of export-led growth amidst the first wave of globalization when compared to the economic catastrophe of the import substitution strategy of the period 1945–1990 demonstrates the advantages of organizing an open economy market system with more emphasis on export-led growth than on import substitution industrialization through import substitution.

The failure of stabilization plans in Argentina, except those plans that were followed by a firm commitment to restore the role of money as a store of value, point to the desirable qualities of a monetary system. A good monetary system sets up a currency that is not only a means of exchange but also a good store of value.

Argentines suffering from inflation and the economic inefficiencies and social conflicts that inflation generates may serve as reminder of the value of price stability.

Finally, just as important as macroeconomic stability is human and social capital investment. Two sets of facts demonstrate the crucial importance of devoting efforts and resources to education, health care, security and justice. The emphasis that the founding fathers of the Argentine national organization put on education was crucial to the impressive development of the country until the First World War. Conversely, in those periods where Argentina relegated the provision of public goods such as education, security and justice while increasing state intervention in markets proved to generate terrible social consequences. The rule of law, security and human capital formation are as important as the economic reforms because without them everything else fails.

Index

Aberanstain, Antonino 53
Administración Nacional de la Seguridad Social (ANSES) 204, 252, 253, 255, 256
agriculture 3, 46, 47, 107, 142, 144, 157, 158, 160, 185, 278; Duhalde, the Kirchners and 245, 248, 249, 252; early expansion of 48; Great Depression and stagnation of 101–4; long-term stagnation of (1945–1990) 110–11; Menem, De la Rúa and 195, 199, 201–3; Peronism and 112, 118, 121, 127; stimulus to (1955) 134–5
Agriculture Department (US) 203, 249
Alberdi, Juan Bautista 43, 52, 191
Alem, Leandro 62, 63, 67, 80
Aleman, Roberto 141, 160, 188, 194
Alfonsín, Raúl 152, 177, 190, 194, 204, 206; Convertibility Plan 195–7; criticism of policies of 188–9; debt management 207; democracy and presidency of 161–2, 164, 167, 170, 171; Duhalde, backing for 225, 227, 229, 240
Alfonsín, Ricardo 241
Allende, Oscar 131
Allende, Salvador 146, 181, 182
Alperín Donghi, Tulio 1
Alsina, Adolfo 55, 57
Alsina, Valentín 44, 52, 53, 54
Alsogaray, Alvaro 141, 153; Menem, De la Rúa and 188, 189, 194, 195, 197
Alto Perú 11, 15–16, 20, 24, 25, 26, 27, 28, 29, 33, 35, 44, 270; Royal Road to, Río de la Plata waterways and 12–14
Alvarez, Carlos 190, 213
Alvarez Thomas, Ignacio 28
Alvear, Carlos María de 26, 28
Alvear, Marcelo Torcuato de 80, 82, 83–4, 87–8, 90, 91, 92, 93, 94, 101, 271
Álzaga, Martín de 20, 26
anarchy, conflict and (1820) 28–30
Angeloz, Eduardo 170, 188, 190
Aramburu, General Pedro Eugenio 130, 131, 133
Argentina Satelital (ARSAT) 253
Artigas, Gervasio de 25, 27, 28
Australia 2, 3, 7, 39, 43, 45, 97, 98, 108, 178, 209, 270, 274, 278; comparative GDP growth in (1820–1850) 38; comparative per capita GDP growth (1850–1929) 45; comparative per capita GDP growth (1913–1945) 79; comparative per capita GDP growth (1870–1913 and 1945–1990) 109; export growth (1870–1913) 46
Avellaneda, Nicolás 45, 48, 49, 51, 56, 58–9, 61, 64
Aylwin, Patricio 185
Azcuénaga, Miguel de 23

Balbín, Ricardo 130–31, 161
Baldrich, Jorge 221
Ballén, Sixto Durán 185–6
Banco Central de la República Argentina (BCRA) 4, 5, 99, 100, 125, ; automatic pilot, post-Cavallo economy on 209; Convertibility Plan 195, 198; creation of 93, 97; debt management 256; exchange rate intervention, 235, 237, 240, 242–3, 252, 256; financial crisis, Bignone's focus on 162, 163–4; financial crisis (2001) 213, 218, 219; financial reform and monetary policy (Martinez de Hoz) 154–5, 156, 158; foreign exchange controls 120–21; growth, inflation and 260; inflation

and crisis (1958) 139; ; monetary and banking reform 118–20; monetary policy 257, 258; Plan Austral (Juan Vital Sourrouille) 168, 169; political and economic instability 137–8; stagflation 153; Wehbe, Grinspan and 164
Banco Nacional 36–7, 56, 58, 62, 64, 65, 66, 67
Banda Oriental 28
Barco Centenera, Martin Del 12
Baring Brothers 30, 36, 38, 51, 53, 57, 58, 66
Belgrano, General Manuel 20, 21, 23, 25, 26, 27
Berro, Bernardo 54
Bidegain, Oscar 148
Bignone, General Reinaldo 152, 160, 161–2; financial crisis, government focus on 162–4
Binner, Hermes 241
Bittel, Deolindo 161
Blejer, Mario 235
Bolivar, Simón 29
Bolivia 18, 22, 33, 34, 35, 37, 84, 93, 170, 173n1, 181, 184, 185–6, 193, 239, 270; Peruvian-Bolivian Confederation 31–2
Bonanni, Pedro 152
Bonaparte, Joseph 20, 22
Bonos de Consolidación de Deudas (BOCONs) 204
Bordabehere, Enzo 92
Braden, Spruille 114
Brady Plan 184, 185, 198–9, 207–8, 209; IMF and accession to, proposal to Menem for 194
Brazil 2, 3, 4, 15, 25, 30, 39, 43, 52, 54, 80,81, 93, 104; comparative GDP growth in (1820–1850) 38; comparative per capita GDP growth (1850–1929) 45; comparative per capita GDP growth (1913–1945) 79; comparative per capita GDP growth (1870–1913 and 1945–1990) 108–9; crisis in, dampening effects of 214, 281; Rosas and 30–2; Duhalde, the Kirchners and 239, 260; economic integrations, negotiations for 162; export growth (1870–1913) 46; foreign policy and 272; Latin American consensus 178, 184–6; Menem, De la Rúa and 192, 193, 198, 199, 201–3, 210, 231; multilateral trade regime in 136; regional trade with, interruption of 34, 36

Bretton Woods 77, 113, 117, 135, 146, 189–90, 271–2
Brown, Jonathan 1
Brown, William 28
Buenos Aires 2, 33, 34–6, 38, 61, 63, 91, 93, 100, 114, 178, 270; anarchy and government of (1820) 29–30; Argentine Confederation and State of 52–4; autonomy for Province of 36–7; Bank of the Province of 57–8, 62, 65–7138; Congress of Tucumán, independence and 28; Constitutional Assembly and Directorates 27–8; counter-revolution and 24–5; crisis of 1876 and 58; Duhalde,the Kirchners and 234, 241–2; expansion of 69; fiscal deficit 273; global economy, integration into 47–8, 55–8, 62–3, 65; Great Depression, effect of 98; Juan Manuel de Rosas and 30, 31, 32; land prices in 66, 70; land tenure system in 71; May Revolution and 22–3; Menem, De La Rúa and 188, 190–91, 208, 210, 217, 220, 222; money and banking (1862–1880) 57–8; Perón and 132, 133, 148; 'Radical Republic' and 82, 85; railroad development in 72; secession from Argentine Confederation 44, 51; Spanish heritage 11, 12, 13, 15, 16, 179, 19–21, 22; territorial expansion of 69; traumatic 30 years (1914–1944) in 78; treasurer role for all provinces 36; Triumvirates 25–6; yellow fever epidemic in 51, 56
Bunge, Mario 1, 86–7
Bush, George H.W. 185, 186, 193
Bush, George W. 225
Bustos, Juan Bautista 29, 31

Cafiero, Antonio 152, 161, 188–9
Caja Nacional de Ahorro Postal (CNAP) 119
Calabró, Vittorio 148
Campaign to the Desert 57, 61, 69, 70
Cámpora, Hector 147, 148
Canada 2, 3, 7, 39, 43, 69, 92, 97–8, 178, 209, 270, 274, 278; comparative GDP growth in (1820–1850) 38; comparative per capita GDP growth (1850–1929) 45; comparative per capita GDP growth (1913–1945) 79; comparative per capita GDP growth (1870–1913 and 1945–1990) 108–9; export growth (1870–1913) 46

286 Index

capital flight 4, 6, 88–9, 95, 160, 185, 213, 257, 259, 261
capital inflows 2, 4, 47–8, 51, 66, 78, 158–60, 182, 198, 202, 275
capitalism 78, 177, 179, 181, 183
Cardoso, Fernando Henrique 185
Carlos III, King of Spain 11–12, 18
Castellano, Manuel Ignacio 85
Castelli, Juan José 23, 24, 25
Castillo, Ramón del 90, 93, 94–5
Castro, Fidel 132, 146
Catamarca 24, 28
Catholic University of Argentina (UCA) Social Observatory 264
Cavallo, Domingo Felipe 1, 2, 162, 224–5, 228, 269; disorderly debt default, attempts at avoidance of 215–22; Duhalde-Cavallo ticket, Kirchner's proposal for 234; first agreement with IMF (May, 2001) 216–17; Menem, De la Rúa and 188–9, 192, 197, 214; second agreement with IMF (August, 2001) 217–19; third attempt-negotiation with IMF to launch Phase 2 of the orderly debt restructuring (November–December, 2001) 219–22
Cavallo Runde, Sonia 1
Central America 239
Centro de Estudios Macroeconómicos de Argentina (CEMA) 230
Charcas 28
Chávez, Hugo 186, 225, 233, 237, 239, 241
Chichas 28
Chile 32, 33, 57, 61–2, 93, 146, 152, 162, 185–6, 231, 272, 277; comparative per capita GDP growth (1850–1929) 45; comparative per capita GDP growth (1913–1945) 79; comparative per capita GDP growth (1870–1913 and 1945–1990) 109; export growth (1870–1913) 46; Menem, De la Rúa and 188, 192, 193, 199, 201; model for Latin America 182–3, 184; Puna de Atacama border dispute with 63–4; 'Radical Republic' and 80–81, 82, 84; reforms in, deepening of (2000s) 239; Spanish heritage 13, 15, 16, 19, 26, 28, 29; stagflation, economic reform and end of 181, 182
Cisneros, Baltazar Hidalgo de 20–21
Civil Registry, creation of 61
Clinton, W.J. ('Bill') 186, 210
Cobos, Julio 241, 252

Cochabamba 24
Colombia 185, 186, 239, 272
Color de Mello, Fernando 185
commercial policies 121, 134–5, 153–4, 169, 199, 246
Commonwealth of Independent States (CIS) 282
communications infrastructure 56, 182, 195, 201, 244, 272, 278
Concepción, Alfredo 164, 168
Confederación General del Trabajo (CGT) 93, 130, 132, 138, 168; Perónism and 114, 115, 148
Confederation 23, 27, 31–2, 37, 44, 47, 48, 51, 57, 69, 270, 273; Buenos Aires State and 52–4
Constitutional Assembly 23, 44, 51, 53, 115, 131, 190; Year XIII and Directorates 27–8
constitutional governments 8; succession of (1853–1910) 44–5
consumer price index (CPI) 5, 224, 243, 244, 250, 256; crises 6–7; crisis (1876) 58–9
convertibility 5, 47, 60, 62, 68, 88, 95, 100, 192, 209, 211, 218, 220, 226–7, 234, 246, 251, 259, 261, 264, 273–74, 275, 279, 281; Convertibility Law 4, 67, 124, 195, 198, 199, 200–201, 203, 204, 222, 227, 228, 230–32, 242; Convertibility Plan (1991) 190, 195–8, 206, 207; destruction of 224–5, 233; establishment of (1883) and suspension of (1885) 65; experimentation with 58–9; IMF in 1990s and 198–9
Córdoba 44, 52, 53, 55–6, 64, 83, 93, 132, 168, 178, 186, 188, 190; expansion of 69; exposition (1871) in 56; land tenure system in 71; Spanish heritage 13, 15, 16, 17, 19, 20, 23, 24, 26, 27, 28, 29, 31
Corrales, Javier 179
Corrientes 23, 24, 27, 28, 31, 32, 44, 54–5, 56
Cortés Conde, Roberto 1, 47, 69, 70, 71, 86
counter-reform 1, 5–6, 241, 272; social security counter-reform 253–5
crises 6–7; 1876 58–9; 1890 66–9; 1949 125–8; 2001: Competitiveness Plan 230–31; convertibility, support for 232; devaluation, rejection of 232; dollarization 230–31; economics 213–15; expenditure cutbacks, government

reluctance on 229–30; exports, stagnation of 231; factors which may have triggered crisis 229–33; peso-ification of dollar contracts, perception of external support for 232–3; public debt restructuring, lack of decision on 232; trigger factors 229–33; crisis management, concluding comments on 279–80
Currency Board 62, 63, 67, 68, 95, 97, 99–100, 198

Dagnino Pastore, José María 144–5, 162, 194
Dahik, Alberto 186
de Garay, Juan 12, 16
De la Madrid, Miguel 184, 185
De la Plaza, Victorino 72, 80–81, 95, 279
De la Riestra, Norberto 59
De la Rúa, Fernando 5, 147, 161, 190–92, 211, 239, 240; disorderly debt default, attempts at avoidance of 215–22; first agreement with IMF (May, 2001) 216–17; origin of Duhalde's decisions, Kirchner's metamorphosis and 229, 230, 231, 232, 233, 234; second agreement with IMF (August, 2001) 217–19; third attempt - negotiation with IMF to launch Phase 2 of the orderly debt restructuring (November–December, 2001) 219–22
De la Sota, José Manuel 217
De la Torre, Lisandro 91, 92, 100
De Mendoza, Pedro 12
De Pablo, Juan Carlos 1, 127, 133–4, 136
debt management 255–6; concluding comments on 275–7; disorderly debt default, attempts at avoidance of (De la Rúa-Cavallo) 215–22; fiscal policy and (1989–1996) 206–8
defensive attitudes 2, 77
deflation 4, 7, 37, 57, 65–6, 68, 90, 101, 124, 211, 274, 279; debt-deflation 239, 259; Great Depression, effects of 97–9, 101; recession, De la Rúa and 192
Del Pont, Mercedes Marcó 257
Del Solar, Julio Gonzalez 164
Del Valle, Aristóbulo 62–3
Della Paolera, G. and Taylor, A. 38, 58, 88, 89, 96
Della Paolera, Gerardo 1
Dellepiane, General Luis 81
democracy 45, 90, 93, 133, 145; Alfonsín and transformation to 8, 152, 160, 161–73; popular and liberal 80

depreciation 4, 65, 66–7, 158, 210–11, 215, 243, 252, 261, 279
Derqui, Santiago 44, 51, 52, 53–4
devaluation 4, 5, 37, 80, 86, 95, 134, 141, 144, 164, 166, 180–81, 184; Duhalde, the Kirschners and 224, 228, 229, 236, 239, 240, 242, 243, 249, 257; Menem, De la Rúa and 209, 210–11, 214–15, 220, 222; Perónism an 124, 125–6, 127, 150–51, 154, 158; rejection of 232
Di Tella, Guido 188–9, 192, 193
Díaz Alejandro, Carlos 1, 86
Diz, Adolfo 153, 154
domestic debt 5, 184
Dorrego, Manuel 30
Drago, Luis María 64
Duarte, María Eva (later Evita Perón) 114
Duhalde, Eduardo 5, 272, 280; decision-making by, origins of 224, 225, 227, 229, 233, 234–5, 236, 238; Duhalde-Cavallo ticket, Kirchner's proposal for 234; economy of 242–5; Kirchners and 239, 240, 241, 243, 245, 246, 255; Menem and 190–92, 206, 209, 210, 222

Economía, Ministerio de 207–8, 212, 213, 214, 216, 217, 251
Economic Commission for Latin America (ECLA) 133
The Economist 231
Ecuador 29, 186, 239, 282
education 15, 49, 51, 56, 82–3, 84, 116, 227, 274, 278, 281; Education Law, Roca presidency and 61; education system 178, 182, 271; importance of 43, 283; secondary education, expansion of 56
Ejército Revolucionario del Pueblo (ERP) 132, 148, 152, 153, 162
electoral reform 70–72
Elio, Francisco Javier de 25
Entre Ríos 25, 27, 28, 31, 32, 44, 52, 53, 54, 55, 56; expansion of 69; land tenure system in 71
Errázuris, Maximiano 63–4
Estensoro, Victor Paz 170, 181, 184
European Union (EU) 282
exchange rates 3, 38, 57–8, 96, 100, 107, 137, 142–3, 184, 275; capitalism without markets and 180–81; democracy, Alfonsín and transition to 163, 164, 165, 166–9, 170; Duhalde, the

Kirchners and 224, 228, 237, 242, 246, 254, 259, 261–2; exchange rate policy (1955) 134–5; fiscal consolidation, IMF and 137; fixed rate system 62, 180, 198, 209, 237, 281; Frondizi's Stabilization and Development Plan (1958) and 138, 139–41; Krieger Vasena's Stabilization and Growth Plan and 144; latent crisis (1958), disclosure of 138–9; manipulation of 278–9; Menem, De la Rúa and 195, 198–9, 205, 209, 210–11; Perónism and 120–21, 149–50, 151, 153–4, 155, 159; rate (1820–1860) 38; real exchange rate 154, 155, 159, 165, 168, 231, 247, 257; Roca and 62, 65–7
EXIN Bank (US) 137
exports 54, 56, 67–8, 77, 85, 88, 92, 94, 100, 101–2, 103–4, 107–8, 143; commercial policy, exchange rate and 134–5; democracy, Alfonsín and transition to 167, 168, 169; Duhalde, the Kirchners and 224, 228–9, 231, 236–7, 240, 245–8, 250–52, 257, 260, 261–2; economic expansion and 46; employment and 281; export growth (1870–1913) 46; export-led growth, need for 282; export performance (1991–1998) 199–200; fiscal accounts and 273; foreign policy and 270, 271, 272; Frondizi's Stabilization and Development Plan (1958) and 138, 139–41; investment, productivity and 278–9; Krieger Vasena's Stabilization and Growth Plan and 144; Latin American consensus (1990s) and 178, 182, 184; Menem, De la Rúa and 184, 192, 199–200, 201, 211; Perónism and 112, 117–18, 120–21, 124–5, 126, 127, 129, 148–9, 151, 153; Spanish heritage and 3, 4, 5, 6–7, 11, 12, 16, 17, 19, 29, 33–4, 36–8; stagnation of 231; terms of trade, exports per capita and (1810–1852) 34
external shocks 4, 7, 8, 77–8, 199

Facundo (Sarmiento, D.F.) 52
Falcón, Ramón 72
Farrell, Edelmiro 112, 113, 114, 115, 118, 121
Federación Obrera Regional (FORA) 64, 71
Federalist League 31
Fernandez, Roque 209
Fernández Meijide, Graciela 190

Fernando VII, King of Spain 19, 20, 23
Ferreres, Orlando 34, 38, 99, 103, 109, 110, 151, 155; democracy, Alfonsín and transition to 165, 167, 170, 171; Duhalde and the Kirchners 246, 247, 249, 250, 258, 259; Menem, De la Rúa and 196, 197, 200, 202, 203, 210
Figueroa, Armando Caro 191
Figueroa Alcorta, José 60, 64, 70, 71, 72
financial crises 56, 60, 62, 156, 161, 214, 252, 273, 278; Bignone's government focus on 162–4; financial and economic crisis (1890) 62; financial crisis (2001) 213, 218, 219; recession growing into (1998–2001) 210–11; *see also* crises
financial obligations 5, 224
financial system 65, 137, 145, 153, 200, 218, 219, 224, 231, 271, 273; halting run on 225; international system 140
First Council *(Primera Junta)* 23–4
First World War 2, 45, 48, 77, 78–9, 80–81, 85, 88, 91, 101–2, 117, 283
fiscal accounts, concluding comments on 273–5
fiscal adjustment, customs duties and 59
fiscal and tax policy reform, proposal to Menem for 194
fiscal conservatism, change to reckless spending from 251–3
fiscal deficit 65, 68, 85–6, 95, 97, 99, 138, 139, 143, 145; Buenos Aires and 273; call for continued attempts at elimination of 224–5; Perón and 107–8, 112, 118, 123, 124; Spanish heritage and 3, 4, 6, 36, 37
fiscal discipline and monetary order (1822–1825) 36–7
fiscal policy 67, 85–6, 98–9, 123, 240, 256, 259; debt management and (1989–1996) 206–8; expansionary policy, negative effects of (1945–55) 123–4; policy arrangements (1956–1958) 138
fiscal resources, interruptions to supply by Potosí 34–7
Fisher, Irving 68, 97–8, 124
Flores, Venancio 54
foreign exchange controls 99–100, 151; government managed foreign trade and 120–21
foreign policy 52, 80, 83, 84, 192, 225; concluding comments on 269–73; foreign relations, Roca presidency and 61–2, 63

foreign trade liberalization, consequences of (1810–1850) 33–4; *see also* exports
Franco, Francisco 116
Frei, Eduardo 182
Frente País Solidario (FREPASO) 190, 214
Frigerio, Rogelio 131, 140, 194
Frondizi, Arturo 3, 130–32, 133, 134, 137, 160; Frondizi-Alsogaray Stabilization and Development Plan (1959) 195; Menem, De la Rúa and 188, 189, 194, 197; Stabilization and Development Plan (1958) 138, 139–41
frontier expansion 60
Fuerza de Orientación Radical para la Jov'en Argentina (FORJA) 90, 93, 114
Fujimori, Alberto 185
Fundación de Estudios Latinoamericanos (FIEL) 178
Funes, Dean Gregorio 24, 25

Galtieri, General Leopoldo 152, 160
Garcia, Admiral Manuel Domecq 83
García Del Solar, Julio 163
García Hamilton, José Ignacio 1
García Vazquez, Enrique 164
Gaviria, César 185
Gelbard, José Ber 1'96, 148–9, 151, 197
General Agreement on Tariffs and Trade (GATT) 137, 185, 272
Gesell, Silvio 68, 97–8, 124
global economy 2, 78, 97, 107, 179, 186, 235, 239, 274, 279; engagement with 77, 108; integration into 4, 7
global recession 5, 68, 241, 257, 261
globalization 78, 107, 108–9, 117, 182, 189, 192; decades of (1850–1914) 43; first wave of 2, 6, 60, 77, 193, 270, 282; opportunities of 8; second wave of 2–3, 77, 271, 282
Gómez Morales, Alfredo 125–7, 148, 149, 151; Menem, De la Rúa and 195, 196, 197
González Balcarce, Antonio 28
governments: management of foreign trade (1943) 120–21; Menem, first eighteen months of 192–3; military coups and 2–3; Perón and government expenditure 107–8; *see also* constitutional governments; individual actors; politics
Great Britain 2, 25, 27, 32, 35, 37, 39, 43, 61, 64, 84, 97–9, 117, 124, 152, 209; comparative GDP growth in (1820–1850) 38; comparative per capita GDP growth (1850–1929) 45; comparative per capita GDP growth (1913–1945) 79; comparative per capita GDP growth (1870–1913 and 1945–1990) 109; export growth (1870–1913) 46; financial relationship with 51, 57, 89, 92, 100; Gold Standard, adoption of 47; invasions by 19–21; trade with 52, 56, 94; *see also* Baring Brothers
Great Council *(Junta Grande)* 24–5
Great Depression 2, 77, 78–9, 80, 84, 85, 89, 90, 92, 94, 101, 117, 133, 271, 274; effect on institutions 95–9
Greece 282
Grinspun, Bernardo 164, 168
gross domestic product (GDP) 4, 5, 38, 66, 68, 123, 143, 167; Duhalde and the Kirchners 226, 240, 245, 251, 252–3, 256, 259, 260, 261; agricultural GDP 127; Mexican GDP 185; per capita GDP 79, 109, 123, 128, 142, 150–51, 202, 210, 261, 279; employment and growth 280–81; fiscal accounts 274–5; Frondizi's Stabilization and Development Plan (1958) 138, 139–41; macroeconomic indicators (1967–1972) 145; Menem, De la Rúa and 203, 204, 206, 207, 211, 212; National Organization and 45, 46, 47–8; Perón and the military 149, 153, 154, 157, 158, 159; public expenditure and fiscal deficit (1955–1972) as % of 139; 'Radical Republic' 85, 86, 87; Yrigoyen, rise of Perón and 97, 98, 100, 102, 103
Group of United Officers (GOU) 94–5, 112, 113
growth 4, 5, 7, 8, 68, 102, 143–4; export-led growth, need for 282; Frigerio's growth strategy 141; Illia, moderate inflation and consumer driven growth for 141–4; inflation and 259–61; Krieger Vasena's Stabilization and Growth Plan and 144; manufacturing industries, growth of 47; performance on, concluding comments on 278–9; productivity, growth and (1990s) 202–4; slow and unstable nature (1945–1990) 108–9; Spanish heritage and 11, 12, 17, 33; stability and (1899–1913) 3, 68–9; United Provinces struggle for 37–9; *see also* exports; gross domestic product (GDP); import-substitution

Guaranteed Banks, Law of 65–6
Guevara, Ernesto 'Che' 132
Guido, José María 131

Hanke, Steve 230
hyperinflation 2, 4, 7, 8, 108, 109, 162, 173n1, 185, 275, 276, 280; Alfonsín to Menem, during transition 170–71, 177; Duhalde, the Kirchners and 232, 233, 239, 264; Latin America, stagflation and hyperinflation in 180–82; Menem, De la Rúa and 191–2, 193, 194, 195; monetary rule and defeat of (1990s) 239; 'stateness,' signal of lack of 180–81; *see also* inflation; stagflation

ideologies: clash between 8; conflicts in interwar period 77–8
Illia, Arturo 131–2, 164, 168, 189; moderate inflation and consumer driven growth 141–4
immigration 37, 48, 51, 52, 56, 182, 270, 280; importance of 43
import-substitution 3, 112, 134, 135, 188, 224, 237, 250, 278–9, 282; growth strategy of, Perón and 107; industrialization growth strategy (ISI) 178
income per capita 4, 108, 278
income redistribution 107, 179, 280
independence, declaration of 28
inflation 3, 5, 6, 7–8, 36, 37, 89, 92, 99, 107, 108–9, 142–3, 282; crisis management, stabilization plans and 279–80; debt management and 276–7; democracy, Alfonsín and transition to 163, 164–6, 167, 168–9, 170, 171, 173; Duhalde, the Kirchners and 224, 226, 230, 235–6, 240–41, 251–2, 253, 255, 257, 259, 260–62, 264; fiscal accounts and 274; Frondizi's Stabilization and Development Plan (1958) 140–41; income redistribution and 280; isolationism and 271–2; Krieger Vasena's Stabilization and Growth Plan 145–6; latent crisis (1958) and 138–9; Latin American consensus (1990s) 178, 179, 180, 181, 183, 184; Menem, De la Rúa and 189, 195, 196, 197, 198, 200, 203, 210; Perónism and 112, 120, 122, 124–5, 126–7, 149, 150–51, 152, 155–6, 157–8, 159; persistence in, onset of 110, 124–5; rent-seeking and 134; Roca and 65, 66,

68; savings and 277, 278; *see also* hyperinflation; stagflation
infrastructure development 30, 36, 38, 92, 97, 145, 178, 182, 271, 272, 274–5, 278; global economy integration and 43, 47–8, 51, 52–3, 58, 60–61, 66
institutional coup (December, 2001) 222
Instituto Argentino para la Promoción del Intercambio (IAPI) 117, 118, 122, 126, 128–9, 134–5, 138
Instituto de Estudios Económicos sobre la Realidad Argentina y Latinoamericana (IEERAL) 86, 87, 102, 103, 136, 139, 142–3, 145, 167, 179; Perón and 121, 122, 125, 127, 150, 154, 155, 157, 159
Instituto Nacional de Estadísticas y Censos (INDEC) 226–7, 244, 247, 248, 256, 261, 262, 263, 264
Instituto Nacional de Tecnología Agropecuaria (INTA) 135
Instituto Torcuato Di Tella (ITDT) 178
International Food Policy Research Institute (IFPRI) 179
international institutions, relationship with (1955–1957) 135–7
International Monetary Fund (IMF) 4–5, 137, 140, 143, 144, 151, 164, 169, 184; convertibility and (1990s) 198–9; disorderly debt default, De La Rúa-Cavallo attempts at avoidance of 215, 216–17, 217–19, 220–22; Duhalde, the Kirchners and 229, 230, 231, 232, 237, 251, 256; Menem, De la Rúa and 194, 202, 209–10, 214; withdrawal of support by, chaos following 5
investment 3, 6, 8, 37–8, 43, 47–8, 66, 84, 92, 100, 143, 173; concluding comments on 269, 271, 272, 274, 275, 277–9, 280, 282; Convertibility Plan and 200–201; Duhalde, the Kirchners and 229, 231, 235–6, 237, 240, 244, 245, 253, 256, 262; foreign savings and (1885–1913) 48; Frondizi's Stabilization and Development Plan (1959) and 140, 141; international institutions and 136, 137; Krieger Vasena's Stabilization and Growth Plan 144, 145; Latin American consensus (1990s) and 179–80, 181, 184; Menem, De la Rúa and 194, 199, 208, 212, 215–16; Perónism and 119, 122, 123, 127, 129, 153, 154, 156, 160; productivity, growth and 202, 203–4

Iran 282
Irigoyen, Bernardo de 62, 63, 80
Italy 46, 48–9, 78, 91, 112, 133, 282

Jauretche, Arturo 92–3
Pope John Paul II 152, 162, 188
Juan Perón-Isabel Perón ticket 147
Juarez Celman, Miguel Angel 60, 62, 65–6, 67, 83
Jujuy 13, 16, 24, 25, 26, 27, 28m 44
Justo, General Agustín Pedro 83, 90, 91, 92, 93, 94, 95, 97, 101, 271; Justo-Roca ticket 91

Kazakhstan 282
Keynes, John Maynard 92, 98, 124; policies based on theories of 180, 232
Kicillof, Axel 241–2, 261
Kirchner, Cristina Fernández de 1–2, 238, 239, 241, 255, 261, 262–4, 272, 275; economy during government of 245–8; spending, from fiscal conservatism to recklessness in 251–3
Kirchner, Néstor 1–2, 5, 7, 148, 191, 206, 224, 225–6, 272, 275; Duhalde and 239, 240–41, 245, 246–7, 255–6, 257, 260, 261, 262–4; economy during government of 245–8; metamorphosis of 233–8; spending, from fiscal conservatism to recklessness in 251–3
Köhler, Hurst 220–21, 230
Krieger Vasena, Adalbert 144, 153, 194, 196, 197; Stabilization and Growth Plan 144–6
Krueger, Ann 221

La Pampa 44, 61; expansion of 69
La Paz 20, 24
La Rioja 16, 24, 27, 28, 31, 32, 44, 54, 55, 93, 188
Lacalle, Luis Alberto 185
landowners 48, 56, 68, 69–70, 77–8, 82, 92, 270, 271, 273; Spanish heritage and 12, 14, 17, 18, 19, 21, 29, 36, 37
Lanusse, General Alejandro Agustín 115, 132–3, 145
Larrea, Juan 23
Las Heras, Gregorio 30
Lastiri, Raúl 147
Latin America 11, 239, 270, 277; Chile as model 182–3; consensus of 1990s in 177–86; ideological discussion (postwar) in 177–80; reform in, course of 183–5; US leadership and consensus in 185–6
Lautaro Lodge *(Logia Lautaro)* 26–7
Lavagna, Roberto 235, 237, 241, 261
Lavalle, Juan 30–32
League of the Free People of the United Provinces 28
Lencinas, Carlos Washington 84
Lenicov, Jorge Remes 243
Leonardi, General Eduardo 130
Leopoldo Melo-Vicente Gallo ticket 84
Lerrik, Adam 232
Letras del Banco Central (LEBACs) 256
Levingston, General Roberto 132, 145
Liniers, Santiago de 19–20, 24, 26
Llach, Juan José 1, 103, 104
López, Estanislao 29, 30, 31
López, Solano 52, 54
López, Vicente Fidel 59, 67
López Jordan, General Ricardo 55
López Murphy, Ricardo 214, 229, 233, 234, 235
Lopez Rega, José 147–8, 149, 152
Luder, Italo Argentino 152, 161
Lula de Silva, Luiz Inácio 260

Maccarone, Roque 214
Machinea, Juan Luis 168, 169–70, 211, 214
Macri, Mauricio 6, 7, 239, 242, 255, 262
macroeconomics 7, 65, 118, 145, 150–51, 169, 178–9, 183–4, 185, 186, 199, 282; populist macroeconomic policies 178, 188, 227
Maddison, Angus 38, 39, 45, 46, 98, 109
Mansilla, Colonel Lucio V. 55, 64
manufacturing 3, 38, 59, 77–8, 88, 107–9, 117–18, 140, 160, 169, 272; Duhalde, the Kirchners and development of 246, 250, 252, 260; Great Depression and slow expansion of 101–4; growth of 47; productivity, investment and 201, 203, 278
market economy 78, 90; creation of, proposal to Menem for 194
Martínez, J. and Díaz, A. 182–3
Martínez, Victor 161
Martínez de Hoz, José Alfredo 153, 162, 194, 196, 197; financial reforms, monetary policy and 154–60
Marx, Daniel 214
Matheu, Domingo 23
Matienzo, Nicolás 91

May Revolution 12, 18, 20, 22, 23, 27–8, 33–4, 72
Melconian, C. and Santángelo, R. 208
Meltzer, Allan 220, 232–3
Mendiguren, Ignacio de 222, 233
Mendoza 12, 13, 16, 24, 27, 28, 44, 55, 71, 84, 178, 241
Menem, Carlos Saul 83, 170–71, 177, 185; Convertibility Plan 195–8; De la Rúa and 188, 189, 190–91, 206, 208–9, 210, 212; diagnosis and plan discussed with 193–4; Duhalde, the Kirchners and 225, 233, 234, 235, 239; government of, first eighteen months of 192–3
Menendez, General Benjamín 115
MERCOSUR (Mercado Común del Sur) 272–3
Mexico 39, 81, 144, 178, 184–5, 186, 193–4, 202, 214, 239, 272; Central Bank of 184; comparative GDP growth in (1820–1850) 38; comparative per capita GDP growth (1850–1929) 45; comparative per capita GDP growth (1913–1945) 79; comparative per capita GDP growth (1870–1913 and 1945–1990) 108–9; crisis in, capital inflows and 4, 281; export growth (1870–1913) 46
migration: population growth and 48–9; *see also* immigration 48–9
military coups: coup of 1930 and effects 2, 77–9, 85–9; coup of 1943 and rise of Perón 90, 107; governments and 2–3
Miranda, Miguel 118, 119–20, 121, 123, 125, 148, 149, 151
Mitre, Bartolomé 44–5, 48, 51, 53, 54, 55, 56, 57, 62
Mizque 28
monetary and bank reform (1946) 118–20
monetary and bank reform (1957) 137–8
monetary expansion 3, 5, 108, 141, 142, 145, 168, 271; Duhalde, the Kirchners and 240, 256–7, 260; Perónism and 124, 126, 149–50, 151, 156
monetary policy 5, 8, 57, 97, 99, 143–4, 181, 183, 193–4, 273, 275; democracy, Alfonsín and transition to 164, 166, 168; Duhalde, the Kirchners and 235, 237, 240, 256–9; Perónism and 120, 124, 127, 154–60; Roca and 65, 67–8
money, concluding comments on role of 275–7
money and banking (1862–1880) 57–8
money and banking (1880–1906) 64–5

money and banking (1914–1929) 88–9
Moreno, Guillermo 261
Moreno, Mariano 21, 23, 24, 25, 26
Mosca, Enrique 82, 93
Mundlak, Yair 178
Mussa, Michael 229
Mussolini, Benito 91, 112

Napoleon Bonaparte 19, 23
National Army, creation of 52
National Constitution, enactment of (1853) 2, 43, 270
National Reorganization Process (1976–1981) 152
National Territories Law (1884) 61
Nicaragua 239
Nixon, Richard 146
North Atlantic Free Trade Agreement (NAFTA) 185

Obligado, Pastor 52, 55
O'Neill, Paul 231
Onganía, Juan Carlos 132, 141, 144–5, 194, 196, 197
Oribe, Manuel 32
Ortega, Ramón 'Palito' 190
Ortiz, Roberto 90, 93–4, 122, 271

Panama 272
Paraguay 44, 51, 52, 57, 84, 93, 116, 185–6, 239, 270, 274; Spanish heritage 12, 13, 14–15, 16, 18, 22, 25, 28, 32, 33, 34; war against 54–5
Partido Autonomista 53, 55, 60, 61, 62
Partido Nacional 53, 55
Paso, Juan José 23, 26–7
Paz, General José María 30–31, 32
Paz, Marcos 54
Pellegrini, Carlos 59, 60, 61, 62, 63, 64, 65, 67, 70, 85, 89, 99, 124, 133
Peña, Roque Saenz 45
Peñaloza, Angel Vicente 54
Pérez, Carlos Andrés 185
Pérez Jiménez, Marcos 116
Perón, Colonel Juan Domingo 112–13, 115
Perón, Evita 112, 114–16, 133, 177–8
Perón, Juan 6, 90, 107–8, 161, 241, 253, 271, 274–5, 280; death of 148; economic policies of 3, 118–19, 147–8, 148–52, 153; government and policies of 112, 113–16, 116–18, 123, 124, 125, 128–9; Menem, De la Rúa and 188, 189, 195, 196, 197; outlawed years

130, 131, 132, 133, 134, 135, 138, 139; Perón-Perón ticket 161; return to government by 147–8, 149
Perón, Maria Estela Martinez de ('Isabelita') 3, 6, 108, 148, 149, 152, 161
Perónism 8, 115, 161–2, 206, 233, 234, 235; outlawed years 130–46; right and left wings of, conflicts between 147–8
Perú 13, 18, 20, 24, 25, 26, 28, 29, 33, 37, 93, 185–6, 239, 270, 272; Peruvian-Bolivian Confederation 31–2
Pinedo, Federico (and Pinedo Plan) 90, 92, 94, 97, 102, 104, 117, 119, 144, 279, 281
Pinochet, General Augusto 181, 182
Pizarro, Francisco 12
Plan Austral (Juan Vital Sourrouille) 163–4, 164–70, 195, 196, 199, 279
politics: chaos following IMF withdrawal of support 5; Confederation 23, 27, 31–2, 37, 44, 47, 48, 51, 52–4, 57, 69, 270, 273; Confederation, Buenos Aires State and 52–4; constitutional governments, succession of (1853–1910) 44–5; democracy, Alfonsín and transformation to 161–73; democracy, return to (1983) 8; 1862–1880 period 55–7; 1880–1906 period 61–4; electoral reform 70–72; government management of foreign trade (1943) 120–21; government of Menem, first eighteen months of 192–3; ideological conflicts in interwar period 77–8; ideologies, clash between 8; institutional coup (December, 2001) 222; international institutions, relationship with (1955–1957) 135–7; metamorphosis of Kirchner 233–8; military coup (1943) and rise of Perón 90, 107; military coups and governments 2–3; National Constitution, enactment of (1853) 2, 43, 270; 1930–1945 period 91–5; 1943–1955 period 112–16; 1989–2001 period 190–92; populist and isolationist policies 2, 6, 7, 92, 162, 177–8, 188, 191, 227, 236–7, 275; public debt and currency regime, professional discussion on 228–9; public utilities and railroads, nationalization of (1946-9) 121–2; 'Radical Republic' and 80–85; system of 2; traumatic years (1914–1944) 77–9; 2002–2015 period 239–42; unemployment and poverty, discussions on 226–7

population 12–13, 14, 16, 25, 26, 33, 34, 55, 68, 100, 206, 243, 262–3; population growth 48–9; well-being of 35
populist and isolationist policies 2, 6, 7, 92, 162, 177–8, 188, 191, 227, 236–7, 275
Portugal 15, 16, 25, 282
Posadas, Gervasio 27–8
Potosí 11, 13–14, 16, 18, 24, 26, 27, 33, 273; fiscal resources from, interruption of supply of 34–7
Pou, Pedro 209
poverty 4, 5, 224, 226–7, 228, 243, 244, 262, 264, 269; concluding comments on 280–81
Prat-Gay, Alfonso 235, 257, 260
Prebisch, Raúl 90, 92, 97, 118, 119, 153, 164, 279, 281; Perón's outlaw years and 133–4, 135–6, 137, 144
prices: controls on (1943–55) 122–3; distortions in, allocative and fiscal effects of 248–51; inflation and crisis development (1956–1957) 138; price controls 5, 101, 118, 128, 138–9, 145, 151, 166, 198, 203, 240, 248, 257, 261–2, 279
productivity 3, 8, 11, 46, 88, 172–3, 181, 184, 231, 245, 248, 269, 271, 280–81; concluding comments on 277–9; growth and (1990s) 202–4; Perónism and 112, 118, 156, 160
public debt 4, 5, 64, 153, 168, 275, 279; currency regime and, professional discussion on 228–9; Duhalde, the Kirchners and 225, 226, 228, 232, 240, 244, 255–6; expenditure reduction, proposal to Menem for 194; Menem, De la Rúa and 207–8, 211–12, 213, 216, 219, 221
public utilities and railroads, nationalization of (1946-9) 121–2
Puerta, Ramón 221, 222, 239
Pueyrredón, Honorio 91
Pueyrredón, Juan Martin de 28, 31
Pugliese, Juan Carlos 170

Quintana, Manuel 60, 64
Quiroga, Facundo 31, 188

'Radical Republic' 80–89; politics immediately before and during 80–85
Ramirez, General Pedro Pablo 94–5, 112, 113, 119
Rawson, General Arturo 113

Recchini de Lattes, Z. and Lattes, A.E. 49
recessions 5, 6, 48, 68, 78, 80, 92, 97, 141, 143, 169, 181; from 1914 to beginning of Great Depression (1929) 85–8; concluding comments on 271, 274, 275, 279; Duhalde, the Kirchners and 224, 232, 239, 241, 257, 259, 261; Menem, De la Rúa and 190, 192, 202, 206; Perónism and 116, 156; protectionism and 59; recession of 1998, causes of 4, 210–11; Roca and 5, 6, 48, 59, 68, 78, 80, 81, 92, 97, 141, 143, 169, 181; Yrigoyen and 81
redistribution 3, 166, 172, 179, 181, 243, 259, 281; strategy of, Perón and 107, 280
Redrado, Martín 237, 257, 260
reforms: counter-reform and 1–2, 178, 188, 190–91, 208, 210, 217, 220, 222, 225–6; electoral reform 70–72; financial reform and monetary policy (Martinez de Hoz) 154–5, 156, 158; in Latin America, course of 183–5; monetary and banking reform 118–20; reversal of (1990s) 225–6; social security normalization, reform and 204–6
relevance to others, concluding comments on lessons 282–3
rent freezes 118, 123
rent seeking 99–101
Repetto, Nicolás 91
Returning to Growth (Cavallo, D.F.) 179
Reutemann, Carlos 217
Reyes, Cipriano 114
Ricardo Balbín-Fernando De la Rúa 147
Rivadavia, Bernardino 25, 26, 30, 31, 33
Roca, Julio Argentino 45, 48, 49, 57, 60, 61–2, 63–5, 68, 71, 80
Roca Jr., Julio Argentino 91
Roca-Runciman Pact 92, 93, 97, 100
Rocha, Dardo 61, 65
Rock, David 1
'Rodrigazo' 149, 156, 161
Rodrigo, Celestino 149, 151–2
Rodríguez, Andrés 185
Rodriguez, Jesús 170
Rodriguez, Martín 29, 31, 33
Rodriguez Saá, Adolfo 222, 224, 225, 233, 235, 239, 240, 255
Romero, Juan José 68
Romero, Luis Alberto 1
Rondeau, Juan 28–9
Rosas, Juan Manuel de 22–3, 29, 30–33, 37, 52, 57, 273

Rozas, Angel 217
Ruckauf, Carlos 217
Russia 282

Saá, Juan 53, 55
Saavedra Lamas, Carlos 20, 23, 24, 25, 26, 93
Sachs, Jeffrey 184
Saenz Peña, Luis 60, 62–3, 64, 67–8
Saenz Peña, Roque 60, 62, 63, 70, 72, 83, 95, 271, 279
salaries (1956–1957) 138
Salinas de Gortari, Carlos 184–5
Salta 13, 16, 24, 26, 27, 28, 44
Salvatore, Ricardo 34, 35
Samoré, Cardinal Antonio 152
San Juan 13, 16, 24, 27, 28, 44, 53, 55, 56, 84
San Luis 13, 16, 24, 27, 28, 44, 53, 54, 55, 56
San Martín, José de 26, 28, 29–30
Sánchez de Lozada, Gonzalo 181, 185
Sanguinetti, Julio 185
Santa Cruz, Andrés de 31
Santa Cruz de la Sierra 24
Santa Fe 44, 48, 52, 56, 62, 81, 82, 241; expansion of 69; land tenure system in 71; Spanish heritage 13, 16, 24, 26, 27, 28, 29, 30, 31
Santiago del Estero 16, 24, 27, 28, 44
Sarmiento, Domingo Faustino 43, 45, 48, 49, 51, 52, 53, 55–6, 58, 61, 82, 271
Sarratea, Miguel de 27
Sarsfield, Dalmacio Velez 52, 55
savings 3, 48, 66, 107, 118, 120, 155–6, 171, 179, 180, 181; concluding comments on 273, 274, 275, 276, 277; domestic savings 179, 274, 277; foreign savings 48, 185, 269, 277; national savings 200; social security savings, spending spree on 123–4
Scalabrini Ortiz, Raúl 92–3
Scioli, Daniel 233, 235, 241–2
Scobie, James 69
Second World War 77, 78–9
Seguridad Social, Secretaría de 204, 205, 254
Sigaut, Lorenzo 160
Siles Suazo, Hernán 170, 181
Sobremonte, Rafael de, Viceroy of Río de la Plata 19–20
social security: counter-reform of 253–5; normalization, reform and 204–6; savings on, spending spree and 123–4

Sociedad Mixta Siderúrgica Argentina (SOMISA) 137
Sociedad Rural Argentina 57
Solberg, Carl 69
soldiers, average height of (1785–1839) 35
Sourrouille, Juan Vital 164–70, 188, 194, 195, 196, 197; *see also* Plan Austral
Spain 11–12, 15–16, 18, 19–21, 24–5, 26–7, 33, 35, 46, 48, 112, 144, 270, 282; immigrants from 49; Perón's exile in 116, 147; recognition of Argentine independence by 52; Regency Council of 23; Supreme Council of 22
Spanish heritage 11–21; British invasions 19–21; cattle hunting *(vaquerías)* to cattle ranches *(estancias)* 16–17; coins minted in Potosí 13; Creoles and Spanish authorities, clashes between 20–21; economic development 13; *gauchos* (itinerant cattle workers) 17, 29; *Guaraní* missions 15–16; hunting of wild cattle 17; indigenous populations, enslavement of 13; Jesuit missions 11–12, 14–16; land ownership 17–18; Montevideo, British occupation of 20; Regency Council of Spain 23–4, 25; Río de la Plata waterways 11, 13–14, 15, 23, 33, 35, 270; Royal Road to Alto Perú 12–14; strongmen *(caudillos)* 17–18, 22, 29–30, 32, 54; trade, control on 13–14; Viceroyalty of Río de la Plata, creation of 18–19; wheat and maize, production of 17
stabilization plans: concluding comments on 279–80; Frondizi-Alsogaray Stabilization and Development Plan (1959) 195; Krieger Vasena's Stabilization and Growth Plan 144–6; Stabilization and Development Plan (Frondizi, 1958) 138, 139–41; stabilization plan (1952) 128–9
stagflation 5, 8, 98–9, 153–4, 162, 164, 193, 241, 261–2, 280; crisis of (1949) 127–8; Latin American consensus and 177, 182, 183–4, 185; 'stateness,' signal of lack of 180–81; *see also* hyperinflation; inflation
Stiglitz, Joseph 232
Stroesner, Alfredo 116
Sturzenegger, Adolfo 179
supply constraints 3
Supreme Central Council of Spain, dissolution of 22

Tarija 24
taxation 3, 4, 5, 67, 95, 107, 135, 144, 151, 180, 273, 277, 281; democracy, Alfonsín and transition to 167, 169, 172–3; Duhalde, the Kirchners and 226, 231, 240, 252; export taxes 134, 153, 167, 236–7, 245, 246, 251–2, 260, 272; Menem, De la Rúa and 194, 199, 216, 219; Spannish heritage and 14, 18, 19, 36
Taylor, Alan 1, 48
Tejedor, Carlos 61
Ter-Minassian, Teresa 209
terms of trade 3, 4, 5, 6–7, 77, 78, 95, 96, 101–2, 135–6, 199, 200, 272; Duhalde, the Kirchners and 235, 239, 240, 241, 245–6, 248; exports per capita and (1810–1852) 33–4; favourable conditions 108; fiscal accounts and 274, 275; Perónism and 121–2, 123, 148–9, 153–4, 155
trade liberalization 36; proposal to Menem for 194
trade union activity 71–2
transportation 16, 18, 46, 92, 195, 201, 243–4, 272, 278; progress in 57, 137
traumatic years (1914–1944) 77–9
Triumvirates 25–7
Trujillo, Rafael 116
Tucumán 13, 16, 24, 26, 27, 31, 44, 56, 93, 132, 178, 190; Congress of 28
Turkey 221, 282

unemployment 4, 5, 6, 81, 86, 95, 153, 206, 224, 228, 236, 269; concluding comments on 280–81; poverty and 226–7, 262–4
Unión Cívica Radical 62–3, 67, 70, 72, 81, 83, 84, 85, 131
Unión Cívica Radical del Pueblo (UCRP) 131
Unión Cívica Radical Intransigente (UCRI) 131
Unión del Centro Democrático (UCeDé) 188
Unión el Pueblo Argentino (UDELPA) 131
Unión General de Trabajadores (UGT) 64, 71
Unitarist Constitution 30
Unitarist League 31
United Nations (UN) 77, 113–14, 133, 193
United Provinces of Río de la Plata 7, 47, 69, 270, 273; economic system of

33; growth struggle of 37–9; Spanish heritage 11, 16, 18, 22, 26, 27–8, 29, 31, 33, 35–6
United States 2, 3, 7, 37, 39, 43, 66, 107, 110–11, 137, 146, 236, 248; comparative GDP growth in (1820–1850) 38; comparative per capita GDP growth (1850–1929) 45; comparative per capita GDP growth (1913–1945) 79; comparative per capita GDP growth (1870–1913 and 1945–1990) 108–9; export growth (1870–1913) 46; fiscal accounts and 274; foreign policy and 270, 271, 282; Gold Standard, adoption of 47; ideological conflicts during interwar period 78; Latin American consensus (1990s) and 179–80, 183, 185; Menem, De la Rúa and 189, 192, 193, 194, 202; Perònism and 113, 115, 124, 158; 'Radical Republic' and 80, 83, 84, 89; split, reunification and 52, 55, 56, 57; Trade Representative (USTR) 185; Yrigoyen, rise of Perón and 90, 92, 94, 97–9, 104
Uriburu, General José Felix 90, 91, 95, 97, 101
Urquiza, Justo José de 23, 32, 44, 51, 52–4, 55
Uruguay 54, 84, 185, 186, 239, 270, 272; Partido Colorado from 54; Spanish heritage 15, 18, 22, 25, 30, 31, 32, 34; Uruguay River 15, 30, 36

Varela, Colonel Hector Benigno 81–2, 85
Varela, Felipe 55
Velazco, Andrés 183
Venezuela 64, 116, 185, 186, 225, 237, 239, 256, 282
Verrier, Roberto 136
Vértiz, Juan José de 19
Videla, General Jorge Rafael 152, 194, 196, 197
Viola, General Roberto 152, 160
Volcker, Paul 158

wage freezes 5, 149, 164, 169
War College (Escuela Superior de Guerra), creation of 63
Wasmosy, Juan Carlos 185
Wehbe, Jorge 164, 168
World Bank 137, 169, 210, 214; World Development Indicators 201, 203
World Trade Organization (WTO) 272
world trade system, importance of integrating into 43

Yacimientos Petrolíferos Fiscales (YPF) 82, 85, 211, 234
Yrigoyen, Hipólito 63, 64, 70, 72; fall of 90, 91, 92, 93, 95; 'Radical Republic' and 80, 81, 82, 83, 84–5, 87, 88; Yrigoyen-Francisco Beiró ticket 84

Zamora, Jaime Paz 185
Zinn, Ricardo 151